music
downtown

ROTH FAMILY FOUNDATION

Music in America Imprint

Michael P. Roth

and Sukey Garcetti

have endowed this

imprint to honor the

memory of their parents,

Julia and Harry Roth,

whose deep love of music

they wish to share

with others.

music
downtown

writings from the *village voice*®

kyle gann

university of california press   berkeley   los angeles   london

The publisher gratefully acknowledges the generous contribution to this book provided by the Music in America Endowment Fund of the University of California Press Foundation, which is supported by a major gift from Sukey and Gil Garcetti, Michael Roth, and the Roth Family Foundation.

University of California Press, one of the most distinguished university presses in the United States, enriches lives around the world by advancing scholarship in the humanities, social sciences, and natural sciences. Its activities are supported by the UC Press Foundation and by philanthropic contributions from individuals and institutions. For more information, visit www.ucpress.edu.

University of California Press
Berkeley and Los Angeles, California

University of California Press, Ltd.
London, England

Library of Congress Cataloging-in-Publication Data
Gann, Kyle.
   Music downtown : writings from The Village voice / Kyle Gann.
      p.   cm.
   Includes index.
   ISBN 0-520-22981-9 (cloth : alk. paper).—
   ISBN 0-520-22982-7 (pbk. : alk. paper)
      1. Music—New York (State)—New York—20th century—History
and criticism.   2. Music—New York (State)—New York—Reviews.
I. Village voice (Greenwich Village, New York, N.Y.)   II. Title.
ML200.8.N5G35   2006
780'.9747'109045—dc22   2004029227

Manufactured in the United States of America
15   14   13   12   11   10   09   08   07   06
10   9   8   7   6   5   4   3   2   1

This book is printed on Natures Book, which contains 50% post-consumer waste and meets the minimum requirements of ANSI/NISO
Z39.48–1992 (R 1997) (Permanence of Paper). ∞

to doug simmons, the best music editor new york ever had

contents

Preface: New Music and the *Village Voice*   xiii

introduction: the importance of being downtown   1

interviews   17

Shouting at the Dead: Robert Ashley's Neoplatonist TV Operas   17

The Part That Doesn't Fit Is Me: Yoko Ono, the Inventor of Downtown   23

Midtown Avant-Gardist:
Philip Glass Sails Columbus into a Clash of Keys and Cultures   28

Trimpin's Machine Age:
A Revolutionary Tinker Revives the Dream of Infinitely Fluid Music   33

Dancing with the Audience:
Carman Moore's *Mass* Attempts to Heal the World   38

Harps from Heaven: Glenn Branca Reemerges from the Thick of Theory   42

Shadowing Capote: Mikel Rouse   50

The Dance Between: David First   55

Raising Ghosts: Leroy Jenkins Brings the African Burial Ground to Life   59

Opera Meets Oprah:
Mikel Rouse Hawks Salvation in an Opera for Real People   63

A Difficult Woman:
A Cosmic Piano Concerto from the Outspoken Composer of *Vagina*   66

Monkey Business: Fred Ho De-Europeanizes Opera with Martial Arts   69

music and/versus society   73

Plundering for Art: Sampling   73

Mozarts Live! "Performing Mozart's Music"   77

Killers in the Audience 79

Letting Euro Go 81

What Normal People Hear: Rose Rosengard Subotnik 84

Dysfunctional Harmony:
Repealing the Suppression of Creativity 86

Don't Touch That Dahl: Classical Radio 88

Spin It Around: New Music in the Public's Hands 90

Paradise at Our Fingertips: *Voltaire's Bastards* 93

What's Your AQ? 95

Dump the Multicult 97

No More Heroes 100

Music of the Excluded Middle 102

Medicine Music: The Uses of Art 104

Who Killed Classical Music? Forget It, Jake—It's Uptown 106

musical politics 110

Paradigms Lost: Rhys Chatham/John Zorn 110

Blurred Out: On Language 114

Rock Rules: Bandwagonism 116

Pulitzer Hacks: Amateur Composers versus the Professionals 120

Composer's Clearinghouse: The Pulitzer Prize 123

Obitchuaries: Critics Take Their Final Potshots at John Cage 125

Totally Ismic: Totalism 127

The Last Barbarian: John Cage 130

Berlitz's Downtown for Musicians: New-Music Performance 132

What Are We, Chopped Liver? The New Generation 134

The Great Divide: Uptown Composers Are Stuck in the Past 136

Y Not 2K? Nostalgia for Modernism as the Millennium Ends 140

Ding! Dong! The Witch Is Dead:
Modernism Loses Its Grip as the Odometer Turns Over 144

aesthetics 147

Let X = X: Minimalism versus Serialism 147

A Tale of Two Sohos: Plato/Aristotle 149

A Secret Manifesto: Fred Lerdahl 151

The Modernist Dance: War in the Brain 156

It's Only as Good as It Sounds: Richard Rorty 160

Noises of Fate: You Don't Need a Sampler to Recontextualize 164

Sounding the Image 168

Waiting for Monteverdi: Minimalism 170

Dads versus Shadows: James Hillman 172

Vexing the Purists: *Vexations* 174

Musical Amnesia Cured! Imagism 177

End of the Paper Trail: Scores 179

reflections on books, figures, and events 182

No Shortcuts: John Cage 182

E.T., Go Home: *Tuning* 186

Composing the Lingo: Harry Partch, American Inventor 188

Morton Feldman's Abstract Expressions 192

One-Note Wonder:
A New York Retrospective for Italy's Saintly Mystic, Giacinto Scelsi 196

Father of Us All: The Critic as Composer 199

Minimalism Isn't Pretty: Tony Conrad Makes a Truculent Comeback 203

Grand Old Youngster: Turning the Century at Lincoln Center 207

concert reviews 210

Maximal Spirit: La Monte Young 210

Big Machines, Little Issues:
The 1987 International Computer Music Conference 214

First Flight: John Adams 218

Admiring the Waterfall: David Garland 220

Yawn: R. I. P. Hayman 222

Searching for the Plague: Diamanda Galas 224

Oceans without Walls: Laurie Anderson 228

Insiders, Outsiders, and Old Boys: New Music America '89 232

Dark Stormy Night: Nicolas Collins 236

Let There Be Noise: David Rosenboom/Trichy Sankaran 238

Music in Time of War: The Composer-to-Composer Symposium 240

Don't Worry, Be Hopi 244

Enough of Nothing: Postminimalism 247

Voltage High: Ron Kuivila 251

Isn't That Spatial? Henry Brant 253

The Limits of Craft: Frederic Rzewski/Philip Glass 255

Opera Is Relative: *Einstein on the Beach* 257

Well-Tuned Blues: The Forever Bad Blues Band 260

Voice of the Unutterable: The S.E.M. Ensemble 262

How Peculiar? The American Eccentrics 264

Flutes and Flying Branches: The Taos Pueblo Powwow 266

The Tingle of $p \times m^n - 1$: La Monte Young and Marian Zazeela 269

The British Don't Have Oral Sex: *Now Eleanor's Idea* 271

View from the Gap: Emerging Voices 273

Bang! Crunch! Who's on First? Twisted Tutu   275

Regarding Henry:
The World's First Multicultural Modernist Conservative Patron Saint
of Outsiders   278

What Our Pulses Say: David Garland   281

Mistaken Memories:
Tony Conrad: One-Idea Composer or Late Bloomer?   284

passings   286

Legacy of the Quiet Touch: Morton Feldman, 1926–1987   286

The Antidote to Publicity: Virgil Thomson, 1896–1989   288

That Which Is Fundamental: Julius Eastman, 1940–1990   289

Philosopher No More:
John Cage (1912–1992) Quietly Started a Spiritual Revolution   293

Index   299

preface

new music and the *village voice*

In the summer of 1979, Peter Gena—my music-composition teacher at Northwestern University—returned to Chicago all excited about music he had heard on his trip to New York City. At a festival called New Music New York, he had heard a group of composers working in the aftermath of minimalism and conceptualism: Rhys Chatham, Laurie Anderson, Steve Reich, Philip Glass, Meredith Monk, Charlemagne Palestine, Charles Amirkhanian, Alvin Lucier, Annea Lockwood, Tony Conrad, Phill Niblock, Richard Teitelbaum, and many others. His enthusiastic descriptions, tinged with contempt for our isolation in provincial Chicago, brought the term *new music* to my ears for the first time.

Peter was also the first person to clarify for me a distinction between what was called Uptown and Downtown music. In 1979, it was an easy distinction to make. The Uptowners, such as Milton Babbitt and Jacob Druckman, wrote complicated music in European genres, heavily dominated at that time by Arnold Schoenberg's 12-tone thinking and its derivatives. Downtown music was simpler and less pretentious, drawing on the nature- and accident-accepting philosophy of John Cage. Conceptualism and minimalism were, then, the two primary Downtown movements; artrock and free improvisation would soon join them.

Downtown music had begun in 1960 when Yoko Ono, a pianist soon associated with the Fluxus movement, opened her loft for a concert series organized by La Monte Young and Richard Maxfield. That concert series included pieces such as Young's *Composition 1960 #7*—the pitches B and F-sharp with the instruction "to be held for a long time"—and Ono's "Wall Piece for Orchestra," which required the performers to hit their heads against the wall. In the years before 1960, all New York music performances took place uptown, around the area where Lincoln Center would soon be situated. The Ono/Young/Maxfield concert series was the first to draw adventurous music lovers downtown, and it offered wild new avenues of endeavor that the uptown classical concert-givers wouldn't have considered music, or at least not "serious" music.

Downtown music remained a local, insider's phenomenon for 14 years, but it burst onto the international scene in 1974 with the appearance of Steve Reich's *Drumming* and other pieces on a prestigious three-record set from Deutsche Grammophon. Philip Glass's old Chatham Square recordings had already been available in record stores that catered to adventurous tastes, and in 1976 his opera *Einstein on the Beach* shook the music world. Nurtured on Cage, Elliott Carter, and Milton Babbitt, people my age had been writing dissonant, atonal music with the most complicated structures imaginable. All of a sudden, music opened up again to a kind of simple creativity. One could enjoy and employ one's god-given musicality without having to make every score intimidatingly complex and abstract. I was hooked immediately and in 1975 wrote a piece with all "white" notes, no sharps or flats, with texts from the writings of Erik Satie.

By 1981 I had finished my doctoral coursework (I stayed at Northwestern University only to study with Peter, because he was such a brilliant and supportive teacher). That summer, Peter called and asked, "Do you want a job?" He had become codirector, with Alene Valkanas, of the traveling New Music America festival, which would be held in Chicago in 1982. I became administrative assistant (glorified secretary) for the festival.

Working for New Music America gave me my first widespread exposure to what was going on in new music across the country. We had a panel of artistic advisers who brought us tapes of music they thought was new, interesting, and worthwhile. George Lewis brought several. One had John Zorn's *Archery* on one side and Rhys Chatham's *Drastic Classicism* on the other. I listened to Zorn's piece and thought, "Big deal, it sounds like Mauricio Kagel. I've heard lots of music like that." But when I listened to *Drastic Classicism,* with its minimalism pounded home by electric guitars, I was blown away. And there, in 1981, were drawn some of the battle lines that I trace in the pages of this book.

Working for the festival, I met the local Chicago critics and, through them, fell into writing for the Chicago *Reader* and then for the daily papers, the *Tribune* and *Sun Times,* as well. My record reviews brought me to the attention of Yale Evelev at New Music Distribution in New York. Some time after Greg Sandow had quit writing for the *Village Voice,* Yale suggested me to then music editor Doug Simmons as a replacement. I had become discouraged about music criticism as a career and was trying to figure out how to go into some other line of work when, in October 1986, Doug called out of the clear blue and asked me to apply for the *Voice* job. I had misgivings because I knew that New York had veered away from the minimalism that had changed my life. But it sounded like the perfect job. And ohh, was it.

The *Village Voice* was—and remains—the only newspaper in America to cover new music, Downtown music, on a regular basis. (I have to admit, however, that I first read serious reviews of Terry Riley and Philip Glass in *Playboy*.) Leighton Kerner had written for the *Voice* since 1961 and concentrated heavily on modern music. Carman Moore, a composer and jazz musician, started writing for the *Voice* in the '60s and was also sympathetic to new and unusual musical forms. But it was composer Tom Johnson who got credit for being the first real new-music critic, giving insightful coverage to hundreds of premieres in Downtown lofts, churches, and other unconventional spaces. Tom wrote for the *Voice* from 1971 to 1982, mostly about composers of his own generation and younger in a flat, phenomenological style that was scrupulous about not imposing external expectations on the music he was hearing. Tom was so supportive of the fledgling scene (although there were a few musicians he gave hell to, notably La Monte Young) that he earned the nickname Saint Tom.

In the late 1970s, Greg Sandow, also a composer, joined the scene and began alternating with Tom in new-music coverage. Sandow, who was more tuned into rock music, meshed well with a scene in which Rhys Chatham was bringing minimalism into rock and vice versa. When Tom left to live in Europe in 1982, Greg took over and wrote until 1985.

Now, in 1986, Doug Simmons (who himself had come from Boston only a year earlier) had the temerity to bring this nobody out from godforsaken *Chicago*, of all places, to fill the chair that had once belonged to Saint Tom and Greg Sandow. On November 14, 1986, I walked into the old *Village Voice* offices on 13th Street wearing a coat and tie and carrying my portable typewriter—the very picture of journalistic naïveté—to find Doug in jeans and a T-shirt. The job description he gave me was remarkable for its brevity, and I can repeat it verbatim: "Go to three or four concerts a week, and write about whatever you want." Then, as an afterthought, "It's expected that you'll concentrate on the Downtown scene." For ten years I followed those instructions religiously. Then, once I began teaching full-time at Bard College, I cut back to half-time on the *Voice* and on the concertgoing as well.

Overcompensating for nervousness, I sharply (and correctly) criticized the New York Philharmonic in my first article, accusing them of faking a Xenakis performance. In the second, I wrote about Philip Glass without once using the overworked term *minimalism* (which I came to call the M-word). My seventh column, "Let X = X," was my first attempt at a think piece, a general article on new-music issues.

In the first two and a half years, I was attacked pretty regularly by Downtown composers who didn't look kindly on this Midwestern upstart passing judgment on them. In my second week of work I heard that I had been branded "unsympathetic to Downtown music." As the 1980s bled into the '90s, however, the Downtown scene and I made peace with each other. One reason was that I had scored some coups, being the first to report on the mysterious demise of Julius Eastman, giving some overdue attention to Morton Feldman, and leveling some recognizably just criticisms at the dominance of free improvisation. Another reason was that the scene changed: the Bang on a Can Festival, which debuted six months after I came to the *Voice*, opened the scene up to other kinds of music, and the Zorn-style free improvisation I had quickly tired of became just one style among many. The major reason, though, I suspect, is that New Yorkers eventually inure themselves to anything, and I became just another irritation they had to live with, like subway noise.

The question the reader has a right to have answered is, What *is* new music? The answer isn't as clear as it was 15 years ago, but to me it still seems clearer than a lot of people think. Many things have changed since I walked into that office. As digital music technology became affordable in the mid-1980s, computer music turned into an often solitary activity. A new generation appeared for whom the classical/vernacular split in music seemed obsolete. Ethnomusicology ceased to be an esoteric discipline and became part of a standard music education. Spinning vinyl records became a performance medium.

But history never turns on a dime, and even technology can't much alter the pace at which artists assimilate new media, forms of expression, and technical devices. Several streams come together in the term *new music*. A major one is minimalism, whose offshoots postminimalism and totalism—defined in essays in this book—continue to dominate recent attitudes toward notated ensemble music. Conceptualism, the practice of basing a piece of music on an idea or concept, remains a potent if transformed force. What is now called world music has made tremendous inroads into the American aesthetic, so that many new-music composers benefit from their training in Balinese gamelan, Japanese gagaku, or African drumming. For many, many new-music figures, computer expertise has replaced traditional musicianship as the impetus for new ideas. And, not least, new music continues to be inspired by the fount of American experimentalism flowing from Charles Ives, Henry Cowell, Harry Partch, John Cage, Conlon Nancarrow, Pauline Oliveros, and other great figures disdained by the classical music establishment. New music is, in short, a grab bag of diverse influences.

In fact, for me, the premise of Downtown music was always a simple one in description, and defined negatively. In Uptown and Midtown circles (see the introduction for explanation of these terms), composers were supposed to proceed according to European precedents. They were expected to master symphonic form and orchestration, use a certain level of pitch complexity, and avoid rhythms too close to rock or any vernacular. Downtown music, by contrast, could be anything. There were standards, and pieces that failed or succeeded according to their own inherent principles, but there were no rules, no formulas for success, no prohibitions, no justifying precedents. The word *music* could never be followed by *must*. This was a conceptual problem for a lot of older classically trained musicians, who felt that without a single standard to judge music against, every piece can be considered good, and all discrimination is lost. But it's not true: some pieces of music raise expectations they do not fulfill, and with the increasing presence of non-European musical traditions, it has become necessary to take a flexible, relativistic approach to different kinds of music and ways of listening.

Uptown, it had become common to justify music theoretically, showing by charts and diagrams that pieces of music were good, even when you couldn't tell by listening what they were about. (This attitude always reminded me of the comment on Wagner attributed to Mark Twain: "Wagner's music is better than it sounds.") Downtown has not remained entirely free of this tendency: there have been composers who felt that the apologetics of free improvisation made improvisation immune to criticism or that music could be justified by its relationship to the vernacular. But I always believed such mandates were a betrayal of Downtown aesthetics. And I once used as a headline the formula for what I felt was the truly authentic Downtown attitude: "It's only as good as it sounds."

Today, new music is no longer the close-knit scene it was in 1970s and '80s New York. Funding has been cut across the board; commercial record companies have become too enslaved to the bottom line to take chances on crazy music; New York City has become Republicanized, cleaned up for tourists, and extremely expensive to live in; there are fewer than half as many new-music concerts in New York today as there were ten years ago; the younger generation is more interested in vernacular music than classical and has never been educated into the Cage tradition anyway; and on and on. But I feel strongly that the composers I wrote about were, by and large, the most important American composers of their day, and, since America has come to dominate creative Western musical activity, the most important composers in the Western world as well. I believe that most of these composers will remain important and that we will look back to them someday as the figures from whose work 21st-century music was born. Thank the gods that the *Village Voice* cared enough about culture to let someone write about them.

As for the selection of columns contained herein: I have written more than 500 columns for the *Village Voice*, of which output this book represents about one-fifth. I'm expected to say that the selection process was difficult, but it wasn't, terribly. Many of the original articles were workaday reviews of two or more performances, their significance exhausted the week they appeared; these obviously have been left out. A few dozen were negative reviews, the kind of criticism least worth passing on to posterity. Some were think pieces based on ideas in progress that were given clearer expression in later columns. I am the kind of writer (there may be no other kind) who can say profounder things the more space he is given to work with, so my longer articles are disproportionately represented here. My column space shrank in the late 1990s (as did the music section and then the *Voice* itself), so few columns after 1998 are included. Think pieces predominate because their significance was not tied to a specific concert; interviews as well, for the same reason. I have corrected typos and errors that the fact-checkers managed to insert but otherwise have avoided revisions made in the light of hindsight. For better or worse, I wanted these articles to ring with the authenticity of the moments they were written in.

I owe more thanks than I can express here to my wife, Nancy Cook, and my son, Bernard, for giving me up to all those thousands of trips into the city to hear concert after concert. A very special thank-you goes to Pat Clinton, former editor at the Chicago *Reader*, without whose generous indulgence and advice I might never have become a critic. It's time to thank Yale Evelev for a recommendation that he may have harbored second thoughts about. I also thank all the editors who worked with me over the years: Joe Levy, Julia Kent, Ann Powers, Robert Christgau, Chuck Eddy, Evelyn McDonnell, and especially Richard Goldstein, new music's biggest fan at the *Village Voice*. I thank Leighton Kerner for being a true gentleman, a gracious colleague, and the most generous classical critic of his generation. I thank Mary C. Francis at the University of California Press for her enthusiasm regarding this project, Kalicia Pivirotto for her help in assembling the book, and Laura Harger and Erika Büky for their friendly and judicious editing. I thank several hundred Downtown composers for providing me with an endless supply of intriguing subject matter, and for the good humor that almost always characterized their relations with me. May they all thrive.

Most of all, I owe an incalculable debt to Doug Simmons, not only for hiring me but also—as my editor for seven exciting years—for kindly and firmly planing away all the pointy-headed academicisms from my writing style and teaching me to write clearly and even, at times, colorfully. Even when the music I wrote about was a mystery to him, he had a genius for relocating paragraphs and sharpening arguments to bring what I was clumsily trying to say into perfect focus. He was my mentor in the world of writing, and my career has been what it has been largely because of what he taught me.

introduction

the importance of being downtown

The emergence of a "Downtown" realm of creative music could have been predicted. In fact, it was. As early as 1945, in "What National Socialism Has Done to the Arts," the Frankfurt School social theorist Theodor Adorno wrote, "The present stage of technical civilization may call for a very ascetic art developed in the loopholes of poverty and isolation, as counterbalance against the business culture which tends to cover the whole world."[1] As World War II was drawing to a close, Adorno launched a warning that the rise of technology had destroyed the ages-old balance between art and science, and that a new technology worship relegated art to the marginalized world of entertainment, leaving it vulnerable to fascistic corporate control. The thread of humanism had been cut, creating a spiritual void through which the values of either fascism or manipulative consumerism could be poured into a mostly unresisting public. Corporate control of the art and entertainment business would push truly creative music out to the impoverished margins of society: thus, Downtown music.

Part of the result of corporate control was the rising fetishism of the classical music business, along with what Adorno liked to call the "reification" of famous musical works. Listening to classical music and attending concerts became a sign of social status—as it really had been in the United States since the 1840s. The orchestra ceased to be a growing, evolving medium and became standardized as to instrumentation and size—partly according to rules imposed by musicians' unions, which thus unwittingly worked against innovation by composers. The encouragement of American orchestral music, common in the early 20th century, ground to a virtual halt in the 1930s as European composers, conductors, and other musicians flocked to the New World to escape Nazi persecution. Classical music became something set off from the rest of American life, its exoticism symbolized by tuxedos and the exaggerated solemnity of those who rearrange the chairs and music stands at Avery Fisher Hall.

A few years later, in a 1953 article titled "On the Contemporary Relationship of Philosophy and Music," Adorno wrote, "Composers have the agonizing choice. They can play deaf and soldier on as if music were still music. Or they can pursue the leveling on their own account, turn music into a normal condition and in the process hold out for quality, when possible. Or they can ultimately oppose the tendency by a turn to the extreme, with the prospect of . . . becoming dessicated as a specialty."[2]

In these sentences, Adorno set out three strategies for musical survival. And one could argue that those turned out to be the three strategies American composers actually worked out for themselves—without Adorno's help, since his article wasn't published in English translation until 2002. Further, one could use Adorno's descriptions to characterize the three streams of musical life widely acknowledged, at least in New York musical circles, as Midtown, Downtown, and Uptown. The Midtown composers, those especially associated with the Juilliard School and the orchestral circuit, can be said to "play deaf and soldier on as if music were still music": that is, they continue to write symphonies and concertos, wear tuxedos and formal attire to concerts, and do their level best to ignore their marginalization in a world in which they are subject to the whims of the star conductors and soloists and made to feel that their music is inferior to even the minor opuses of the dead masters such as Brahms and Mendelssohn.

Among prominent Midtown composers one could name John Corigliano, Joan Tower, John Harbison, William Bolcom, Christopher Rouse, Ellen Taaffe Zwilich, Stephen Albert, Joseph Schwantner, John Adams in his later music, and others who write orchestral and chamber music in intuitive, nonsystematic idioms comparable in form and feeling, if not always in musical materials or style, to European works of the 19th century. The term *Midtown*, a kind of back-formation following the more widely publicized Uptown/Downtown split, refers to the association of some of these composers with the Juilliard School and Lincoln Center (against which *Uptown* has acquired an association with Columbia University).

The Uptown composers could be described as "oppos[ing] the tendency by a turn to the extreme, with the prospect of . . . becoming dessicated as a specialty." Out of context, this is a rather vague statement, but Adorno wrote at great length about this strategy in a better-known 1955 article, "The Aging of the New Music." For Adorno, the midcentury avant-gardism dedicated to dissonance and musical fragmentation (represented by Stockhausen, Boulez, Nono, and others heavily influenced by Anton Webern) was a *critical* movement, a music that criticized the new position of music: a negation of musical expectations, a refusal to fit into a social role that had ceased to be authentic. Avant-garde music,[3] he wrote, "has its essence in the refusal to go along with things as they are, and has its justification in giving shape to what the conventional superficies of daily life hide and what is otherwise condemned to silence by the culture industry."[4] Already by the mid-1950s, however, Adorno felt that this music had been tamed and watered down by a false positivism, a cheerful and unreflective overdependence on technique, and a renewed striving after verifiable masterpieces. Though still using the rhetoric of negation, it had lost its critical edge.

Adorno wrote from a European viewpoint. In America the problems were the same, but the perception quite different. Twelve-tone music and its related forms worked their way into university music departments, meeting with tremendous and well-documented resistance at first but eventually finding a home there. This was music made to be analyzed, and if its presence in the concert hall was problematic, its use in the classroom created a continuing intellectual excitement. Uptown composers often acted surprised and hurt that the classical-music organizations gave their music an increasingly cold shoulder (Milton Babbitt, chief spokesperson for the field, sadly called the university "our last hope, our only hope"),[5] but actually their music became the musical culture of academia, with its own concerts, stable of expert performers, and well-funded support system. An endless supply of students made academic musical culture self-propagating, ensuring its survival for many decades hence. (One could quote Chomsky: "Institutions of dominance have a nice way of reproducing themselves.")[6]

As leading Uptown figures one could name, besides Babbitt, Elliott Carter (independently wealthy and curiously absent from academia for most of his career), Roger Sessions, Donald Martino, Mario Davidovsky, Charles Wuorinen, and Leon Kirchner. There is a general consensus that the Uptown scene began to lose steam in the mid-1980s with the defection of many younger composers from any allegiance to 12-tone technique, although there has been a rallying, characterized as the New Complexity, centered on the cult figure of the British composer Brian Ferneyhough.

This brings us to the third strategy, the one that forms the subject of this book: "They can pursue the leveling on their own account, turn music into a normal condition and in the process hold out for quality, when possible." What Adorno calls "leveling," which acquires a derogatory tone in his writings, was for Downtown composers a determination to reintegrate their music into the normal flow of daily life. In the most obvious respect this meant rejecting the formality of classical orchestra concerts, the tuxedos and the distant proscenium stage, and equally rejecting the internal framing devices of classical music itself. For a while Downtown music took this tenet as literally as possible: it was a movement that began in private lofts in Manhattan, performed by composers in their own living rooms.

The very terminology of Uptown and Downtown came from the anomaly of Yoko Ono having presented concerts in her loft on Chambers Street in 1960. "In those days," as Ono told me in an interview, "there was only Town Hall and Carnegie Hall." Performing music downtown was a strange experiment.

Downtown music was a deliberate rejection of Uptown elitism. Most of the early figures in Downtown music, including La Monte Young, Steve Reich, Philip Glass, Pauline Oliveros, and Rhys Chatham, had been educated in situations that brought them into contact with the complexity of the European avant-garde and with the American 12-tone movement. Glass, studying in a Paris dominated by Pierre Boulez, later described it as "a wasteland, dominated by these maniacs, these creeps, who were trying to make everyone write this crazy, creepy music";[7] the colorful phrase sums up a reaction typical among those who gravitated toward the Downtown scene. And yet what Downtown composers admired in and shared with Uptown ones was the felt necessity to flee from mass culture, a belief that whatever was being hawked commercially must be contaminated. Downtown music was never elitist like Uptown music, in the sense of employing an extravagant and difficult-to-follow technical apparatus. But it could at times be as austere, from the audience's point of view, and as baffling in its covert rules.

In fact, patent surface differences in social sphere obscured a strong point of commonality between Uptown and Down. While Midtowners generally proclaimed a faith in intuitive musicality and traditional expressiveness, those at Manhattan's opposite ends pursued avenues of speculative theory, though in different areas. Uptown was fascinated by the 12-tone row; Downtown by the harmonic series. Postserialists at Columbia worked out large-scale permutational systems that you couldn't hear; those at Roulette and Experimental Intermedia, just as frequently, drew cascades of notes from inscrutable algorithms, or let a progression of sounds be dictated by digital machines or software. What Downtowners rejected in Uptown music was the artificiality of the 12-tone row and its attendant pitch-set permutations, preferring more "natural" ordering devices such as chance, machine logic, natural numbers, and the harmonic series. Both sides gave lip service to the importance of being able to hear what was going on in the music, Downtowners perhaps more vociferously. But in practice, both sides knew that they often performed for sympathetic audiences of friends and fellow practitioners, and that opacity would be forgiven.

Meanwhile, Downtowners rejected the formality and the implied upper-class status of both Uptown and Midtown music. Midtown composers seemed to revel in dressing up to the gills for world premieres, trading public and effusive compliments with the performers, and generally setting their music off in a make-believe world that imitated 19th-century conventions of patronage and royalty. By contrast, Downtown composers were often so committed to the "normalcy" of their music that they would perform in whatever torn T-shirts they had happened to throw on that morning. Their rejection of music's "specialness" even extended to musical technique itself; all the hard-learned conventions of tonal harmony, the finer points of orchestration, the fetishization of notational detail common in Midtown music seemed like precious attempts to inflate one's self-importance and musicotechnical expertise. Midtown composers seemed, socially and in their music itself, like people who had been impressed by glorious biographies of great composers of the past, and were desperately trying to live a life that no longer existed, or persisted only artificially. Downtown composers were committed to making their music part of everyday life—and, in Adorno's poignant phrase, "hold[ing] out for quality, when possible."

At the same time, Downtown composers shared with Midtown ones a feeling that music should not ignore the audience, that it should be made for a particular venue or body of listeners. Midtown composers had a clear clientele to whom they pitched their music: the classical music organizations and performing ensembles, the in-place orchestras and string quartets, Lincoln Center, chamber music organizations. Downtown composers had a more difficult time figuring out where their audience was: at first it did not exist, nor were alternative institutions available. The commercial success, in the late 1970s, of Philip Glass, Steve Reich, and John Adams built up an audience for new music, but one that younger composers have had a difficult time tapping into (for complex reasons which I have frequently speculated about in articles). Downtown music gave rise to its own performing venues altruistically run by local heroes, usually in fairly rough New York spaces never originally intended for music: Roulette, the Knitting Factory, Experimental Intermedia, and others more ephemeral. Eventually, the hipper "legit" spaces—the Brooklyn Academy of Music (BAM) unparalleled among them—figured out that the music most conducive to pleasing a sophisticated audience of nonmusicians came from the Downtown scene. And this may be the place to emphasize once again that Downtown music was not only a New York phenomenon: Chicago, San Francisco, Los Angeles, Seattle, and many other cities have their own scenes of "Downtown" composers.

After all, what separates Downtown music most from both Uptown and Mid is the provenance of its source materials. Generally speaking, Downtowners believe in drawing for musical ideas on their personal experience and environment, not on the heritage of European music they were taught in school. In this respect, Downtown composers share a philosophy and sensibility with most American visual artists, novelists, and playwrights, who don't have to struggle as much with and against the Great European Tradition as composers do. There is much talk of "the vernacular" among Downtown musicians, meaning mostly the pop music young Americans are commonly exposed to in public settings. It is often asserted as a principle that one's music should draw on vernacular sources in order to provide the presumed audience with a point of recognition. Often parallels are drawn, correctly or not, with the great classical composers like Mozart and Schubert, who are alleged to have drawn on the "vernacular" or folk music of their own place and time. Downtown electronic composers tend to use samples and noises found in their environment or locatable in some immediate cultural sphere. When a Downtown composer does make reference to European music (one could cite as examples Kitty Brazelton's *Fishy-Wishy*, based on Schubert's "Trout" Quintet, or Eve Beglarian's *Machaut a Go-go*), it tends to be with a sense of irony or at least self-conscious quotation of something foreign and distant, as one might make a reference to Balinese gamelan patterns. There is a strong sense that, however one may have been trained, true art should be directed toward, and drawn from, one's everyday life and experience—*not* a musical tradition from a long-ago era and a distant continent.

The most important thing about Downtown music, however, is revealed in the fact that Adorno was able to predict its eventual existence as early as 1945. For Downtown music—whatever its excesses, whatever its unconventional sounds and methods, whatever its detractors say about it, whatever legitimacy those with further Uptown sympathies wish to deny it—was a deeply felt and collective response to an oppressive economic and cultural situation.

In the 1950s, the American business class succeeded in imposing its values on the rest of America, and, incipiently, on the rest of the world as well. The deluge of propaganda that the corporate world poured into the media after the widespread strikes that followed World War II, in order to wrest worker allegiance away from the unions and portray business values as American values and therefore sacred, has been abundantly documented.[8] As Adorno spent his career pointing out, business ethics destroy the "use value" of a work of art—in other words, what a work of art can potentially mean to a person or a people—and substitute "exchange value," what someone will pay for it. The process had been going on for decades, but in the 1950s there was a particular triumph of business culture—vastly reinforced in the Reagan 1980s—that reduced art to mere entertainment, diversionary but not particularly necessary or reliable as a source of truth or self-knowledge. Whether a work such as *Le Sacre du Printemps* was capable of changing the course of history, or making an entire culture take a new look at itself, was no longer important. All that mattered was how much someone would pay for the recording.

The Midtown response—not to pin it down geographically, but just to generalize it as a term—was to pretend that nothing had happened. The Midtown composers were angry that their symphonies could not command as fees as high or performances as frequent as the symphonies of dead people like Dvořák, Brahms, and so on, but they held out, hoping that the state of affairs was temporary. The Uptown response was to withdraw from the commercial market entirely and set up a separate support system with academia as its basis. There has always been a little hypocrisy in the Uptown venture, since most of the Uptown composers thought, on no particularly logical grounds, that commercial success, or at least fame, ought naturally to follow success in academic circles. Unfortunately—from the Downtown point of view—withdrawing from the commercial market also seemed to mean withdrawing from nonmusical society.

This was the crux of the dilemma and the massive challenge that Downtown composers instinctively agreed to take on. The Downtowners did not want to remove themselves from engagement with the wider society, as the Uptowners had; nor did they consent to be hypocritical, as both alternative groups seemed to them. They sought, for the most part, to create a nonelitist music that nonmusicians could understand (although this theoretical goal was, admittedly, sometimes abandoned). And yet they wanted to create an ever-renewing music that would not fall into the categories defined by the commercial music industry. To avoid submitting to commercial pressures, and to get by without the support of the classical music organizations, they had to make their music virtually self-sufficient. And thus they created what to many more-traditional musicians seemed like Adorno's "very ascetic art developed in the loopholes of poverty and isolation, as counter-balance against the business culture which tends to cover the whole world."

After 1985 commercial pressures were about as difficult to avoid in Downtown Manhattan as rhinoceroses. As the recording industry put more and more of a stranglehold on the creativity of pop musicians, Downtown composers were in less and less danger of "selling out." The increasing emphasis on profit over cultural value since Ronald Reagan was elected has resulted in a continual increase in the amount of instant appeal necessary to attract a recording company's interest in a piece of music. A label that might once have been satisfied to sell 500 copies of an avant-garde record suddenly insisted on sales of 2,000 compact discs a year, then 5,000, then 20,000. As every intelligent pop-music fan knows, the idea of taking a chance on an unknown band and nurturing it through several sleeper albums in hopes of a long-term payoff has become a laughable anachronism. Adorno's predictions of the corporate world's damnable impact on culture took 40 years to become obvious, but they have been abundantly vindicated.

When I was a student in the 1970s, a lot of the new music I was most excited about was on major record labels like Columbia, Deutsche Grammophon, and Nonesuch. By the time I started at the *Voice* in 1986, these labels had little new music to offer, and I was reviewing discs on new-music specialty labels like Lovely Music, New World, and New Albion. By the mid-1990s, New World and New Albion especially were passing by much of the most interesting new music, which was coming to me on tiny labels like O.O., Atavistic, and Mode—not regularly available in record stores, but findable on the Internet. By the turn of the century, most of the music I was crucially interested in came to me on labels produced by the composers themselves, like Mikel Rouse's Exit Music, sold out of boxes in the composer's basement. The feeling that during the course of my lifetime new music has been pushed from the mainstream to the totally unfunded periphery of society is very palpable. Without the explosion that has taken place in self-publishing technology, there might appear to be no new creative music being made at all.

All aesthetic differences and stylistic quarrels aside, this is the economic background against which Downtown music must be understood. The two central issues from which the rainbow of Downtown styles became diffracted are accessibility and distribution. *Accessibility* refers to what kind of music you make in response to this economic problem, *distribution* to what you do with the music to get it to its audience.

Accessibility is the code word for the major aesthetic disagreements that have occasionally wracked Downtown. The minimalist who writes pretty, predictable music believes in seducing the listener in hopes of eventually gaining a wide audience. The free improviser who makes ugly, wrenching, transgressive music doesn't care about a wide audience but only about devoted listeners who are "serious," no matter how small a group that vague word might define. (The conceptualist who creates no tangible musical result may be happy with no audience beyond a few friends; this was a more sustainable aesthetic in the 1970s, when rents were cheap.) The issue is, who is your audience? Do you write for your friends? for like-minded disaffected outsiders everywhere? for musical "intellectuals" (whatever that term may connote)? for people with lots of money (certainly a viable strategy)? for devoted music lovers? for all humankind? Given a group of strangers assembled in front of your stage, do you feel an impulse to seduce, engage, enlighten, challenge, or insult them? On such decisions hinge many more technical and stylistic musical issues. Across all musical boundaries, there is a cause-and-effect relationship between musical idiom and size and depth of audience.

Yet complicating that relationship is the problem of distribution. Suppose you write music that could appeal to thousands of music lovers, but you can't get your music out to those thousands. Isn't it partly true that the public will accept whatever is sufficiently hyped to them by the culture industry, and that bad music is as easily sold as good? A revealing moment came in the late 1980s when Nonesuch sent out thousands of copies of Górecki's *Symphony of Sorrowful Songs* (a rather maudlin effort, to my tastes, but one easily enjoyed, and which had been composed much earlier in 1976) to British taste-makers and found themselves with—surprise!—a classical best-seller on their hands. How many new-music compact discs, given the same treatment, might garner the same results? Not all of them, surely—there is a limit to the number of nonmusicians (and even musicians) who are going to have a blast enduring the noise onslaught of Borbetomagus. Even a gorgeously sensuous work like John Luther Adams's *In the White Silence* will prove too featureless and intentionally nondramatic for some listeners, especially those with the most "classical" tastes. But composers are haunted, with good reason and much anecdotal evidence, by the suspicion that there is a large, untapped new-music audience out there, invisible beyond the unscalable wall of corporate distribution tactics. I get this feeling myself frequently: giving a lecture, I'll play examples of music by Adams, William Duckworth, Beth Anderson, Elodie Lauten, and others and afterward be mobbed by people asking me where to get those CDs. Few people are aware that such beautiful music exists; play it for them, and enthusiasms sprout full-blown like desert plants after a rain. Many of the CDs I play *aren't* available, however, and the potential audience goes home disappointed, giving up after a quick Internet search.

And so distribution strategies vary both in relation to and independently of accessibility issues. It was an instructive Downtown morality tale in the late 1990s when the Bang on a Can festival signed up an exciting deal with the recording giant Sony, didn't deliver the kind of sales Sony was hoping for, didn't get treated very well, and finally retreated to form their own label, Cantaloupe. The message was clear: the corporate world is not friendly to new creativity, and even if you can crowbar your way into it, you may be better off promoting your music yourself. "The compact disc," as Charles Amirkhanian likes to say, "has become a composer's calling card." Many composers find it easier—and very nearly as lucrative—to pass out their discs for free or for a small charge at festivals, conferences, and solo concerts than to try to market them through retail outlets. Some composers seem happy to remain part of a closed scene, with few outside the local Downtown audiences taking notice. Others keep chasing after traditional means of music distribution, such as publishers and major labels; many of these composers seem to end up bitter. Some band together to form ensembles, festivals, or record labels, with considerable short-term success but a pretty much inevitable burnout rate. Still others use technology to become entirely self-sufficient, creating their own CDs and (in the extraordinary case of Mikel Rouse) even complete films. Even in the case of such success stories, it can be heartbreaking to see so much hard work run up against the impermeable barrier of commercial distribution.

As for my critical coverage of this scene, I might as well admit that, although as a historian I try to be even-handed, as a critic-cum-struggling-young-composer I very definitely took sides. I was generally on the side of accessibility; I fancied myself not believing that music should appeal to the ignorant masses, like that of the New Age tinkler Yanni, but rather imagined an ideal audience of tens, perhaps hundreds of thousands, the sensitive people who might occasionally attend a play or see a museum exhibition because it sounded interesting, readers of books. It seemed to me that music, without necessarily being pretty or familiar-sounding, should be clear, distinct, and transparent enough to get its idea across to these people. I became the enemy of anything murky, accidental, confused, insular, or self-indulgent—anything that threatened to keep new music confined to a cultural ghetto. Steve Reich and Philip Glass had broken out of the Downtown ghetto and become famous and widely heard. I harbored similar ambitions and imagined that every composer shared them, which is of course not true. I felt that to win over audiences took a certain amount of musical discipline. John Zorn, in both his music and his entrepreneurial activities, was the herald of the opposite point of view: that composers should ignore audiences, make whatever kind of music appeals to them, and rely on distribution to maintain a presence in the general culture. But I have never been an extremist nor a purist. There are plenty of "ugly" and transgressive pieces of music for which I hold a secret fondness, and plenty of favorite composers—Stefan Wolpe, for one—whom I know the general public will never take to its heart.

Overall, I believed, and believe, in the importance of a healthy musical and artistic culture to which all contribute: composers by making their music as clear as possible and listening to it with an objective, audience member's ear; listeners by taking chances and not always contenting themselves with music they've heard before or that sounds like something they've heard before; and presenters, publishers, and record labels by nurturing new and outlandish-seeming work, even, *yes*, to an extent that might result in short-term financial loss. There is no more leeway for self-indulgence on the part of a record label than there is for an individual composer. We all have a responsibility to create a lively and sustainable society. To make loads of money from old and familiar music without nurturing new artists and cultural expressions is like cutting down forests wholesale without planting any new trees. It leads not only to a cultural dead end but eventually to an economic one as well.

Having outlined some philosophical and economic background for Downtown music, it remains only to provide the more usual history of styles and movements. Hardly a unitary phenomenon, Downtown music resembles not so much a tradition or social group as a battlefield on which various groups reign ascendant from time to time. First came the conceptualists, around 1960. They reveled in the verbal instruction piece, what came to be jocularly known as "the short form." "This piece is little whirlpools in the middle of the ocean," wrote La Monte Young in his *Composition 1960 #15*—in fact, that enigmatic line and whatever visions it stirs constitute the entire piece. Young's *Composition 1960 #5* instructs one to "turn a butterfly (or any number of butterflies) loose in the performance area. . . . The composition may be considered finished when the butterfly flies away." Other conceptualist works were more radical, like Takehisa Kosugi's *Music for a Revolution:* "Scoop out one of your eyes 5 years from now and do the same with the other eye 5 years later." Or Nam June Paik's *Danger Music No. 5:* "Creep into the vagina of a living whale." And yet other conceptualist pieces could be quite entertainingly performed, like Robert Watts's *Trace,* which consisted of musicians setting their sheet music on fire, or Yoko Ono's "Wall Piece for Orchestra" of 1962, in which performers hit the wall with their heads.

One of La Monte Young's most (in)famous pieces was *Composition 1960 #7,* which consisted of the pitches B and F-sharp and the instruction "to be held for a long time." This, along with his Trio for Strings of 1958—whose notes were held for minutes at a time—was the beginning of a new movement that around 1970 would acquire the name *minimalism*. While the early minimalists, some of them all but forgotten today, were a noisy, loud, austere bunch, musically speaking, the Johnny-come-slightly-latelys of the movement, notably Steve Reich and Philip Glass, wrote music that was, for the time, shockingly pretty. Whereas conceptualism had been perhaps the ultimate anticorporate music—how could you sell something that was only an action directed by a quizzical aphorism?—minimalism, with its return to ensemble music, however lightly notated, was far more marketable. Tape-delay pieces like Terry Riley's *Persian Surgery Dervishes*, tape-loop pieces like Reich's *Come Out* and *Piano Phase*, and additive-process pieces like Glass's *Music in Fifths* seemed to offer the basis for an entirely new era in compositional technique and a basis for a new music that owed nothing to European influence. Within a few years, works like Reich's *Drumming* and *Music for 18 Musicians*, Glass's *Einstein on the Beach*, and Laurie Anderson's *O Superman* were winning a wide audience of fans who had been turned off by most contemporary music.

This is where the term *New Music* came in, popularized in the late 1970s and confirmed in 1979 by the New Music New York festival at the Kitchen. To this day, many of us continue to use *New Music* as more or less synonymous with *Downtown Music*, if a little less restrictive and New York-based—even though its vagueness and likelihood of being misunderstood out of context are a perennial frustration.

The early 1980s saw minimalism turn establishment. Reich and Glass started getting commissions for orchestra pieces and conventional opera-house operas, works that were rarely as compelling, innovative, or exciting as their earlier, homemade ensemble music. As younger, classically trained composers puzzled about what to do with all this minimalist input, free improvisation rushed in to fill the leadership vacuum. Already in 1979, a saxophonist named John Zorn, back from studying in Saint Louis, had written instruction-based improvisation pieces called *Archery* and *Pool*. In 1984 his work in this area would climax with *Cobra*, an improvisation piece in which each performer at some point played traffic cop for the others, bringing a fresh spontaneity and turn-on-a-dime precision into a genre often too bloated with clichés. This represented a 180-degree spin away from minimalism and, generally, a shift of Downtown activity away from classically trained composers to jazz-based musicians. Where minimalism had sought to supersede modernism, free improvisation was modernism returned with a vengeance, out to conquer new territory. Quite shockingly to many of us, Zorn revealed in interviews that he was as contemptuous of Cage, Oliveros, and minimalism as any Uptowner could be and that he took his cultural clues not only from free jazzers like Albert Ayler and Anthony Braxton but also from European avant-gardists like Mauricio Kagel and Karlheinz Stockhausen.

In the summer of 1986 Zorn had his popular breakthrough with *The Big Gundown,* a Nonesuch record of crazy Downtown arrangements of film music by Ennio Morricone. In November 1986 I started writing for the *Village Voice.* In May 1987 the first Bang on a Can festival debuted, organized by the composers Michael Gordon, Julia Wolfe, and David Lang. Bang on a Can signaled (as perhaps my arrival did as well) the beginning of another turnaround, which would become full-blown by 1990. Now the scene was flooded with composers of notated music that was far more complex than minimalism but heavily indebted to it. The conceptualists and minimalists had exhausted the possibilities of solo and composer performance, and the younger artists wanted to write for large ensembles again. In the ensuing outpouring two streams became audible, which I've defined (though I didn't invent either term) as postminimalism and totalism.

The term *postminimalism* has been used by many writers to refer to music that reminds them of minimalism but is somehow different, usually less strict. My use of it is much more specific. In the late 1980s I began noticing a tremendous amount of music that used steady pulse throughout, simple but nontraditional diatonic tonality, and simple but not obvious numerical structures. That this music was a spin-off from minimalism was clear, but it also incorporated influences from older classical music and several world traditions, including bluegrass, gamelan, African drumming, Japanese gagaku, and others. The first examples of this well-defined style included William Duckworth's *Time Curve Preludes* (1978–79), Janice Giteck's *Breathing Songs from a Turning Sky* (1980), Peter Gena's *Beethoven in Soho* (1980), and Daniel Lentz's *The Dream King* (1983). Spread geographically from coast to coast, and mostly born in the 1940s, the exponents of this style formed no unified scene and mostly didn't know one another (I introduced many of them to one another). The ideas of postminimalism, though, were clearly "in the air."

Totalism—named by some composer's girlfriend who has vanished into myth, but the name stuck—was a mostly New York movement of younger composers born in the 1950s. Totalism began in Mikel Rouse's works for his Broken Consort ensemble, such as *Quick Thrust* (1984), Lois V. Vierk's *Go Guitars* (1981), Michael Gordon's *Thou Shalt!/Thou Shalt Not!* (1983), and my own *Mountain Spirit* (1983—my output being divided between totalist and postminimalist tendencies). This was a style based in minimalism's limitations of pitch material, but using minimalist patterns as a springboard for considerable rhythmic and tempo complexity. The totalist composers (myself excepted, actually) envied the propulsive energy of rock and were also often trained in some aspect of non-Western music. Pounding rhythms, either in complex polyrhythms or changing tempo abruptly in a kind of gear-shifting effect, are a common totalist characteristic. Nine-against-eight is a particular favorite, achieved in ensemble performance by keeping an inaudible quarter-note beat going while half the ensemble plays dotted eighth notes and the other half triplet quarters; it can be amusing to watch a totalist ensemble nod their heads in unison to a beat no one is playing. I've written at length elsewhere about the differences between postminimalist and totalist music,[9] and the essays in this book offer further explication.

So what about today? The New York scene has changed since the mid-1990s, and, as my professional activities have shifted from journalism to academia, I am no longer its foremost chronicler. My own sense of obsolescence as a critic dawned on me the day DJ-ing was declared an art form. It's not that I don't believe someone could make worthwhile art from spinning vinyl records and CDs: I imagine many possibilities, and I'm floored by the technique involved. (How do they manage to get all those beats from different records in sync? Incredible.) It's that, listening to various acclaimed DJ artists, I have trouble telling them apart stylistically and can't tell what their aesthetic aims are. I can't distinguish a great DJ artist from a mediocre one; they all kind of blend into gray for me. Their apologists come with armloads of postmodern deconstructionist jargon whose content I'm suspicious of. But, unlike the traditional classical critics who saw themselves as the gatekeepers of the canon, I raise no red flag against DJ artists. I'm positive, from talking to them, that their music is an authentic expression. I am simply not the person to write about it. I'm from the wrong generation, and it may not be my music to understand. Perhaps an opportunity to understand it better will come my way.

Will Downtown music continue to exist? Indubitably. As the United States, under pressure of corporations and rightwing fearmongers, becomes a country of petrified conformists, the possibilities for nonconformity expand, and it becomes more crucial than ever to have a music scene where the nonconformist can feel welcome. The bigger question is whether any semblance of Downtown tradition will remain unbroken, or whether the current scene is a total shift toward musicians whose reference points are overwhelmingly from popular musics. As a scene, Downtown music has endured discontinuities before, and may even thrive on them. Perhaps a more urgent question is, will Downtown music continue to be written about? One palpable cultural tragedy of recent years is the steadily declining space in newspapers for arts coverage, which has made getting a concert reviewed— once a matter of course in New York—a rarity on the order of winning the lottery. If you have a music scene and no one writes about it, does it make any noise?

Above all, please don't surmise that the word *Downtown* encompasses anything doctrinaire: it is basically just a set of survival strategies. "The present-day composer refuses to die," quoth Frank Zappa, and as long as composers are determined to survive—as long as there is a corporate behemoth to survive against—there will be a Downtown.

notes

1. All the Adorno articles I mention can be found collected in the volume *Essays on Music: Selected, with Introduction, Commentary, and Notes by Richard Leppert, New Translations by Susan H. Gillespie* (Berkeley: University of California Press, 2002). Quote from 384.

2. Ibid., 136.

3. Interestingly, Adorno called it New Music, but this not very widespread usage was discontinuous with what came to be called New Music in the late 1970s in America. In the 1950s, *contemporary* and *avant-garde* were the more common terms, at least in America.

4. Ibid., 181.

5. Milton Babbitt, *Words about Music* (Madison: University of Wisconsin Press, 1987), 183.

6. Noam Chomsky, *Understanding Power: The Indispensable Chomsky* (New York: New Press, 2002), 226.

7. Quoted in K. Robert Schwarz, *Minimalists* (London: Phaidon Press, 1996), 114.

8. See, for instance, Alex Carey, *Taking the Risk Out of Democracy: Corporate Propaganda versus Freedom and Liberty* (Urbana: University of Illinois Press, 1995).

9. See, for instance, my book *American Music in the Twentieth Century* (New York: Schirmer, 1997) and my article "Minimal Music, Maximal Impact" on the New Music Box web site, at www.newmusicbox.org.

interviews

shouting at the dead

robert ashley's neoplatonist tv operas

OCTOBER 8, 1991

For several years in the '70s, Robert Ashley told me, he never gave a thought to what he was going to do in a performance before he stepped onstage. That Zen-like reliance on the moment contrasts markedly with the months of 12-hour days that he's putting into rehearsing his two labyrinthine but comfortably vernacular operas—*Improvement (Don Leaves Linda)* and *eL/Aficionado*. Now, no amount of thought is enough; there are always new tracks to overlay, further details to hone, new sounds to refine. And, most disconcertingly, new operas springing from the old.

It remains an underground secret that Ashley is the only *original* opera composer of the late 20th century, the first since Harry Partch to tell the European tradition to go to hell. If his operas follow each other in tumultuous succession, it's because they don't carry the opera house, with its sung dramatic libretto, on their backs. If they're agonizingly slow to come to production, it's because no institution (least of all the TV stations they're written for) has seen the inevitability of Ashley's vision. When Ashley and cohorts present *Improvement (Don Leaves Linda)* and *eL/Aficionado* (see "In Ashley's Dreams," below), they'll be his first complete premieres since *Atalanta* in 1986. And yet, he's already created the narrative framework for his next 50 operas. That's right, *50* operas.

Just as you can't be around John Cage without being touched by his humility, you can't hang out with Ashley without getting a buzz off his boundless enthusiasm. The sources for his operas (call them performance novels if *opera* raises too many expectations) range from ancient Buddhist texts to modern wacko fanzines; no document is too low- or highbrow to spark his interest. Ashley's current mega-opera-in-progress is *Now Eleanor's Idea,* and each of the four operas it comprises is grounded in a piece of literature that's meant a lot to him. Part one, *Improvement,* is based on Frances Yates's books about Neoplatonism, occult traditions of the Renaissance, and Giordano Bruno (the philosopher burned alive in Rome in 1600 for heresy). *Foreign Experiences* is drawn from Carlos Castaneda's Don Juan series.

Part three, *Now Eleanor's Idea* (the mega-opera's "title song"), dramatizes *Low Rider*, a southern California magazine devoted to cars that have been customized to ride close to the ground. Boasting the motto "Low and slow," the mag features a pretty girl perched on a car on every page, and Ashley borrowed from its lovelorn column for his libretto. *The Immortality Songs*, as Ashley said while sharing a couple of Te Amos at his Tribeca studio, "are about corporate mysticism. I subscribe to *Fortune* magazine, and read it cover to cover every month. Great insights. I read *Forbes* and the business section of *The New York Times*. It's an amazing culture, a religion, the church of the corporation."

Ashley's best-known opera is *Perfect Lives*, whose structure originates in the *Bardo Thodol*, the Tibetan *Book of the Dead*. Monks shout the *Bardo Thodol* into the ear of the recently departed—on the theory that hearing is the last sense to die—to guide the deceased through the Bardo, the 49-day passage between death and reincarnation. There are seven chambers in the Bardo, and seven sections to *Perfect Lives*. "In each chamber there are your antagonists, the bad guys. They shout the Tibetan *Book of the Dead* to warn you about those characters. If I'm shouting into somebody's ear over the microphone—that's what I'm sort of doing—I'm warning them about these characters." The description links *Lives* with Ashley's 1964 anticlassic *The Wolfman*, a nightclub piece in which he screamed into a microphone with maximal amplification. He's always been a shouter.

Perfect Lives, though, isn't about Tibet, it's about the Midwest. "The Bardo is like Dante: down, down, down. I modeled *Perfect Lives* on Midwestern evangelism, which goes up. It's an inversion. In Pentecostal evangelism, especially in the Midwest, you start in the most banal place. The preacher says, 'You don't really have to be here, except that you're in deep trouble, and I'm going to lead you.' And it gets more and more intense, until you get to the penultimate place, then he lets you down and you go out."

Such layers of meaning give Ashley's texts a resonance beyond the surface narrative. Knowing the *Book of the Dead* connection, for instance, adds chilling poignancy to Isolde's calm last words in *Perfect Lives*: "Dear George, what's going on? I'm not the same person that I used to be." *Improvement*, in which "Don is Spain in 1492 and Linda is the Jews," carries out Ashley's conceit on the double significance of 1492, the date not only of Columbus's discovery, but of Spain's expulsion of the Jews.

"The Jews went around the corner to northern Italy and got involved with Lull, and Ficino, and Bruno. And all of Neoplatonism, all of alternative science, came from those Jews. Spain went into total decline with that moment. The Spanish energy went to the New World, and the Jewish energy, the north African energy, all that mysticism from the Cabalah and Moorish philosophy, went to Italy and left Spain open. It's as if they separated, and Neoplatonism went through European intellectual history, and came in through New York and the East Coast; the other part, this other energy we don't even have a definition for, went to South America. And [in *Now Eleanor's Idea*] they meet, they are united, in the great future in Los Angeles."

Because his literary structures are so central and so intricate, as a musician Ashley is rampantly misunderstood. Much attention has been given to the role improvisation and collaboration play in his operas, and little recognition to the brilliant integrity of his formal designs. The elaborate scores and charts for each work, when published someday, will make a fascinating study. *Improvement*, for example, like Act I scene 4 of Berg's *Wozzeck*, is based on a passacaglia, a 17th-century instrumental genre that weaves variations over a repeating ostinato. In this case, the passacaglia is a 24-note row (containing every pitch except D) over two chords, B-flat minor resolving to F minor. As it repeats, the duration on each note varies according to Linda's situation; when she speaks, it's usually one note per line, but when she's oppressed by her antagonists, it slows down to eight, 11, even 31 measures per note. You can hear the passacaglia accumulate, for secondary characters chant the notes of the row previous to the one Linda sings.

Why the antique form for a TV medium? Because when Ashley was writing *Perfect Lives*, he was reading Frances Yates's *Giordano Bruno and the Hermetic Tradition*, and was taken with the occult Renaissance concept of the universe mirrored in the structure of its smallest particles.

"The idea is that the pattern for the whole is contained in the smallest part. If you study anything in enough detail, you get the pattern of the world; then that pattern, in effect, explains everything else. And the proportions are the same. That's Neoplatonism. You can know everything, but you have to have a model. I got fascinated with the idea that all of *Now Eleanor's Idea* would be based on passacaglias. The passacaglia is like the Renaissance Theater of the World, you can assign notes to meanings. And by bending the passacaglia around, you can have the notes represent landmarks, whether you go fast or slow."

eL/Aficionado is based on a 16-note passacaglia, and also on a modal/harmonic concept Ashley developed from the playing style of his pianist, the inimitable "Blue" Gene Tyranny. (Tyranny's presence colors all of the operas, but Ashley calls *eL/Aficionado* "my tribute to 'Blue.'") Over the piece's chord progression is superimposed a series of modal structures; each mode or scale has points of dissonance and consonance with the harmony it accompanies, and varying tensions color each moment of the piece. The opera is a solo vehicle for baritone Thomas Buckner, and though Buckner improvises throughout, a look at the score shows that the limits of his improvisation are minutely determined, and require extreme concentration to satisfy.

That's what gets overlooked about Ashley's music, because of its casual, boogie-woogie surface: its strict correlation of structure and detail is as fanatical as in any Stockhausen work of the '50s or '60s. And, now 61, Ashley belongs to Stockhausen's generation. "I find it interesting to force those rules on the piece. Of course, I'm a serialist! What else would I do? I force it because I want it to give me back that information. It's an amazing job to assign to yourself and make it sound good. You have this moral obligation to the music. I can no more depart from that design than I can change notes in Mozart. Because otherwise I wouldn't learn anything. That's Giordano Bruno. If this is the model of the world, you have to live with it."

Another structural key to the operas is their common division into 22-minute segments, intended to make them viable for commercial TV. *Perfect Lives* exists in a gorgeously produced video version, which Ashley once hoped to get aired on PBS (the "Petroleum Broadcasting System," he calls it). "PBS had projected this idea of being experimental, that they're different from commercial television. Actually, they're worse, because they're a perfect form of the kind of bureaucracy government creates."

Still, he firmly suggests that television is American opera's only honest path. "I put my pieces in television format because I believe that's really the only possibility for music. I hate to say that. But I don't believe that this recent fashion of American composers trying to imitate stage opera from Europe means anything. It's not going to go anywhere. We don't have any tradition. If you've never been to the Paris Opera, never been to La Scala, never been to the Met more than once, we're talking primitivism. How can you write the pieces if you've never been there? It's like Eskimos playing baseball. It's crazy! It's nuts! It's superstition.

"The form is related to the architecture. La Scala's architecture doesn't *mean* anything to us. We don't go there. We stay home and watch television. We go there like we go to the Statue of Liberty, but it's from another time, like the pyramids. It'd be delightful if the Metropolitan asked me to do an opera. I'd do it, but I wouldn't deceive myself for one minute that I was doing a piece that had any meaning compared to Verdi. That guy went to the opera every night of his life. If you're going to play baseball, you have to play baseball every day for your whole life. You can't go to a baseball game once, then play baseball. You can't go to the opera 10 times and then write an opera."

Ashley's cut deeply into one of new music's most pervasive self-deceptions, and explained why we're watching the European tradition writhe through a miserable demise (in John Adams's recent *The Death of Klinghoffer*, for example). It'll be a while before the electronic media take advantage of the forms Ashley has custom-made for them, forms that half-a-dozen younger composers have already imitated. But when the 21st century glances back to see where the future of opera came from, Ashley, like Monteverdi before him, is going to look like a radical new beginning.

in ashley's dreams

Ashley's interconnected TV operas may contain fewer characters than Wagner's *Ring*, but the relationships among them are complicated by dreams, discontinuities, conflicting points of view, and metaphors. First, there was a trilogy: *Perfect Lives*, *Atalanta*, and *Now Eleanor's Idea*. That last one has split into four suboperas: *Improvement (Don Leaves Linda)*, *Foreign Experiences*, *Now Eleanor's Idea*, and *The Immortality Songs*. *The Immortality Songs*, in turn, has sprouted 49 subsections, the first of which is *eL/Aficionado*. Here's a Cliffs Notes guide to *Improvement (Don Leaves Linda)* and *eL/Aficionado*.

The source opera for all the characters is *Perfect Lives*, recently released on Lovely Music last month; the libretto has just been published by Archer Fields and Burning Books. In *Perfect Lives*, the singer Raoul, piano player Buddy, Captain of the Football Team Don, and his sister Isolde conspire to commit the perfect crime: remove all the money from the Bank for one day, then return it. Buddy's dogs create a ruckus, Isolde distracts the Bank Manager. The bank tellers—Jennifer, Kate, Eleanor, Linda, and Susie—each see something different.

There's more to *Perfect Lives*, but the robbery is the moment from which the other operas take flight. (Coincidentally, the flying saucer in *Atalanta*, looking for the world's greatest woman but 8,000 years off schedule, picks up what it thinks are Atalanta's three golden apples—actually Max Ernst, Bud Powell, and Willard Reynolds—and deposits them at the bank during the confusion.) Linda and Don are married and have a son, Junior Jr., but Don is rumored to have had an affair with Eleanor. Eleanor calls herself Now Eleanor, because people always address her, "Now,

Eleanor . . ." The night after the robbery, these four characters dream, and their dreams are the *Now Eleanor's Idea* operas.

Improvement (Don Leaves Linda) is Linda's dream. Don runs off with Now Eleanor, leaving Linda in the rest room of a turnoff on the way to the airport. Linda sees Don's abandonment as "more acceptable to me, more generous on his part, more friendly, because it is clearer and, thus, more humorous, more human, than had it come hidden, ambiguous, timid, and without confidence in me." The airline ticket-counter agent (actually Linda) interrogates Don, then (as Don) questions Linda. Linda becomes the companion of Mr. Payne, an Italian man who tap dances, but—after a lengthy discourse on the philosophy of pasta—declines his proposal of marriage in an all-night delicatessen. That's Act I.

But this is dream-as-allegory: "Don is Spain in 1492 and Linda is the Jews." In Act II, Linda goes to the Big City, where she encounters popular opinion in the "Tarzan Song"; this is the Jews' urban experience. Meeting a doctor at a party, Linda tells him a dream she had, which he pompously analyzes; that's Marx and Freud. She finds a place of her own in the country (Zionism) and plays a game of bridge in which each hand regresses through Jewish history: Hitler, the labor movement, the burning of Giordano Bruno, and finally the lost continent of Atlantis. This finale brings in ideas from Barry Fell's *America, B.C.*, which documents ancient Hebrew expeditions to North America. (The *Improvement* libretto is published in the Burning Books collection *The guests go in to supper*).

eL/Aficionado is Don's call-in to Junior Jr.'s talk show in Junior Jr.'s dream, *The Immortality Songs*. Don's an agent for the Agency; he doesn't know who sends him on assignments, but he can't refuse. *eL/Aficionado* recounts four assignments, actually archetypal dreams, the first of which has already been performed in New York as "My Brother Called." Here the agent is instructed to go to a café, use the phone, and describe everyone who comes in in the code language of personal ads. In scene 2, he's to go to a house and memorize it, but warned that the house contains something mortally dangerous, something he'd never recognize as such. He describes the house in the language of real estate ads, until in the last room he sees— his mother.

Scene 3 has the agent instructed to interrogate the Kid, a 10-year-old, and find out what makes him tick. The Kid, "spiritually much bigger than he is," tells him that a dog will appear at the window, and that "when you see the dog, you'll know who's in charge here." In the final scene, the Kid has regressed into preverbal infancy and is on trial for a genetic flaw: being antisocial. He's a born revolutionary.

The operas are Ashley's history of America. They begin in his youth, the year 1942, which he transposes to 1492. *Atalanta* is the East Coast, where people remember their ethnic roots and stories of the Old Country. *Perfect Lives* is the Midwest, where ethnic backgrounds are vaguely remembered in the form of sayings. The libretto is made up largely of overheard adages. *Now Eleanor's Idea* is the West Coast, where people's sense of their roots has disappeared. As you progress westward across Ashley's America, you forget where you came from, and all that's left of your history is what's embedded in your language.

the part that doesn't fit is me

yoko ono, the inventor of downtown

AUGUST 11, 1992

Take a naive, rebellious, Downtown, avant-garde artist. Marry her to a media star. Expose her to the glare of daily public scrutiny. Do you expect her to win popularity contests?

Or put it another way: Would John Cage's music be better liked if he'd married Madonna?

Yoko Ono's is a life out of context, a little chunk of Tribeca seen through a telescope. Ryko has restored some perspective with a six-disc set of her music: 105 songs and pieces from 1968–85, 20 of them never released before. *Onobox*, as it's marketed, is a focal point for looking at the deep differences between the pop and avant-garde worlds, whose uneasy intersection is Ono's fated terrain. Today, at an Italian café near the Dakota, still pretending to hide behind the world's most recognizable sunglasses, Ono calls the box a "second life for my music." Her career needs a new reinterpretation to go with it.

Let's start near the beginning. In the late '50s, the great atonalist Stefan Wolpe contracted a rising young Japanese composer, Toshi Ichiyanagi, to play in one of his mammoth three-piano pieces. At the Carnegie Hall dress rehearsal, Wolpe introduced Ichiyanagi and his wife—our heroine—to John Cage. (Edgard Varèse was nearby, too.) Ono had been pushed by her banker father into the classical music career he wasn't allowed to pursue. When keyboard chops didn't materialize, she trained to sing German lieder and Italian opera instead. "One of the things that attracted me to Toshi," she says, "was that he was a successful pianist, whereas I was a failed pianist."

If all thumbs, Ono was brilliant at sniffing the winds of change. In 1960, she invented Downtown: she was the first to rent a loft to present concerts, which she organized with minimalist (and Velvet Underground) forefather La Monte Young. "In those days," she recalls, "there was only Town Hall and Carnegie Hall. When I first thought of renting a loft, my friends in classical music, Juilliard people, advised me not to do it downtown. They said, You're crazy, you're wasting your money, nobody's going to go there. Anybody who's interested in 'serious' music goes to midtown." Ono, Young, and Jackson Mac Low were among the performers at those historic concerts. John Cage and Marcel Duchamp were in the audience.

Ono spent the '60s publishing and performing conceptual instruction pieces, typified by "Wall Piece for Orchestra" from her 1964 book *Grapefruit:* "Hit a wall with your head." (Performing it this March in Brooklyn, the S.E.M. Ensemble gave head-banging new meaning, standing with their backs against the wall and knocking their heads in unison at the conductor's downbeat.) A 1966 manifesto stated the aims of her "silent mind" music: "If my music seems to require physical silence, that is because it requires concentration to yourself—and this requires inner silence which may lead to outer silence as well. I think of my music more as a practice (gyo) than music. . . . My works are only to induce music of the mind in people." Artist/entrepreneur George Maciunas coined the term Fluxus for the Downtown conceptualists she worked with, but Ono, no joiner, resented the label. "My feeling was that to group these people together was a political move."

Marriage to John Lennon in 1969 flung Ono into the public eye, but the deliberate naiveté, the antiprofessionalism, that the Fluxus artists adopted was not calculated to steel someone for mass fame. "I was always just interested in what excited me at the time," she explains. "I thought being an artist was to create because you were inspired, not because it becomes a profession." Robert Palmer says in his superb *Onobox* liner notes that meeting Lennon was a tragedy for Ono's career, that it distracted her as she was just getting recognized as an artist. Well, yeah: had she kept up the Fluxus work, maybe today she'd be as famous as Alison Knowles or Yoshi Wada. Had she struck it rich in the conceptual art biz, she could afford to live in Alphabet City. Maybe. Don't waste any sentiment on Ono's career. She rode Fluxus as far as it went.

In fact, the 1966 trip to London, where she met Lennon, looks in retrospect like an instinctive escape from Fluxus's dead end. Her switch to rock, sneered at by her classical friends, was another ahead-of-its-time move; Laurie Anderson and Rhys Chatham led new music down the same path years later. "I didn't think the avant-garde was finished," she says. "It wasn't a logical conclusion. I just kept pursuing what was exciting, and I bumped into rock." Nor does Ono feel that her acceptance level was any higher when she was performing for avant-garde friends than it was in the pop world. "Even in friendly circles, people refuse to understand. I wouldn't say that I communicated better in the avant-garde. Some people understood it, some didn't, it's always 50-50, isn't it?"

The first Ryko disc, *London Jam,* contains the fruits of initial contacts with Lennon's friends, Ringo Starr and Eric Clapton among them. Ono was so wary of renewed criticism for these experimental improvs that she nearly left the disc out of *Onobox,* but critics are agreeing that it's her most compelling music. The pieces that rockers find *most* forward-looking, though, sound timid to me. Lennon was proud of his guitar playing on "Why," but the repeating rock bass lines over which Ono vocalizes in "Why" and "Why Not" *tame* the shrieking the B-52's claim as inspiration and mute the effect it must have had solo in a darkened, 1961 Carnegie Hall. (Ono credits her operatic training for enabling her to compete with electric guitars.) On the other hand, the vocal pieces over drones and non-melodic textures, like "Greenfield Morning I Pushed an Empty Baby Carriage All Over the City" and "Touch Me," have a well-honed intensity that would sound timely at the Knitting Factory in 1993.

And when the Beatles turned to Stockhausen for inspiration, Ono was ahead of them. Her "Paper Shoes" collage of 1970, with its freight train modulating into ecstatic drumming into a thunderstorm, is worthy musique concrète, introverted and better sounded-out than the *White Album*'s "Revolution No. 9." In "Head Play," Ono's suggestive breathing over audio circuits built by Fluxus composer Joe Jones creates a texture that would become pervasive in electronic music of the '70s. And there's something sweetly prescient about "Toilet Piece," a 31-second recording of a flushing toilet: a touch of Fluxus pointing to new music's sampled future.

Working with Ringo Starr and Eric Clapton gave Ono a focus that set her apart from a Fluxus crowd that looks homogeneous in hindsight, but it caught her between conflicting standards of success. In the avant-garde milieu she had come from, selling 500 copies of a record would have been counted glorious vindication. Yet, pointing to the *Somewhere in New York* album (excerpted on the last disc of *Onobox, A Story*), with its once-censored photo pasteup of Nixon and Mao dancing nude, she says, "This was the album that ruined John's career. For John, not to be in the top 40 was a terrible failure.

"I was excited by what I did with *London Jam.* Then we put out this record called *Yoko Ono/Plastic Ono Band,* and it was like, no sound coming back: the sound of one hand clapping. It was debilitating, in a way. I didn't think, Oh, this is not the way to go to get a sound back, and therefore I shouldn't do this. But maybe I was affected on a deep subconscious level. I started to get all these incredible—well, incredible is an adjective I should not use, maybe—inspirations for songs, and I wrote them down." Consciously or not, Ono set aside her wild standards and tried to conform to new ones. The remaining five discs are full of rock songs, though she says her formula (perhaps learned from the *White Album*) was to get across one "weird" piece on each disc.

If there's a common thread between Ono's Fluxus concept pieces and songs, it's the use of words to evoke visual images. Every Ono work begins as a text, which may then turn into a film, a performance, a painting, a mental image, a jam session, or a song. There are overt links, in fact, between her instruction pieces and lyrics. A 1967 piece from *Grapefruit* called "Water Talk" ("you are water / I'm water / we're all water in different containers") is the precursor to the jaunty 1972 song "We're All Water" ("There may not be much difference / Between Chairman Mao and Richard Nixon / If we strip them naked"). Another love song, "Have You Seen a Horizon Lately," comes from a concept piece that continues, "Measure it from where you stand and let us know the length."

When I mention the ubiquity of word-pictures in her work, Ono brightens as though she'd been waiting for someone to notice. "I have a strange kind of cross-line there [pointing to her brain] between the visual and the auditory. When a song hits me and I put it down, there's a visual image as well. Of course, when I hear sounds I see color and picture and everything." Even sonically, Fluxus fingerprints dot the songs. "Yes, I'm Your Angel" begins with a radio, environmental sounds, footsteps, a door opening. Ono began her composing career by notating bird songs, and birds turn up here in intros and fadeouts. The art/life boundary is often fuzzy: the opening of "It's Alright" is a tape of son Sean pleading, "Mommy, you have to wake up." It's as though Ono wants you to get a picture in your mind before the song starts, and the music is there to carry the visuals.

Perhaps it's not so much that Fluxus pervades Ono's rock as that the talents that made her an interesting conceptualist limited her songwriting to some static, if unconventional, archetypes. Many of the songs arise from strong verbal concepts, few from musical inspirations. The tics that repel many rock fans are well known. She did not inherit, by marriage, Lennon's gift for melody. In lieu of melody, she often has a spurt of words on each downbeat. Her model for ballads is not the Beatles, but the 1930s theater of Brecht and Weill. Her pitch inflections show the influence of her mother, who sang traditional Japanese styles; they aim at a speech quality, but to the Western ear they can sound counterintuitive, if not out of tune.

But when Ono unleashes her oddness, she can evoke striking musical images, often resulting more in chants than songs. "Namyohorengekyo," never before released, is a charming setting of a karma-releasing Buddhist chant popular in the early '70s. In it Ono gets an unearthly sound by over-dubbing her voice at close intervals and then omitting tracks to get the chords she wanted. "Let the Tears Dry" uses overtone melodies of whirled tubes as background for an encouraging chorus about grief and hope. I don't think it's my avant-garde imagination that the "weird" songs are the best, the most honest. It delights her that I like "No, No, No," a grinding feminist song full of staccato, tritone dissonances, and the weepy, buoyant synthesizer glissandos in "Spec of Dust."

Is this an apology for Ono's music? Well, if honest intentions made art great, we'd have a lot more great art. As an avant-gardist, I'm tempted to say, She's one of us; don't hold her to pop rules. For instance, I find "Walking on Thin Ice" (admittedly a rock-critic favorite) a string of rhyming-dictionary and beatbox clichés, but it opens an intriguing formal problem by breaking out of verse and ending with a prose poem; listening, I'm left cold, but reading, I think, "Wow, what an odd idea." The *Onobox* has its share of such ear-disappointers, though it also offers tuneful, painfully honest love songs like "Nobody Sees Me Like You Do" and provocatively philosophical dances like "Hell in Paradise." Which 35 of the 105 songs you'll hate depends on where you're coming from. Hearing the *Onobox* sideways by way of the Beatles, though, rather than forward from Fluxus, leaves much of Ono's sensibility unexplained.

Ono tells me a revealing story. She didn't meet her father until she was two and a half. The first thing he did, she remembers, is examine her fingers for pianistic potential. The pressure ruined her; she never learned to stretch wide enough to play octave passages well. Ever since, her life has been a spark of genius bouncing off a wall of expectations symbolized by men: her father, Ichiyanagi, Cage, Maciunas, that Man Among Men Lennon, and finally the public she's still trying to reach. The aggrandized Father Figure looms shadowlike over her work, and not only in the ambiguous yearnings of the feminist songs. This latter-day Alma Mahler (another composer who kept marrying artists) is so conflicted between feverish originality and a desire to be liked that more than once during our interview she makes a defiant statement about how unimportant it is to be understood, then recoils and says, "No, I take back what I said."

"There were always people who felt, that was very Fluxus, or that was not Fluxus. Or, that's not rock. Or, what I thought was poetry, no, that's more like prose. Something maybe doesn't fit, but that part is me. You always end up being yourself. You think you've reached so far, and you look in the mirror and you're the same you. I got cold feet a couple of years ago and said, Do I want to go on like this? Keep on creating? Part of me thinks as long as I enjoy it it's fine. The other part of me thinks it's very hard to keep on being me." Listening to *Onobox*, you can hear Ono's originality flare into fireworks, then drown in commonplaces, over and over.

Ono's come to the café from a recording studio, but she won't hint what she's working on. Her most recent visual work, on display last month at Mary Boone Gallery, is a sculpture called *Endangered Species: 2319–2322:* a group of bronze, slightly melted human figures, supposedly people dug up centuries from now. Along with the figures are sculptures of their "thought forms," or dreams, objects that materialize their reactions and fears. It may be her first visual piece in which the concept not only inspires humor and insight, but a real emotional response. Ono's only an amazingly young-looking 59. Rockers are through by that age, but not artists. There's a lot more to Ono than *Onobox*.

midtown avant-gardist

philip glass sails columbus into a clash of keys and cultures

OCTOBER 27, 1992

As his reputation has it, Philip Glass writes "going nowhere" music. His music sure seems like it's going somewhere to me: to the Metropolitan Opera first, then Brooklyn Academy of Music, the Joyce Theater, and the Public Theater. Once upon a time Glass electrified the Soho loft scene with his virtuoso ensemble's austere, multilinear process pieces, which pioneered breathtaking approaches to superfast, irregular rhythm. Then in the '80s, he seemed to retire into the mainstream (yawn), forever to churn out predictable reams of arpeggios and scales in 4/4 meter (in a wild moment, maybe 6/8). Suddenly, he's back. The "'70s composer" we had forgotten about is all over New York, inescapable. Why Glass? Why now?

Maybe it's music's version of the Perot phenomenon. If neither Uptown nor Down has much use for Glass at the moment, that may show how out-of-touch both parties are. Musicologist Susan McClary, in her recent book

Feminine Endings, cites Glass as a victim of the business's macho bias. Since his music avoids forward motion or climax, she argues, it flouts the expectations of our traditionally patriarchal sense of form. Twelve-toners dismiss it as theoretically wimpy; improvisers concur that it's not "kickass" enough. General audiences don't necessarily give a damn. They want it to sound good.

But is Glass an audience's composer or an impresario's composer? The latter may love him for a nonmusical reason, his meticulous professionalism. Commissioned by the Met to write a Columbus opera, *The Voyage,* he turned in the score, parts, and piano-vocal score to the Met library months early, July of '91, for this month's premiere. "The Met's not used to doing new composers," Glass explains in the kitchen of his East Village brownstone, "and I thought it would do everyone a favor to have the music in early. The choral director might like to start rehearsing in the spring, I didn't know. It's a great reputation to have. People know they can count on you." If you were a producer risking millions on a new opera, isn't that attitude the first thing you'd want in a composer? (In 1986 the Met canceled Jacob Druckman's opera because he was so far behind schedule.)

One of the savviest and most articulate musicians I've ever met, Glass realizes that even his best fans tend to like only half his output. Admitting to a split between his "lyrical" and "rigorous" sides, he notes that hardcore new-music types lament his downhill slide after his 1974 classic *Music in 12 Parts.* Others prefer the lyricism in *Songs from Liquid Days* and *Hydrogen Jukebox.* Glass has emphasized the lyrical in recent years, and now he's betting that *The Voyage* will bring some "rigorous" listeners back to the fold. Premiering on the 500th Columbus Day, *The Voyage* is an oblique Columbus portrait, with a libretto by David Henry Hwang of *M. Butterfly* fame, who previously worked with Glass on *1,000 Airplanes on the Roof.*

Glass's operas have never favored realism. *The Voyage* takes Columbus as one in a series of exploration metaphors. In Act I a spaceship lands on earth in 50,000 B.C., and in Act III scientists receive signals from outer space. "We play on the cultural confrontation which has been on everyone's minds," explains Glass, "in an allegorical rather than literal way. When you deal with a subject allegorically you bring less baggage and can think more clearly. Columbus and the Indians is such an emotional issue, it's hard to get anybody to disagree about it. Everyone knows he didn't behave very well. But if you can't go beyond that, you get stuck in Indians and us and white people and black people.

"At the end of Act I David wrote a beautiful scene where the commander, who's a woman, meets the natives. She does an aria in which she talks about, 'I wonder what they expect from me, what do they think I'm going to do for them, who do they think I am?' Then the chorus sings the same words back to her. It becomes evident that there is no objective way for cultures to see each other, that every point of view will be subjective. It's a statement we might not have come to had we dealt with Columbus and the Indians per se. David is first-generation Chinese American, and doesn't write from that white European male viewpoint that we now know we've suffered under."

In Act II, Columbus appears, but "never arrives. It's not the 33rd day at sea, it's the 32nd day. In fact, our opera takes place October 11. I may not have told the people at the Met that." The opera's prologue contains a character based on Stephen Hawking. "What interested me was a scientist who does it in a wheelchair, who travels to the very edge of the universe. Explorers are not necessarily Indiana Jones characters. They can be artists or scientists, the explorations can be spiritual, mental, or physical. I wanted to extend the range of the opera that way. The second act is Columbus as Noah, Ulysses, the Flying Dutchman, people who *have* to find courage because they are so alone, whose only resource becomes themselves. I'm interested in courage, and in doubt. They go together."

Act III jumps to the year 2092, with two scientists looking for life in outer space. They discover crystals that, when put together, amplify radio signals, and begin receiving messages from another solar system. In a humorous scene with cheerleaders, a band, and the chorus as spectators, astronauts leave to seek the source of the signals. "As the astronauts say goodbye, David made a nice point I wouldn't have noticed: every time we leave, we're leaving somebody behind. This is the side of discovery that we forget about, that it's about parting. We have a final scene with Columbus in 1506. He's dying, Isabella's already dead, but he has one last duet with her, and finally explains himself."

Musically, what's new? *The Voyage* isn't enough of a departure to convert inveterate Glass-haters, but its subtle advances in complexity are pervasive. Rhythm is once again a big issue. The score relies heavily on syncopating 3/4 meter as 6/8—no big deal in itself—but Glass milks that tic further than you'd think. The growling, whirlwind prologue keeps several rhythmic levels going at once, setting up nice tempo tensions of three against four. Elsewhere, phrase lengths expand from 7/8 to 9/8, melodies repeat in intricate cycles of 49 beats, in the jumpy way of Glass's early process pieces such as *Music in Similar Motion* and *Music with Changing Parts.* "The ideas I concentrate on gradually become secondary," says Glass, "background instead of foreground. Certain kinds of additive rhythm I've used a lot are still there, but instead of being the subject of the work, they create the context for other things. If you listen carefully you'll say, 'Oh yeah, that's five plus four plus three, Glass always does that.' But it goes by so fast that you'd have to know my music to be aware of it. Whereas, in *Music in Similar Motion*, that would be the whole piece."

Such details are linked to the structure of the story. "The only way music can be profoundly successful," Glass contends, "is if the musical language is part of the *argument* of the piece. The argument of *The Voyage* is sketchy and a little abstract, but there's enough of one. Finding a way of working on a musical idea *through* the dramatic idea is the key to doing opera." For instance, *Einstein on the Beach* of 1976 is about combining a functional harmony and a rhythmic structure into a unified entity; that's most audible in the "spaceship" scene. *Satyagraha* of 1981 is a series of seven chaconnes, the chaconne being a Baroque-era form of continuous variation over a repeating harmonic progression. Robert Ashley has also based operas on the chaconne, with dissimilar results; it's natural, Glass notes, that "my generation, which is interested in repetition, is drawn to a formal device in early music also based on repetition."

Glass calls *Akhnaten* (1983) his first experiment in polytonality, the music being in several keys at once. "What I was trying to do in *Akhnaten* was make the perception of the harmony ambivalent. You could analyze a particular number in several keys, but not two at the same time. It was like an optical illusion, such as in Albers, where you could look at it two ways, but not both ways at once; it can't resolve itself. It was my first extension out of a triadic harmonic language which had been fairly simple up until then."

The Voyage, his ninth opera, extends *Akhnaten*'s polytonality into a metaphor of coexisting cultures that can't blend. The entire work is based on a familiar but theoretically problematic chord: the augmented triad (C, E, G-sharp). "The piece is an exploration of what an augmented triad really is. The sound of the crystals is the augmented triad. It's never out of earshot for long. People say a right angle doesn't exist in nature; in a certain way, an augmented triad doesn't exist in nature. It's an invented, conceptual chord. And by the time I wrote the epilogue, I finally saw what it is. We find it in polytonal music. It can be explained as a natural result of an extended diatonicism towards bitonality. That made me feel good, because I found a new way of thinking about music through thinking through this process."

Got that? In this respect Glass is no different from Schoenberg, who wrote his Chamber Symphony No. 1 to try out all possible resolutions to a chord made of stacked perfect-fourth intervals. Such thinking can make

Glass's music thrilling. For example, the clash of A-flat major and E minor in the Epilogue to *Akhnaten:* those incommensurate keys won't blend, and their repeated seesawing finally balances them in your ear like two plausible but contradictory thoughts. This is why his music still requires repetition, and why, at its best, it repays attention to subtle relationships of harmony and voice-leading (the melodic ways in which harmonies connect). One thing Glass learned from studying with Nadia Boulanger—the century's most famous composition teacher, who also taught Copland, Barber, and other celebrated Americans—was to be meticulous about voice-leading. Nestle an A-flat major triad inside an E-minor one, and you can see where that influence survives.

The Voyage goes even further. In its opening moments, the lower strings spin out E-minor scales while the chorus repeatedly enters on an *E-flat major* triad. That's a common Glass contrast, but rarely if ever has he held the dissonance in such a sustained way. As it repeats, that gritty effect sounds more and more transparent, and key clashes related to it color the opera. (If you're looking for the augmented triad, take the E-flat from the E-flat triad, the B of the E-minor triad, and their common note G.) In the final scene, as Columbus dies in a monastery, Dominican monks sing a flowing chant that rolls into a thread the chord relationships we've been hearing all evening.

Glass felt freer to write such dissonant choral parts and rhythmic difficulties because of the Met's expert forces. "The Met's such an ideal situation," he sighs. "Most opera orchestras aren't that good. You write difficult music for them at your peril; especially the kind I write, where there's no place to hide, you can hear everything. With most orchestras I've held back, with this orchestra I didn't. And they're working very hard." It's the audience who *doesn't* have to work hard, because after three hours those chord clashes have been turned through every possible perspective in slow motion. Envious composers complain that Glass's music is diluted by repetition, but it lays out complex information at a pace listeners can take in comfortably.

In fact, Glass's music is not only going somewhere, it's on a route no one else is taking. From *Music in Fifths* through *The Voyage*, Glass has retraced the history of musical materials from Gregorian chant to impressionism, getting a little more complex with each major work. After all, he came to John Cage's influence not from the more common direction of Ives and Schoenberg, but via Boulanger and Darius Milhaud; not from a chromatic, complex tradition, but from a tonal, diatonic one. His is a *conservative* background, not even Uptown but Midtown, diffracted through the '6os avant-garde, and there aren't many other examples. (It's a kick to run across, in music libraries, the Coplandy scores Glass published before his conversion.)

When Glass talks history, you hear names other composers don't mention. One of Glass's profs, Vincent Persichetti, wrote a book on polytonal harmony, but Glass traces his interest in polytonality to Milhaud, whom he studied with one summer at Aspen and admires profoundly. "He made a subtle contribution to 20th-century music. We tend to concentrate on the biggies, like Boulez, Stockhausen, Bartók, and forget other influences which may be subtler but more lasting. Like Debussy. I think about him more now than I ever did. Not a popular idea.

"History's curious, because our interests change, and as they change, our evaluation of the past changes. There were 20 years where no one listened to Bartók. Now we're hearing him again. There's no final judgment of history, because we judge music from the point of view of the present, and the present will always be new." This season, the present is Glass, and as *The Voyage* plays, history seems to shift uneasily. Adventurer in a wheelchair, or maybe an armchair, is a good image, for he's slowly exploring music's microcosm.

trimpin's machine age

a revolutionary tinker revives the dream of infinitely fluid music

APRIL 20, 1993

SEATTLE—A black frame ominously straddles the lidless grand piano in Trimpin's studio. It supports a quartet of precision-cut metal bars, from which dangle golf tees, bronze discs, rubber wedges, and other trinkets. This is the Contraption IPP 71512. The number refers arcanely to one of the machine's earlier incarnations, and IPP stands for Instant Prepared Piano. When finished, the Contraption will insert its tees and wedges between the piano strings at the whim of a computer, switching automatically between prepared and unprepared piano. Trimpin, who's been giving me a demonstration, leaves to answer the phone, and I absentmindedly touch a button on a black box. With a whirring growl that scares my hands into my pockets, the Contraption rises and rotates to an expectant halt. I sense its indignation at being called to life by the hand of a tyro.

You can see the Contraption played by its creator at the Kitchen (April 16 and 17), where Composers' Forum is bringing Trimpin (who goes only by his last name) back for his second New York appearance. Trimpin's first gig here, New Music America '89, was incredible, he filled a room with saxophones, xylophones, violins, drums, pianos, and other instruments, all playing themselves without human intervention. Trimpin makes computer music, but he uses no electronic sounds. His ensembles have no amplifiers or loudspeakers. His works rarely involve human performers (though at the Kitchen, he'll guide part of the Contraption by hand while the computer plays it). A genius at circuitry and machinery as well as acoustics and musical structure, he manufactures orchestras that play themselves.

The Kitchen concert will be a mere taste, for it would take days to do Trimpin's artistry justice; also a bigger pile of moola, for his equipment is expensive to transport. One of his installations was a six-story-high xylophone running through a spiral staircase in an Amsterdam theater; microtonal melodies zipped from the ground floor to the sixth floor with lightning speed. Another was a water-fountain fugue, with precise, computer-dripped rhythms echoing each other across a roomful of glass receptacles. For a dance piece, Trimpin designed costumes that squeaked and squawked. The dancers' shoes contained small bellows that played tuned duck calls, while under their armpits were air blowers that played reeds as the dancers flapped their arms in a satirical rendition of *La Traviata*.

Trimpin has computer-mechanized every instrument of the orchestra, and, not interested in duplicating efforts of live musicians, he extends the instruments' capabilities. His cellos, for instance, play much slower, longer, perfectly even bowings than any live hand could achieve. His timpani mallets don't merely beat the drumhead: "I can place the beater on the skin," he explains, "and vibrate it very rapidly so that the lower frequencies build up gradually. You get tremendous harmonics, and a sustained note on the timpani. No human could keep the pressure that fast and precise."

Trimpin's visions laugh at physical limitations. One upcoming project is a gamelan suspended in air. Magnets hold the iron bells up, a beam of light holds them down; as soon as a bell rises too close to the magnet, a photo sensor breaks the circuit, turning the magnet off and keeping the bell suspended in oscillating stasis. Since the bells don't touch anything solid, their ring (incited by mechanical mallets) has a phenomenally long decay, and, Trimpin claims, as they vibrate, they start to spin. His next commission is for a quartet of bass clarinets, which he will deepen an octave or more downward by two- to three-foot extensions. Extra keys will spiral around the instruments as closely as possible for a scale of tiny microtones. And since humans only have 10 fingers, a computer will play those extra keys, allowing for impossibly fast microtonal glissandos. All the clarinetists do is blow.

Trimpin's spacious, cluttered studio combines a machinist's shop with a Dr. Seuss world of imaginary music. On a high shelf rest eight timpani mounted on their sides to accommodate mechanical mallets. On the wall is a Siamese-twin trombone, slide on one tube, valves on the other, on which two melodies can be played at once through a split mouthpiece. By a window is a double bass with a brass mouthpiece sticking out of the side: the instrument actually has a baritone horn *inside* it, so that you can play the horn, which resonates inside the bass body, while bowing the bass. Overhead are fiberglass tubes with metal horn bells at one end, duck calls at the other. Mechanical xylophones and maracas on hinges surround the room. Hanging from the ceiling are tuba parts, cellos, violins, French horn bells, rubber tubes, a manikin, and several naked baby dolls. The entire room is strung with ribbon cable.

The studio is an extension of Trimpin's childhood. He grew up in Germany near the French and Swiss borders, on the Rhine near Basel, speaking the near-extinct Allemanish dialect. With his thick beard, long hair, and etched features, Trimpin has the look of a 19th-century hermit/saint. You could also imagine him working on the crew of a salmon-fishing boat in Alaska's Bristol Bay, which is, in fact, exactly what he occasionally does when his grants and commissions run out.

"As a kid I had my own workshop and tools," recalls Trimpin, whose father was a brass and woodwind player. "I was constantly cutting instruments up and exchanging sections. When I studied the flugelhorn I wanted to make a longer bell, or increase the length of the tubes. One day when I was eight, my father said, 'Let's go in the forest and play some music.' It sounded strange, but I said, I guess I have to go. It was a great experience. It was not very interesting music, simple duets for flugelhorns, but those echoes! I will never forget this first awareness of what acoustics are. From that point I was always determined to go beyond what you could play normally. At 10 or 12 years old, I would go to the junkyard and pick up old shortwave radios, stack up 10 into a sculpture, and hook them up to antennas of 300, 400 feet. I liked the weird sounds you got from turning the knobs between stations. I had to do this in secret, because my parents would have thought it was too dangerous to work with 220 volts."

Trimpin's early teachers declared him incapable of learning because his mind ran in such odd channels. Nevertheless, he studied metal work and electronics at apprenticeship school, then decided to go back into music. For a music therapy course, he invented a light-sensitive keyboard for handicapped patients that they could play by moving a light pencil with their mouths. Like all German artists, Trimpin waxes eloquent on the superiority of European educational methods and art habits, but his high-tech needs drove him to America; he took a studio in Seattle 13 years ago.

"I came to this country for junk: high-tech equipment which is disposed of or obsolete, but still has certain parts I can use. Everything on the Contraption is a found object. In Europe there was no place to buy surplus material, or used equipment. You had to buy it new. And this was too expensive, especially over there, and especially in the early days of the computer. The optical disc reading system I was using to run my pieces was too slow and limited. I was paralyzed. I couldn't go on."

He went to Seattle, he says, because it sounded like a nice place to live. Trimpin sees himself continuing the ancient art of mechanical music, a tradition that has abruptly shifted direction in this century. The Romans had water-powered mechanical organs, and the earliest surviving instructions for building a self-automated instrument (a set of flutes) are found in an Arabic manuscript from 890 A.D. Mechanical instrument design leaped ahead with Robert Fludd in the 17th century, and automatic organs became a popular plaything of 18th-century aristocrats. Composers who wrote for mechanical organs and orchestras included C. P. E. Bach, W. F. Bach, Haydn, Mozart, Beethoven, Salieri, and Albrechtsberger (Beethoven's composition teacher). Superseding the 19th century's automated orchestras called "Panharmonicons" (for which Beethoven wrote *Wellington's Victory*), the player piano became a staple of bourgeois homes, its popularity peaking in the early 1970s with the production of a quarter-million a year.

But with mass marketing of the phonograph around 1930, mechanical instrument sales screeched to a halt. "It was easier to change a record," notes Trimpin, "than a roll or cylinder. Automated instruments were made for entertainment purposes, and were never accepted as musically respectable. The composers who wrote for them—even Stravinsky, who wrote for player piano—never used them as a tool to go beyond what a normal instrument could do."

As so often in music history, the medium's death as an entertainment venue coincided with its birth as an art form. In his *New Musical Resources*, written in 1916–17 but published in 1930, Henry Cowell outlined rhythmic complexities outside the realm of human performance, but suggested using the player piano to realize them. Nine years later, Cowell's book fell into the hands of a fiery, Texarkana-born composer named Conlon Nancarrow, who was just leaving New York for Mexico City to avoid harassment from the government for his Communist Party affiliations. In 1948 Nancarrow returned to New York briefly to buy a player piano and a roll-punching machine, and began punching out the most rhythmically complex music ever written, his 49 Studies for Player Piano.

"When I first heard Nancarrow's music, I got addicted," says Trimpin. (He confesses a similar obsession with Anthony Braxton.) "But I thought, what a pity, to have just one instrument. His music would be so different if the voices were separated, or different in timbre." Trimpin tried to look Nancarrow up in Mexico City, but didn't meet him until Nancarrow was invited to Amsterdam for the 1987 Holland Festival. Trimpin had built a box with a player-piano mechanism that could convert the hole punches of piano rolls into MIDI computer information. Nancarrow was skeptical. Trimpin said, "Look, I have this machine that could read your rolls, and I would love to have access to them. He said he didn't think a computer could read this stuff, because some other people had already tried it. I brought him to my studio and took a typical player piano roll to show him how the computer could pick up the precise notes and durations from the roll. And he couldn't believe it. He said, 'How can this work?'"

That fateful meeting put Trimpin at the center of the musicology and preservation of Nancarrow's music. He's got the data from all of Nancarrow's rolls stored in his computer, and even a machine that can repunch the rolls from MIDI information. (Now, should Nancarrow's studio ever burn down, the rolls aren't lost forever.) At the Kitchen, Trimpin'll play some music by Nancarrow that has never been heard publicly. Nancarrow's assistant, Carlos Sandoval, recently discovered more than 40 rolls that Nancarrow had tossed aside, and Trimpin copied them during a November trip to Mexico City. Among them are unfinished pieces, preliminary sketches, and works intended not for player piano, but for the abandoned, roll-run percussion machine Nancarrow tried to build in the '50s. Among the "lost" rolls Trimpin might bring us is a bluesy, ostinato-filled sketch for Study No. 41, far too complete and exciting a piece to have thrown away.

Although Trimpin had made mechanical music before he'd heard of Nancarrow, their lives and aesthetics are full of parallels. (Even Trimpin's studio, with its multiple keyboards, ubiquitous drawers, and personalized clutter, feels like Nancarrow's.) Of his Contraption music, Trimpin says, "The whole piece isn't so much based on compositional material as on the texture of the piano, what you can do with sounds." That's true of Nancarrow's music, too: both composers work, not with detailed pitch syntax, but with large-scale symmetries and layered sound structures. Like Nancarrow, Trimpin is fascinated by different tempos competing at once, and he sees them as a way to explore spatial acoustics.

"When two instruments play the same pitch just slightly off from opposite directions, they cancel each other out, and the sound location moves from one side to the other. It would be interesting to see how this cancellation works with close tempos. I'm convinced that the relationship between pitch and tempo goes into the acoustic dimension. I can't prove it yet. What I have in mind is a sphere with acoustic instruments in circular configurations, both vertical and horizontal; say, eight or 10 octaves of marimba bars in one row, wood blocks in the next, brass in the next, and so on, with the listener in the middle."

As for amplification, Trimpin isn't against it on principle, but because of electronic sound's limitations. "We have all this fancy digital recording equipment, and we still use a loudspeaker design which is nearly a hundred years old, this big magnet with a magnetic coil and a physical membrane. It's laughable. Digitally, every detail gets recorded, but the output lacks the resonance of the instrument. The future of loudspeakers is a different design that resembles more the acoustic resonance of instruments. Then we can talk about physical response."

A revolutionary potential of Trimpin's technology is that it could someday offer composers the chance to hear their works played by a mechanized orchestra, freed from dependence on conductors, orchestra managers, and recalcitrant or inadequate players. But that day is a ways off. "I'm still five or 10 years from the point of having other composers work with this array of instruments. It looks simple because we're used to MIDI instruments which are pre-programmed, more idiot-proof to operate. It's not like telling a musician to play *ff* and then crescendo. You have no idea how time-consuming it is to communicate all this information to a so-called intelligent instrument."

Nevertheless, electronic music had offered us a dream of an infinitely fluid music, fluid as to tuning, timbre, spatial location, rhythmic structure, speed. Because of the limitations of electronic sounds and loudspeakers, that dream didn't materialize. But now, with Trimpin's spatialized, computer-run orchestras, the dream is back.

dancing with the audience

carman moore's *mass* attempts to heal the world

AUGUST 9, 1994

You could be a new-music devotee and never have heard of Carman Moore. Conversely, you could be a fan of Moore's Skymusic ensemble and unable to name another living composer. At once pop and classical, Uptown and Down,

Moore has had impressive orchestral commissions (one for the New York Philharmonic from Pierre Boulez himself), yet has been little written about. He's been active in New York for three decades, but you won't hear his music played by the Uptown groups, at Downtown spaces, or even at new-music festivals: steering a maverick path, he's taken it directly to the people.

The *Mass* began to take shape three years and 11 months ago, when Saddam Hussein invaded Kuwait. Moore had wanted to write a piece celebrating the end of the communist/capitalist conflict, but Gulf War tensions shocked him into conceiving a renewed prayer for peace. "I felt so personally offended," he says from his apartment overlooking Lincoln Center, "that that kind of thing was starting up again." Focusing on the ways in which baby-boomers, despite their early ideals, have failed to nourish today's youth, Moore made children's choirs the centerpiece of his *Mass*. · He recruited singers for this production from a wide range of communities: the New York Muslim Youth Choir, the Seamen's Church Institute Choir, the LaGuardia High School choir, the Chinese-American Children's Choir of Northern New Jersey, and the Hare Krishna Choir from Long Island. Total number of singers: 200, split evenly between children and adults, including as soloist Cissy Houston, Whitney's mother and an old friend. Twenty-five dancers will perform as well, all accompanied by the 13-piece Skymusic ensemble.

Moore's lived in the same apartment for most of his life—31 years out of 57—after going to grad school at Juilliard, a block away. There he got the full conservatory shtick, studying with Vincent Persichetti, Hall Overton, and the Italian master Luciano Berio. While at Juilliard, though, he took a left turn Downtown, becoming involved with the Judson Church, where Claes Oldenberg, Jim Dine, and others staged the first happenings. "We were having all-night, nonjazz jam sessions," Moore recalls. "Despite being trained to the teeth at Juilliard, we were banging on bottles, blowing whistles, stomping on the floor. Terry Riley was there and would get a bunch of people at the organ, making noise all night. I got some confidence in improvisation doing that, not based on the jazz idea of running changes, but leading people through the maze of their subconscious. In a short time, banging bottles disappeared and I found I could use the Juilliard stuff and still improvise something totally new."

Moore's involvement in the burgeoning Downtown scene was verbal as well as musical: from 1967 to 1974 he wrote criticism for the *Voice*, discussing Uptown and Downtown new music, jazz, and pop with ecumenical open-mindedness. His talent with words had already brought him second prize in a *Voice* poetry contest ("I won a year's subscription and some books signed by Marianne Moore and Robert Lowell, the contest judges"); it more recently enabled him to write the libretto for his *Mass*, which, like Leonard Bernstein's, departs from the Catholic liturgy for dramatic effect. (Moore claims his own spiritual viewpoint is closest to Taoism, which has no church, no clergy, and no bible.) Along with the "Kyrie eleison," "Gloria," and "Alleluiah" of the traditional mass, there are also songs detailing society's ills:

> Till everything is possible and everything is mine,
> And everything is multiplied many, many times, . . .
> Till everything's identified and all is broken down,
> And I've the key to everything and everything's in town, . . .
> Till everyone is specialized and knows just what to do,
> And every law is averaged and all the people too, . . .
> Progress. Progress. This is Manchild's dream.

The most literary part of the *Mass* is a "meditation on the 20th century" in which sampled voices representing major world figures—Queen Victoria, Gertrude Stein, Albert Schweitzer, Jung, Hitler, Gandhi—speak and argue, opening with a quote from Queen Victoria's diary for New Year's Day, 1900. The music accesses styles from Gregorian chant to hip hop, but the only actual musical quotation is "The Blue Danube."

Such a mixture of conservatory polish and eclecticism hasn't endeared Moore to either jazz or new-music circles. Complaints: he's too versatile, he wanders from style to style with no personality of his own, his music is too soft-edged, too New Agey, his improvisation too restrained, his pop moments too sentimental. Of his attempt to rap in his *Mass* (in a song called "The Future's on Fire"), Moore admits that "the nicest thing some people had to say about my rapping was that it was 'genteel rap,' so I'm going to step back [and not do the rapping myself]." For all his use of vernacular idiom, Moore has a smooth classical sensibility and is not the type to turn raw emotion loose.

And yet most of the complaints are ways of saying that Moore is an audience's composer, rather than a musician's or critic's. You don't win friends in the field by coloring outside the lines. Pretty as Moore's music often is, it never lacks a formal rigor and directionality that distinguish it from New Age mindlessness. The only thing the *Mass* shares with minimalism is its leisurely, audience-friendly information pace. Underneath the simple surface lies an elaborate, Juilliard-trained sophistication. More than once I've listened to a simple Moore tune and found myself absorbed in some writhing background counterpoint that few in the crowd probably noticed. He weaves in subtle nuances for the expert listener even when he's circling an easy chord progression for the layman; wasn't that sort of new music's goal all along?

While speaking of careers, I suggested to Moore that perhaps reliance on specialist new-music groups and spaces encourages a suicidal isolation from nonspecialist audiences. "Well said," he replied. "I tend to think I wasn't accepted by these different places, but in reality, if I had forced it, I'm sure I could have made a home with any one of them. I had a feeling Boulez wanted me to be his protégé, to write his way and stay close artistically, but I wasn't interested. The piece I wrote for him had the flavor of [serialism], but it also had blues in the second movement. The *Mass* was written with the audience in mind, which is precisely the opposite of what I was taught—though not in so many words. But because I haven't been tied up with these places and people, I have indeed thought about the public, and I play with them in mind." At Skymusic's concerts you'll see that pay off. New-music aficionados don't show, but invariably a couple hundred enthusiastic and unfamiliar faces do.

One song from the *Mass* begins, "So why do we rage so, / My brothers, my sisters . . ." If Handel's *Messiah* just flashed through your mind, Moore's got you where he wants you. "I know people know 'Why do the nations / So furiously rage together,'" he confirms. "I'm acknowledging that and having fun with it. When I write something I'm trying it out on some part of myself that knows, or thinks it knows, what the listener is probably thinking." Moore's favorite head-trick is to mix and match genres. "For example, the 'Alleluiah' starts out as an Episcopal choirboys' song. I know the audience is going down that road [of thought]. Then at a certain point I slap a bass underneath it, and it starts to sound like it's going to become gospel. And then I let the gospel rip. It's the same tune, you just shift the environment. That's doing a dance with the audience. There's a piece called 'Hymn to Mother Earth' in which the accompanying instruments are from the Arabic world. The male choir is singing in neo-Gregorian chant style, and there are two Senegalese griots who are wailing away above the thing." One beautiful song with the line "To make a perfect harmony / Every bird must sing" allows the ensemble to improvise a panoply of birdsongs.

Such an ecumenical attitude runs against the currents of liberal identity politics that demand that minority artists express only a specific cultural viewpoint. In this respect, Moore is typical of musicians in general, for music isn't conducive to explicit political statements, and, almost perforce, musicians remain closer to the idea of a universal language than playwrights and visual artists. "This is part of the wave of balkanization that's going on worldwide," he says of such recent thought. "I hope it's temporary, because it really is about the illusion of separation that makes us forget that we're all just people. My work is going totally the other way, toward finding the language that we can all speak. Otherwise, we're going to end up starting wars that don't need to be started.

"Because the idea of 'making one world' has a lot of momentum, of course you get the fundamentalist breakout that is trying to say, 'Oh my god, my past is threatened.' The fears are based on not trusting the Tao, you know? Not understanding that all things are in growth and change at all times. To resist that is to cause yourself pain. If an Arab wants to do blues, or a Chinese person wants to do hip hop, culturally that's very exciting to me. If the music is so fragile that it's going to collapse if someone else is doing it, then it's not an authentically strong music. To have somebody of gift and thoughtfulness do a, let's call it a meditation on what somebody else does, is, I think, flattering."

Mass for the 21st Century realizes Moore's most global ambitions yet. Sections of the work have been performed at the Cathedral of St. John the Divine, where Moore is artist-in-residence, and after this Lincoln Center premiere, Skymusic will tour the piece in Trinidad and then Japan, for the 50th anniversary of the end of World War II. He's seeking funding for a "set of celebrations" in South Africa for the first anniversary of Nelson Mandela's election. "The activity of the *Mass* project is to go to places, form choirs and dance companies, incorporate local musicians. Like going to India and forming a choir with both Hindus and Moslems, or whatever. The *Mass* is meant to go out as a healing force." Whether it heals or not, it will reach more ears than if Moore had followed the usual composer's track.

harps from heaven

glenn branca reemerges from the thick of theory

NOVEMBER 22, 1994

Had he kept tinkering with theoretical systems, Glenn Branca says today, he might be as lost to history as his hero, the German theorist Hans Kayser, whose beautiful spirals and pyramids adorn the sketches for Branca's symphonies. "A lot of people think I've already dropped off the face of the earth," he adds with a melancholic edge. But if Branca hasn't been very audible in New York these last few years, it's not for lack of work.

Most of his commissions come from Europe now, and his projects are usually too mammoth to be easily repeatable. "I spend months writing a piece, it gets one performance for 700 people in Graz or Linz, no proper recording, and it's gone. My Symphony No. 8, commissioned by Expo '92 in Seville, was heard by an audience of tourists who had come to the world's fair. That was the end of it." Not quite—that symphony, along with Branca's Tenth, will shake the Kitchen November 16 through 20. The king of the multiple electric guitars strums again.

Enjoying his outcast role even as he distances himself from it, Branca, at 46, indulges his past reputation with weary reluctance. He just wants to write for European orchestra now, though he dreams of augmenting that orchestra with sitars, bagpipes, sarangis, tambouras, steel drums, hurdy-gurdies. He scored Symphony No. 10 for guitars only to fulfill a commission. Even so, he realizes he's in the lucky position of having two audiences to satisfy, and that he's been edging away from the more enthusiastic one.

Like Debussy, whose music has always appealed to both sensuous traditionalists and 20th-century analytic types, Branca captures the ears of both underground rockers and new-music intellectuals. But while the erstwhile punk rockers who love his blasting volume and blazing momentum show up for his orchestra pieces, he's not sure they'll buy his new incarnation. Meanwhile, the intellectuals who dig his tuning systems and overtone effects will be harder to impress in the saturated, more traditional orchestral genres.

Also, like La Monte Young, Branca derives some legendary panache from being a classical composer whose aesthetic once altered the course of rock. Thurston Moore and Lee Ranaldo played in his guitar ensemble in the early '80s, and eventually carried some of his motionless harmonies and odd tunings into Sonic Youth. Branca, however, doesn't relish the fact that part of his fame comes from this long-ago connection ("Is that enough about Sonic Youth?" he asks soon after I bring up the question). Nor, as he tells it, are they thrilled to still be tagged with this early influence.

"I didn't see Sonic Youth as ripping me off. They saw me going in this direction of extended instrumental pieces, and they thought there was a lot of potential for this kind of sound in commercial music. So they put the sound back into the context of rock songs, which I had left behind previously." Still, Branca remains not only a guiding light for alternative rockers, but a supportive friend. He helped Sonic Youth survive years of obscurity by releasing their first records on his Neutral label, and at last month's concert at CBGB's Gallery by the Branca-esque noise band Blastula, he was among the 10 people in the audience.

What he's saying about his own music, though, isn't what rockers expect to hear. "I'm more interested in thinking in terms of structure than of sound," he muses in his crowded Soho studio, crammed with books, computer equipment, Mahler and Wagner recordings, and a stack of guitar cases. (Apologizing, he claims his apartment is even smaller.) "In doing that I find myself failing on the side of sound sometimes.

"I'm trying to work with an idea of nonlinear music. This is why I consider myself a minimalist. Minimalism does not progress from left to right. It's about what happens *inside* the music. I'm trying to allow the music to change organically, so that you have the sense that you're experiencing the whole piece at once. One complaint I get from classical musicians is that there isn't the kind of change they normally expect. I use no crescendos, no accelerandos, no dynamic markings whatsoever. It's all played at the same level. But overt or obvious dynamic techniques distract the audience from listening *into* the music." It's a kind of '70s-style theory carried to '90s levels of subtlety. But is it enough to sustain his fans once the drums and hall-shaking vibrations are stripped away?

For someone who so symbolizes a musical crossroads, Branca keeps his worlds almost schizophrenically separate. To rock critics he'll talk Aerosmith, the Ramones, the Dolls, Henry Cow, and Orchestra Luna (the Boston band he claims David Byrne ripped off to create Talking Heads). With me he uses a different set of references, equally obscure: Krzysztof Penderecki, Dane Rudhyar, Hans Kayser. Originally, though, those worlds crept into his consciousness in parallel. Growing up in Harrisburg, Pennsylvania, his first love was Broadway musicals (especially Steven Sondheim's notable flop *Anyone Can Whistle:* "Absolutely brilliant, very strange and atonal"). He didn't care for rock until "a Kinks song that was very repetitious jumped out of the radio at me. 'You Really Got Me,' and 'All Day and All of the Night,' and a Paul Revere and the Raiders song called 'Just Like Me': they all had this same kind of uptight repetition. It wasn't until years later that I realized I was attracted to the repetition itself."

His first highbrow experience, in the '60s, was a PBS performance of a piano cycle by Olivier Messiaen. "That hit me right in the forehead. I started doing musique concrète. My parents would buy me cheap reel-to-reel tape recorders, which would break a few months after I got them, so they would get me another, and another. I had three or four, all with different defects, so I made tape collages with all these *RRRngrrr RRRngrrr* sounds.

Then I heard Cage doing these wonderful noise collages, better than anything I had ever imagined."

Branca saw himself, though, as a theater person. After a year in London, he moved to Boston and founded the Bastard Theater. "It was totally abstract. I wasn't interested in anything remotely resembling a play, even though I had written a couple of plays. At first I used records for the music, but I finally decided I wanted to write my own. The actors played instruments I collected off the street: metal pots, broken-down piano sounding boards, sometimes a broken trombone, anything I could get my hands on. The budget would be like $40. I wish I had recordings of that music, but we only had one tape recorder, and we used that to get tape effects like live delay."

Moving to New York in 1976, he started a collaborative venture with Jeffrey Lohn, who had a first-floor Soho loft perfect for theater. Then, Branca remembers, "one day, in the middle of painting this loft black to turn it into a theater, I could no longer hold down the desire to start a band. Jeff said, 'Let's do it together.' He had a performance artist friend named Dan Graham who said, 'Why don't you play as part of this performance piece I'm doing at Franklin Furnace?' That gave us three weeks to find the instruments, find a drummer, and write all the songs. But we were young and had a lot of energy."

The resulting band, Theoretical Girls, "started out doing slightly skewed punk songs. Then we realized we could use more experimental ideas from our theater pieces. We never imagined that people would like it. We didn't care. But the stranger the music got, the bigger the audience got.

"Jeff and I got into an incredible competition as to who could make the most outrageous, completely ridiculous piece. I plugged a recording of white noise into the p.a.—a *wall* of white noise. Then we played a jagged version of 'You Really Got Me' by the Kinks underneath it. In one piece I wrote, each musician played at a different tempo. I played a fast Chuck Berry thing. The bass player did a sort of reggae pattern, at not only a different tempo, but a different feel entirely. The drummer was instructed to play something completely off with everything he heard. It sounded fabulous. These ideas are hardly revolutionary, but at the time they were pretty strange for a band at CBGB."

In fact, Theoretical Girls ended up at CBGB only because they had built up an art-world audience first, at Franklin Furnace, the Kitchen, and other such spaces. "We were boycotting the clubs at first. They paid the bands practically nothing, and were really sleazy about it. Eventually CBGB didn't have any choice but to book us, no matter how much they hated our noise music, because we made money for them. The art band thing became what was exciting. Even Robert Longo and Richard Prince, everybody who eventually became major visual artists, had bands. Then we were wiped out by neo-abstract expressionism. The art world lost interest, and the whole thing went *phffft.*"

Here, the story gets difficult to tell. The history of the artrock scene of 1977 to 1982 is still too touchy a subject to straighten out, mired as it is in one of those archetypal sibling rivalries like Boulez versus Stockhausen and Glass versus Reich. Everyone agrees that Rhys Chatham, then music director of the Kitchen, played bass during one song at a couple of Theoretical Girls gigs. Branca says this was Lohn's idea, to get Chatham to invite them to play at the Kitchen. If so, it worked. Meanwhile, Chatham hired Branca at least twice as a replacement to play with his guitar ensemble, Tone Deaf. Let us kill here and now all allegations (made by critics, not themselves) that either was ever a member of the other's band. Chatham, in his 1977 *Guitar Trio,* was working with overtones of a single pitch on several guitars. Did Branca steal that concept and make a career out of it? Chatham thinks so, but admits that he had no copyright over it as intellectual property. Branca says that's ridiculous, that he was already doing similar things anyway.

The primary problem seems to be that Branca got records out more quickly, inducing critics to give him all the credit for ideas he and Chatham were developing in tandem. Clearly, each had brought his own stuff to the party, and both admit their subsequent musics were quite dissimilar. It's safe to say that, since Chatham came from a classical background and Branca from rock, and both ended up making long ensemble pieces for electric guitars, that elusive substance called influence was exploding in all directions. But Branca's world had different rules than Chatham's. Word spreads rapidly in rock, sluggishly through classical channels. And this version of the feud doesn't even figure in Lohn, whose background was philosophy, and whom I remember best for his perky choral setting of Wittgenstein's *Tractatus,* minimalistically neoclassic. Today, like Chatham, Lohn resides in Paris, and is reportedly composing again.

Whatever the case, Branca soon abandoned Theoretical Girls and his other rock band the Static, and turned the corner of his own creative life with *Instrumental for Six Guitars* of 1979. The incredible din of electric guitars playing cluster chords took him by surprise. "I hadn't intended to imitate Penderecki—he was just about my favorite composer at the time— but I had Penderecki from heaven. I've still never figured out how this acoustic phenomenon in the last section of *Instrumental* occurs. The motivation of the early pieces was to get that sound to come out more: more voices, more trumpets, more harps from heaven. I started using denser harmonies, bigger clusters, and the closer and bigger they got the more I heard it. It's psychoacoustic. Part of it is the fact that the ear is being absolutely overloaded with sound. You start hearing things that aren't there. The mind starts to invent what's happening."

In researching overtones, Branca discovered Hans Kayser (1891–1964), who devoted his life to exploring properties of the whole number series and its ramifications for acoustics. In 1982, Branca's girlfriend turned him on to the French-born American astrologer-composer Dane Rudhyar, whose book *The Magic of Tone and the Art of Music* contained a virtual recipe for the sonic-spiritual experiences Branca was trying to create. In a section called "Holistic Resonance," Rudhyar speaks of producing "nonharmonic waves of sound in which the sense of individual notes and tonality is lost." He talks about "pleromas of sound," in which the pitch field is articulated by sonorities conducive to various psychic states.

Kayser's charts and Rudhyar's feeling-states have become central to Branca's aesthetic. He likes talking about his Ninth Symphony more than the others, but what he says about it applies to the Eighth and Tenth as well: "In Symphony No. 9 I interpolate 15 different types of change and variety and contrast. Each one has its own chart over the course of the piece: key change, mode change, rhythm change. They change at different times, to give you the feel that there's no obvious change coming at any one time, that there's a solid-state field occurring, within which the changes happen. Once I get it up on the computer and can play it through the sampler and hear it, I can play with it. I'm not strapped in by some kind of Cagean idea, or a mathematical formula that has to play itself out. I've done that kind of work, and seen the limitations of it.

"I'm not working with the harmonic series anymore. I went so deeply into process and mathematically determined music that I ended up coming out the other side. I realized that I was either going to become a theoretician or mathematician or philosopher, but I wasn't going to be a composer. What's important is to come back to intuitive composition, but from a perspective of process and what we've learned."

Branca sees his reemergence in New York as coinciding with the more composition-oriented aesthetic of the '90s, epitomized by composers like Michael Gordon, Mikel Rouse, David First, Evan Ziporyn: "The New York school started with Fluxus, which was basically antimusic written by nonmusicians. Minimalism was very conceptual, related in some ways more to visual art than to music. The next movement was artrock, which was still conceptual. The movement that's happening now is the first real Downtown composed-music movement, the first to come more from a music orientation than from visual art or conceptualism. Composers who would have been Uptown 20 years ago are now attracted to the Downtown scene, and are bringing their ideas about composed music. This is the most sophisticated development of the New York school, the first real group of trained musicians.

"I've been talking about this composition scene all through the John Zorn period. I knew it was coming. That's how movements work in this town, they go in opposites. If you've got an improv scene, the next thing has to be rigorous composition. Plus, I knew Gordon and his boys were coming. I have an ear too. We released his first record on Neutral."

Branca's grand, lumbering Symphony No. 9 (with chorus weaved into the orchestra) may be his greatest work so far, as spiritually contrapuntal as Górecki's Third Symphony or Arvo Pärt's *Passio*, but far more complex and mysterious. It's coming out on Atavistic, as part of the slew of new Branca CDs being unleashed in the next six months, including Symphonies Nos. 5, 8, and 10, and the American release of *The World Upside Down*. I've heard Symphonies 8 and 10 only on tape, which as Branca concedes can be like kissing your lover over the phone. For all its pulsating backbeat, the Eighth Symphony's first movement is remarkably conventional in the way it sustains harmonic tension through chromatic lines continually wandering through dissonant chords—like disco Wagner. It was originally written for string orchestra, as the beginning of an opera based on Georg Büchner's *Woyzeck.* The second movement is more heroic, resolving into triumphal chords.

By contrast, the Tenth—the symphony that put Branca one up on Beethoven, Dvořák, Bruckner, Mahler, and a few other jokers—is less obvious, more mystical in its ever-writhing swirls of slow counterpoint, more unpredictable as to where its excruciatingly slow climaxes will peak. I can promise you Virgil Moorefield's drumming will be as ecstatic as ever, and that even the deaf will register these guitar melodies through their feet and rib cages. There's plenty of empty space (filled in only with the momentum of drumming) for classical critics to scoff at, but to dismiss three minutes of Branca because it doesn't go anywhere is like dismissing the first three minutes of *Das Rheingold* because Wagner only knows one chord. Branca's art is one of immense gestures with little surface detail. That's why his static, one-chord-banging techniques seem, for me, curiously oversized in the context of Sonic Youth's songs, like a steel girder in a gazebo.

One virtue I won't let anyone deny Branca is his self-critical ear. I've seen him go through a tape of one of his symphonies—the 7th, I think it was—saying, "That doesn't work . . . this section is nice . . . that's a total flop . . . this didn't sound right at all . . . here's a part that came out just the way I wanted it." And he's right every time. Unlike so many composers who feel their every note is golden, Branca holds each measure to high standards, damns the experiments that fall flat, and revises symphonies after premiering them by jettisoning entire movements. If you like some parts of a Branca piece and don't like others, he may agree with you.

Of his Symphony No. 9, Branca says, "That is the first piece in which I rigorously tried to start working toward the idea I have of what music should be. It's just the beginning of it, and people wouldn't necessarily hear it, but I hear it." That's an amazing disclaimer to make about your *Ninth Symphony*, unless you're Franz Joseph Haydn and have 95 more up your sleeve. (Branca might.) The thing is, good '70s Downtowner that he is, he puts his music before the public whether it's ready or not. He knows you don't make a career in Downtown Manhattan by sitting for years at a time in your studio meticulously polishing, but by giving your public the performances it's demanding whether they're ready or not.

Some classical types thought Branca's sound sculptures were interesting until he became pompous enough to call them symphonies. Yet Branca's symphonies do pursue, in their stripped-down way, the kind of large-scale harmonic motion we associate with the symphonies of Bruckner and Brahms. In Branca's orchestral works, there *is* an amateurish, rough-hewn surface to the orchestration. On the other hand, every orchestra piece he's written has surpassed in originality and interest any of the pieces by Zorn, Glass, or Chen Yi on the Brooklyn Philharmonic's recent new-music program. His textures are brash and simple, but they don't sound like anyone else, and in the long run, they work. Autodidacticism has its rewards, and Branca is an artist whose weaknesses are married to his strengths.

He's also one of those composers, like Cage, Alvin Lucier, Pauline Oliveros, and La Monte Young, who lets himself be instructed by nature. He likes to tell critics that he taught himself to compose by sitting in front of a speaker with a guitar, listening to loud feedback for 45 minutes at a time. That's a way of saying that, in a good old American tradition, he bypassed history and went straight to the essence of sound. If you're writing large works without any classical training, it's extremely hard to avoid stumbling into pitfalls and clichés—unless you submit yourself to some kind of rigorous discipline and keep your ears honest. Whether you think Branca's self-imposed disciplines have been sufficient, or his ears honest enough, is yours to decide at the Kitchen this week.

shadowing capote

mikel rouse

FEBRUARY 7, 1995

La Côte Basque was Truman Capote's undoing. He used to sit in this elegant French restaurant on 55th Street with the other celebrities, soaking up gossip about who was sleeping with whom, who shot her husband and got away with it, who was caught in flagrante with a German shepherd. Then he published it all in *Esquire* (in a story called "La Côte Basque"), and none of his friends ever spoke to him again. Now, decades later, two other relocated Southern boys—Mikel Rouse and myself—have returned in search of Capote's ghost. We're collecting vibes for Rouse's new opera inspired by Capote's *In Cold Blood*, which he'll premiere at the Kitchen this week.

That's "inspired by," not "based on." Rouse is so fascinated by Capote's achievement that he ventured not to set the book to music but to retrace Capote's steps, to become Capote through music. Accordingly, he spent years (since 1988) sifting through the New York Public Library's Capote archives and drew his libretto from the same newspaper accounts, official depositions, interview transcripts, letters, and diaries the author used as a basis for *In Cold Blood*—not a word of the libretto originated with Capote. The result, called *Failing Kansas*, is a nonnarrative, deliciously tuneful, more abstract response to the same horrible event that caught Capote's attention: the heartless murder of the average, upright Clutter family in Holcomb, Kansas, by a pair of shiftless ne'er-do-wells named Dick Hickock and Perry Smith. Rouse performs the opera solo with elaborate taped musical background, plus a film by Cliff Baldwin, a longtime Rouse collaborator who has structured a film to fit the music the way composers usually cut music to fit a film. For those who have trouble calling a multimedia electronic song cycle with one performer an opera, Rouse admits, "It's like performing a 75-minute pop song."

Capote claimed, with *In Cold Blood*, to have invented a new art form, the nonfiction novel (not with total justification, for there were arguably predecessors). "Without trying to be pretentious," Rouse continues over his Chef's Cassoulet Toulousan with white beans and delicate duck sausage (normally he's a connoisseur of truck stop food and Southern barbecue), "I wanted to come up with something as new as the nonfiction novel. I spent a year and a half making sketches and thinking about it. I tried speaking the text, but a lot of people had done that, and my music is too complex to be a background for someone talking. Then I asked, what would happen if I was talking in rhythm? So I made the first section, 'The Last to See Them Alive,' and it knocked me out. It changed the course of everything I've done."

He called his technique *Counterpoetry* on the analogy of counterpoint: he overdubs himself speaking in rhythm so that the listener hears several texts simultaneously, or else the same text in different rhythmic settings at once. (Spreading far beyond the opera for which it was intended, Rouse's Counterpoetry has become the basis for all of his songs, notably the ones on his recent disc *Living Inside Design* [New Tone].) *Failing Kansas* contains four major scenes linked by five interludes, and the big sections follow a crescendo of Counterpoetic technique. The interludes provide relief from the verbal denseness, and the postclimax is a disarmingly simple rock tune.

Knowing *In Cold Blood* will help you catch references, but unlike Richard Brooks's remarkably faithful 1967 film, Rouse doesn't stick with the book. Where Capote intercut masterfully among scenes of the family, the roving killers, and the frustrated police investigators, Rouse spends most of his opera inside the minds of the murderers—an interesting choice of strategies, considering he's the son of a Missouri state trooper. Much of his libretto centers around the experiences that turned Hickock and especially Smith into killers. Rouse chants, "She had a flashlight and she hit me with it," referring to the nuns who beat Smith for bed-wetting, and one interlude is taken from a letter Smith's father wrote to the parole board, damning his son while ostensibly defending him. A big parrot that Smith repeatedly dreams will save him is a recurrent motif—"Yellow like a sunflower, taller than Jesus." "Fortunes in diving!" shouts an ad that inspired one of Perry's get-rich-quick schemes. The murdered Clutters hardly appear, and in Baldwin's poster for the opera, they appropriately fade out of focus behind the vivid title lettering.

"Having grown up in the South, I'm sensitive to Capote's issues," Rouse explains. "He was the most talented writer of his generation but was denied a lot of the accolades and awards that go with that stature because of his background—which was that he was basically self-taught. But beyond that, did I relate to the Clutter family? Yeah, I knew tons of people like that, growing up on the farm. Did I relate to the murderers, Dick and Perry? In some ways even more. When I think of the friends of mine who are dead now, because they grew up on the wrong side of the tracks, I think, 'How did I get here?' When one of my good friends laid across a railroad track and is dead. Another guy I knew killed himself in Russian roulette.

"The murderers were the people who were left behind to tell the story. I'm not trying to advocate sympathy for the murderer. But in terms of where we are, with 'three strikes you're out' and Pataki being governor, *In Cold Blood* is relevant because it's saying there are no simple solutions. What Capote makes clear in that book is that everyone had a potential for something. These guys had complex lives, and they could have been something. The murders are senseless, no doubt about it. But why don't people say, when something's senseless, that there's not an easy answer? They say, 'It's senseless, let's kill them.' It's crazy."

In making this opera, Rouse has fallen into an almost karmic relationship with Capote, periodically reinforced by odd coincidences, such as a friend stumbling across a rare edition of a Capote book and giving it to Rouse, or his meeting someone who had just visited the Clutter house. "The fact that these guys were on death row for five years meant Capote didn't have a finished book until he knew the ending. It also meant that he got to know them. At the end of it all, he went to the execution, and Perry gave him a 100-page letter, which no one's ever seen. Capote was a wreck for days afterward. He stayed in his room and couldn't stop sobbing.

"I think everything you want comes with a price, and he paid the ultimate price. He wrote one of the most important books in American literature. He delved so far into the human psyche in trying to keep true to this new art from that he destroyed himself. He never recovered."

Rouse's upbringing in Poplar Bluff, Missouri, was so down-home rural that his favorite pastime was jumping from a horse onto a moving train. (His name is pronounced "Michael," by the way; he changed the spelling himself, deliberately, in grade school.) A triple-threat artist who studied painting and film at the Kansas City Art Institute and music across the street at the University of Missouri at Kansas City, he has always written his own lyrics and still carries a sketchbook to draw whatever scene he finds himself in, in a fresh caricatural style. Being in the boondocks helped him get his start. When Talking Heads played Kansas City in 1978, Rouse's rock band Tirez Tirez was the only local group progressive enough to open for the Downtown scenesters. "David Byrne liked us," Rouse recalls. "The next time they came into Kansas City, he called and gave me tickets to come backstage. The first time we played CBGB's, in 1980, he showed up, and after that it got easier."

Tirez Tirez relocated to New York in 1979 and performed until '87. In the meantime, Rouse had also formed Broken Consort, the keyboard-sax-bass-drums quartet for which most of his instrumental music is written (their most compelling disc to date is *Soul Menu*, also on New Tone). New music's best songwriter since David Garland, Rouse is one of the few composers equally at home in theatrical vocal music and abstract instrumental genres. "Others, like the noise music and improv people," he notes, "were using vernacular instruments, but I was the only one using jazz-rock instrumentation fully scored right down to the drum set. That's the first thing I set out to do."

Once in New York, Rouse taught himself rhythmic techniques from A. M. Jones's two-volume tome *Studies in African Music*. Believing it was possible to learn perfect pitch through hypnosis, he found a willing hypnotist, Jerome Wahman, and got more than he bargained for: Wahman was also one of supposedly 50 people in the country qualified to teach Schillinger technique, the quasi-mathematical methodology for composing that Joseph Schillinger developed from natural number patterns, which was adopted by composers as diverse as George Gershwin and Earle Brown. "Schillinger was never a system like 12-tone music," says Rouse. "It was a set of vocabularies you could use to help your composition whether you were doing a pop tune or whatever, in any style. It got a bad rap because Tin Pan Alley songwriters used it. I was drawn to it because it was so naturally the way I thought. Everything I'm doing now is totally intuitive, but still framed by the method. Listen to 'The Corner' [the climax of *Failing Kansas*], where it's happening on so many multiple layers you'll never get all of it."

Rouse got considerable notice in the early '80s. Then, like everyone else writing carefully notated music, laid low during the late '80s while free improv dominated the scene. One of his biggest triumphs came last winter, when Ulysses Dove's dance piece for the Alvin Ailey Dance Company, based on Rouse's 1984 work, *Quorum*, was presented with six dancers at City Center; the piece has been taped for national PBS broadcast March 1 on *Great Performances' Dance in America*. *Quorum*, innovatively scored for the once-groundbreaking Linn drum machine, is probably the first work to take the drum machine outside the context of pop and use it abstractly. A source work for Rouse's rhythmic ideas, it was originally an hour and 45 minutes, but "that was the pretension of youth," Rouse confesses. "For the dance, two 11-minute sections were enough."

Rouse has also found himself in the forefront of a movement called totalism, a word coined by composers tired of critics misidentifying them as minimalists. Totalism's idea is to have your cake and eat it too, by fusing the accessibility of minimalism with the complexity of serialism. In most cases, the complexity is invested more in the rhythm than in the melody or harmony. "Minimalist harmony," theorizes Rouse, "is welded to the rhythm and doesn't have that multiple element that happens with pitches in totalism. In the music I'm doing now, the rhythm dictates the harmonic progression. I get traditional cadences and resolutions, but totally dependent on the rhythm. Totalism also focuses more on the overall structure for the piece, something that minimalism lacked."

The simplest, most recognizable level on which Rouse's totalism works can be heard in "Answer," the sixth section of *Failing Kansas*, where he cycles three phrases over and over: "I know the form," "The secret is," and "People are dumb." He sings them on a pattern of four pitches: A, F-sharp, E, F-sharp Since three phrases don't fit onto four pitches, they go out of phase. Phrase one is on A, two on F-sharp, three on E, one on F-sharp, two on A, three on F-sharp, and so on. Listening casually, you think it's a simple repeating pattern until you try to sing along, when you realize it's as difficult as patting your head and rubbing your tummy at the same time. The music is so tuneful that the most illiterate top-40 fan might think he could hum along with it (until he tries), yet the dense rhythmic layers contain Nancarrovian intricacies that would require the score and a calculator to unravel. Singing his Counterpoetry songs, Rouse looks calm and suave from the elbows up, but if you look at his fingers you'll notice he's counting beats like a madman.

You don't need to be aware of the numerical tricks to enjoy the music, but they keep the surface lively and surprising. Years ago Rouse had sent me a tape of "The Last to See Them Alive." In it he speaks the text of "In the Garden," a hymn every Protestant remembers from childhood. I couldn't figure out why the rendition seemed so moving until our dinner at La Côte Basque, when he pointed out that he retained the 6/8 meter of the hymn in his speaking, but the musical accompaniment is in 4/4 (the eighth-note being equal in both meters). The emotionalism I attributed to mere nostalgia was at least heightened (if not created) by the tension between the two beat patterns. Such tricks draw your ear into the music the way optical illusions draw your eye. The totalists have resuscitated the medieval insight that music is the medium that can translate numbers into feeling.

In April, La Côte Basque is leaving the location it's occupied since 1941, and the historic atmosphere will be lost; the fact added urgency to our dinner.

Needless to say, we weren't seated in the place's prestigious front room where Capote set his fateful story, but it did gratify us that our waiter, an older man, remembered seeing him around. And if I picked up any scandalous gossip sitting there, I'm not telling. I know where my bread's buttered.

the dance between

david first

MAY 2, 1995

The fascinating thing about a David First performance is that your eyes and ears have to part ways. Though the musicians hardly move, a cacophony of tones swirls around the hall. It's impossible to tell who's responsible for what sounds. Some of the tones aren't even being played; they take place inside your inner ear, or else result from patterns drawn in the air by colliding drones. The drones—on synthesizers, winds, strings, whatever— slowly glissando toward and past each other as the chair seems to sink from beneath your body and the hair on your neck points skyward. It's a conscious attempt on First's part to recreate the kundalini energy of meditation, and it succeeds in making acoustic phenomena that are dry in the description vividly theatrical in experience. And now, April 27 through May 7 at La Mama, First is turning to the theater, against his previous better judgment. His opera *The Manhattan Book of the Dead* fuses the three pillars of his career—rock, free improv, and acoustic experimentation— in a moving response to the AIDS crisis.

First of all, uptown critics, etc., please note: once again, this isn't an opera in the 19th-century European sense. If you come predetermined to be disappointed if the work doesn't contain linear narrative, exciting emotional scenes, soprano arias, period costumes, and so on, then do everyone a favor and stay home. If God engraved the permanent meaning of the word *opera* on the back of the Ten Commandments, Moses forgot to record the fact, and Downtown composers, like many generations before them, have invented their own definition. In this case, the piece comprises dance, video imagery, the thrilling baritone of Thomas Buckner (who commissioned early installments of the work), and First's incandescently writhing ensemble conducted by the perfectionist Petr Kotik.

Whenever I'm obliged to wrap up Downtown music in 25 words or less, First is one of the hardest composers to place. He seems nowhere and everywhere. He has a free jazz background—he got his start playing guitar in Cecil Taylor's band at Carnegie Hall in 1974, at the age of 20—and usually improvises his music, but he's too far into drones and acoustic effects to fit the improv crowd. He favors microtonal pitch bendings, but with an antitheoretical practicality that alienates him from alternate tuning circles. I've called him a totalist because his complex numerical structures give him much in common with Glenn Branca, Mikel Rouse, Michael Gordon, and Ben Neill. But he's the only one in that crowd who doesn't use a backbeat drawn from a rock vernacular, and his reason is, paradoxically, that he's spent much of his life as a rock guitarist and songwriter.

If First is one of the hardest artists to classify in a scene where unclassifiability is a major career goal, all those kinships with diverse fields also make him one of the most widely admired Downtowners. His popularity may stem partly from his self-effacing humor, a blend of modesty and chutzpah that's made him the funniest press release writer in the business. His releases include mock interviews (with interviewers who say things like, "Well, Dave, you're looking great") and rave *Village Voice* reviews dated 15 years in the future. When I have to pause in ripping through my mail for a long chuckle to subside, there's usually a First concert coming up.

First grew up in Philadelphia, that city where artistic and blue-collar worlds seem peculiarly intertwined, and whose proximity to New York inflicts a special kind of crucifixion on local artists. His father, an electrical engineer, introduced him to heterodyning oscillators and sum and difference tones, acoustic phenomena that retain seminal importance for First's aesthetics. One of his first bands, an instrumental trio called the Note Killers, shared a bill with Branca in their 1980 first New York gig; he describes them as "free jazz meets Steve Reich meets Jimi Hendrix." In the three bands he's had since moving to New York in 1984—the World Casio Quartet, Echoes of God, and Joy Buzzers—First has pursued pitch-bending experiments and free jazz. Before 1985, though, when he switched his focus to the drone-continuum pieces he's best known for, he considered himself mainly a rock songster.

First's rejection of a rock beat came just as everybody else was adding one to their music in order to entice pop listeners. In a move reminiscent of an heir giving away his fortune to find out who his true friends are, First rebelled. "Rock wasn't some new toy to play with for me. I knew how it worked. I could do it any time I wanted to. You can do whatever you want on top, put a beat underneath it, and it becomes palatable. That wasn't a challenge. I wanted to make sure my music was interesting without it. And if it wasn't interesting to whatever scene there was, that seemed irrelevant.

I was annoyed with the crossover thing. 'We're serious, but we're going to have some fun, too.' OK, maybe the world was too serious a place. But I had already done things with beats all along.

"Plus, I really wanted to understand harmony, and that sensation, and I felt it was only masking it to put a beat under it." By "that sensation," First means the out-of-body experience of hearing thick, sustained tones slowly moving into and out of consonance. From playing the blues, he knew the irrational acoustic phenomena that result from sliding pitches out of tune. He formed the World Casio Quartet (Casio made the cheapest tunable keyboard in the mid '80s) to explore the effect more systematically. Appropriately, his major disc to date is titled *Resolver* (O.O. Discs). "The idea of kundalini energy is to try to draw your energy up your spine into your head. When I was playing around with resolution of pure tones, I realized it was that same energy. If you slowly glissando into those intervals, you get something you don't get if you start out with pure tunings: a shock goes through your system."

In a way, First has taken what Alvin Lucier, La Monte Young, and others have done, and gone on to the next step, bringing something pure and abstract into workable and immediate performance situations. In hallowed Downtown tradition, he has turned his lack of formal training into an asset. Because he approached tuning not theoretically but from experimentation, he discovered what the pure-tuning thinkers missed: that the movement from *near*-consonance to consonance can be far more arresting than simply pure tuning. "Perfection becomes boring," he points out. "When you take people from one to the other, they experience the difference. I reach out and grab them and pull them in, rather than say, it's here, you find your own way in. That's why I use glissandos. I like the dance between."

Rhythm came afterward. When First bought one of the first cheap samplers on the market in the mid '80s, he realized something that has fascinated American musicians since Henry Cowell: that, like waves and particles, pitch and rhythm are different aspects of the same thing. If you play two rhythms against each other at a relationship of four against five, for example, and speed up both equally, you'll eventually arrive at pitches a major third apart, such as C and E. That's when First began formalizing his tuning knowledge, because in order to add multitempo rhythms to his harmonic continuums he needed to know what the mathematical relationships were. For a couple of years all his pieces were basically fantastically enlarged manifestations of the harmonic series, as if heard through a microscope. And, like Branca, Rouse, and many others, he became disaffected with physics. "I thought I was Pythagoras Jr., in tune with nature and unlocking the keys to the universe. But you hit a wall, and it becomes no longer art. Because art is man's subversion of nature, not his surrender to it. Artists have egos, and if they do something they consider a collaboration with God, they want half the credit."

In his best works, such as *Jade Screen Test Dreams of Renting Wings* (First has a whimsical way with titles; one section of the opera is "Chrome Sun Hat's Beautifully Thought Out Regrets"), he notates the pitch and rhythmic systems for the other players in often idiosyncratic ways, with numbers indicating how many fractions of a semitone sharp or flat to play. Then he improvises within the result as a self-styled loose cannon, subverting the total harmony by bending it to create acoustic illusions. The results can be uncanny. Unlike Lucier's delicate sound sculptures that require intent listening, First's continua are aggressive in their effect, deploying acoustic beats the way other composers would melody. Unlike Young's sine-tone installations, they work theatrically as performances. And unlike Branca's symphonies, there's no rock beat to distract from the sonic phenomena. First has diverted an esoteric stream of American music into viable concert performance.

If First's reputation has taken longer to gel than some of his less principled crossover cohorts, his development has also been slowed by the number of aesthetic irons he keeps in the fire. When I first heard him in 1987, his sound constructions still retained awkward vestiges of rock drumming, splintered to near-unrecognizability. The impressive thing about *The Manhattan Book of the Dead*, though, is that for the first time he's successfully brought all his strategies into one arena. The undulating drones (many aided by E-bows placed on the piano strings) will be warped by First's synthesizer and mirrored by elaborate rhythmic systems especially written for the machine-precision fingers of pianist Joseph Kubera. Also, for his first theatrical piece, First decided a return to rock was in order, and wrote several honest-to-goodness pop tunes. Text and libretto, written by First, are pretty minimal; the piece seems very musically conceived. He reread the Tibetan and Egyptian books of the dead as research, and wrote his own response to loss and death rather than anything directly about AIDS. When asked what he had lost that led him to write the piece, he replied cryptically, "My youth." The only explicit AIDS reference is the use of male dancers as the opera's two lovers, one of whom dies and brings the survivor the book of the dead.

For First, the truth is more in the sound itself than the program. "I never believed in doing theater. People told me for years, do things with lights and film, because that will give people another hook into your music.

I said, no, this has got to be taken straight. If they need that, they should-n't be there. But after the first performance of the 'Separation Chant' [the opera's penultimate scene], people came up to me with red eyes, emotion-ally moved. I realized I could have formal structures that appeal to me in an intellectual way and physical way, but also engage people emotion-ally." A lot of Downtown composers are struggling with this move from sound to content. Few have negotiated it with so much integrity or musical success.

raising ghosts

leroy jenkins brings the african burial ground to life

MAY 21, 1996

In most situations I've seen him, composer Leroy Jenkins is soft-spoken and retiring. Not this day. Entering in mid-rehearsal May 3, I find him con-ducting wildly and chattering rapidly, intently absorbed and aggressively in control. He's working at this point with only the instrumentalists in his new cantata—percussionists Thurman Barker and Wilson Moorman and pianist Joan Harkness—and he's singing every vocal line in the score. In fact, he seems incapable of not singing; every time he quotes a phrase, even in conversation, he sings it, and the melodies jump up and down athleti-cally like grasshoppers on a hot day. So does Jenkins, leaping like a 24-year-old with such abandon that at one point the baton accidentally flies out of his hand. Wiry and only slightly gray, he looks about 50. He's 64.

What's missing is the violin. I've never seen Jenkins without his instru-ment before. He's identified with a raspy but fluid violin tone so individual that I think of him as his own section of the orchestra. I've never heard a work of his he didn't play in; even in his opera *The Mother of Three Sons* (with choreographer Bill T. Jones), his growling timbre rose reassuringly from the pit. But the new work he's premiering at the Kitchen May 16 through 26, *The Negros Burial Ground: a cantata for the departed,* has no place for a violin.

Also unusual for Jenkins is the work's overtly political nature. With a libretto by Ann T. Greene (whose evocative poetry he also set in *Three Sons*), the piece is a history of the 18th-century slave graveyard unearthed beneath a Wall Street lot in 1991. As Jenkins howls this angry, obscenity-laced but eloquent libretto, you realize where his newly unleashed energy comes from. Beneath his polite exterior, he's furious about his place in white society. *The Negros Burial Ground* is his opportunity, at last, to make a statement.

It's a statement no one is better equipped to make, for few zigzag over the line between black and white music as many times a day as Jenkins does. He grew up in Chicago, studying violin and playing clarinet in the marching band and bassoon in the concert band at Du Sable High, a school famous for turning out musicians such as Johnny Griffin and John Gilmore. He then got a scholarship to Florida A&M University, one of the black Southern schools that encouraged musicians in the '50s. There, while supporting himself playing saxophone in bars, he learned the Bach unaccompanied violin sonatas from a European-trained teacher who played them with him in unison. After an exhausting teaching stint in Mobile, Jenkins returned to Chicago and got involved with the AACM in its heyday, working with Anthony Braxton, Muhal Richard Abrams, Leo Smith, and Roscoe Mitchell. After a few European gigs, he settled in New York in 1970.

Then in the '80s, the jazz scene took a conservative turn, and suddenly Jenkins couldn't get gigs. "[Wynton] Marsalis was in, and people started talking about going back to classic jazz," he recalls. "We couldn't play in clubs. As soon as we'd walk in, the jazz guys, the beboppers, would walk out. We'd come in and make a big sound, and they didn't go for it. They'd say, 'Oh, the noisemakers.' They wanted [chord] changes. Our music was a result of [Ornette] Coleman and [Cecil] Taylor. And we prided ourselves on taking it further, because we studied Cage, and Xenakis, and Schoenberg, and all those guys. They were the ones who broke away from the old way in classical music, so we had to study them to see how we could break away."

To survive the Reagan drought, Jenkins turned to the new-music scene, for he knew that classical composers had been interested in Coltrane's and Coleman's innovations. (Actually, I first heard him at New Music America in 1980.) He began writing notated scores, the first a string quartet for the Kronos. Then choreographer Bill T. Jones brought Jenkins's music to the attention of German composer-entrepreneur Hans Werner Henze. "Europeans are great," Jenkins enthuses. "I've sent the piece to other people, and they say, 'Aw, it's too jazzy.' It's not jazz, but what else do they expect me to deal with? I'm classically trained, but my background is jazz and gospel. I visited Henze in his villa for two weeks. I got sick, we had so much wine and rich food. He's a real bon vivant, like Cecil [Taylor]. My stomach was ruined." Henze convinced his board to commission *The Mother of Three Sons*, which was premiered in Aachen at the Munich

Biennale, with subsequent productions at the New York City Opera and Houston Grand Opera. Now, Jenkins has one more commission lined up after *Burial Ground:* a theater work called *Editorial* that's inspired by Willie Horton's role in the Bush-Dukakis election but is more generally about the black man as fall guy.

All this makes Jenkins something of a late bloomer, and his ongoing adaptation to his new-music role has had humorous moments. "When I was writing *Mother of Three Sons*," he says, "I was talking to Muhal and Henry [Threadgill], and Henry asked, 'Are you working on a [piano] reduction, Leroy?' I said, 'Reduction? What's that?' Muhal said, 'You don't know what a reduction is?' So they told me, and I said, 'Gaaaahd daaaamn.' So I had to go back and write the piano score. That's how I found out. All the books I had read about it, nobody said anything about that."

Yet, though Jenkins admits having learned from composers as diverse as Wuorinen and Glass, when asked which ones have influenced his own music, he pointedly omits white names from the list: Abrams, Threadgill, Alvin Singleton. And he's thrilled that, at 73, George Walker has just become the first African American to receive the Pulitzer Prize for music. "I thought it was about time, man. It was great that he got it, and the piece he got it for, *Lilacs*, is fantastic."

Jenkins met Greene through Bill T. Jones, and called her when the Kitchen approached him for a commission. The controversy about the African Burial Ground was boiling at the time (the *Voice* devoted a 1993 cover story to the issue), with African American groups charging that their heritage was being stolen from them by scientists who had no personal interest in it. (The remains were finally handed over to Washington, D.C.'s Howard University for study, though their fate is still in dispute.) Greene did the research and developed a story (see "Hierarchy of the Dead," below) about fictional and nonfictional oppressed African Americans in the 18th through 20th centuries. Jenkins came up with the form. "At first they were calling it an opera, and I looked at them and said, 'Jeez, an opera, what do they have to act? This is a storytelling thing. People telling the stories of how they died.' You don't enact 'How I died'—who knows? So I decided since there were so many voices, we'd make it a cantata, because that's what a cantata's about."

The music in *The Negros Burial Ground* is nervously dissonant but not atonal, with blues melodies shooting up from clusters and dense chords whose repetition manages a kind of tense stability. Call it Billie Holiday meets Bartók. "I didn't want to do anything atonal; I had to be very careful because of the singers. The harmonies are based on made-up chords.

They don't have the first, third, fifth, seventh, and all that stuff; they skip around. That's how I'm able to disguise it, by having one voice here, maybe a 13th way up here. I just try to be sophisticated about it.

"Much as I love Duke [Ellington], I don't want to sound like him. I don't think anybody's been compositional in jazz since Duke, except for the AACM. I'm not trying to be avant-garde, or thinking about any particular time. I'm going from note to note, just trying to find something that's going to be interesting and exciting. Especially these days, I'm not classified at all. I don't know where to draw the line."

hierarchy of the dead

To spin a libretto for Leroy Jenkins's cantata *The Negros Burial Ground*, Ann T. Greene speculated about the bodies found at the site, including a woman whose remains showed traces of a musket ball through her torso. In search of characters, she conflated two events from 18th- and 19th-century New York history. The first was an insurrection led by African slaves and Native Americans; the second, an alleged conspiracy in which tavern owner John Hughson was going to lead slaves to take over the city and kill all whites. Historical figures from this latter event appear by name, including indentured servant Mary Burton, who precipitated a witch hunt by pointing fingers and basking in the resulting celebrity.

The piece's larger intent, however, hits closer to home. Three central characters are African Americans who were killed by the police during Ed Koch's final years as mayor, and who appear as newcomers to the slave burial ground. One is 67-year-old Eleanor Bumpurs, who was shot in the face by cops evicting her from her apartment; another is Michael Stewart, a graffiti artist held in a chokehold by transit police, who went into a coma and died; the third is Edmund Perry, a brilliant 17-year-old Harlem graduate of Phillips Exeter, who died of gunshot wounds to the stomach after allegedly mugging a plainclothes cop in Morningside Park. "These were embittering and controversial events," Greene says, "one of the by-products of which, I think, was the election of David Dinkins. They created a schism between blacks and Hispanics and white liberals who supported Koch. Liberal politics changed forever in those years." The action is united within a West African social structure; here, the world of the dead has its own hierarchy, with the elder male rulers and decision makers at the top.

The Kitchen is offering two forums with which to get feedback on the issues the cantata raises. "I'm hoping that some of the people deeply involved with the fight over the burial ground will come," Greene says. "I want to hear from people who feel a sense of possession about this, to get a dialogue going."

opera meets oprah

mikel rouse hawks salvation in an opera for real people

NOVEMBER 5, 1996

Dennis Cleveland is cool and in control. In white sport coat and dark glasses, waving his microphone like the magic wand it is, he mediates among his puppets, his performers, his guests on the first-ever new-music talk show.

Dennis Cleveland is really—though his show makes you question what reality is—New York composer Mikel Rouse. And for all his slickness, Rouse is a product of rural Missouri, the boot-heel region down near Arkansas. As a teenager, he ran away from home to join a carnival. He learned how the shell games worked, how the ball tosses were rigged, how the whole show was cynically set up to create a false reality. It was good preparation. For now, 20 years later, he's tackled two of society's most unreal phenomena—talk shows and opera—and fused them into a talk-show opera, *Dennis Cleveland*, premiering at the Kitchen this week through November 2.

For years Rouse has mentioned his dream of having his own, liberal-biased talk show, and he's finally, sort of, done it. Even before he started work on *Dennis Cleveland*, he took an English friend to see *Geraldo* because he wanted to give her a massive dose of American culture. As the guests poured out their private neuroses and screamed epithets at each other, Rouse glanced at his friend and saw her crying and laughing at once, mumbling, "This is *so* fucked up." Since then Rouse has returned to *Geraldo* and sat in on *Ricki Lake* and *Gordon Elliott*, plus a few local shows. "I like kitsch," Rouse admits in his Hell's Kitchen apartment, where he's been rehearsing his singers. "Talk shows were a phenomenon that started 15 years ago, then 10 to seven years ago started going further and further in a ritual direction. I was already working on a set of pieces about people looking for some type of meaning or faith or awakening through popular culture. When I zeroed in on the talk-show thing, I realized that was the format I was looking for."

A lot of composers have drawn elements from pop culture, but few have embraced it so whole hog as Rouse. For his first opera, *Failing Kansas,* he spent five years researching the murders that were the subject of Truman Capote's *In Cold Blood* and couched the vernacular he found in a cool rock idiom of subliminally intricate cross-rhythms. For *Dennis Cleveland,* he wanted something more topical. He began by taping talk shows on dozens of hours of DAT tape, feeding sound bites into his computer and analyzing and mimicking inflections. Found phrases from real people—for example, "If you don't love me the way I am, then you can go"—became the ostinatos and rhythmic patterns of *Dennis Cleveland.* Ironically, Rouse thought this new opera would be a cinch after the research-intensive *Failing Kansas.* The Capote opera, though, had one performer: Rouse. *Cleveland* has 19. The piece represents a major leap in Rouse's compositional ambitions. He's not only negotiating a film version but hoping to take the piece to Off-Broadway.

What's more, participating in talk-show audiences opened up Rouse's ideas of what theater could be. "When I sat there and looked at it as a theatrical experience instead of a live TV taping, it opened up whole new vistas in terms of breaking down the fourth wall. Here you've got a multimedia situation where there's no separation between the people onstage and the audience for two reasons. One is the lighting. The other is that the only thing that makes the person onstage more of an expert than the person in the audience is that he's onstage. More importantly, the show is being taped live, and the audience can watch the live taping on the monitors as it's going down. They're doing two things at once: they're live participants within the action, but they can also watch the thing on TV. The minute I stepped back from that and looked at it as a theatrical experience, which of course nobody in that audience does, it was mind-blowing."

The result was an overhauling of the operatic genre. Just as the cameramen in a live taping are seen by the audience, *Dennis Cleveland* contains cameramen who are both functionaries and performers. The libretto appears on cue cards that Cleveland/Rouse is reading, and the audience can read them too, just like the supertitles at the Metropolitan. Singers will rise from among the audience to sing, and the audience will watch themselves on video screens. If talk shows are a mirror of society watched by the participants as in a mirror, then *Dennis Cleveland* is a mirror mirroring mirrors. "Finally," the poster for the piece announces, "real opera for real people."

That's not to say it's a light, easy piece. The overarching viewpoint for the opera comes from *Voltaire's Bastards,* a wide-ranging critique of modern culture by Canadian novelist, historian, and businessman John Ralston Saul. Saul writes about the corporatist takeover of the Western world, the dismantling of democracy by multinational corporations, and the consequent increased reliance on the illusions of mass culture as a source of personal meaning. Talking about TV, Saul (who is reportedly flying down from Toronto to see *Dennis Cleveland*) wrote:

"The most accurate context in which to place television programming is that of general religious ritual. . . . Like television, [religious rituals] eschew surprise, particularly creative surprise. Instead, they flourish on the repetition of known formulas. People are drawn to television as they are to religions by the knowledge that they will find there what they already know. . . . After watching the first minute of any television drama, most viewers could lay out the scenario that will follow, including the conclusion. Given the first line of banter in most scenes, a regular viewer could probably rhyme off the next three or four lines. . . . There is more flexibility in a Catholic mass or in classic Chinese opera."

Accordingly, Rouse/Cleveland is both host and priest. When he yells to two audience members to "Come on down!" Rouse wants you to think of a televangelist eliciting conversions, but also of prize-hawker Bob Barker on *The Price Is Right*. The piece's conceit is that each audience member tells a confession, but by the end you realize that the confessions tell the story of Dennis's own life.

Like Burt Lancaster in the film version of *Elmer Gantry*, he's selling salvation, but painfully aware that he hasn't found the meaning of life himself. "All of my life I've been loveless," he repeats as a refrain, but turns it into an advertising slogan by ending, like a lettered phone number, "L-O-V-E-L-E-S."

Rouse's artistic subtext is that he's trying to revive what he calls "the broken promise of *Einstein on the Beach*," the promise that opera could shed its European pretensions and relate to everyday life. (The piece is dedicated to that genius of operatic vernacular, Robert Ashley.)

"I'm taking a format that everyone's familiar with," Rouse explains, "and placing it in a new context. It takes the intellectual snobbery away from opera immediately, and puts you in a frame of mind to accept new information. It's always been a strategy of mine to provide some area within the format, whether it's the production of the CD or the use of a rock groove or whatever, that the audience will be already familiar with. If they've got that, you can slip them more complex information under the door."

For Rouse himself has something to sell: rhythmic complexity. Counterpoint. Thematic unity. Aesthetic richness. The idea that music can be popular in format and yet still perceptually challenging, that we can, in effect, upgrade the daily discourse of American life. It's a John Ralston Saul idea as well. Rouse hopes that maybe, just maybe, a few of those people in the talk-show audiences will see *Dennis Cleveland* and start to think about the fact that we who complain about what goes on as observers are also participants. We may be watching the show, but we're also the actors. We let the media tell us we're helpless, but we have the power to change the world.

a difficult woman

a cosmic piano concerto from the outspoken composer of *vagina*

MAY 20, 1997

Gertrude Stein called America "the oldest country of the 20th century," and where women composers are concerned, we're still several decades ahead of Europe. I can list 80 American women composers off the top of my head, but past Betsy Jolas, Sophia Gubaidulina, and Victoria Jordanova, the European names dry up quickly. Maria de Alvear tells me the number is growing, but when pressed she remembers only a half-dozen. And none of them is as original, powerful, and shocking as the German-Spanish composer who—though little known at present—has as striking an individual musical profile as any European under 50. New York heard de Alvear once before in a lengthy piano and trombone work at the Kitchen, and we'll hear her again May 15 at Merkin Hall, when her piano concerto *World: Ceremony for Two Pianos and Orchestra* is performed by the S.E.M. Ensemble, along with works by Pauline Oliveros, Alvin Lucier, and Petr Kotik.

We're being treated to the premiere of a major European work because de Alvear, who was born in Madrid and lives in Berlin, hasn't been able to get it performed in Europe. Her unconventional notation—often without rhythms, just streams of unattached noteheads—is a stumbling block there. Because she grants so much freedom to the performers, the music requires intense concentration, and more rehearsals than European groups are accustomed to offering. The Berlin Philharmonic agreed to play one of her pieces because it looked easy, then came back and told her it wasn't easy at all. Worse, de Alvear writes confrontationally personal music along sexual themes, with titles like *Sexo* and *Vagina*, often using her own speaking voice to declaim lyrics designed to disturb the audience. The combination of musical unconventionality and sexual forthrightness drives Europe's male musicians away in droves. As she explains the scene:

"I have more problems not from being a woman, but from being a strong woman. It's not easy for anyone, even another woman, for a woman to have authority. And I do have authority. Men want us to be nice and harmless composer women." As in America, she says, women composers succeed more easily by being unoriginal. "It's so nice when a woman composer sounds like Pierre Boulez; everyone understands that. There are no problems with the musicians, no problems with the score, no problems with the press. But when a composer sounds like me, and uses titles like *Vagina*, it's a big problem, because nobody wants a woman to be a problem. They accept a man being a problem, but not a woman."

De Alvear's authority is palpable. She exudes tremendous self-confidence (though vulnerability as well), an exact knowledge of what she's after musically, casually saying of her own works, "That's a very magical piece" or "This one is really great." The authority comes from her sense of spiritual mission and the experiences she's put herself through to achieve it. Every year she spends a month or so at a Native American retreat in Appalachian Tennessee, meditating with her spiritual guides and confronting her fears and demons in a rigorous physical regimen. Though she's told me stories about the retreat, she doesn't want to name it in print, nor publish details of her exercises. She is quick to insist, though, that the retreat "has nothing to do with this Carlos Castaneda stuff. It's very normal, very realistic and quotidian. No mystical dream world. They make you work on yourself, go through fears, and stuff like that. I don't like this guru type of thing."

The Tennessee retreat is only part of de Alvear's involvement with indigenous peoples. Last year she made a death-defying trip to the isolated town of Chatanga on Poluostrov Tajmyr, Siberia's northernmost peninsula, 400 kilometers from the North Pole. Her purpose was to record the songs and stories of the fast-disappearing Nenets people. Reaching the peninsula required a seven-hour flight from Moscow followed by military transport, and once she was there, polluted water gave de Alvear a stomach ailment that nearly killed her. In spiritual terms, the ordeal was worth the struggle. "I learned the rules of music," she says. "I learned how the magic of music works, and why it is medicine for certain kinds of people. What happened in Siberia is what happened in America 150 years ago, the genocide of the native people. The children had to go to boarding schools, the parents had to work in artificial cities, everybody got alcoholized. It was prohibited to speak their language. They are losing their culture. There are only 800 of them left. These are the caretakers of the land, the earth. We need that because we're the destroyers. I have to be a messenger to my people, the European people."

As messenger to Europe and America, however, de Alvear doesn't indulge in Third World exoticisms. European in instrumentation and harmony, she insists on imparting the medicinal effect of spiritual music via the conventions of her own culture. Her one recording available here so far is *En Amor Duro* (hat Art), a long, meditative piano piece played by her favorite pianist, Hildegard Kleeb, for whom the piano concerto is also written. Other works I've heard on tape reveal a mesmerizing cross of *Sprechstimme* and performance art, postserialism, and Feldman, a transcendent hybrid of a type Europe has never heard before. In *Sexo*, de Alvear harangues in four languages over sadly pulsing chords. In *Vagina*, she chants over clouds of tones: "You and I, we are going to teach these people a lot about sex. . . . Do you trust me? Good. So lay back and relax. I know it is difficult, but try to stop your mind and feel your body. Do you feel? Good. Now you know the difference between feelings and emotions." Can you imagine Europeans brought up on post-Schoenbergian abstraction responding to such a personal onslaught?

The piano concerto, she says, is similar in intent, but more metaphorical, portraying the cosmos in layers of sound. Aside from Kleeb's solo, there is a second piano in the orchestra played by Joseph Kubera, with certain notes tuned a quarter tone off to provide perspective. De Alvear's music is slow, she explains, to allow the performers time to make the most beautiful sound possible. "I try to put goodness in the world. Beethoven did that, Mozart did that. For Europeans, criticizing society is their way of dealing with problems. My way is different, although I do that too, in a more happy and tender way. All that criticizing creates negative energy, though, always telling the people how bad they are. *Sexo* begins telling how terrible life is, and ends telling people the possibilities to make it good. *Vagina* is about a woman who has a little girl inside of her, and the whole piece is this woman making the little girl grow up. My music has a lot to do with psychology, but I call it spirituality."

Part of de Alvear's problem is that she's spearheading the same kind of spiritual revolution that John Cage and Pauline Oliveros did here 30 years ago, and her complaints about Europe echo those of Downtown composers about the classical academic establishment. Europe's big names, like America's, "protect" their students from music they despise, music outside the accepted European forms. "It is difficult to be different in Europe," she explains, "because the quality there is so good. To be different, you have to be a bad composer, you have to go through the shit of being bad. You have to begin from zero and invent. The big fight is to raise your quality so that you reach the level that is in Europe." She studied with Mauricio Kagel, who encouraged openness and originality, and, like many others, claims that his students are Europe's most interesting young composers. She also admits that she hears better women composers in America, for they have the courage to go their own way. Even here, though, few composers of either sex exhibit the unstoppable self-directedness of Maria de Alvear.

monkey business

fred ho de-europeanizes opera with martial arts

NOVEMBER 25, 1997

Fred Wei-han Ho knows how to cut your carotid artery with his hands, and how to snap a man's spine in three seconds. His expertise in such maneuvers isn't recent; it dates back to his 1974–75 stint in the Marines as part of an elite special corps trained in hand-to-hand combat and stealth assault techniques. But I find the relationship of that training to his baritone sax playing too evocative to ignore. He won't describe the spine-snapping gambit (and I sure don't want a demonstration), except to say that it requires a kind of intensity exploding out of stillness, from a storehouse of *chi:* internal energy. That explosive quality is evident in every phrase Ho blurts out of his booming sax. And as he and I discuss his upcoming opera next week at BAM—*Journey Beyond the West: The New Adventures of Monkey*—it strikes me that that Marine stint, distant as it seems, is a focal point of Ho's life.

Ho is at the forefront of an attempt to create an Asian American musical and operatic aesthetic. A snappy if eccentric dresser known for his purple suits and trademark wide mohawk, he directs two ensembles, the Monkey Orchestra (performing at BAM) and the smaller Afro Asian Music Ensemble. His solution to the dilemma of Asian American hyphenation is to infuse a basic jazz idiom with strong doses of Asian sonic iconography. Gongs and pitch-bending squeals dot his scores, and his favorite sax technique is an altissimo wail that he achieves without fingering, through sheer lip pressure and, well, *chi*. He writes his vocal works in non-Western languages—Cantonese, Mandarin, Tagalog, Farsi—and is counting on tai chi–trained choreographers. "Martial arts," he insists, "is going to kick the ass of modern dance."

And so *Journey Beyond the West*, of which we'll hear the first three acts, is narrated in Chinese. You won't have trouble understanding the story, for it is told in unmistakable terms—Ho calls it a "visual comic book"—through choreography. The basic plot is traditional: A cowardly priest is sent on a dangerous journey from China into India to find and bring back the Buddhist scriptures. Three companions protect him—Monkey, a trickster figure, expert in martial arts but arrogant and conceited; Pig, whose appetites for food and sex are uncontrollable, once an admiral but changed into a pig for trying to seduce the emperor's daughter; and Ogre, persecuted in youth by humans and harboring a rage that can only be satiated by slaughter. As Ho admits, it's kind of a Tang dynasty *Wizard of Oz*, but overlaid with his own politically inspired additions.

A superficial glance suggests that Ho is not alone in creating an East-West fusion; Asian-American composers are thriving at the moment. Tan Dun's opera *Marco Polo* and his *Symphony 1997* for the reversion of Hong Kong made recent splashes, while Chen Yi, Jhou Long, and Bun Ching Lam receive frequent commissions. Ho, however, points out crucial differences between himself and the others: none of them were born in America, none of them grew up with racism, all of them came here as professionals with doors opened for them by Columbia University and other institutions, and all of them work within a Eurocentric concert tradition. He's complained in print that Asian artists and companies are given precedence over Asian Americans "because they are considered 'safe'—their work will not confront issues of racism, oppression, project resistance, and struggle, as the expressions of oppressed nationalities (so-called peoples of color) in the U.S. tend to do."

The only other prominent East Coast figure in Ho's situation is Jason Hwang, also born in the U.S. Hwang comes from Chicago's chaotically improvisatory AACM tradition, Ho points out, whereas he comes from a big band tradition. Yeah, it flashes on me, *that's* what makes Ho's sound so original: instead of the individualistic free-for-all of most Downtown improv, his groups always blend for a powerful sonic kick. His whole ensemble's got *chi*.

Ho did so many projects in the Bay Area during the '80s that everyone assumes that he came here from California. Actually, although he was born in Palo Alto, he grew up in Amherst, Massachusetts. The racism he confronted there, and the domestic violence in his household, conditioned the thrust of his career. (Music against misogynist violence is one strain in his output: a recent suite is titled *Yes Means Yes, No Means No, Whatever She Wears, Wherever She Goes.*) Despite a turbulent childhood, he lucked out during high school in the fact that jazz greats Archie Shepp, Max Roach, and Reggie Workman lived and worked in Amherst. Ho missed no opportunity to sit at their feet, attending workshops and analyzing band arrangements by Thad Jones and Duke Ellington. He gravitated toward jazz, he says, because:

"As a teenager I was trying to find an example of something that was not part of the white world. The catalytic impact of the Black Power movement, and Malcolm X, and the Black Arts movement sought to challenge white supremacy in America. I came of age during the Asian-American movement of the early '70s, and I'm trying to forge a unity between the two great social movements that had an impact on my life. Music that's been called 'jazz' said a lot to me because it came out of the experience of an oppressed people. At the same time, it spoke to the beauty and passion of people who in spite of their oppression affirmed their humanity."

Then came the Marines. Ho's racist instructor used him for target practice and (this was the Vietnam era) would point to him and tell the other men during workouts, "Here's what the gook looks like." Finally, Ho—a big guy—knocked the instructor unconscious during a training drill. Harvard was next and hardly better. "The main impact Harvard had," he recalls, "was making it clear that I did not to want to join the bourgeoisie— to be a manager or some lackey of the governmental or corporate ruling structure. It became clear that privilege doesn't equate with talent, ability, intelligence, or hard work. Privilege is simply privilege." Ho steered a wide path around the Eurocentric music department, majoring in sociology.

After college Ho became a construction worker and started working with nonprofessional musicians at community centers. Though he's done the usual new-music-circuit gigs, he considers his "guerrilla accomplishments" the center of his musical life—playing for the Asian-American Creative Music Festival in Boston, Yale University's Minority Freshmen weekend, the Guadalupe Cultural Arts Center in San Antonio. He's belonged at times to the Nation of Islam, I Wor Kuen (an Asian American group modeled after the Black Panthers), and the League of Revolutionary Struggle. A portrait of Ho on his wall was painted and sent to him by a Puerto Rican nationalist prisoner incarcerated in Wisconsin. "What I'm trying to do is to try to change the American musical landscape . . . to develop a new American music that is anchored in the traditions of people of color in this society. To de-Europeanize the world."

In the fourth act of *Journey Beyond the West*, the one we won't hear yet, Monkey returns to his homeland to find that the jealous gods have corrupted it, capitalist style. Monkey has a choice: he can proceed directly to Nirvana, or he can form a revolutionary movement to liberate his homeland and change the world. "Naturally," I venture, "he chooses to stay and fight."

The slightest grin breaks across Ho's impassive face. "Of course," he replies.

music and/versus society

plundering for art

sampling

MAY 1, 1990

There's three composers at this party, see? I put on the new Carl Stone CD *Four Pieces* (EAM) and ask them to guess the tune. After minutes of quizzical staring, one says it's got to be Schubert. Another says, can't be, that's a pop singer's voice. The third's on his knees, ear against the speaker.

Composers one and two are both right. Carl Stone's *Shing Kee* was made by sampling a recording of classical pieces sung by Japanese pop singer Akiko Yano. Stone sampled her singing "Der Lindenbaum" from Schubert's *Winterreise*—stored several hundred thousand bits of it in digital form—and in *Shing Kee* he plays the samples back, using the computer live to add a few milliseconds at each repetition. What one hears first is a hazy, pulsating piano harmony. A windy sound enters and slides upward on repetition. After 90 seconds you realize the wind is a voice—that slow, breathy slide to the pitch is the hint it's a pop singer. A stunning aural illusion, the gradual lengthening proves vividly how dependent our perception of pitch and timbre is on duration.

Digital bit by bit, the wind expands into the syllables *ahhh meyyy,* which, not being German, convinced composer three that it wasn't Schubert. In the next few minutes, you gradually discern enough of the piano's triplet to stir a vague memory. Then, at 8:30 on your second counter, a four-second sample ending in a familiar trill gives you the only clear ID in this 16-minute piece; got it!, that's "Der Lindenbaum." Stone grabs a three-second excerpt and, over the next six minutes, slows it down by slight increments to 20 seconds, in voluptuously receding curves. In the final two minutes, Schubert's trill, inconclusive in the original, waves its good-bye diminuendo, stretched from a quick ornament into an evocation of eternity.

Sampling—digitally recording performed or prerecorded sound for potential manipulation—has hit the music world like a sonic boom and opened

up thousands of unforeseen possibilities. Line-hook your sampler to a CD
player and the world of recorded music is your oyster: Coltrane's horn,
Phil Collins's drumming, Fischer-Dieskau's voice all at your disposal. It's
also created a legal miasma. Copyright laws are well defined for *printed*
material, scores and sheet music, but ill-prepared to deal with actual sound.
When, in 1972, George Crumb wanted to quote Rachmaninoff's *Rhapsody
on a Theme of Paganini* in his *Makrokosmos I,* the piece was still in copyright, so he switched to Chopin. Had he *sampled* Rachmaninoff, the legality would have become murky.

The CD that has most violently thrown sampling's legality into question is *Plunderphonics* by Toronto composer John Oswald. With few exceptions, the entire disc consists of stolen sounds: a chord from "Sgt. Pepper,"
Dolly Parton's voice, Ligeti's *Atmospheres,* a few Metallica tracks. *Le Sacre
du Printemps* is broken into unrecognizable violent chords, then a section
of the piece is sped through dizzying fast-forward. The beginning of the
finale of Beethoven's Seventh is suspended in a cartoonlike loop, unable to
burst past the opening chords. Music boxes plink four easy-listening tunes
at once, layered beyond discrimination.

What got Oswald in trouble was his use of Michael Jackson: "Dab," the
CD's longest cut, is a transparent satire on "Bad," looping obvious chords
and bass lines from the song. Worse, for the cover Oswald pasted Jackson's
face over a naked woman's body. That got the attention of the Canadian
Recording Industry Association (CRIA), which in December demanded that
Oswald cease distribution. Eventually, CRIA's lawyers convinced Oswald's
that he should turn over the remaining copies to be crushed; Oswald had
printed a thousand, 700 were already sent out. Money was never an issue,
since Oswald had paid for production out of pocket, mailed the CDs free of
charge, and stated in the liner notes, "This disc may be reproduced, but neither it, nor any reproductions of it, are to be bought or sold." Even so, a few
copies have been located in used record stores, and alternative radio stations
(including WFMU) have been giving the disc copious airplay.

Justifying CRIA's stance, president Brian Robertson said, "The Oswald
issue, in our view, went way beyond sampling as we've known it in the
past. The Michael Jackson track was not sampling, it was copying. A whole
section was sampled, you could clearly hear the original. Polygram has
estimated that by 1995, up to 50 percent of the industry's income is going
to come from rights, not from retail sales. There has to be a structure of
legal protection."

"It was compounded," Robertson continued, "by the graphic changes
made to the Michael Jackson image on the cover. That underscored for us

that the recording was exploitation, not individual creative expression. And it seemed to be sheltering behind sampling." Oswald opted not to spend the next few years fighting a multibillion-dollar corporation, and in February CRIA destroyed the remaining copies of *Plunderphonics*, making the disc a collector's item. Oswald admits, "The project isn't compromised by having 300 fewer copies of the CD."

Sampling's legal limits remain blurry. Carl Stone quoted me an alleged "fair use" rule stating that, formerly, one could use up to two seconds of a recording without violating copyright. But Lawrence Stanley, an attorney for Tommy Boy Records who defends rap groups in their use of samples, laughed at the suggestion. "Nice rumor. There has never been a ruling. There is no standard, guideline, or anything. Basically, it falls under the copyright act. It has to do with the nature of the use, the amount of the sample used in relation to the work as a whole—for example, whether or not the sample was used sporadically in the piece or was the 'hook' of the song—and whether or not it's for profit."

So sampler composers use a variety of strategies to avoid copyright penalties. Stone got prior permission to use Yano's voice from her Japanese label. On the same CD, *Hop Ken* samples *Pictures at an Exhibition*, though the unspecified exact recording would be difficult to track down. Nicolas Collins, whose music is based entirely on found material (and who dedicated a recent performance to Oswald), utterly transforms the stuff he steals, layering it with other stuff. Of his 1985 album *Devil's Music*, he says, "Since my material came off the radio at random, in principle I didn't even know where it's from, so I couldn't have gotten permission. The record was clearly a copyright violation. But if something was too recognizable, if a line was clearly a Madonna vocal line, I didn't use it in the final mix."

Stanley points out a weakness in the argument. "If it's unrecognizable he has no problem. But do you know De La Soul's album *3 Feet High and Rising*? There's a song on it called 'Transmitting Live from Mars.' We're in court on it in California. It's a bar-and-a-half sample of Flo and Eddie, used together with a how-to-speak-French record and an organ line from Wilson Pickett's version of 'Hey Jude.' The master was slowed down, so even the pitch was changed. They're suing us under the California bootlegging statute. It's not recognizable to most people, unless you play it right next to the original. What's unrecognizable to me may be recognizable to someone else."

On much of *Plunderphonics*, recognizability is precisely the point. The liner notes meticulously credit each sample. Stone and Collins, Oswald points out, "do the same thing that some rap artists do: they don't credit their sources, which is a strong form of protection. Because you're not admitting in the same language used by law that you're doing something, only in the language of music. At this point no one has been able to establish in court that a person actually did sample something, as opposed to putting together a very accurate facsimile. My thesis—that you should credit your sources, as in journalism—puts me in an awkward legal position."

So far, not a single case of copyright infringement involving sampling has gone to trial: the few that went past the complaint stage have been settled out of court. Most artists are savvy enough to get advance permission before releasing a sampling album, allowing the sampled artist the option of either a fraction-of-a-cent-per-disc royalty (preferred when a major band is involved) or a lump-sum buyout. Robertson gripes that Oswald made no attempt to get permission. In defense, Oswald says, "I wanted to start this project with an example in which there were no holds barred by anything other than my aesthetic choices. People warned me that the cover would probably get me in trouble, but I wasn't willing to exert any self-censorship or make any compromises."

"Fortunately," Stanley notes, "a lot of this has to do with economics. Someone like Collins, people aren't going to be interested in suing him because he's putting out his records on independent labels. Even Nonesuch is not really big enough to go after." Thanks to small-time economics and the unrecognizability factor, copyright violation doesn't seem to threaten the experimental music community, Oswald's case notwithstanding, to the extent it does rap groups. Still, a few artists are worried. Linda Fisher plans to exclude her recent sampling piece *Big Mouth* from her upcoming CD, because it uses lines from Warner Bros. cartoons. Even Stanley cautions staying away from television theme songs and film music. Collins makes a distinction of intent between the new music's use of sampling and commercial music's use:

"Sampling in pop music seems to me to be about throwing a little flag up—say, James Brown for a dance record—without looking into the timbral or musical essence of the material. Other people steal for purely pragmatic reasons. They steal terrifically recorded horn sections because it saves them money in the studio. The difference between that and what Carl Stone or Oswald or I do is that we use sampling technology to reveal the double character of found material. On one hand a sample refers to something, it has the cultural associations of the pop record it comes from. At the same time it's an exploration of the textural and timbral essence of real-world sounds, which are often more luscious than anything you could generate with a synthesizer. Pop music uses the sampler as a tape recorder, new music uses it as an instrument."

Plunderphonics meets Collins's criteria only intermittently. Some of the cuts are well below party-game level, certainly the warped but otherwise straight version of "White Christmas" or Dolly Parton's transformation into a man by slowing and lowering her voice. And the lethargic version of *The Andy Griffith Show* theme is barely cute. Where Oswald experiments, though, especially in the *Le Sacre* reconstruction and a Cagean reworking of Glenn Gould's recording of the *Goldberg Variations,* makes for fascinating results. Still, artistic merit aside, "Dab" could never be mistaken for "Bad," and that Oswald would have lost a court case is by no means a foregone conclusion. Oswald and Stanley agree that *Plunderphonics* might have fared better in the U.S., where copyright laws grant more leeway to satire.

As usual, the copyright office may take decades to set clear legal guidelines for the new technology. For now, if you want to use a Milton Babbitt sample in your next tone poem, for heaven's sake don't put a nude Babbitt photo on the cover. And in the meantime, name that tune.

mozarts live!

"performing mozart's music"

JUNE 18, 1991

The atmosphere at Juilliard's "Performing Mozart's Music" symposium was a little stifling for a Downtown electromusic fan. But every so often I have to check into the "real" classical music world—in this case, the May 20–24 symposium, which overlapped with the annual meeting of the Music Critics Association—to try to figure out why so many classical music buffs disparage all modern music without listening to more than a millionth of it.

I had no objection to learning more about a man who wrote some wonderful music 200 years ago. What bothered me was the frequent feeling that I was in church, that Mozart was a god, and that self-appointed priests were getting their strokes by making him one. A doctrine of textual inerrancy ruled; musicologists catalogued dots and strokes as though Mozart sweated over every note, as though it would be sacrilege for a performer to add anything interpretive to what Mozart had set down. Haydn proclaimed that Mozart "has taste, and a profound knowledge of composition"; for me that sums up Mozart's advantages exactly, but one academic quoted Haydn with contempt for so pedestrian a recognition of suprahu-man genius. (Symposium director Neal Zaslaw sprang to Haydn's defense.) Old men, failing to make a point in words, would croak out *bada-dum, bada-dum, bada-DEE-dum* with lifted eyebrows as though the first 10 notes of the G-Minor Symphony, no matter how cracked, ought to confer enlightenment. Even recording engineers got into the act. Sony isn't trying to turn a buck, you know; it's upgrading its equipment to carry on Mozart's holy work in ever more glorious fidelity.

Don't get me wrong. I didn't find either musicology or criticism in a deplorable or corrupt state. The best scholars were fascinating and talked as though old Wolfgang were just a particularly expert composer whose working methods were open to study and explanation. Robert D. Levin's ear-opening analysis of improvised passages in the concerto solos made Mozart seem *more* of a genius, not less, while also making him seem human, shrewd, practical, and overly busy.

The danger I sensed came from the duller 50 percent (including some of the famous folks), for their Mozart worship had an egotistical undercurrent. Demystifying Mozart empowers us all and advances music, but holding him up as a mystery empowers only the person who puts a stop to discussion by saying so. Not everyone gets to be a great composer or thinker, but everyone can draw prestige from appreciating great music that has been predigested via an immense subintellectual framework. People with no light to shine themselves make gods in order to gain self-importance by reflecting their light. The bigger the sun, the better they shine, and the more viciously they resist the possibility of other suns. When that happens, scholarship becomes a suction hose to siphon power away from performers, and criticism becomes a stick to whip modern music with.

What are a god's job requirements? First, he has to be dead. If you decide to reflect the light of, say, La Monte Young, there's the risk that he might embarrass you by forgetting your name. If a god-candidate is still alive, you need permission to orbit him, and in the flesh Wolfgang might have offended some of the people who spoke of his music last week in hushed tones. In fact, a god must be long dead, for recent stiffs leave friends behind, which creates a hierarchy: some people reflect more light than others. A friend of mine once studied with someone who had met Brahms, so even Brahms isn't cold enough for safe worship.

It would embarrass the priests to learn that there are Mozarts in New York today, for it would imply that they wouldn't recognize a Mozart who wasn't predigested for them. Therefore, in their minds modern music must a priori be inferior, and one or two (or 15 or 50) unsatisfactory pieces are

enough to prove it. Beyond his undeniably "profound knowledge of composition," Mozart's greatness is partly something we've conspired to
create, by other composers imitating him, by molding our thought framework around him. Someday, Morton Feldman's music, too (which has its
own perfection), will be so thoroughly chewed that every literate person
will know how to think about it without listening to it. Not many people in
America today have taste *and* a profound knowledge of composition, but a
few do. That most new music stinks is utterly irrelevant: if the same hadn't
been true in Mozart's day, we'd be celebrating his contemporaries as well.

The people who attended "Performing Mozart's Music"—scholars,
record company execs, orchestra managers, performers, critics—run the
music business. Some of them I have a lot of faith in, but others obviously
derive a sense of importance from being Mozart's (or Bach's, or Beethoven's)
accessories that no living composer, no matter how talented, could give
them—that Mozart himself couldn't give them if he were alive.

The self-interest that directs the music business, when it doesn't have to
do with money, comes from vanity, and new music's inevitable uncertainty
threatens vanity. We need to recognize (composers in self-defense, bigwigs
in self-criticism) that the distribution of new music squirms under the
thumbs of thousands of reflected-light people who have a vested interest in
keeping alive the myth that there are no more Mozarts, and in *making* that
myth come true by preventing living composers from getting the practical
experience Mozart had. Mozart appreciation enriches everyone. But
Mozart worship is antagonistic to all future creativity, and it stems, not
from love of music as it pretends, but from ego-inflation.

killers in the audience

JANUARY 14, 1992

I get the feeling that if J. S. Bach were around today writing the *Goldberg
Variations,* audience members would tell him, "Jo, don't you think you're
limiting yourself, writing harpsichord pieces to put Count Keyserling to
sleep? Where is the grand statement? Where is the universality? Don't
you *want* to be as profound as the masters were?" I like to think J. S. would
be very Downtown in his reply: "Look, man, I had a gig."

Ten years ago, in the composer/audience split, my sympathies were
with the latter. I felt that most composers had sold out to aurally irrelevant

theories, and that the few interesting ones were failing to make their ideas clear enough for nonmusicians to perceive. Credo: I believe in a nonmusician audience, as an ultimate goal for both criticism and composing. The blame-the-audience gambit, fair or not, had failed in six decades to advance musical culture one iota in any direction.

Then in 1987 I got a rude shock when a NY Phil audience walked out en masse on John Adams's accessible and cogent *Harmonielehre,* after warmly receiving a tepid Anton Rubinstein concerto. That was too revealing. And lately, after lectures, I've been attacked for *liking* new music, with the naysayers lacing their comments, with platitudes about universality and claiming Shostakovich (that mediocrity!) as the Last Great Composer.

Whether composing has seen better days or not, *listening* is a lost art.

Composer Stuart Smith reports that a few years ago he came across the international statistics on musical literacy. In Great Britain 55 percent of the population could read music, in France and Germany 60 percent could, and in eastern Europe and Scandinavia the figures approached 90 percent. The musical literacy rate in the U.S. was .25 percent—one-fourth of one percent. Now, many passionate and intelligent music lovers can't read notation, and you can't draw a one-to-one correspondence between literacy and sophisticated listening. Nevertheless, the figures say something about what the American composer is up against.

Those numbers suggest why the best American composers (most spectacularly, Feldman and Nancarrow) are hailed as titans in Europe before they're heard of here. Since even young Americans play more in Europe than here, they have to keep a double standard. They're as subtle as, and more original than, European composers, but here, unless they shut themselves up in the university (which demands kissing a particular set of asses), they play to an audience unwilling to follow anything it hasn't heard before. Smith, gigging in American jazz clubs, grew contemptuous of "accessibility" when he noticed the better he played, the colder the audience became. No wonder composers give up on the audience.

Literacy isn't the whole story, for classical buffs are absolutely, absolutely the worst. The industry has made them consumers and destroyed any feeling for music as a historical process. They want masterpieces signed, framed, and delivered. They recognize a masterpiece not by its internal logic—that would require listening—but by its similarity to previous masterpieces. They treat universality as though it were an overcoat a composer must put on to appear in public, and talk about feeling as though the model for all feeling were Tchaikovsky's *Romeo and Juliet.* Dislike of dissonance and discontinuity was their old excuse, but suave and pretty

Harmonielehre showed that that was a red herring. What they wanted was the ego-reinforcement of reified Culture, and no living composer can give them that.

Compositionally, we do not live in a bad time. As I hear them, Carl Stone's *Shing Kee*, Nic Collins's *Dark and Stormy Night*, Larry Polansky's *51 Melodies* could go down in the books as paradigms for new aesthetics, like *Piano Phase* or *Le Marteau* or *Pierrot Lunaire*. I listen to Laurie Spiegel's *Sound Zones*, "Blue" Gene Tyranny's *The Intermediary*, Rhys Chatham's *An Angel Moves Too Fast to See*, and I think, wow, what a great time to follow music. The Downtown scene bubbles with hotter ideas right now than it has in 12 years. So why are public and critical interest deader than ever?

The real history of American music remains a secret. The reason is simple: History is made mostly by nonacademics, and written by academics. The latter market their textbooks to other academics who buy them only if their own name's in the index. In a recent *Times* think piece, David Schiff (author of a worshipfully uncritical book on Elliott Carter), divided the 20th century into pop and 12-tone music. That's like calling the 19th century an era of parlor songs and pompous symphonies, and leaving out Wagner and Schumann. When the Newspaper of Record (deadeningly conservative now that John Rockwell's on the sidelines) denies that the hundreds of new pieces I dearly love exist, how do I escape critical solipsism?

Perhaps the problem is the composer and audience blaming *each other*. Say they don't owe each other anything. Psychologist James Hillman insists that, instead of the other way around, "man is a function of psyche and his job is to serve it." Music is part of psyche; it exists not *for* either audiences' pleasure or composers' vanity, but both exist to serve Music. And what they owe Music is to keep it alive, in themselves, in public, and in history. Bad pieces exist, but listening happens one performance at a time, without comparison. The audience member who says that great music is dead is its murderer.

letting euro go

JANUARY 21, 1992

Allow me to talk about my ethnicity for a moment, such as it is. The Ganns sailed from Alsace-Lorraine to Philadelphia in 1751. Musically as well as genealogically, I feel my ancestors came from Germany, but were here for the revolution. Mozart and Schubert nourished my childhood, but when I discovered Ives at 13, and Cage at 15, I felt I had come home.

As a Euro-American, I feel the claims of two traditions. The claims Bach and Mozart make on me are in terms of consistency of language, contrapuntal integrity, smoothness, emotiveness, assimilation of one's inherited technique. The Americans, Cowell, Partch, Young, et al., make a different set: inventiveness, attention to sonic reality, rethinking music from the ground up, independence from habits, clichés, or methods developed by others. The two sets of claims are mutually contradictory. To create your own technique (America) and internalize it too (Europe) is a Herculean psychic task; Carl Ruggles achieved it, and Morton Feldman, sometimes Conlon Nancarrow.

Every musician trained in two or more traditions suffers the difficulty of competing claims. Invariably, one set takes precedence over the others; the '80s could be defined as a collective failure to recognize that. When the claims that European and American listening make on me can't both be satisfied, I automatically drop the Euro side of the hyphen. That's where other classical critics must differ from me: they put the Euro first, and usually last. I assume that a composer will polish up his or her ideas in late career, but originality has to be there from the beginning, or it's not worth warming up my word processor. For me, Uptown music can be summed up as polish without originality. The Eurocritics at the *Times* and *New Yorker* obviously prefer that condition to its reverse.

The American postrevolution composers are so diverse—Oliveros, Rzewski, Tenney, Branca—few people realize that they constitute a tradition. I've called it the American experimental tradition because Peter Garland does, but you might as well call it American classical music, an indigenous tradition of large-scale concert music—as long as you distinguish it from the Euro-aesthetic of the 12-toners and neo-Romantic symphonists. Am-class got buried during World War II when Stravinsky, Schoenberg, and Hindemith immigrated stateside, and it's been digging its way out ever since. The "new music" fad of 1979–83 gave it a temporary foothold in public cognition, but that's been lost. Now BAM, seeking alternatives to "Eurocentric" programming, can think of only African and Asian musics.

But the proof of a tradition is that it can make claims on you, that its collective virtues can come to seem indispensable. It don't mean a thing if it ain't got that—whatever. For Am-class, that whatever equals independence, originality, sincerity. Being a postrevolutionary American composer virtually entails creating your own philosophy along with the music.

Anything less homebuilt—serenades with a first and second theme, a pitch trick thought up by some dead Austrian—don't mean a thing.

Uptown's Europhile symphonies and 12-tone pieces sound lousy to my Am-class ears. European-based music is rhythmically infantile, still grappling with the four-bar antecedent/consequent in 4/4 meter. Its rhythmic complexity is ornamental, the beat obscured by a virtuosic gruppetto; or else pulse is so ephemeral as to be irrelevant. It clings to the climaxes and catharsis of Europe's "golden" moment, the Romantic era, and where it lacks emotive content, it substitutes hectic virtuosity. Actual Europeans compensate for this rhythmic lack with a harmonic and instrumental sophistication that Americans rarely possess even uptown. Still, György Ligeti tries to ape Nancarrow's rhythms, but he just doesn't have Nancarrow's American jazz ear.

Am-class, on the other hand, since Cowell, has taken its beat from all the world *musics* that have found their way to this continent. Cage set Am-class securely on the basis of rhythmic structure, like the music of most other continents, rather than on Europe's harmonic structure. This being a classical tradition, those various world beats are abstracted (for the sake of manipulation) in a way that removes them from the more tactile world of rock and jazz. Uptowners have long derided Am-class for its pitch simplicity, and have convinced critics that music with 12 pitches per octave is more "intellectual" than that with seven or 10. But Am-class, determined to shed every vestige of Europe, is redefining tuning according to the overtone series so that its works now typically include from 16 to 72 pitches per octave; that ought to turn the equation around.

Failure to recognize Am-class as a distinct tradition results in reviews written on mistaken premises. No critic would be so stupid as to apply European criteria to Indian classical music, but it happens to American classical every month. Sometimes dramatically, as last fall when the *Times*'s Edward Rothstein reviewed a very different African American work, Leroy Jenkin's *Mother of Three Sons,* by the most stiff-lipped, prim European standards (horrors, a bare-breasted soprano!). But it happens to whites, too, that a composer trying to rethink sound is lambasted for not having a soothing emotional curve. New music is often perceived as a shady middle area between classical, rock, and jazz. It isn't. It's understood that way because classical critics recognize its structural aims, pop critics sympathize with its Americanness, but neither understand both. It occupies its own space and proceeds from its own common, unstated assumptions.

I hope that by the 21st century Cowell will have been dead long enough to be understood as the cofounder of a new stream in music history.

American classical music will never have a public as long as it is represented as a deficient aberration of a European tradition. What I want for the new year is: no more reviewing American music by European standards. Or as one early American critic put it, DON'T TREAD ON ME.

what normal people hear

rose rosengard subotnik

JULY 28, 1992

"I don't think about the audience when I write," smirks a composer, "because there's no such thing as *the* audience. Everyone listens differently." If you're rooted in reality, your brain should now flash COP OUT! COP OUT! There sure as hell *is* such a thing as *the* audience; I sit in the middle of it 150 times a year. A surgeon might as well say, "I don't use anesthetic, because there is no such thing as *the* patient. Everyone responds to pain differently."

What do "normal" people hear in music? Rose Rosengard Subotnik thinks it's time composers quit ducking the question. A Brown University prof, she's America's leading scholar on Theodor Adorno's music writing, and she's assembled her musical essays, the best I've read in years, into *Developing Variations* (University of Minnesota Press). Subotnik is a post-Adornoite aware of the thinker's Eurocentric bias against pop music. Indeed, she concludes that rock is doing its job in the 20th century better than art music is. Her mentor is spinning in his grave.

In the book's last essay, "The Challenge of Contemporary Music," Subotnik tips over a problematic imbalance in musical society: composers don't hear the way audiences do. Most listening habits evolve haphazardly, but universities teach musicians a specific skill, *structural listening,* unknown on the outside. "Structural listening," she explains, "amounts to following and comprehending the unfolding realization, with all its inner relationships, of a musical conception." It's a Schoenbergian tendency, grounded in analyses of symphonies of the Great Masters, to hear form as autonomously self-referential. (Consider a visual equivalent: an artist looking at a Mapplethorpe photo of a guy with a whip up his ass and seeing only planes and diagonals.) Further, it "treats the individual user's mental framework, in a Kantian sense, as a kind of universally grounded, and hence ideologically neutral, epistemologically transparent structure."

She's nailed it. Grad school implanted that paradigm in me, though I usually relax and listen a little more viscerally unless I have particular incentive to dig up a piece's deeper relationships. Not even composers listen that intensely all the time, but they do learn to write *as though* that's how civilians listen. Worse, they're drilled that Mozart was great *solely* because of his formal achievements, and so "have located musical significance not just metaphorically but literally . . . in the structure of their works." As a result, they've lost touch with reality. They create structures that they *know* are solid, then wonder why nobody listens. The only audience that doesn't exist is the "ideologically neutral" audience school led them to expect.

The demand for structural listening, Subotnik argues, alienates people, for it denies the sensuous and stylistic listening modes they naturally and enjoyably bring to music. For many composers, especially older ones, that's the audience's tough luck; they shoulda gone to music school. But structural listening is a privileged paradigm only in academia's Never-Never Land. Subotnik underlines its Kantian fallacy, that the listening mind is a blank slate on which the piece of music writes its structure detail by detail. "Kant's efforts to preserve a universal basis for human communication," she continues, "have proven futile against the power of irreducible differences in perceptions, structuring principles, and values among differently situated individuals and cultures." Our clash of backgrounds, our growing awareness of relativity, have smashed the blank-slate hypothesis, and with it structural listening's frail claim to normalcy.

All right, so what do non-grad-music-school-trained people hear in music? "What the public hears," Subotnik answers (and she's taught enough Intros to Music to know), "is what is always heard, not autonomous structure but the sensuous manifestation of particular cultural values." Those cultural values are communicated through gesture, melody, style, rhythm, sophistication of technological surface, and, perhaps most importantly, how the music varies previously familiar archetypes. In classical music (this is precisely what separates it from pop), structure is *part* of the value-expressive element, but not even in minimalism is it the most immediate part.

Here's an insight that applies as well to Deadheads as to Elliott Carter snobs. You like Milton Babbitt's music? It's probably not so much because you can hear the way he juggles hexachords as the fact that 12-tone music expresses the "serious intellectual" values of the scientific/academic community you identify with. (Subotnik enjoys pointing out how lay listeners subvert 12-tone info flow into mere ambiance.) Like Downtown improv?

Fancy yourself a rebellious anarchist, as long as you have a collective to back you up. Like Mozart? That elegant European ethos lifts you above hoi polloi. I like new music, successful or not, that tries things never heard before; I want to think of myself as independent, as having escaped the inauthenticity of mass consciousness.

Make up your own examples. Every genre has its better and worse pieces. The point is that structure is secondary. It gives music staying power, by putting logical force behind the emotions, but it's not what makes people want to listen in the first place. Even Mozart, Subotnik claims, believed in an "artless art," whose formal tricks were intended to remain a trade secret. Thinking that a neutral design by itself can justify a work is (to use a handy French term) the composer's *professional deformation.* Audiences want to hear their cultural values confirmed, elaborated, perhaps even challenged. Composers need to deschool themselves, think themselves into that perspective, and realize that, to most people, exquisite grammar ain't worth beans if you don't have something important to say.

dysfunctional harmony

repealing the suppression of creativity

SEPTEMBER 14, 1993

Jung believed in five instincts: hunger, sex, aggression, flight, and creativity. Everyone deflects, satisfies, or represses these instincts in various ways. Americans (especially Republicans) suppress creativity even more than sex. As a result, we live in a musically dysfunctional society. Concertgoing is a penance. Musicians gripe about rock's limitations, but the possibility that we could have some more evolved music as collective cultural expression seems so quixotic it's never entertained. Our official classical scene is a sham in which professors give each other awards for writing tedious music. Composer and audience have mutually acquiesced to a rotten marriage of frigid noncommunication.

The suppression of creativity is pervasive. I do it myself. I'm a dysfunctional drawer too embarrassed to even doodle, but I once followed the exercises in Betty Edwards's book *Drawing on the Right Side of the Brain,* and within minutes was turning out amazing duplicates of Picasso drawings. Today I can't draw a recognizable cat, but there may be a Rembrandt inside me wishing I'd step out of the way. As Edwards says, we're born knowing how to draw but it gets schooled out of us between ages 10 and 13. And in this increasingly visual culture, music is even more squelched. Believing ourselves uncreative, we project creativity onto some safe, distant target. Artists, we reassure ourselves, are *different*, selected by God, not normal.

Which is why we worship Mozart. It's comforting to believe that *real* creators lived far away and long ago. Recognizing oneself in a new work requires summoning up the creativity within us, but kowtowing to History's Hallowed Warhorses makes no demands at all. The person who idolizes the "divine genius" of Mozart denies, projects, and is out of touch with his own creativity. I've analyzed Mozart's music, and I know his tricks—he was brainy, but not divine. That's why music's worst enemy is the classical establishment, whose every nuance hinges on a genius myth that dumps water on the average Joe's inner spark. (And it's why *Amadeus* is such a wretched, smarmy film, gratifying our most self-defeating delusions.)

Psychologist James Hillman, in *The Myth of Analysis*, asks: "Why must the person who lives largely in terms of the creative instinct be damned out of common humanity? And the reverse: why can't the common man change his heroically romantic nineteenth-century concept of genius, so charged with ambition and envy, and be done with this fantasy of the extraordinary personality? Has not each of us a genius; has not each genius a human soul? Could we not find a similar extraordinariness within ourselves in our relation to the creative instinct as we experience it?"

To acknowledge creativity in those proximate to us is dangerous, for it shines a light on what we keep locked up. That's why Cage struck a nerve. When an interviewer said to him, "If music's that easy to do, then I could do it," Cage responded, "Have I said anything to make you think I thought you were stupid?" One of Cage's aims was to erase the line not only between art and life, but between artists and nonartists. And in fact, no such lines exist. Asian and African cultures, unlike our own, acknowledge the universal need for artistic expression.

Art communicates via empathy. We all, in childhood, tried to draw a human figure, and remember how hard it was to make it come alive; that's why a figure drawn well takes our breath away. Same with sports: we feel in our muscular imagination the delicacy needed to curve that ball's trajectory into the basket. If you'd never tried it, watching it wouldn't mean much. Most teenagers try their hand at poetry, and many attempt a song, one reason rock persists. We can imagine the effort that goes into a well-set lyric enough to admire someone who does it better than we can. But how many people attempt to write smooth polyphony, or instrumental music, or auditory shapes on a canvas of time? In our educational systems, no one.

The average American has no concept of what's involved in polyphonic or textural musical creation, and therefore can't admire the results.

And how could they learn, with composers today trained to express creativity on such rarefied, picayune levels? I recently sat on a grants panel whose requirements included a residency in which the composer spent a few days with the audience, and I thought, Here's the future of music: a new breed of composer/teacher/creativity-facilitator to replace the lonely-genius-who-writes-in-isolation paradigm. It is as immoral for composers, as the carriers of our culture's musical creativity, to ignore their social responsibility as it is for weapons designers and bioengineers. The composer must not only trumpet her own hyperdeveloped musical sense but tap the listener's more modest one. To have an audience is to unlock a collective creativity.

Composers have to learn, as some have, to gear their art toward present-day categories of listener empathy. That won't make their music weaker, only clearer. Europeans and music professors will scoff at it for being too straightforward, not complex enough: fuck 'em. They're part of the problem. At the same time, audience members have to acknowledge that their knee-jerk negativity toward new music arises from insecurity about their own stifled fantasies. Their job is not to judge, but to exercise their imaginations within the music. As in any marriage gone sour, each partner has made the other what it is. Moving toward health is going to require self-inspection and remedial attitude work on both sides. And lots of courage.

don't touch that dahl

classical radio

JANUARY 25, 1994

I never set out to become a critic. For years I tried to break into radio as a classical DJ. But growing up I acquired something that would keep me off the highbrow airwaves forever: a Texas accent. C&W stations might have embraced me, but classical radio didn't think its audiences would swallow that an Andy Griffith soundalike could distinguish Buxtehude's cantatas from Bach's. They were probably right. Southern drawls are linked with stupidity, and not just in the North, where the abhorrence of biases and stereotypes extends to every cultural group except Southerners. (I winced at the *Voice*'s recent cover story on Texas cheerleaders, which sneered at the kind of people I grew up among as though they were an inferior species.) Luckily, I took refuge in print. As long as I don't write "Philip Glass is fixin' to give a concert," I can pass undetected.

Classical DJs can't talk about Charles *Ahves*. (*Ah* being the standard, inaccurate, Northern transcription of the Southern long I. If I were to transcribe the Northern pronunciation of the name, I'd use two syllables: I-yeeves.) Instead, they twist their lips around horrific locutions like Clode Daybyoo-sih and Sairzhe Rrrrachhmahneenoaff, meticulously avoiding any phoneme that could be mistaken for one used in American English. What disaster would befall if they were to lapse into an American consonant? The same thing that would happen if they advertised Budweiser and Ford pickups instead of Saabs and chummy little banks that offer free checking for minimum deposits of only $500,000: their upscale listeners would be jolted back to the fact that they live in a democracy where they're forced to mingle with hoi polloi.

We low-income classical fans find it revolting that in America such music is a class thing, escapist, elitist, and pitched toward the rich. You can close your eyes and ignore that at concerts, but on radio it's inescapable. I'm an avid classical buff—I own all of Cavalli's recorded operas, and two sets of the complete Franz Berwald symphonies. Ravenous for new repertoire, the more obscure the better, I should be classical radio's ideal target. Yet every classical station I've ever followed has made me feel like an intruder in a foreign, snobbish, anti-intellectual world. I used to wake up each morning to allegedly the country's best station: Chicago's WFMT. Every day, within 10 minutes, I'd slam it off in disgust at some absurdly affected overpronunciation, smarmy ad, or symphonic movement played out of context. Until New York's WNCN switched to a rock format a few weeks ago, I had my clock radio set to it. But much of the music it favored wasn't classical in any meaningful sense, just 19th-century pop music for orchestra. I don't miss it.

Why should we have radio stations devoted entirely to the music of dead Europeans anyway? For the generations growing up today, Europe is just another continent. I see that as a positive change. It's obvious that if libraries contained only 18th- and 19th-century European literature, and librarians were determined to keep them that way, they'd be dropping faster than armadillos on a back road. If our theaters recreated only dead European plays, nobody'd stand in line for tickets. But in America, any classical music that grows from native soil has been jerked out as a weed. The genre has been kept a pristine Euro-transplant, treasured for its exotic snob value, not its relevance.

Hardly anyone born after World War II buys the elitist conception of European culture that classical radio traffics in. The very word "classical" is so suspect that composers I know refuse to use it, except privately and in desperation at communicating what they're aiming for. We have no qualms about preserving the classical musics of India or Japan; outside the West, the word simply refers to a social function, a formalized, ritual music played for its own sake, as opposed to music for religious services, virtuoso improvisation, dance, theater, films, or popular songs. So defined, a classical music (fused, however, with dance or theater in certain cultures) has existed in most of the world through most of recorded history. As we used to sing in a record store I worked at, "Hey, hey, my, my / Classical music will never die," because the need for a formalized music is rooted in the psyche. But a tradition with no indigenous roots must eventually wear out its welcome.

I dream of a classical music that doesn't exist in official America: one that could be announced by a Texan drawl without incongruity. A music that would go as well with Dos Equis and chili (*real* chili, not Northern tomato soup) as with Chablis and escargot. A music that connects to everyday life, like that of Ives, Partch, and Cage, rather than whisks listeners away to some make-believe salon where a fictionalized Chopin sends the ladies swooning. One in which *classical* is a neutral notion, dissociated from class and money, a matter of duration, attention, and function.

We now have a healthy, exciting, American classical music rooted in local vernaculars. Admittedly, it's not a music that will provide the featureless background wash that radio listeners abuse Beethoven for. Nobody I know writes music to put the ear to sleep. Even so, a lot of new music by Harold Budd, Laurie Spiegel, Jon Gibson, and others is more suitable for the ambient listening mode radio encourages than German symphonies ever were. NPR and college radio, bless their hearts, intermittently provide that new music an outlet. I'm sentimental because 24 years ago Dallas's WRR set me on the right track by airing Terry Riley's *In C*. But classical radio will have to be totally revamped before it will become viable again. In the foreseeable future, it has no meaningful part to play in the dissemination of interesting music.

spin it around

new music in the public's hands

FEBRUARY 22, 1994

TACOMA—Not only have I heard the future of music, I've performed it. It's at the Tacoma Art Museum through February 27, an installation called *PHFFFT-ARRRRGH* by Seattle's genius composer-engineer Trimpin.

Four sets of 12 tubes ending in organ pipes hang from the ceiling. Accordion reeds bleep through cylinders and tuba bells, one splatting like a snare drum, another rumbling like tuned thunder. A wheel mounted with duck calls spins slowly overhead, powered by a silent fan. Other duck calls honk through bass clarinet bells, also spinning. Air is the only sound source. The tones are uniformly pure, reedy, attackless. Though they shoot from all directions, you can't pinpoint them in space; they seem to be inside your head. Nothing is amplified.

At the center of the room, wired to a hidden computer, are two knobs anyone can turn. One sends sounds rippling around the room, the other modulates the tones to different keys. You can activate this colossal hurdy-gurdy yourself, or you can press a button and Trimpin's computer will treat you to preprogrammed sequences in which massive chords moan, squeaks spin, and tone complexes echo from one side of the hall to the other with a 20-millisecond delay. *PHFFFT-ARRRRGH* is coming to Lincoln Center May 17, but, typically, it will be scaled down for a smaller room where its spatial effects will be less astounding. New York's too crowded to fit the best new music in.

I had come to Seattle for a project called Music in Motion, spearheaded by Joseph Franklin of Philadelphia's Relache Ensemble. I can't review it because I was one of the composers involved, but suffice it to say that it's an attempt to get audiences involved in the creation of new music from the ground up, not just hearing the finished product as a fait accompli. For example, January 28 at the Henry Art Gallery, Seattle postminimalist Janice Giteck presented fragments of a work in progress, then asked for audience comments. The crowd was composer-heavy (Seattle may have more recognized composers per capita than any city in the country: Alan Hovhaness, Stuart Dempster, David Mahler, Jarrad Powell, William O. Smith), but several "real people" made some interesting points, in some cases with considerable heat. I asked myself, What would happen if we tried this Downtown? My guess is, the composer's buddies would show up, smile sweetly, and shout, "Nice piece!"

We in New York are sheltered from the hurdles new music faces out in the world. Hey, we give concerts, our friends fill the seats, what's the problem? All we know is, the NEA's slitting our throats because the rest of the country hates our guts. Out in Seattle, Chicago, Philadelphia, new music groups put tremendous work into outreach because they *have* to establish contact with strangers. We don't. Organizations out there can't afford to present work without closely scrutinizing its impact, nor abandon audiences to a passive position. Funding's been slashed, and the arts are in national disrepute. Seattle's premier new music presenting organization, Soundwork Northwest, just ceased operations, which for New York would be like Roulette, the Kitchen, and Experimental Intermedia all going under at once.

Why so much resentment against artists? All stupid right-wing rhetoric aside for a moment, maybe because, in terms of that basic instinct for artistic self-expression that every human has to satisfy at some level or another, artists are the haves, and everyone else is have-nots. The creativity and aliveness that *ought* to permeate the life of every McDonald's fry cook and Arthur Andersen accountant are ruthlessly stamped out by the structures we live under. At Mobil Oil, my dad got in trouble for putting his name plate on the unorthodox side of his desk. Last year I visited my best friend from high school; he used to write piano music, I'd perform it. Now he spat anti-NEA vitriol as eloquently as William F. Buckley, while I wanted to crawl under the table. What he finally admitted, though, was that he envied artists for living out the dream he once had, while he played it safe and became a computer analyst. That admission may say more about the arts in America than all Donald Wildmon's followers could.

If only one segment of society were allowed to have sex, would they become popular by flaunting it? That's pretty much the position artists are in vis-à-vis creativity. The solution, of course, isn't to squelch the only group enjoying fulfillment, but to spread it around. That's why, outside New York, the old we-give-concerts-you-sit-and-listen format is losing fans. No one wants to watch artists do what's denied to themselves, nor, because it's been denied so long, do they know how to appreciate it anyway. In the grant panels I've been on lately, art for art's sake is a discredited corpse. Artistic quality is a low priority, for unheard masterpieces are a dime a dozen. Funders want to see residencies, artists working with non-artists, spreading around their expertise, their technology, their creativity, educating the young, expressing communal needs rather than individual ones. Non-artists—so present institutional thinking has started to run— hate artists *because* this is an art-starved society, and artists are hoarding it all. We've got to divide some loaves and fishes.

Twirling the knobs at the Tacoma Art Museum, I fell into an asymmetrical pattern of honks and whistles that so mesmerized me I couldn't stop. Oblivious, I kept up the motions for maybe five minutes. Trimpin had put a complex sonic experience in my hands, and I was shaping it for myself in some way that resonated more deeply that I could fathom. As I reluctantly left off, I wondered: Had I just become the archetypal audience member of the 21st century? The revolution in the way "serious" or classical music involves, confronts, and seduces its listeners has begun. New York, with its massive institutional inertia and captive audience of fellow artists, is out of the loop.

paradise at our fingertips

voltaire's bastards

MARCH 8, 1994

Late in World War I, the British lost 250,000 men at the Passchendaele swamp. On paper, the area looked perfectly defensible. But when Chief of Staff Lancelot Kiggel, who had helped propel those soldiers to their deaths, visited the swamp afterward for the first time, he broke into tears and cried, "God, God, did we really send men into that?"

That's my favorite example from the book I'm recommending to everyone lately, *Voltaire's Bastards: The Dictatorship of Reason in the West* by Canadian historian and novelist John Ralston Saul (Vintage). Saul exhaustively chronicles how the West's worship of rationalism exploded out of control, creating an interlocking network of rational structures that impose order without responding to real-world needs. Rightly understood, reason is only a set of tools: amoral, susceptible to misuse by the greedy, and subject to correction by feeling, experience, imagination, and common sense. But we live as though *rational* were a synonym for *good* and *justifiable*, with the result that our corporate technocrats make themselves rich and comfy through purely rational methods.

There are three ways composers can respond to the advancing rationalistic administration of society Saul describes. The Uptown solution is to become a mirror of the corporate technocrats, to refine composing into a smooth, rationalist, analyzable, and predictable activity. Milton Babbitt and Brian Ferneyhough have this down literally to a science, complete with contempt for the common herd. They may send listeners into a swamp of notes that looked good on paper, but they can prove the validity of their work with charts, diagrams, and Pulitzer prizes, and will fit snugly into society without challenging the status quo. (In a variation on this pattern, women composers such as Ellen Zwilich might spread a little "lyricism" into their music as a sop to keep the savage audiences quiet.)

The Downtown response is to shout expletives at the technocrats, to insult rationalism with antirationalism. John Zorn and Karen Finley are the handiest examples, but Downtown galleries are full of others. This type of artist is prized by both the reigning powers and their victims because they provide the illusion of challenging the status quo along with the guarantee that they won't make a dent in it. Because, by being merely *antirationalist*, they have implicitly accepted the technocratic terms of the debate, and agreed to make only a negative contribution. They perform the same function for corporate America as the mudhead figure at a Hopi dance, siphoning off the negative energy so the ceremony can proceed as planned.

The third response is to grab the power the Republicans have so kindly handed us and save the world. If artists have the capacity to destroy our nation's moral fabric, we must have the capacity to heal it, right? And if the West's problem is its exclusive, blind reliance on rationality, we artists have paradise at our fingertips. Every antidote to hyperrationality, every compensatory human function, is elicited by art: sensory experience, in the corporeality of clay, thick paint, and the rumbling of immense drones through the floor; feeling, in the ability to pinpoint the pain beneath the surface of appearances; imagination, in the interplay of mutually contradictory ideas and logically impossible forms; the unconscious, in the images that escaped our knowing control and even the common sense and humanism Saul describes so warmly.

So, we've got the antidote, how do we administer it? In a healthy society, it would be enough to hone our skills, present our work onstage, bow, and go home. Surprise—we're not in a healthy society. Those poor schmucks listening out there haven't opted for conformity, they've had it pounded into them. They've internalized the message that creativity is a bad thing, that everything, their "entertainment" included, is supposed to flow without a hitch according to the rational procedures of the powers above. A stockbroker or factory worker who functions as a whole person, using all her human faculties, gums up the works. An artist who does not function as a whole person is a waste of time. We can't just show people a finished product, nor does it help to "educate" them in that old rationalist name/ date/style manner; we have to teach them how to rediscover and develop the faculties they knew how to use as children. We have to sell wholeness, instruction manual included.

As Saul writes, "The wordsmiths [substitute *composers*] who serve our imagination are always devoted to communication. Clarity is always their method. Universality is their aim. The wordsmiths who serve established power, on the other hand, are always devoted to obscurity. They castrate the public imagination by subjecting language to a complexity which renders it private."

He quotes Baudelaire: "Any book which does not address itself to the majority . . . is a stupid book."

By that criterion, only a couple dozen composers have quit serving established authority. Meredith Monk, Carman Moore, and Toby Twining present their creativity on levels so clear and infectious that listeners are carried away despite themselves. Pauline Oliveros and Layne Redmond offer workshops that put sound creation in the audience's hands. Trimpin and Ron Kuivila build sound installations that allow the listener to influence the result. Laurie Spiegel, via Music Mouse, has made her music available to be reshaped by others. Even the MTA is subverting rationalism with its wonderful "Poetry in Motion" campaign, which some days is the best thing about New York. These are tentative steps, but it may be that the revolution we need—the artistic seduction of America—can only proceed one liberated listener at a time.

what's your aq?

JANUARY 17, 1995

From the first paragraph of the first article in the *Times*, I found the whole issue of *The Bell Curve* surreal. The minute I saw "correlation," "IQ," and "income" in the same sentence, I knew Charles Murray was peddling major-league bullshit. If, as he claims, ghetto African Americans can't dig themselves out of an economic hole because their IQs aren't high enough, then the corollary is that a high IQ tends to assure economic success. In the *Times*, he estimated an average $6,000 increase in salary per 15 IQ points. Now *there's* an occasion for a rich belly laugh. Allow me to say a word for the high-IQ/low-income types who feel marginalized by this debate, as indeed they feel by much of American life. The most brilliant people I know have a hell of a time finding a toehold in this economic system. The smarter they are, the more outcast, and the less money they have.

The intelligence at issue may be simply an ability to flow with rationalist structures, in fact a kind of self-effacing mediocrity, an abasement before logic and authority. John Ralston Saul defines such intelligence in his *Doubter's Companion* as "mechanistic, rational and linear. It tends toward narrowness, is fearful of the uncontrolled idea, person or event, as well as intuitive or creative characteristics. . . . Controlled mediocrity is more intelligent than either original or sensible thinking because it is responsible to existing structures." If we limit intelligence to this kind of rationalist thinking, then it's true the most intelligent artists do best economically. The composers who justify their music with charts and diagrams give each other Pulitzer Prizes, and have tenure. The composers who write listenable music, however, have a wider-ranging, creative intelligence that doesn't fit smoothly in the music world's structures.

The quality that can best be correlated with income, it seems to me, isn't *intelligence*, but *acquiescence*. Those who ignore the evidence of their feelings and senses and say yes to authority and the status quo are the ones who move up society's ladders. And there is, interestingly, a correlation between narrowly rationalist intelligence and acquiescence. The psychologist Alice Miller has detailed how, in a heavily disciplinarian environment such as is typical in the West, the smartest infants learn to acquiesce to avoid becoming the victims of their parents' violence. They internalize authority, squelch their individual sense of reality, and develop what has been widely documented as the authoritarian personality. Stupid babies, by contrast, may stick to their guns, do what they want, and get beaten (or ignored, or humiliated) repeatedly. Later, they may go into life expecting to be beaten up, but they don't surrender their sense of self in order to be spared. The leaders of the Third Reich were smart guys, but with no internal compasses. So in this culture there is a certain logic to the brainiest composers writing the most unrewarding music, and moving up career ladders the fastest. Having internalized authority so early, they never paid attention to the evidence of their own ears and emotions, but they had a good eye for the rules.

But what of those who regain their sense of self later in life, or who, because of whatever benevolent providence, never lose it in the first place? After grad school I was all set to go the academic route, but I had trouble acquiescing. Perhaps because I was nurtured in Mozart and Schubert literally in the cradle, I never lost my sense of musical reality. I did learn, as an undergrad, to listen to some serialist mess by Wuorinen or Davidovsky and nod, "Yes, yes, a very well-crafted piece," and I really could tell "good" 12-tone work from "bad." But I always had misgivings about music whose communicative aspects seemed so much to beg for special pleading, and for whatever fated reason—native stupidity, perhaps—I was too honest to squelch those misgivings as they grew larger and more disturbing.

Eventually I noticed that the Pulitzer pieces were all dull, and that orchestras performed not the exciting new music, but that which followed European formulas. The composers who had Murray's kind of intelligence overlooked these facts. Having forfeited their sense of self and learned to acquiesce, they patterned their music after that of the prize winners. I, on the other hand, finding 80 percent of the contemporary music scene a hoax, couldn't utter three sentences without blowing the whistle on some cherished conventional wisdom. Inability to acquiesce rendered me somewhat unhirable, except at a newspaper staffed by similarly reality-dependent misfits.

At an academic conference a few years ago, I heard a lecture by a theory professor analyzing some of Elliott Carter's music. Afterward, I overheard him say casually to a colleague, as if it puzzled him, "You know, you find all those wonderful structures in Carter's music, but when you listen to it, you can't hear them." Had I given that lecture, I would have been incapable of saving the most crucial point for 10 minutes after it was over. That professor and I had both analyzed Carter's music, and were both disappointed that the brilliance on paper never reached the ear. But while I refuse to admire the emperor's new clothes, he acquiesced in public and doubted in private. He probably makes more money than I do, but is he smarter? Maybe. Certainly by Murray's standards.

In a way I'm only repeating what others have abundantly said, that creative intelligence is much more than this linear, mechanical measurement we call IQ. But more emphatically, I suggest that, even for true high-IQ types, making it in the American system requires suppressing (or being out of touch with) one's creativity and sense of reality. If anybody wants to do some *real* research, I can probably persuade the geniuses I know to reveal their bank balances. Perhaps they and the ghetto people share a similar reluctance to acquiesce. Sorry to cast a shadow on Murray's statistics, but I can't help it. I have a low AQ.

dump the multicult

JANUARY 24, 1995

Privately, musicians I know shrug off multiculturalism as an ideology by which organizations make a grand, Republican-defying show of doing their social duty. Few, I suspect, realize how much multicultural ideology disadvantages music in multiarts funding and presenting situations. Were it simply a matter of ethnically diverse programming, it would hardly differ from what liberal organizations have been doing these last 15 years.

But the politically correct these days won't countenance a lesbian play directed by a heterosexual woman (who obviously "can't do justice" to a lesbian vision). They'll damn a black-and-white gay theater group for failing to incorporate the Hispanic point of view. Even worse, music gets dismissed out of hand as unworthy of funding because, not being "text-driven," as the multicultists so benignly put it, it rarely expresses an explicit identity-politics agenda.

In practice, though, multiculturalism has resulted in a cartoonish paradigm for how art reflects the artist's cultural background. A work of art does not parrot the opinions and viewpoint appropriate to the artist's ethnic and sexual identity, though multicultists pretend it does. Consequently, they can't account for (nor reward) whites who play jazz or sing Indian ragas, African Americans who write string quartets, or Asian women who get educated at Columbia and write postserial piano concertos. One group having trouble in the arbitrary new climate is a fine Balinese-style gamelan, ultra liberals all. When only white performers play in the ensemble, they're condemned for "appropriating" the music of people of color. And yet, when that group first formed, there *was* no other gamelan in New York, and its members had been instrumental in creating a fertile cultural interchange, bringing over Indonesian musicians, and spreading Balinese techniques in new music. That's a sad example, but even black jazzers, Chinese *pipa* virtuosos, and American Indians playing native flutes get pushed to bottom priority simply because nonverbal music doesn't parade its political point of view.

I've focused more on women composers than any critic I'm aware of, and have profiled a high percentage of the new music scene's African Americans. I've written about more gay composers than you'll ever know, because I never mention the fact unless it's relevant to the music, and it's damned difficult to distinguish a gay piano piece from a straight one. That's precisely the point. You can't necessarily tell from anyone's *music* what *anyone* is. And while music is the most universal of the arts, the others harbor a bigger dash of universality than current deconstructionist theories admit. (I'm open to the fun of reading signs of Schubert's homosexuality into his music—you could find evidence he was a pipe smoker if it's what you're looking for. But it's my rusty finger technique that makes me unfit to play the Schubert sonatas I love so much, not my sexual orientation.)

In multiculturalism, the arts, considered a padded playground for lunatics, are being used to illusorily solve a nonartistic social problem, by offering ethnic groups a comforting semblance of representation in an area of life in which representation is pragmatically meaningless. It's a cynical substitute for real social change, letting politicians off the hook. If it further endangers people's ability to understand art by replacing aesthetic criteria with political ones, well, that satisfies two right-wing agendas at once, doesn't it? Artists who hype multiculturalism have internalized the principle that art doesn't matter.

When Republicans deny art's importance, the Left can't save it by conceding it's unimportant and wrapping it around politics to justify it. In America making any art, no matter how "apolitical," is already a protest. Putting endless time and work into a disciplined, unremunerative activity for the potential benefit of audiences unknown constitutes sufficient defiance of capitalist imperatives. Artists, people of color, gays, and feminists have a common interest in banding together to protect themselves from the elements in America who wish the earth would swallow them all up. But artists are ill-served in this coalition if other minorities' needs and aims take precedence over art. If artists won't stand up for the inherent importance of art, who can be expected to?

All the multicult's counter-commonsensical, sloganeering ideology is the Left's version of the hardened rationalism that the Right hammers us with. As one rationalism against another, it doesn't provide a true alternative. Art does. The Left of the '90s seems to be slowly shedding this tendency to form its attitudes in reaction to (and therefore as an unconscious imitation of) the Right's. This, I think, is what's happened at the Kitchen. In the '80s, under politically correct director Bobbi Tsumagari, performance art thrived, while music was reduced to trendy entertainment. Performance art, of course, is the Johnny-come-lately genre whose theories are tailored to fit multiculturalism's equation of social identity and artistic content. Under new director Lauren Amazeen, the Kitchen has returned to putting art before politics and the music programming has improved 500 percent. The performance artists, naturally, feel abandoned.

I don't buy this "the Left is dead" stuff for a minute, but the part of the Left that formed in reaction to the Right has always been dead. I'll continue celebrating women, gay, and minority artists at every opportunity, because I champion those who've been unjustly neglected no matter what the reason. But since I believe in music more than I believe in liberalism, democracy, God, kindness to animals, or practically anything else, I'll fight any ideology that relegates music to the bottom of the artistic hierarchy. If the Left can alienate a group as congenitally liberal as avant-garde musicians, it may have some rethinking to do.

no more heroes

JANUARY 31, 1995

Recently my clock radio awakened me in the middle of an 18th-century minuet. Between phrases of the undistinctive theme, the violins were tossing in twinkly motives that didn't seem to have anything to do with the rest. Consonant but contextually inappropriate chords popped up at random. The phrases repeatedly led my ear to places they had no intention of cadencing. Of course the composer, I quickly realized, was Franz Josef Haydn, the symphony his 88th, and I was waking up to the agreeable sensation of having my leg vigorously pulled. And yet people give me quizzical looks when I refer to Haydn as an experimental composer. Within the limits of 18th-century musical language, he was not only an experimentalist, but a surrealist, isolated in his secure post at Esterházy and having a blast seeing how much he could get away with. There is no P.D.Q. Haydn because Peter Schickele couldn't have beat Haydn at his own game.

Today it's difficult to hear Haydn this way, at least when awake. Those chords, those timbres, those tame motives are so worn with use that their Monty Python-esque logic disappears behind a nuanceless disclaimer: ELEGANT, DULL, POWDERED-WIG MUSIC/CONSIDERED GREAT/DO NOT LISTEN CLOSELY. But this time Downtown music flashed to mind, for Haydn's fragmentation, unexpected superimpositions, and surreal humor were the Imperial Austrian version of what Manhattan's improvisers have been doing these last 10 years.

Musical shock is a drug. As with most drugs, the system gets used to it, and you have to increase the dosage to keep reaching the same level of pleasure. Beethoven nearly expunged his teacher Haydn from collective memory because he upped the shock dosage so much so fast (yet without, except in his last works, coming up with much that Haydn hadn't already tried on a more subtle scale). After Beethoven's Fifth, it's hard to be surprised by Haydn's "Surprise." Subsequently, the heroes of each new generation had to up the discontinuity further, from Berlioz to Wagner to Stravinsky to Stockhausen to John Zorn. Zorn's *For Your Eyes Only*, played by the Brooklyn Philharmonic this fall, and the CD collages of David Weinstein's Impossible Music group continue the trajectory of Haydn's experiments, now expanded from the level of incongruous chords to that of interruptively clashing cultures. But a system can take only so much of a drug, and past a certain maximum, there's no longer any way to increase the dosage. Rock's had a hell of a time trying to match its original shock, which was so explosive it rang for 20 years. Rap has upped the ante only by resorting to the extramusical: obscenities and politically incorrect sentiments.

This is where my generation comes in. The minimalists, in a sense, had also shocked listeners with their length and intensity of focus, but on a deeper level they had flattened out the musical context to make a milder buzz once again possible. The tiny surprises that arrived within the predictability of Steve Reich's *Come Out* could, if you narrowed your focus, be as bracing as the clangorous style shifts of Luciano Berio's *Sinfonia*. True, that focus quickly became too small, but the realization was enough. It convinced my generation that our musical drug dependency was unnecessary, and that we could create a saner, more natural music that didn't continually have to look upward for the next notch. And just then, Morton Feldman stepped out of the one-upmanship of history with such serene, pianissimo(!) self-assurance that he seemed a prophet of a new age. Minimalism's Feldman-influenced offshoots, postminimalism and totalism, no longer offered visceral shock, but subtlety and surprise in contexts that once again required closer listening. The new music could still be zany, but without necessarily outshouting Haydn.

On top of our music criticism machine, at the point where events on the new-music horizon are registered, is a hero-detecting device. It hasn't picked up many signals lately, and the heroes it has located seem questionable. It might still be possible (and a lot of people are counting on it) to continue in ever wilder discontinuities and juxtapositions. We could throw together Eskimo throat singers, Gregorian chant, and steel drum bands into ever grander Wagnerian apotheoses, and as I write someone is probably doing it. But by now the gambit is so obvious that the very success seems trivial, like swallowing enough goldfish to get into the *Guinness Book of World Records*. Context is everything, and if you take chords in Haydn as analogous to cultures in today's collage music, it's not clear that, within the limits of their respective languages, the wildest genre-clashers ever surpassed his brilliance at putting down the exactly wrong chord in the most expectation-deflating spot. Other composers, rather than withdraw from the drug entirely, have gone back neo-Romantically to imitate old heroes in hopes of reminding us of earlier highs.

No phallic thrust surges ahead forever. Western Man is not going to continue his physical domination of the planet much further with very satisfying results. Neither Christianity nor communism is going to convert every last heathen. New rationalisms are not going to solve problems the old ones created, without getting back in touch with reality. The age of heroes is over. That isn't necessarily a sad prospect. Great music doesn't need heroes (listen to Bach, after all), and the best music of our time is attuned to the social movements that balance macho aggressiveness with an appreciation for stasis, receptivity, and natural flow. Critics think there are no new-music developments because they're not picking up shock-increasing heroes on their radar screens, but they can call this the end of history only if they're up-front about equating history with one-upmanship. I disconnected my hero-detector long ago, and I'm celebrating a decade I find more musically exciting than the four that preceded it.

music of the excluded middle

JUNE 27, 1995

After Pierre Boulez swept through town recently, Peter G. Davis noted in *New York* magazine how preferable his cogitative complexity was to the reiterative blandness of Philip Glass and Henryk Górecki. Well, yeah. Our computer-operating society does love to define choices in terms of binary opposites. We think either O.J. was innocent or he was guilty. We either think the federal government's a menace or we want handouts from it. We believe either in the high, Eurocentric culture defined by dead white males or in the political protest art of women and people of color. The musical spirit of our time is either Elliott Carter or Chuck Berry. We are pressured to take sides. Those of us who perceive advantages and partial truths in both camps find it difficult to even express our ideas without having them roll automatically into one of the two great troughs society has hollowed out.

I receive monthly notices of musical grants and awards. They invariably fall into two categories. One type, such as the Guggenheim, lists only white, male, mostly tenured academic composers teaching at prestigious universities. The other type, such as the New York Foundation for the Arts, lists predominantly jazz and women composers, the latter mostly performance art–oriented types attacking the patriarchal mainstream. This is true progress: 10 years ago, only the first category existed. Institutionally, the music world seems neatly divided in half. Yet I rarely find any of the composers I write about on either list. Likewise, in my weekly rounds I never hear music as simplistic as Górecki or as intellectually pretentious as Boulez, but for our official musical institutions these extremes are the whole show.

New music is a protest against cultural schizophrenia. A lot of this music is made by liberal, feminist, anti-imperialistic white males who wouldn't cross the street to save the European tradition from extinction. (Many of them consider their music "multicultural" but can't prove it under current definitions.) Some is made by women who write abstract music that doesn't necessarily telegraph the gender of the composer. Some is made by African Americans working outside jazz, not dealing explicitly with the black experience. All of it goes beyond any vernacular, none of it is classical in the old European sense, and it falls through a crack wider than the Grand Canyon in America's conception of music. What's disturbing from the new-music standpoint is that, now that we have a multicultural ideology on the left to balance the elitist ideology on the right, the chasm has widened. For years Downtown composers ferreted out a middle way, how to make music intelligent without being elitist, fun without being stupid or conventional, and socially relevant but still universal. And as the culture wars further polarize us, that middle way turns out more and more to be frowned upon by both sides.

If I wrote about "Pitch Set Complementarity in the Music of Roger Sessions" or "The Survival of Slave-Song Inflections in Early New Orleans Jazz," universities would eat out of my hand. But La Monte Young? Meredith Monk? Julius Eastman? Too white and not white enough, too vernacular and not vernacular enough. Both camps see this lack of one-sidedness as a failure, but it was new music's plan all along.

The music I hear weekly suggests that certain antinomies are within striking distance of being transcended. They are, after all, illusory. The sterile academicism of the music professor and the crass commercialism of the pop star are mutually necessary antipodes, opposite results within a shared framework. Likewise the defender of European white male tradition and the sexually explicit political artist. When one side changes character, the other shifts to adjust. (Look at the close-knit, mongoose-and-cobra dance of Republican senators and Downtown performance artists, each changing strategies in response to the other.) The hope that we will collectively embrace one half-truth and abandon the other is contrary to psychological reality. The point is to defuse the polarity, not to make one side win.

And in the end, all such antagonisms get resolved in the same way: the belligerents eventually die, and the subsequent generation, full of its own concerns, doesn't give a damn. Forty years ago the bitterest, most inescapable musical controversy was whether to follow Schoenberg or Stravinsky. Which composer won? Both, and, more importantly, neither. Composers now graduating from college already see no incongruity in fusing techniques from M. C. Hammer and Luciano Berio. Music becomes more interesting when commercialism and intellectuality interpermeate each other than when they're neurotically separated.

The relentlessness with which other critics pound away at their pet side of these binary choices makes me feel like I'm writing too soon. We're in a fin-de-siècle period, after all, in the mood to deal with endings, not new beginnings. I guess each side wants the world tilted its way when that mystical 2000 mark hits, so critics try to write off new music as an ephemeral or confused phenomenon rather than the diversity-friendly new mainstream it feels like from the inside. But every week I hear a future in which High and Low Culture are no longer opposites but arbitrary points in a fluid continuum. A music in which the abstract and spiritual is assumed to have its political and culture-specific aspects—and vice versa. A music whose engaging surface can attract the most casual listener even as its underlying intricacy offers plenty for the musically educated. The aspirations of an entire generation are wrapped up in that much-maligned term: totalism. The word implies that we can put brain, body, and heart together and have it all, if the skeptics will just shut up and listen.

medicine music
the uses of art
AUGUST 22, 1995

In San Francisco's Chinatown a few weeks ago, I ran across a crowded little shop that sold CDs of Chinese medicinal music. Since I'm fascinated by music made for utilitarian purposes, I loaded up my credit card. The discs treat hypertension and excessive yang of the liver and kidney, and the liner notes include directions for listening (30 to 60 minutes before going to bed, at 45 to 55 decibels, do not "use the walkman" while driving) and testimony by doctors about how far the blood pressure can drop with proper exposure. The stuff is so rhythmically square it does make me drowsy. If this is health-producing, Downtown music must be propelling me toward an early grave.

I was in San Francisco to speak on a panel about multicultural funding for the arts, presumably to present the "art for art's sake" point of view. That was ironic for, as hinted above, I don't believe in *ars gratia artis* at all. Kant's equation of artistic beauty with disinterested contemplation, however nobly intended, relegated art to a position of uselessness that has led in a straight line to the current NEA crisis. Because the purposes of art lie outside the sphere of reason, a one-sidedly rationalist society has had no choice but to place art outside the domain of practical life, with disastrous results. The prophecy is self-fulfilling: many 20th-century artists, internalizing the rationalist worldview, have obligingly created truly useless works. (The more rationalist, the more superfluous—anybody know a use for the Babbitt string quartets?) But this fallacy is peculiarly Western. Those who write about art of other cultures, like Ananda K. Coomaraswamy and Ellen Dissanayake, show that no Asian or African society has ever considered art useless, much less called it so *approvingly*. The fact that we do is evidence that our idea of art is royally screwed up.

Uptown critics cling to the fallacy that art is useless, elitist, something apart from everyday life that the masses can never comprehend. If they are listened to, arts funding is doomed. The multiculturalists, unable to argue outside the rationalist framework, have responded with a strategy that is brilliant, but only temporarily effective. They've discovered a use for art new to the history of aesthetics: art can embody and express the viewpoint of minorities and oppressed societal groups against the monolithic dominant culture. A masterstroke, it's paralyzed the elitists. But it claims usefulness for only a small amount of art: that made by women, African Americans, gays, and so on, explicitly expressing their concerns *as* women, African Americans, and gays. This definition is based on an unspoken paradigmatic medium; performance art. The further a medium gets from performance art, the less helpful the definition is. And music lies at the opposite pole.

Once we step outside the rationalist and materialist dogma, uses for art crop up in profusion. Art can cure liver ailments. It can solemnify and create appropriate atmosphere for ceremonial occasions. It can provide therapeutic physical activity. Perhaps its most common use among people in our society who cherish it is that it offers symbolic images around which our psychological needs crystallize. I just got around to reading *Anna Karenina,* and am astonished at the precision with which Tolstoy portrays psychological patterns of marriage and sexual affairs, imprinting me with deeply resonating images: a very useful book. In certain situations fragments of poetry I memorized years ago leap to mind, ordering and clarifying my experiences and assuring me that I'm not the first to have them. The role of music in this process is more difficult to pinpoint, but no less real. Mahler's Sixth Symphony, its intensity almost unbearable in calm periods, has gotten me through some of the darkest moments of my life, which is more than I can say for such "useful" objects as my computer. (In fact, my computer has caused some of my darkest moments.)

It's embarrassing to speak this way. It seems somehow soft-headed, as though we're begging for premises not commonly accepted. But when we ashamedly back off from describing art's emotional and psychological value, we capitulate to the corporatist, bottom-line-obsessed rationalism in whose limited terms art's importance can never be justified anyway. Deep down, we all know that art's value is no more computable in dollars or statistics than is the human dignity of the homeless, or the education of children. As in so many crucial areas, scientific methods do not apply. We can't possibly predict which artworks are likely to prove useful in the future; we can only guess based on feelings and experience. The Left has wasted a lot of print defending *specific* works of art, some not terribly defensible, when what was needed were assertions of art's beneficial and always unpredictable impact. Letting corporatist thinking set the terms of the debate will keep us forever vulnerable. Suppose in the future "studies show" that all the multicultural art we funded didn't solve any social problems? Bye-bye funding, and how can we protest? It was our idea.

The multicultural argument is a stopgap measure, as is the argument that the arts provide jobs and generate tax revenue. Let's use those lines on politicians too stupid to understand better ones. But *entre nous,* let's keep in mind that even nonpolitical art enriches our lives far more than nuclear bombs, computer gadgets, and countless other objects touted as practical. The fact that many people don't avail themselves of art is meaningless; some people don't use buses, but buses are still useful. Saving the NEA is a necessary but modest and puny goal. We have to transform our notion of "usefulness" until it includes all those intangibles that we know we need but can't calculate in dollars. In so doing, we will turn this upside-down culture right side up.

who killed classical music?

forget it, jake—it's uptown

JANUARY 21, 1997

By the time I got there a crowd had already gathered. There, in the middle, was the body, stretched out with a reel's worth of high-grade tape wrapped around its neck, and still soiled with the muck of the East River. It was a ghastly scene, but nobody seemed particularly upset; in fact, several people were smirking. "If it had been united, it could never have been defeated," somebody chuckled near me. I looked up; it was Fred Rzewski. Alvin Lucier said nothing, but cordoned off the body with a long thin wire that hummed ominously. John Adams pushed his way through the crowd and grabbed my arm. "This is the work of Arab terrorists!" he snarled. That was a knee-jerk reaction; he was still bitter about the Klinghoffer episode.

Classical music was dead. And I didn't need to call the American Symphony Orchestra League to know that they were going to want somebody to pin charges on. I needed answers.

When I got to my office, there was a livid message on my machine from Charles Wuorinen. "You know who did it!" he screamed. "Those damn minimalists! They've been out to kill classical music for 30 years!" Charlie's kind of a nutcase, but hell, it was a lead. I popped around to Steve Reich's apartment. "Sure, I had a fling with classical music in the '80s," he admitted nervously. "But ever since *The Cave,* I've been strictly into electronics." "I buy your story, Steve," I crooned to calm him, "but the League's going to want to see proof. You gonna come out to show them?" "Come out to show them?" he repeated. I saw he had gone into one of his phases, so I left him there.

I knew Terry Riley was out of the loop, and Phil Glass had been pretty cozy with classical for the last few years; I made a mental walk-through of his entire output and couldn't find a motive. So I paid a visit to the Big Kahuna, La Monte "Hillbilly" Young. He had an alibi, too. Problem was, it was six hours long. Classical music died a quick death; Young couldn't have pulled off a job like that in under a month.

I waltzed around to Bob "Wolfman" Ashley's digs. I knew he hadn't done it—the guy never touched an orchestra in his life—but he was a big man in the underground, and he seemed to know things other people didn't. When I asked if he'd heard anything, he didn't even look up from his vodka, just moaned, "If I were from the big town, I would be calm and debonair. The big town doesn't send its riffraff out." That didn't mean anything to me, so I kept mum. When he saw I wasn't going to leave, he drawled over his shoulder, "You ever know classical music to give a woman a fair deal?" I shook my head. "*Cherchez la femme,*" he muttered bitterly. Then, more slowly, "She was a visitor."

Ellen Zwilich's landlady suggested I try her at the Pulitzer Club. After I stiff-armed my way past the bouncer, a blur in white gloves ran out in a hurry, clucking, "Oh dear, oh dear! I shall be too late!" I saw enough to recognize David Del Tredici. Once in the street, he disappeared into a manhole.

I resisted an impulse to follow, but that was suspicious. When I cornered Zwilich, though, sipping martinis with Joe "Fluttertongue" Schwantner and Jack "Jack" Harbison, the trio looked as morose as piano tuners at a synthesizer trade show. "You think we were involved?" she laughed sardonically. "That's right, we bumped off the goose that laid the golden eggs." Elliott Carter must have gotten wind that I was there, for suddenly two Columbia grad students appeared from behind and gave me an expenses-paid whirlwind trip into the back alley.

I dusted my pants off and decided I had barked up the wrong tree anyway. The Pulitzer gang was high on classical music's payola list; as long as they kept their yaps shut, it'd come across with the occasional concerto commission. The only broad big and outside enough to pull a stunt like this was Pauline "Ma" Oliveros. Oh sure, she talked peace and good vibes, but there was something about the way she squeezed that accordion—as if she meant it. But this time I wasn't going direct. I looked up an old connection named Annea "The Torch" Lockwood. I figured any dame who started out her career burning pianos wouldn't scruple to help deep-six an entire genre.

"It was just another random killing," she insisted when I tracked her down at a sleazy East Village gallery. "John Cage is dead, hon," I countered. "Try again." "Look," she stammered, "you're going after small game. Classical music was drowned out, right? You need a louder suspect. Know a schmo named John Zorn?"

Zorn had crossed my mind, but I had seen his victims before: so cut up that you couldn't tell what piece came from which body. This wasn't his style. I thanked her for the tip, though, and headed for the Knitting Factory in search of a joker named Branca. I could hear his electric guitars as far away as Washington Square. Word on the street was that he was calling his pieces "symphonies" even though he didn't use an orchestra. Sounded like a takeover. He had good reasons for wanting classical music out of the way. When I got there, an old guy named Nancarrow was guarding the box office. "Branca may be backstage and he may not," he stated mechanically, in two tempos at once somehow.

As I stepped into the back, the blast of a high-decibel shriek knocked me against the wall, where I got a blow on the back of my head that made me hear Stockhausen's *Zyklus* and Varèse's *Ionisation* at the same time, with encores. When I came to, a harpy from hell with cavernous eyes and sharp claws was leaning over me. I made a quick grab for my .45 (I never carry a gun, but just for the heck of it I often make a grab for one), when the demon spoke: "Sorry, didn't mean to rattle you, sport."

"Oh, it's you, Diamanda." Nice Greek girl from San Diego. Had a funny thing about makeup, though, and a voice that could bounce your eardrums off each other. "Geez, try not to sneak up on a guy."

"I'm going to save you a lot of trouble," she said, lighting a cig by breathing on it. "Nobody here had anything to do with classical music getting waxed. It was a suicide."

"Suicide?" I coughed, still caressing my noggin.

"Think about it," she urged. "Tried to starve itself to death. A tiny, self-imposed diet of the same German and Russian food over and over. Cholesterol in the high 600s. Didn't want to grow. Refused to eat anything new. Kept trying to pretend the 20th century never happened. Severe personality disorder. It never established any roots here anyway—still obsessed with the old country, and acted so hoity-toity to cover up its insecurity. Suicide was the only way it could save face."

"You're sure of that, huh?"

"Sure I'm sure. I could see it coming. That's why I quit playing Mozart concertos and singing Xenakis 15 years ago."

Something about the way she said it—in a piercing wail three octaves above middle C—made me think that was the best explanation I was going to get. I went back to my office and was greeted by another blinking light on the machine. It was Susan McClary; there was no such thing as classical music in the first place, she claimed, it was just a construct invented by white males to subjugate women and minorities. "Let her believe that if it makes her feel better," I thought, clicking her off in midsentence. I poured myself an inch or two of cheap whiskey, parked my loafers on the desk, and snapped my fingers to a kickass rendition of 4'33" that the city was playing in the street below.

musical politics

paradigms lost
rhys chatham/john zorn
MARCH 28, 1989

To write: that is to sit in judgment over one's self.
HENRIK IBSEN

For a decade now, we in new music have put up a brave pretense that, in their extended, experimental forms, rock, jazz, and classical music are now all part of the same jovial, late-20th-century urban mix. There are times, however, when that pretense does unconscious harm, when we might achieve a kinder, gentler music scene by admitting that, thrown together as we are by a love of unconventional music, the pleasures we seek from it are still irreducibly diverse. Such a time came in February, when two highly visible young new music figures, Rhys Chatham and John Zorn, gave major performances, Chatham at the Kitchen February 16–18 and Zorn at Town Hall February 25.

Chatham's compositions threatened, once, to draw rock and classical music into a unified stream. It hasn't happened, nor is he likely to further facilitate such a change. As rock, his music has often been disappointing, and is growing more so. His *Drastic Classical Music* and *Guitar Trio* brought what was at first an intriguing minimalist focus into rock, but heard within the history of rock, their materials, their speed guitar riffs and drum patterns, weren't terribly original; nor, in more recent works such as *Minerva* and *Die Donnergötter,* has he developed them in any way a rock fan would find innovative. As a result, 10 years after he grabbed popular attention, it's now easy to dismiss Chatham, quite correctly as far as it goes, as a throwback to Deep Purple or Blue Oyster Cult.

But to ears accustomed to classical music, materials and a performance-specific quality of energy mean nearly nothing. Classical music plays with relationships between macro- and microstructures, each determining the meaning of the other; in a funny way this is as true of Cage as it is of

110

Haydn, which is why improvisation in a Cage work sounds grossly inappropriate. "Structure is the most expressive part of music," someone once said, and it sums up the classical attitude. Idiosyncratic performance energies threaten structural relationships, which is why, since Haydn, classical music has increasingly squelched the performer in favor of the composition (and never more than in the "improvisatory" works of the '60s). Music written to satisfy classical assumptions about "the integrity of the work," even for electric guitars, will sound, as one critic wrote of Chatham's retrospective, "rigid and overcontrolled." To rock-immersed ears, that reproach clings to the entire classical tradition.

But what a classically trained musician will hear in Chatham is enormously different. His achievement is that he expanded minimalist form to accommodate the volume and the inertia-laden, resonant materials of rock. Originally, *Drastic Classical Music* did little more than shift minimalism's perceptual focus from pattern to acoustics. *Minerva,* on the other hand, constitutes an eccentric but provocative exploration of the cadence, a formal marker that classical composers have agonized over for 800 years, but which rockers have always taken for granted. Still more recently, Chatham's brass pieces have abandoned rock except for the backbeat, and have distilled his formal ideas even further. In terms of what a rocker is used to listening for, Chatham has backslid, but in terms of the structure/material relationship a classically trained musician instinctively hears, his music has grown in complexity and subtlety. Today, the pieces that first propelled him to fame seem like rough sketches next to the elegant clarity of his present work.

Perched to one side of another fence, Zorn's music has achieved a popularity that draws a panorama of blank stares in many new music circles. I've had composers with classical credentials ask me why he's made such a career out of ideas that are 25 years old, and I've been lost for an answer. Heard with the material-slighting classical ear, Zorn sounds like a throwback to the European avant-garde '60s. The open form, the "pure structure" he advocates, celebrated its 30th birthday some time ago, and it's been almost two decades since Christian Wolff abandoned the rule-oriented game pieces Zorn has imitated. *Archery* is nearly indistinguishable from Mauricio Kagel's *Acustica* (1968), *Cobra* represents no conceptual advance over the old Everest recording of Cage's *Variations IV.* Stockhausen opportunistically attached his name to the Beethoven bicentennial by emptying out his *Kurzwellen,* refilling it with Beethoven recordings, and renaming it *Opus 1970,* and as far as expressive structure goes, Zorn's contribution is equally superficial.

What musical interest is here must be found elsewhere. By bringing the '60s' "Available Forms" (to use Earle Brown's handy phrase) into improvisation, Zorn's stabilized and concentrated the fragmentational tendencies of AACM experimental jazz; in a way, he's done for experimental jazz what the 12-tone system did for atonality, enabled it to create large structures whose parts are audibly connected. It's a necessary technical achievement, and if *Cobra* isn't a piece I could listen to over and over, well, neither is Schoenberg's Violin Concerto. Compared to Kagel and Stockhausen, Zorn's structures sound naïve and not pushed into sufficient variation, but they have to be that way, or else there would be no room left in them for the improviser's role. Take a different model: next to the idiosyncratic language of Roscoe Mitchell's *L-R-G, Cobra*'s more flexible, more communal possibilities begin to sound like an interesting development. And, significantly, Zorn has achieved most of his success in circles where *Acustica* and *Kurzwellen* are not familiar points of reference.

The thing is, both Chatham and Zorn appear to be on the fence between musical paradigms. What each is really doing, though, as becomes more apparent with every performance, is using material from one paradigm to solve a problem in another. Whether you hear either as innovative depends on what musical history you're closest to, and the increasing split in critical reaction suggests that, though the underlying paradigms may be obscured, they still exert a decisive influence. Our ears have different histories, and the ear without a history belongs to a dilettante. When my rock critic friends think Chatham's music is stagnating while I find it more brilliantly insightful every year; when my jazz critic friends can't get enough of Zorn, while to me he sounds like the P. D. Q. Bach of the '60s avant-garde ("his plagiarism limited only by his faulty technique")—*then* it's time to dust off William James's pragmatic motto, "Where there's a contradiction, draw a distinction."

It's not a new problem, just one we haven't dealt with openly. In the '60s, Dave Brubeck was held up as worthy of classical attention because he used, among other things, 5/4 meter; classical fans, some of whom knew that quintuple meter could be traced back further than Handel's *Orlando*, shrugged. Harlem jazz greats of the 1920s must have given that same shrug when Darius Milhaud made classical music history by weaving their jazz syncopations into a French ballet. It's a musico-critical axiom: when a musician infuses new life into Tradition A by stealing from Tradition B, Tradition A fans may hear a breakthrough, but Tradition B fans just wonder what the fuss is about. The jazz, rock, and classical genres have stolen from each other for decades, which was fine because, until recently, it was implicitly assumed that they're not playing in the same ball park.

Let no one think I'm saying that musicians should run back to their pigeonholes. There are plenty of pieces around with true crossover appeal, and certain music—Varèse, and Coltrane's *Ascension* come to mind—has had a tremendous influence in more than one history. Artists allergic to labels, I suspect, have mostly been burned by thoughtless or insufficient categorization: as when experimental improv people are assumed to be playing "jazz," and get misreviewed because they are lumped into a paradigm from which they've moved away. Art will always wreak havoc with boundaries, and the artist who categorizes his or her *own* work imposes deadly self-limitations. Let not the artist usurp the critic's work.

But in criticism—which after all need not parallel the real world—*descriptive* taxonomy allows us to concede that we're still seeking diverse musical pleasures, and that some of those pleasures play off of histories that have become highly elaborate. New paradigms split off from their parents like amoebas, and the postminimalist model is almost invariably misreviewed by classical critics who think it's trying to sound like classical tonality. Any particular paradigm is a slippery thing that changes with every piece that refers to it, to the point that even "the late-18th-century concerto" is merely a fiction. Ultimately, all standards resolve into one—"Did you have a good time?"—but penultimately, paradigms are the different ways we've discovered to have a good time. Far from being the bane of new music, we need a critical taxonomy as the only weapon with which to defend excellent composers from intelligent critics. It's the discipline that will eventually transmit new music to the broader public it desperately needs.

Zorn and Chatham are coming from and going to different places, with different objectives and different ideas of what makes music pleasurable. They're hardly crossover composers: Chatham has sworn off marketing himself as a rocker, and Zorn, apologizing that his *Hu Die* for two guitars and speaker (in Chinese) was meant to be played in bars rather than concert halls, begged his Town Hall audience to "make some noise." To enjoy music while making noise or while keeping quiet—that's an irreducible paradigm difference, for if the classical model assumes *anything*, it's uninterrupted attention. *Hu Die*, high on atmosphere, low on information, *would* have sounded better as background music, and was coolly received. Zorn was far more engaging in his club musician persona with his band Naked City, and the most satisfying point came when they played "Snagglepuss," a hilarious jazz sendup of the discontinuous structures which sound so forced and pale when he uses them with highbrow pretensions. Chat during Chatham's *Minerva*, though (as if you could), and you'd miss the spread-out melodic structure that is practically the piece's only virtue.

So let's admit that, when Chatham steals a '70s rock sound to fashion a new classical form, rock fans have little reason to be impressed. And when Zorn appropriates early-Stockhausen structures to give jazz riffs new meaning, the avant-garde is unlikely to sit up and take notice. There's no reason to force music back into narrow categories; the Great Experiment isn't over, and we have no idea how much might be left to gain from audience crossover and the confluence of ideas. But in criticism, both public and private, it might ease discourse to keep some of the old labels we had so optimistically thrown away polished and handy in case we need them. We're not really arguing over whether Chatham or Zorn are talented musicians: they both are. Our argument is between highly evolved contexts for musical meaning that no one is so foolish as to want to give up.

blurred out

on language

SEPTEMBER 5, 1989

In the mail today came a press release announcing a new kind of fish that, believe it or not, swims in water. Actually it was about a new music performer who is *blurring boundaries,* and since this is at least my 2,000th blurring-boundaries release this year, it's time for some sort of homage to the genre. Here's one: *blurring boundaries* and *breaking down barriers* have become ultimate '80s clichés. If I were to get a release saying "Composer X conscientiously respects the boundary between roots-rock reggae and Eskimo throat songs," I'd say, *here's* an original.

Each decade's hard-earned convictions degenerate into the following decade's vacuous truisms. The '50s invented "total organization," the '60s religionized it into dogma. The '60s fought for "let the sounds be themselves" and "Eastern influence," ideals the '70s abused to justify any silliness. People whose gray matter was in high gear in the '70s gave us blurring boundaries and breaking barriers. Tired composers, critics, and PR people tout these aims as a priori virtues requiring no further explanation.

One problem is, the words have ceased to mean anything. Is what separates classical music from jazz really a *boundary,* i.e., something they share that neither spills over? Or is it more like what separates a rose bush from a cactus: divergences in function, evolved growth patterns, and suitable climate? They both have thorns, and you can trim a rose bush into saguaro shape, but can you really cross-pollinate them to create a hybrid? Or is something "in between" necessarily a new form altogether, requiring its own habitat and survival strategies? I ask because so many take these hazy horticultural issues for granted, seduced by the vernacular into substituting a few handy, agreed-upon phrases in place of thought.

For decades, we've had a model for music that blurs boundaries among European classical, Middle Eastern, and Far Eastern musics: Alan Hovhaness. The worst examples from his prodigious output float along in noncommittally exotic A minor, the lowest common denominator of mutually prime traditions. Having erased boundaries, he often had nothing positive to pencil on the blank page. An increasing amount of "world music" is stamped with that unpattern, but to paraphrase a wisecrack of Nietzsche's, if you don't know what you're free *for*, it's not much help to know what you're free *from*. Lucia Hwong's pleasant dance music at this summer's Serious Fun! similarly illustrated that to cross a boundary guarantees nothing. It had a rock beat, some jazz riffs, African rhythms, an Asiatic melody, no personality. Anthony Davis's improv-tinged opera arias the same night succeeded better, because instead of screwing generic elements together, they lit off down their own, in-between trail.

Breaking down barriers is an even bigger joke. No audience as sophisticated as BAM's assumes the presence of any type of perceptual barrier. For an audience in Waco, Texas, on the other hand, certain barriers may always exist, and that's no reason to despise Waco. To think about your work in terms of breaking barriers is not to deal with the real audience that's out there listening, but to jerk your knee. The only barriers back in place are those beyond which music spread outside the concert hall into the environment, because breaking *those* down made it difficult to get gigs. The barrier no '80s artist wants raised is the one between him and his record contract.

Both clichés sprout from a truism no earlier culture or century would have understood: that rules, boundaries, and limitations "get in the way" of artistic expression. This chestnut, a chief ingredient in *EAR* magazine's pablum, is contradicted by almost every good piece made in 700 years, yet gets lip service even from people whose work shows that they don't subscribe to it. "One should recall," wrote Nietzsche in paragraph 188 of *Beyond Good and Evil*, "the compulsion under which every language so far has achieved strength and freedom—the metrical compulsion of rhyme and rhythm." He develops that theme into a sonata: "All there is or has been on earth of freedom, subtlety, boldness, dance, and masterly sureness . . . in the arts . . . has developed only owing to the 'tyranny of . . . capricious laws.'" (That's why I'm excited about the Jesse Helms obscenity fight: art hasn't had a *visible* enemy in 20 years.)

It's hardly safe to assume that what an artist slaps into a press release indicates his or her most heartfelt artistic aims; but someone who's thinking carefully about his or her work isn't likely to describe it in the same terms as 300 other people. This stagnating decade is crashing toward its final cadence, and it's time to dig out the new ideas that are buried under the avalanche of potboilers. One potent '80s notion is just intonation, tuning in accordance with the harmonic series; will that idea become fatuous in the '90s (and can one prevent it by pointing out the probability)? At the very least, we can apprise those who babble about boundaries and barriers that their artistic statements look exactly like everyone else's. Those B-words convey not individuality but conformity. That you're working without boundaries goes without saying, but what are you working *within*?

rock rules

bandwagonism

JANUARY 23, 1990

"No more Cage! Zorn is the Rage!" chanted Tony Conrad through a megaphone in 1989, as part of a performance of Cage's *Songbooks*. It was a fitting homage to the decade's major musical movement: bandwagonism.

Let's provide some historical context: God knows, it was a rare commodity in that kick-ass decade, the '80s. New music started out (remember?) as a movement of disaffected classical composers with a new, nonelitist experimental attitude, their own vocabulary, and their own genealogy of influences. Thanks to Laurie Anderson, Philip Glass, Mary McArthur, and Rhys Chatham at the Kitchen, John Rockwell at the *Times,* and Tom Johnson and Gregory Sandow here at the *Voice,* it became hip circa 1976 and stayed hip until almost '82. It was born in lofts, the Kitchen gave it a home, and then in the late '70s other homeless knocked on the door. Garrett List programmed jazz improvisers at the Kitchen, Chatham brought in rock. New-music aficionados were scandalized, but those were good impulses; the lines drawn between those genres stemmed from a snobbishness that had no place in the new liberal scene.

Had an equilibrium been maintainable, everything would have been hunky-dory, but one side inevitably swamped the other. The jazz groups were infinitely recombinant; needing little preparation, always able to rehearse with the same core of players, often *disdaining* rehearsal, the improvisers could give 30, 40 gigs a year without breaking a sweat. By contrast, the classical people were lucky to come up with a new piece every other year; parts had to be copied, ad hoc ensembles formed, rehearsal time managed for people whose schedules weren't in sync, money found to pay players who weren't part of the gang. The classical new musicians were a more fragile strain of plant, which is why they needed sanctuary in the first place. And, fatally, they turned out to be the kind of liberals Robert Frost complained about, too broad-minded to take their own side in a quarrel.

Consequently, the Bermuda grass spread. Spaces veered to the jazz side in a crescendoing spiral of economics and fashion. Bars like the Knitting Factory, where music a priori has to be aggressive enough to compete with the serving of drinks, became typical new-music joints. Robert Ashley (a new musician if there ever was one) despaired of a New York hall for his new operas and started premiering them elsewhere. Chatham (*here's* a bit of irony) wrote a quiet piano piece and had no place to play it. The Kitchen, forgetting that its tax-exempt status assumed a mission to improve public taste, got scared away from a movement that suddenly wasn't hip, and booked what it thought rock audiences would flock to. One subtle New York experimentalist, accepted onto one of the worst festivals the Kitchen ever presented, was asked to "play something loud." New music, decreasingly viable in New York, decentralized, and led a quiet existence in Los Angeles, San Francisco, Minneapolis, Urbana, with tenuous toeholds at the Alternative Museum and Phill Niblock's loft in New York.

Remember pluralism? That was a hairy, '70s notion, the idea that instead of a mainstream we'd have different musics coexisting side by side. Pluralism got lip service in the '80s, but Downtown ceased to be a place where you were likely to hear just about anything and became a place where what you were going to hear was loud improvisation—not that that was the only game in town, but the spaces were no longer set up for anything else. The music was mainly made by fifteen 35-year-old white East Village males who played BAM every year and the Knitting Factory every week, a different member in front at each gig. (They were called *the usual suspects* in so many *Voice* choices, you may have thought that was the name of their band.) The music they played—why, it ranged from free improv informed by aleatory structures to aleatory structures filled with free improv. On a really wild night, after a few beers, they might even say TO HELL with the aleatory structures and just do free improv. I used to wander up and down Houston Street in a daze, wondering what I'd hear next.

When the kick-ass decade crowed about pluralism, it meant a plurality of standards, not musics. As so often in the '80s, a specious liberalization turned out to be a retrenched exclusionism. The '70s rule on women was, women aren't composers; the '80s rule was, they can be composers as long as they also sing, dance, or do something else "feminine." African Americans could now become known for nonjazz music as long as they made a jazz career first. (One of the best composers I know of, a black whose music isn't jazz-derived, reportedly spent the last few years living in a public park.) A severe ageism was in, and midcareer composers were severely out. If you were born before 1951 and weren't famous by 1979, you didn't exist. Dary John Mizelle, Annea Lockwood, Carman Moore, Daniel Goode, and four dozen others spent the '80s working at the height of their creative powers, but so what? As Chatham lamented, we were now playing by rock rules, and one rock rule is that you peak at 23. One 30-ish guitarist, who did more than his share of Nonesuch records and Lincoln Center gigs, wrote to chew me out for continuing to review what he called "'70s composers." Since he's an "'80s composer" himself, I assume he retired this month.

So where were the critics in all of this? Some were dazed, others AWOL. In the '70s, the classical critics had been successfully intimidated by serial composers, so when minimalism, an idiom with few pretensions, became a growing force, they were thrown for a loop. They blustered awhile, as taught, about the importance of incomprehensibility, and when opportunity arrived to change the subject, they grabbed it. What did they do? They spent 10 years arguing the fascinating question of whether Handel's music sounds better when played on 200-year-old woodwinds. Answers to that provocative inquiry spanned the entire range from "I think so" to "I'm pretty sure." Apart from isolated high points (I loved Will Crutchfield's noble defense of Charles Ives in the *Times*), classical critics tried to look busy, and few had the guts to stay in a tortuous dialogue where their viewpoint was badly needed.

Into the vacuum poured rock critics. They could quote Adorno, which put them over the heads of their colleagues, and they started paying attention to experimental music 15 minutes after the premiere of *Einstein on the Beach*. Their observations were refreshing, but since they had missed out on the eight or nine centuries that preceded 1976, they cheered every reinvention of the whistle. With all the best intentions, they celebrated a decade of déjà vu, of recycled '60s collage technique misread as a new wrinkle in Western music. To them, quotation was a revolutionary act, noise a new phenomenon, improvisation a renaissance; they praised rockers and jazzers for doing what the classical people had done 20 years earlier, and then—irony of ironies—called the classical people "conservative" for having moved on to something else.

The problem went beyond criticism. I was told of a young composer who was wowed when a performer bowed a cymbal—that horrendous cliché's been abused for 25 years. It was an inevitable dilemma: music of the last 50 years has been so sparsely disseminated that only specialists know its history. Successful '80s composers were the ones who turned public ignorance into a career advantage. It's now easy to impress an audience by filching '60s tricks that survive only in *Source* magazine, David Cope's textbook, and out-of-print records. Not for nothing was John Zorn the Reagan era's quintessential composer: he made us feel good about macho progress again, he achieved his greatest success with yuppie audiences, and he did it by recycling ideas two or three decades old. In the kick-ass decade, every other concert was another Grenada, an assault on defeated territory.

The '90s *have* to be better, but it's going to take leadership: composers, presenters, and critics who use their ears instead of their reflexes. Trickle-down theories don't work. The fact that Laurie Anderson, Glass, and Zorn have become recording stars doesn't translate into more gigs for Beth Anderson, William Ortiz, and Lois V. Vierk; quite the contrary. Organizations who've done their Kronos gig think they've paid their new-music dues, so as the famous get famouser, the obscure get obscurer. And the music, as Glass demonstrated for us, doesn't get better just because the names get bigger. The number of "homeless" composers, i.e., those who have almost no venue at which the *type* of music they make is welcome, has swollen.

The '90s are going to be the decade of women composers. There are too many brilliant ones, they've been shamelessly ignored, and they've got a huge body of work you haven't heard yet. Those floodgates can't stay shut much longer. BAM, Serious Fun!, and other series organizers take note: Laurie Anderson, Meredith Monk, and Pauline Oliveros no longer count as women. You've been using the same three people as your token women for over a decade, and nobody buys it anymore. If you want to prove that you aren't systematically excluding females, you're going to have to come up with some new names, and I've got a long list if you need it.

A 1989 press release enthused, "BAM is interested in developing the NEXT WAVE beyond Eurocentric programs to include the culture and artists of Asia, Africa, South America, and the Near East." As a good liberal I'm supposed to applaud. But what that release says without saying it is that American concert music, which stood in the shadow of European music for decades, now stands in the shadow of Third World ethnic musics. American composers are going to have to take back the "next wave" themselves, because no one's going to hand it to them. To do it they're going to have to stand behind and articulate their own principles, their own post-Cage, post-whatever tradition—to polemicize, even at the risk of seeming illiberal. We need not a monthly press-release reprint like *EAR* magazine, but an adult, literate journal capable of putting new ideas in a broad context.

My bet is that *perestroika* will require a new term. Except when it signifies new rock, as it probably does to most people, *new music* has come to mean two things: free jazz (which we already had a perfectly good term for), and music that steals from Third World musics. If your music extends the tradition you grew up in or studied, or grows not from tradition at all but from a formal idea, process, method, electronic circuit, or computer program, you're not making new music, and there's no way to popularly explain what you *are* doing. (I notice I've been falling back on *avant-garde*, whose militaristic veneer is a clue to its European male orientation.) The term *new music* and the festival named for it have become means of excluding not only the very composers, but the *type* of composers, they were fashioned to represent.

Any term can be subverted, but for now I favor *alternative music*—with connotations not of *more advanced* or *better*, but being outside of established genres or major-label record contracts. The name still lacks punch, though it holds out a hope that the '90s will nurture a more spiritual, self-forgetful, *musical* attitude toward music than the '80s did. Any better ideas?

pulitzer hacks
amateur composers versus the professionals
JULY 30, 1991

This is an American story.

Morton Feldman dies after a lifetime of writing original music, maybe 18 years of writing truly great music. Then the recordings come out. Four years after Feldman's death, 11 hours of his music appear on CD from seven different labels.

Same season, Shulamit Ran wins the Pulitzer Prize for music: a prize never given to Feldman or any of his associates. Ran is the young composer whom radio interviewer Charles Amirkhanian once asked, "How does it feel to be writing in a style whose other practitioners are men in their sixties and seventies?"

There are two types of American composers, and have been ever since Charles Ives and Daniel Gregory Mason. Type A, the original, invents a new kind of music that exerts tremendous underground influence. He/she often works outside music (dry cleaning, insurance, and computers are popular), dies, gets canonized in the press, and develops a cult. Type B lives the *official* composer's life: awards, orchestra residencies, pat-on-the-head reviews, commissions, widespread influence not on other people's music, but over their careers. No one listens to type B's self-serious music with love or enthusiasm, and once he/she dies, it is forgotten.

Feldman described the two types with an accuracy I can't improve on: "The real tradition of twentieth-century America, a tradition evolving from the empiricism of Ives, Varèse, and Cage, has been passed over as 'iconoclastic'—another word for unprofessional. In music, when you do something new, something original, you're an amateur. Your imitators— these are the professionals. . . . The imitator is the greatest enemy of originality. The 'freedom' of the artist is boring to him, because in freedom he cannot reenact the *role* of the artist."

Of amateurs: "An amateur is someone who doesn't stuff his ideas down your throat." Of the professional composer: "He writes a piece occasionally. It is played occasionally. . . . His pieces are well made. He is not without talent. The reviews aren't bad. A few awards—a Guggenheim, an Arts and Letters, a Fulbright—this is the official musical life of America. You can't buck the system, especially if it works. And this system does work. . . . These men are their own audience. They are their own fame. Yet they have created a climate that has brought the musical activity of an entire nation down to a college level."

A friend of mine once got stuck on a plane next to Milton Babbitt, who explained to him that Charles Ives *really*, after all, wasn't a professional composer. Now, in one leap, Feldman the amateur has surpassed Babbitt (whose articles often make fun of Feldman's early work) in the record catalogues.

At a conference two years ago, I overheard a professor who had just delivered a lecture on the structure of an Elliott Carter orchestral work admit to a colleague that while Carter's music analyzes beautifully on paper, you can't hear in the music the nice things you've analyzed. His colleague sorrowfully agreed. And once Carter's *academic* reputation crumbles, he's nothing more than the Daniel Gregory Mason of his generation.

Ives won the Pulitzer, you'll object. To do it he had to expunge the "experimental" parts from his Third Symphony, so that for 40 years we heard that symphony in a bowdlerized version. Instead of influential experimentalists—Feldman, Partch, Cage, Reich, Oliveros, Young, Ashley, Tenney—the Pulitzer has gone to many names that would be unknown even to new music fans: Sowerby, Toch, La Montaine, Bassett. Given to academic composers by other academic composers, the Pulitzer has become a Reward for Conformity and a Compensation Prize for Ineffectuality. But it gives the public the idea that the winners represent the best modern music, and an excuse to conclude that American music sucks.

As David Mamet wrote, "In this time of decay those things which society will reward with fame and recognition are bad acting, bad writing, choices which inhibit thought, reflection, and release: and these things will be called art." The music Pulitzer and our official scene carry out the program of decay.

The amateur originals envy the support system that the professional imitators have built, especially the money. (One piss-poor Pulitzer product I know of gets $100,000 a year teaching composition one day a week.) What fragile support system the amateurs had developed is falling apart. New Music America's gone. BAM, after five years on the John-Zorn-and-his-friends wave, has decided no new "next wave" is coming, and has returned to the wave before last. Cage's publisher, C. F. Peters, no longer publishes younger composers who aren't academic atonalists. Amateurs used to hope for the MacArthur "genius" award, which first went to actual geniuses (Conlon Nancarrow and Ralph Shapey); lately it's been following the Pulitzer around.

What the amateurs *do* have is flashy record labels like Lovely Music, New Albion, Hat Art, and Wergo. They don't pay to put their music on vanity labels like the pros do, because they (a) don't have the money, and (b) write music that's satisfying to listen to.

When the grand irony becomes obvious, the experimentalists get to say, "I told you so." The en masse CD arrival of Feldman's music is such an opportunity. It shows that, though we give prizes to 12-tone ideologues, the music that excites our passion and wonder is that of a more honest, less doctrinaire, less "professional" composer. The sad thing is that those opportunities rarely come except after somebody dies.

I'm tired of seeing artists I love live unrecognized, *then* upon death be celebrated as though everyone knew they were hotshots all along. Let's dismantle the academic hegemony over our official musical life until the day arrives when no great, influential composer is ever again denied commissions, residencies, or performances on the basis of being an "amateur."

composer's clearinghouse
the pulitzer prize
MAY 5, 1992

Leo Sowerby, John La Montaine, and Bernard Rands are giants of American music. If you believe that, the Pulitzer Prize board has a bridge to sell you. What smelled about this year's award was no fishier than what happens every year, only more public. The board overturned the judges' recommendation of long-scorned Ralph Shapey and gave the prize to a 64-year-old San Francisco prof I'd never heard of, Wayne Peterson. Fallacies clashed: the jury insisted only experts could judge new music, while the nonmusician board imposed what they felt was a more audience-relevant standard.

In reality, it was business as usual. The one great Pulitzer composer was Charles Ives, and his 1947 winning strategy illustrates the prize's historic timidity: at Lou Harrison's urging, Ives expunged the "experimental" parts of his Third Symphony and sent in the bowdlerized version, which did the trick. Since then, the prize has bypassed nearly every creatively influential, innovative, or audience-friendly composer: Cowell, Partch, Cage, Feldman, Ellington, Ornette Coleman, Nancarrow, Oliveros, Johnston, Reich, Glass, Riley, La Monte Young, Rzewski, John Adams, on and on. The music Pulitzer isn't awarded to dissenters, originals, or outsiders. A consolation prize for ineffectuality, it has often gone to composers who remain known only for having won it.

This year's jury made a daring first choice, for Shapey, a garrulous, profane, and outspoken critic of the musical establishment, doesn't fit the Pulitzer mold. Though he teaches at the University of Chicago, he never earned a degree, and until his midforties he lived by freelance conducting and teaching violin in New York for about $2,500 a year. On the wall of Shapey's Chicago apartment hangs a sampler reading, "Prizes are for horses, not artists"—a Bartók quote. It has long been speculated in print that Shapey might decline a Pulitzer, and perhaps the board sniffed potential embarrassment. (Shapey once wrote FUCK YOU across a Guggenheim application.) Yet Shapey would have been the most intrepidly original recipient since Ives.

In choosing their own winner among the jury's recommendations, this year's board claimed to represent lay ears, but historically the juries have been so far out of touch that by the time their selections reach the board any audience relevance is ruled out. With few exceptions, the board/jury decisions have distinguished not the year's best composition, but the best by a white male East Coast university professor. As Ed Rothstein hinted approvingly in the *Times,* all Pulitzer winners of recent decades share a Europe-imitative, expressionist, serial/neo-Romantic aesthetic. (Rothstein also repeated the error that the Pulitzer music jury had never before been overruled.) Excluded from consideration are minimalists, postminimalists, experimentalists, jazz- and world-music-influenced composers, and all others who don't write in European forms with a complex pitch vocabulary. And how could that situation change? The judges are often previous winners, ensuring a continuity of aesthetic bias. The question is not, should the prize be decided by experts (as a *Times* headline put it), but whether it should be decided by the same inbred group year after year.

George Perle, the jury's spokesman, is an excellent and brainy composer, but one with a narrow definition of what constitutes good new music. His jury mates, Roger Reynolds and Harvey Sollberger, hardly represent diverging viewpoints. For historical reasons, 12-tone composers can't judge minimalism as well as minimalists do 12-tone music; most minimalists, taught 12-tone technique as students, never denied the style's validity, whereas academics refuse to recognize minimalism or experimentalism because neither springs from European premises. The field of serious composition is politicized, but many composers, especially outside the university, have more ecumenical tastes than the stuffed shirts favored by the Pulitzer. If the board wanted an audience perspective in its juries, it might call on composers who perform for a living: Steve Reich, Pauline Oliveros, Muhal Richard Abrams. Variety of background could make for interesting choices. Wouldn't you be intrigued to hear a piece that Milton Babbitt and Anthony Braxton finally agreed on?

"So what?" my friends say. "Let the academics have the Pulitzer. No one takes it seriously." I want to agree, but that's only true among musicians. I was once the sole musician on a panel about to give a grant to a composer of miraculously dull squeakfarting specifically because he had won a Pulitzer. The grant died when I described the prize's pitiful past. After decades of academe's "It's better than it sounds" argument, few nonmusicians have the confidence to distinguish good new music from schlock. Lay listeners (far more than the audiences for theater and novels) rely on the type of certification prizes provide when they pour money into the field, whether through record buying or grant awarding. And the view of American music the Pulitzer list offers them is jaundiced, monochromatic, and depressing.

Given that any national prize for "best piece" will be a lottery, wouldn't it have more credibility if all composers had a chance at it, rather than as the permanent ideological property of a partisan group? Music patron Paul Fromm, in his last years, realized that relying solely on the advice of academics had led him into an artistic dead end, and he enlarged his circle of associates in order to sustain his new-music impact. The Pulitzer is now in that boat. Its current gap between expert advice and popular appeal is going to yawn wider unless the jury process expands to include more diverse composers than the dying breed of Eurocentric expressionists, ignoring all but two of the many streams of American music. What are they afraid of—that a piece audiences enjoy might accidentally win?

obitchuaries

critics take their final potshots at john cage

OCTOBER 13, 1992

> So it always goes with very great men. At each are fired all those
> accusations of which the opposite is true. Yes, *all,* and with such
> accuracy that one must be taken aback by it.

ARNOLD SCHOENBERG

New music doesn't often get glimpses of itself in the mainstream mirror. John Cage's death spotlighted our ignored field; suddenly avant-gardists saw their activity reflected in the national consciousness.* Cage had put his message across during his life better than any composer since Wagner. Critics from Los Angeles to Rome not only hailed him as the most influential American composer of his time, but showed a surprising awareness of the receptivity to sound he promoted. Textbooks so routinely misexplain

---

*See John Cage's obituary on page 293 of this volume.

4′33″ (reactions of the provoked audience, and so on) that I was braced for caricature. Yet for one week, everybody understood, often in personal terms, how the piece brought about a change of focus.

Some clichés were inescapable. Schoenberg's comment about Cage being "not a composer, but an inventor—of genius" was overplayed. Who'd trust an old-school German's insights into a brash American student 38 years his junior? And *Time* magazine's Michael Walsh calling Cage "one of the century's seminal theoreticians" was interesting, considering Cage didn't propose any theories. But most critics described even the wilder pieces respectfully, cited Cage's "impish humor," and proudly recalled meeting him.

Cage's death also provided the first new-music controversy in years. A few critics couldn't contain their irritation over Cage being taken seriously and wrote negative thumb-suckers. You might expect that the big-city thinkers understand Cage and summed him up fairly, while those in the hinterlands reacted with horror, right? Quite the opposite. Uptowners at the *Times,* the *New York Observer,* and *New Yorker* saw the funeral as an opportunity to kick the corpse. At the *Times,* only Bernard Holland (whose Messiaen obit was also lovely) really grasped Cage's aesthetic. But three critics (including the *New Yorker's* anonymous one) saw his demise as a chance to head an entire scene off at the pass.

If they simply hadn't liked his music, I'd say, "It's a free country." Instead, they made up a fictitious devil to exorcise. Cage advocated anarchy in the sense of the absence of coercive government, and by extension the absence of hierarchic musical structures, but the Uptowners recast him as a dynamite-tossing Bakunin. Edward Rothstein, in a September 20 *Times* Sunday piece, projected the image of a free-wheelin', irresponsible, cowboy composer, then acted indignant when Cage didn't measure up. Rothstein glanced at Cage's scores and triumphantly announced, as though he'd uncovered an embarrassing contradiction: Aha! Cage used "oddly elaborate techniques" in his music. "Cage didn't want liberation from law," Rothstein sneered, "he was actually always seeking to submit himself to it."

Well, yeah, thanks for noticing. Asked for 10 words that defined his life's work, Cage picked, among them, *discipline.* He was a Schoenberg student, a postserialist, a superbly rigorous artist, and a Virgo. Even the Cage quotes Rothstein picked were about liberation from tastes and dislikes, not law. And Rothstein's contention that, with regard to his public persona, "Cage was almost never innocent" was bile, neither substantiated nor musically relevant. Where did Rothstein get the idea that Cage pretended to reject rules? Not from *Silence,* but quite possibly from his colleague John Rockwell, who in August characterized Cage's music as "anything goes." Rockwell's Cage-as-passive-liberator, "letting [notes] happen every which way" to achieve "Instant Zen," is no more grounded in reality than Rothstein's Cage-as-fake-cowboy. How many *Times* critics does it take to screw Cage? Two: one to misinterpret him and the other to attack the misinterpreted image.

Rockwell's well-meant superficialities were also a springboard for Hilton Kramer, who waited scowling in the wings until September 14, when he registered his disgust in the *New York Observer*. Kramer quoted Cage as saying, "I don't like meaningful sound," blithely perverted that into "He preferred meaninglessness in all things," and then castigated Cage admirers for using meaningful sentences to eulogize him. For seven paragraphs he skewered "Cage's obituarists," but he seemed to mean only Rockwell, for he quoted him nine times and no one else. (So he *doesn't* read the *Voice*. I'm devastated.) Kramer then snorted that there was "nothing of significance in [Cage's] philosophy that had not been anticipated and propagated by Marcel Duchamp." Cage, who wasn't a philosopher until critics declared him one, had said the same thing, only he mentioned Thoreau, not Duchamp.

This is shoddy homework, getting your facts from colleagues instead of going to the source. Rockwell's a smart fellow who's taken it from both sides in this slugfest, but his misconstruals of Cage have been shrugged off in new-music circles for years. There are inconsistencies and statements to argue with in Cage, but to find them, go to a real Cage scholar like Richard Kostelanetz or William Brooks. Enjoy Cage's music or not, but don't dump on him for failing to be what he never claimed he was. And if you can't even explain why he was important enough to merit *four* articles in the *Times* after he died, what credibility do you expect to have reviewing the hundreds of composers who take Cage as a starting point? Cage's death was an illuminating moment for new music: it showed us who's listening and who's just gunning.

totally ismic

totalism

JULY 20, 1993

When I first heard the word *totalism*—from musicians hanging out at Rudy's bar, Ninth Avenue at 45th—I instantly knew what it meant. We haven't had a new musical ism for years, but those who listen carefully hear a collective language percolating. Please set aside your reservations about labeling for a moment: an ism is merely an infinitesimal point of crystallization that music turns toward, crosses, and moves past without pausing. The light that draws artists to a common point is there whether we tag it or not. Let's concede it a name, and see what happens.

Totalism? As the term implies, it's an attempt to have and eat the cake, a short circuit to the no-win choice between serialism and minimalism. Composers born in the '50s feel like survivors, their noses bloodied in a pointless battle between a commercially successful music of simpleminded patterns on the one hand, and on the other, a cult of stupid pitch tricks that tried to pass off complicatedness as intellectuality. Meanwhile, the organic complexity of jazz and Third World musics beckoned, attractive but inaccessible to those whose backgrounds had already conditioned them.

Totalists liked the impulse of minimalism, and took from it some ideas about rhythmic structure. But their music doesn't repeat, its rhythmic patterns have a multilayered intricacy, and they're weary of their new Downtown complexity being written off as minimalist by critics who divide the world into only two camps. Minimalism's gradual process turned into an adaptable compositional tool, too, but totalist structure is global, not linear, and totalist processes are rarely gradual, as minimalism's are.

Ergo, totalist music *always* has a steady beat—more likely, a plurality of steady beats. What passes for rhythmic subtlety with Elliott Carter and his followers is a mishmash because their music never articulates the grid against which complexity can be perceived. Totalism uses the grid, and thus has a Nancarrovian urge toward overlapping pulses, each with the feel of rock or world music. Evan Ziporyn's *LUV Time* (on *Bang on a Can, Volume I*, CRI) uses two grids at once: one Balinese beat in strident piano chords, another in a slow drum, around which three saxophones run circles. The grid in Mikel Rouse's *High Frontier* shifts like an optical illusion: is it 5/4, or 4/4 with quintuplets?

Likewise, the melodies recurring every five and a half beats over a 4/4 dance tempo in Ben Neill's *Downwind* are totalist. At the trickiest moment in Michael Gordon's *Four Kings Fight Five* (on *Big Noise from Nicaragua*, CRI), seven tempos are going at once, including an eight-against-nine pattern in the violin and viola, and another eight-against-nine, three times as fast, in the clarinet and bass clarinet. The different tempo drum beats that play against each other in David First's *Jade Screen Test Dreams of Renting Wings* are totalist too, though First's glissandoing pitch continuum stems from somewhere else.

How does totalist harmony work? Instead of returning to old tonality like the neo-Romantics, totalism has reconceptualized tonality. Where a traditional tonal piece has a single pitch as its tonic (say, D in the key of D), totalism offers the concept of a "tonic sound complex," a harmonic/rhythmic/timbral image from which the piece starts and to which it may, in the end, return, or not. The music ignores academic hairsplitting about pitches in favor of a gestalt-conscious approach to musical images drawn from Stravinsky and Feldman. Fights about consonance versus dissonance lose their sting.

For example, it might be said that the "tonic image" of Rouse's *Hope Chest* (on *Soul Menu*, New Tone) is two phrases in overlapping rhythms of seven and eight beats, respectively. The tonic of Gordon's *Thou Shalt!/Thou Shalt Not!* (also on *Big Noise*) is a 9/8 rhythmic figure with F and A in the violin and a low E in the bass clarinet. Ziporyn's *LUV Time* has competing tonic drone-tempos in the piano and drums, for in totalism, tempo can take over functions once reserved for harmony. Since pitch and rhythm are ultimately governed by the same numbers, they're subject to the same controls, and a piece can modulate to a new tempo as well as a new key. That idea came from Henry Cowell long before Stockhausen ripped it off, but only totalism has made it an audible structural principle. Totalism is rhythmically polytonal.

The movement also comes with a built-in Uptown/Downtown split. The Bang on a Can festival, run by Yalies with a soft spot for Europe, likes dramatic conflict in its totalism, a dialectical battle between opposing textures. For example, *Thou Shalt!* pits triple rhythms in strings and winds against interruptive quarter notes in the percussion, and one of them has to yield. Asia-leaning totalists, such as Rouse and Neill, are content to unfold a single system of relationships with no need for first and second themes; they descend from La Monte Young, who said, "Contrast is for people who can't write music." They even have different record labels, CRI for the Eurototalists, the Italian New Tone label for the meditationists. Keep an ear on this fracture to hear if the opposition eventually outweighs the shared interests.

These composers may deny totalism as Debussy did impressionism and Glass minimalism. (Ism: a club everyone talks about and no one belongs to.) Fine; that won't erase the fact that a distinct, technically definable type of composition has emerged in the last five years. As Haydn and Mozart demonstrated, composers working toward the same vision steal insights from each other, and when they do, the pace of a music's growing sophistication accelerates. Isms help music survive, because they concentrate public attention long enough to let new perceptions emerge. Coining a word doesn't change music, but it does give audiences a context in which to hear that music anew.

the last barbarian

john cage

NOVEMBER 9, 1993

Raphael Mostel tells a story of returning to the Bang on a Can festival with John Cage after a dinner break. As they made their way to their seats, some friends urged them to come sit in the back, claiming, "The sound is better back here." Cage laughed and went to his previous seat, saying, "Imagine, a sound being better."

October 4 through 9, the Center for Contemporary Art in Warsaw presented a conference on Cage, "Days of Silence," to which I was invited. An impressive cross section of the Cage Industry was there, polishing up a new vision of him not likely to penetrate New York's atmosphere for a few years yet. Marjorie Perloff showed how evocative Cage's mesostics become when you take them seriously as poetry. Susumu Shono talked about the arithmetical ingenuity with which Cage framed his sounds. Gordon Mumma aired a tape of Cage performing a Satie Nocturne with a marvelously emotive rubato. (On a more gossipy level, Cage had vouchsafed to Thomas Hines some 11th-hour revelations of his early homosexual experiences, though since he was never secretive about it, only private, he can hardly be outed.) The edited Cage is a slick artist in whose work randomness plays only a minor role.

The undercurrent, though, was that the Industry is rescuing Cage from us infidels who came later. The first mention of minimalism inspired a feeding frenzy; Klaus-Heinz Metzger opined that while it may have been valid for 18th-century music, "repetition shouldn't exist anymore in art . . . it becomes false, the thing that must be avoided." General cheers greeted his proposition that "minimalism's repetitions steal from a person the one thing he has left, the vanishing moments of his lifetime." (Makes you want to sue conductors who repeat expositions.) Cage was a towering genius, but feh! These younger composers, they depart from the true path. The Industry has made Cage the next in Europe's series of Great Men (presumably the last, until the next one), and excommunicated the rest of us, exactly as Cage was excommunicated for 40 years. (He still is in most universities and at one major New York newspaper.)

I shouldn't have been surprised. Some people have a deep-seated need to be the guardians at the gates of culture, and to be a gatekeeper, one needs barbarians to storm the gates, whether they exist or not. Historically, one by one, the barbarians are allowed inside to become the guarded. Deciding whom to let in is a popular academic power play. But I had thought of Cage as the ultimate barbarian, our aesthetic Attila the Hun. Let him in, and whom are you going to keep out? "'Chance' and 'system' are other words for *puer* and *senex*," writes psychologist James Hillman, associating chance with the eternal-youth archetype, system with the rigidity of sterile old men. That means Cage is music's ageless bad boy, and if you're going to turn him into a bronze statue, naturally you have to push chance into the background.

To me, identifying with Cage sufficiently to explicate his work means relinquishing the idea that gatekeepers are necessary. He, of course, would have never made any such pronouncement against minimalism. His biographer Mark Swed tells me he was disturbed by the idea of literal repetition. Of course he was; that was his generation. Cage's irrationality, however iconoclastic, was grounded in a Western concept of objective rationalism that my generation finds no longer tenable. Feminism and Eastern cultures, among many other things, have taught us that objectivity is an establishment-serving hoax, so we've embraced subjectivity with our eyes open. And as our worldview includes African and Balinese musics, so it includes repetition. Now that the battery's dead on Europe's Hegelian goal drive, sitting still can once again be perfectly authentic.

Cage was born too early to sympathize with that subjective worldview, but he never railed against it the way the Euro-establishment composers do. He wasn't threatened by younger composers. He responded to minimalism by writing one of the minimalist masterpieces, *Hymnkus,* a work that squeezes its pitches into two octaves, within which each instrument repeats its line over and over, verbatim. He digested every new idea and technology as it came along. We loved him because, if he didn't like our ideas, his worst possible response would be to steal them and make them more interesting. He didn't set up criteria for what music must or must not do. Other famous composers bless only their imitators, but Cage blessed those who went their own way.

This was the argument I had in the late '80s with Downtown composers from diverse camps. Several of them were running around shouting, "To be valid, music *must* incorporate the vernacular music of its day." But the minute we Downtowners lay down mandates for what music must do, we become no better than the Uptowners, just their mirror image. (Besides, that's reactionary bullshit. A lot of fantastic, timely music has made no reference to any vernacular: Ruggles, Varèse, Feldman, Lucier, Tenney.) If Cage's life had a point, it was that *must* follows *music* only in the dictionary. For me, preserving the Cagean integrity of Downtown entails expelling *must* from our vocabulary. Let us have bad composers and good within each idiom, but no more excommunications.

The sad thing is realizing that even Cage couldn't change the world. The man who proclaimed that the gates of culture do not exist is now tucked away safely within them, another icon to terrorize the youth with. But—senator, I knew John Cage. And the next time some codger tells me that his generation of composers was better than these youngsters today, I'm going to laugh and say, "Imagine, a generation being better!"

berlitz's downtown for musicians

new-music performance

JULY 26, 1994

Suddenly people are playing Downtown new music who never have before: virtuoso soloists, members of the Albany Symphony, even the New York Philharmonic. It's great when they get it right, but there's often a translation problem, a clash of cultures. We need a primer for classically trained musicians on how to approach this Downtown tradition that has so little to do with the Euro-classical style. Ultimately, such a treatise will have to be written by performers, but a critic may presume to set out some initial guidelines.

When the music is postminimal, rock-oriented, totalist, or from some other minimalism-derived genre, classical types have trouble believing that a composer could really want a melody in which every note is the same volume. Postminimal composers, influenced by rock and computer sequencing, often write melodies or bass lines of straight, even dynamics, or pieces in which dynamic shifts are sudden rather than gradual. Classical players, taught to curve, climax, and taper every phrase, find that unmusical. As a result, they'll do to Terry Riley's *In C* what the NY Phil players did in May: add crescendos, climaxes, and accents in an attempt to turn it into a "real piece." Blech. Riley notated the piece blankly because it sounds good blank.

There are actually different sets of problems, for classical players come in diverse shapes and sizes. Those accustomed to Romantic repertoire at least assume that they'll have to do a certain amount of interpretation. Performers who specialize in Uptown music of the Babbitt/Carter school have the hardest time going Downtown, for they expect composers to notate every possible nuance in scores full of sforzandos, crescendos, slurs, and diminuendos, sidestepping the issue of interpretation altogether. Grad schools teach young Uptowners to hand-feed every minute bit of information as though performers were computers, for Uptowners assume that their music, written for posterity, will be performed by players unfamiliar with its tradition. They think, mistakenly, that a score is a piece of music.

Downtown scores, on the other hand, are often nearly devoid of dynamic markings. An Uptown performer will say, "I see you haven't put the dynamic markings in yet," and the Downtown composer replies, "Yes, I have, it says right there at the beginning: *p*." There are many reasons for this, some practical, others philosophical. One is that Downtown composers reject the idea that music can be taken out of context. Downtown music isn't made for martians to make sense of centuries hence, but for a living tradition in which the composer is present and involved. In addition, Downtowners, trying things no one's tried before, like to experiment in rehearsal. Frequently they combine acoustic with electronic instruments, setting up a balance problem that notated dynamics won't necessarily solve. Like Duke Ellington, they take the performer's personality into account, which means the performer has to have one.

What works against Downtown composers in this situation is that Uptown performers have come to equate a heavily nuanced score with professionalism, so that, faced with a lightly marked piece, they conclude that the composer doesn't know what he or she really wants, and is therefore amateurish, illiterate, and careless. Look at *In C*, or Christian Wolff's *Snowdrop*, or Mikel Rouse's *Copperhead*, or Nick Didkovsky's *Amalia's Secret:* you won't see any dynamics, just notes. Unedited, J. S. Bach looks the same way. Riley and Wolff, like Monteverdi, don't even specify what instruments to use. Downtowners know that music's essence can't be notated, and that texts are always ambiguous anyway. And they have faith that, if the work is written well, the player will come up with his or her own concept of it, perhaps adding felicitous strategies that the composer wouldn't have thought of. Only unclear works need to be notated to death. To Downtowners, an *excess* of notation shows unprofessionalism.

I mentioned these concerns to Lois Svard, a classical pianist known for being the first American to perform the Ligeti Etudes, but who has also recorded music by several Downtowners. "It's the same problem performers have approaching early music," she said. "The only music they teach us in college is classical and romantic, and to play anything else we have to learn a new tradition. Duckworth's music is deceptively simple. It looks straight minimalist, but there's all kinds of nuance built in. On the recording I gave it more nuance; these days I play it straighter, which I think he'd probably prefer. For Ashley's *Van Cao's Meditation* you have to choose where to put nuances, nothing in the score gives you a hint. 'Blue' Gene Tyranny doesn't mark his scores much, but when we recorded *Nocturne With and Without Memory* he was very specific about the color of every note, or how long to delay something. But those are things you can't get across in notation anyway."

So for all you classical performers who are taking the plunge into new music, welcome to Downtown. Our composers have different rules. They want the players to feel the piece in their gut, not just spit back out what's on the page. They may get inspired in rehearsal and change everything. They may play a piece *ff* today and *pp* tomorrow. They're not sitting in classrooms looking at other people's scores, they're out getting practical experience the way Mozart did. Future musicologists will have one hell of a time reconstructing their music; that's not their problem. But they write the way they do on purpose, and they're goddamned serious about what they're doing. Assume that, or get lost.

what are we, chopped liver?

the new generation

SEPTEMBER 13, 1994

May I cheerlead for my generation a moment? We're feeling neglected. In the early '80s, BAM and Lincoln Center showcased Glass, Reich, and Laurie Anderson, then moved up through younger composers like John Zorn, Elliott Sharp, and their roster of friends. When it came my generation's turn, those institutions twiddled their thumbs, avoided new music for a couple of years, then went back to Glass and Reich. Why's everybody afraid of *our* next wave? Generation X, which oughta be called Generation Whine, is already clamoring for its moment in the spotlight, while we boomers, who allegedly already run everything, can't even get onstage.

By my generation, I mean artists born between 1954 and, maybe, '59. If the mid '70s weren't the hottest time to be in college, they did offer a bracing friction between intellectual freedom and respect for tradition, both of which seem in short supply on today's campuses. After college, when I first came to New York, I felt like a minority of one on nearly every musical issue. But once people my age began seeping into the new music scene and running parts of it, I found that, far from being unique, I was typical to the point of banality. Composers I know who went through college in the '70s came out with strikingly similar experiences.

For example, they found 12-tone music's intellectual pretensions empty, its arrogance toward the audience reprehensible. On the other hand, they learned serial technique inside and out and can apply it at will. They were excited by the way early minimalist music reached out to audiences, but disliked the pandering, 4/4 regularity of the minimalism that came afterward. So they avoid minimalism's strict repetition and candy tonality, often opting for dissonance, but within harmonies that shift only gradually. They met John Cage and were charmed, but saw no point in duplicating his achievements in randomness. They do agree with his conviction that music's formal foundation should be rhythm, not harmony—especially with such a wealth of rhythmic traditions to choose from in America. My generation's music is bullish on rhythm.

They were the first to study African, Asian, and pop musics in college side by side with the European tradition. As a result, they sneer at the hypocrisy of professors who eschew pop and jazz in public and tap their feet to it in private. At the same time, they realize using pop materials can be a cheap audience bid, and have seen that no matter how many electric guitars the avant-garde uses, it rarely weans many fans from rock. They improvised in college, which was the cool thing to do at the time, consider jazzers among the great musical minds, and weave jazz riffs into their music. Nevertheless, they tend to agree with Cage and Boulez that improvisers get stuck on their favorite licks, and they got deadly tired of the improv clichés of '80s New York. Besides, they're too interested in form not to notate music. Formlessness, they learned, is finite.

In short, they're an "in-between" generation: in between the 12-toners and the minimalists, in between hermetic complexity and populist pandering, in between the classical establishment and the vernacular, in between Uptown and Down. Survivors of the music ideology wars of the '70s, they grew up with extremism on all sides. Now they're leery of musics that claim absolute truth, and of ideas that become more important than the music. They recognize all the lures, but they've seen all the pitfalls. They want music to honestly express its culture, though they're aware that most obvious ways of doing that lead to shallowness. Their upbringing resulted in not a *school* of composers who've agreed on a direction music should take, but rather a disenchanted generation whose experiences have shown them the directions music *shouldn't* go in. And rather than continue the macho battle of either/or bequeathed them by their professors and populist role models, they've taken a 90-degree turn onto a path where those battles no longer rage.

That might be, in fact, the reason for their current neglect. Economics is one factor: my generation came of age artistically the year the recession hit, and now institutions no longer take risks. But I suspect there's something deeper, that artists born in the mid '50s are the first to drive home a glacial change of direction in the arts. Every previous generation has been able to hype itself as the "next step" in a linear historical progression toward more and more fragmentation, chaos, eclecticism, and conceptualist acrobatics. Minimalism upped the ante on conceptualism's in-your-face outrageousness, just as conceptualism had leapfrogged over serialism. The '80s improvisers capitalized on the rhetoric of modernism, though they were repeating so much history that the slogans roared thin and unconvincing.

My generation's composers aren't going to be more outrageous, more chaotic, more macho in their modernity than what went before. That dialectic is played out. They are synthesizers, reintroducers of structure, speakers of a new language *more*, not less, coherent than that of their predecessors. They don't get press because critics and institutions haven't been able to single out any one figure for his or her one-step-ahead hipness. The critics are still looking for the moribund technicolor opulence of autumn leaves, while these composers bring the opening buds of a new spring. Before you hear this generation at BAM or Lincoln Center, administrators will have to learn to take postmodernism at face value. In the future, newness will have less to do with chutzpah, hype, and one-upmanship than with consolidation, structure, communicativeness, and subtlety of language. Meanwhile, the new music is here whether it's heard or not.

the great divide

uptown composers are stuck in the past

JULY 9, 1996

The Grand Canyon is located between 20th and 59th streets, running east to west. You can't see it, and inhabitants of both rims claim it's been shrinking every year. They have vested interests in saying so. The Uptown colonials don't want to feel like a bunch of stodgy old farts, and the Downtown savages don't want you to know how broke they are. But teaching a graduate seminar (on music since 1945) this past semester to students molded at Eastman, Harvard, Princeton, Columbia, Rutgers, Oberlin, and other prestigious centers of higher learning, I got nimble at jumping that canyon on a weekly basis. I can calculate its size to the inch, and I can tell you it's getting wider. Yes, Virginia, Uptowners are different from you and me.

Uptown/Downtown isn't really the exact distinction. The difference lies between those whose only exposure to new music has come from within academia's ivied walls, and everybody else. Students from today's best-known music schools possess an amazing mixture of sophistication and ignorance. Play them some Milton Babbitt and they can talk fourth-order combinatorial hexachords and z-relations like they were throwing around baseball stats. Show them a simple 13/8 ostinato by Meredith Monk, how-ever, and they stare at you like you're trying to sell them prime Florida real estate, down payment in cash.

These were grad-school composers in their midtwenties, already involved in professional life. They had never heard a note of Robert Ashley. Never heard Meredith Monk. Didn't know who Harry Partch was. Were skeptical about music John Cage wrote over 40 years ago. Didn't believe in using synthesizers. Hadn't heard Glenn Branca. Had heard of Morton Feldman, but thought it was hilarious that he worked in a dry cleaner's until he was 46. In short, any musical trend that appeared after 1970 was news to them (except the guy from Oberlin, my own alma mater, who had gotten a wider experience), but man, could they talk Boulez and Stockhausen! And why should they believe me, who spoke of things none of their other professors ever mentioned? Teaching these students was like landing on one of those Pacific islands peopled by Japanese guerrillas who'd never heard that World War II was over.

I've tried to believe that Uptown has its own developing philosophy par-allel to Downtown's, but that really isn't the case. Instead, universities all over (except for the one that was open-minded enough to hire me, I must say) are determined to freeze the state of music circa 1964 in cryonic sus-pension. George Rochberg once asked his teacher Luigi Dallapiccola what was going to come after 12-tone music, and the old man replied, "Nothing. This is our language. There is no need for anything else." That's the oper-ative attitude. It's not that Uptowners still write 12-tone music—they boast that they've transcended the "row" concept, and they have to boast because you can't tell that by listening. But they do believe that the tenets of high modernism, like the Third Reich in 1933, are here to stay for a thousand years. My friends in other arts find this incomprehensible, for in no other field do academics insist that history has reached a stopping point.

The trap is that students are taught to analyze music according to pitch sets. The music of high modernism—Bartók, Webern, Babbitt, Stockhausen—is a blast to analyze this way. You dive into pages of chaos, and as you go deeper, all the notes gradually sort themselves out perfectly. It's as satisfying to slide the last pitch into place as it is to finish a devilishly hard crossword puzzle. You become proud of knowing how that music works internally. Pitch-set analysis becomes the criterion of musical greatness. Music that makes no claim to pitch-set perfection is threatening, because it denies you what you do so well. The smarter the composer, the more unwilling to give up that thrill. That's why the top-notch schools turn out the driest, dullest, most out-of-touch composers.

Relinquishing such a finely honed technical skill in order to become something as vulnerable as an artist requires a rare courage. One raucous Downtowner I know who graduated from Princeton and Columbia tells me that coming out as a lesbian was easier than coming out as a Downtown composer, and cost her fewer friends.

But pitch analyzing a piece to see whether it's any good is like determining whether a novel is great by analyzing its grammar with Venn diagrams. Pitch-set consistency no more guarantees art than correct grammar does truth. I analyzed Babbitt and Stockhausen for these students because I know that stuff cold, but the music I really loved—Monk's *Atlas*, Partch's *Castor and Pollux*, Michael Gordon's *Four Kings Fight Five*—I hardly knew how to start analyzing. I don't know where Monk got her notes— from the ether, I guess. We need to rethink what musical analysis consists of, because the best music of the last 30 years doesn't lay pitches out in nice, neat rows. We've got to learn to analyze music in terms of content, expression, rhythmic structure.

If I needed a telltale sign of Uptown's spiritual emptiness, the students handed it to me in their lack of new heroes. When I was in high school 25 years ago, my new-musicky friends and I glommed up every recording by the hot composers of the day: Babbitt, Carter, Ligeti, Boulez. Whom do twentysomething Uptown composers rave about today? Babbitt, Carter, Ligeti, Boulez. The composers they're influenced by are all septuagenarians, at least. The midcareer Uptowners—Schwantner, Zwillich, Harbison, Shulamit Ran, Wayne Peterson—who get patted on the head by classical critics inspire no enthusiasm from young composers, because they're so obviously imitators, not originators. Why would anybody model their music after Zwillich's bland pastiche instead of going directly to the masters on whom she modeled her work? In three decades, the only name that has tentatively joined the Uptown pantheon is Brian Ferneyhough, whose music the average music lover is hard put to distinguish from Boulez's.

Meanwhile, Uptown composers in their thirties, having sensed that attachment to a stagnant style is a dead end, circle over the Bang on a Can festival like vultures, snarfing up hints on hipness. In the new Uptown career map, Downtown is the shortcut to Tanglewood. But these Johnny-come-latelies, still disdainful of Philip Glass and La Monte Young, never bothered to study that seemingly simple music, and so their attempts to hitch a ride end up superficial. They can't see that serialism morphed into conceptualism, and conceptualism into minimalism, or that Schoenberg-Cage-Young-Glass-Branca was a logical if bumpy progression. And so they write Hollywoodish orchestration assignments with titles like *Zeke's Wild Adventure at the Underwater Bordello* that have no feeling, urgency, or theoretical depth. You can't suddenly jump over 35 years from a calcified scene to a healthy, vital, growing one without going back and living what you missed. Downtown music may look wild and crazy, but it's driven by a compelling sense of history.

Toward the end of his life, following a teaching stint at Eastman, Henry Cowell complained about the partisanship of composition professors, about their refusal to expose students to styles of music different from their own. "What composers need," Cowell wrote, "is breadth of experience, instead of judgments as to what somebody may believe to be 'good' or 'bad,' 'right' or 'wrong,' in music. How else can a composer learn to live in the world around him, here and today, unless all of today's possibilities are freely offered for his choice? Some of these will 'speak' to him, and many will not: but why should he be protected from any of them?"

It's clear that at the nation's best music schools, young composers are routinely "protected" from new music. The lucky ones, those who fail to obtain academic jobs, will be pushed out of the nest and find that they have 30 years of history to catch up with; the others will spend their lives bitterly shoring up the status quo against the "barbarians" by inheriting control of the Guggenheims, the Grawemeyer Awards, the Pulitzers, the university jobs. All those students should ask themselves now, while there's still time: What are my professors protecting me from? And why?

critic 1, composers zilch

One of the defining moments in the death of Uptown occurred this spring. Rutgers University held a symposium March 31 on Stravinsky, and invited Charles Wuorinen, Milton Babbitt, Claudio Spies, and Richard Taruskin to be on a panel. The first three are among the most distinguished Uptown composers and theoretical brains; Taruskin is an erudite, rabble-rousing critic and Berkeley musicologist whose book on Stravinsky is due out any day now. Before the panel could take place, however, Taruskin put one of his famous attack pieces in the March 10 *New York Times*. Titled "How Talented Composers Become Useless," it deconstructed two new CDs of complex serialist music by Donald Martino.

Taruskin's argument was that serialist music contains a basic flaw: the composer puts in elegantly arcane pitch structures, but all the listener gets out are gross, undifferentiated gestures contrasted by loudness and register. Rather than facing this disjunction of intention and result squarely, the composers hold laymen in contempt, brag about the difficulty of their music, and then hypocritically complain because laymen don't appreciate their genius. Yet serialist music isn't dying from lack of public interest. It survives on an artificial life-support system within academia, dependent for its continued existence on brainwashing each new generation of young composers.

Taruskin's logic was elegantly inescapable. Had there been anything contradictable in what he said, or any more elevated criterion he had failed to take into account, Babbitt, Wuorinen, and Spies should have walked onstage with him and defeated him in a quick, clean, three-against-one debate. Instead, all three *withdrew* (Wuorinen did so before Taruskin's article appeared). The panel was canceled and replaced with a group of performers who had worked with Stravinsky, with Taruskin participating from the audience.

If there were any truth at all to Uptown serialist dogma, would three of its greatest sages run in cowardice from a single music critic speaking common sense? Let's honor these dour old men for the important moment in history they represent. But let's admit that that moment was nothing more than a fascinating dead end.

y not 2k?

nostalgia for modernism as the millennium ends

APRIL 6, 1999

The music that has constituted the "contemporary music" of my lifetime so far is a music violently opposed to nostalgia. As Pierre Boulez, one of its leading architects, wrote, "If you do not negate, if you do not make a clean sweep of all that you have inherited from the past, if you do not question [your] heritage and adopt an attitude of fundamental doubt towards all accepted values, well!, you will never get any further." And again, "When one has had one's fill of experimenting, there comes a nostalgia for the past. . . . [S]uch nostalgias have no interest for me; they are . . . unable to contribute to a future." The very music, as written by Boulez, Elliott Carter, Milton Babbitt, was structured to defy nostalgia, to defeat memory, to so baffle comprehension that one couldn't even think back to the beginning of a piece from the end of it.

How charmingly ironic, then, to end the 20th century in a wave of nostalgia for that very music. Schoenberg's *Moses und Aron*, at last trotted out by the Met as though they'd just discovered the 20th century, is reviewed sentimentally by critics who tout Schoenberg the way the Republican House managers touted the Rule of Law—aware that the public isn't really behind them, but determined to act proud of their lonely principles. Boulez is named to the composer's chair at Carnegie Hall, extending his influence in a city and time ultimately as foreign to him as he is irrelevant to them. David Schiff and Paul Griffiths in the *New York Times* lament that composers no longer write incomprehensibly complex music. I was drafted to a panel on modernism recently in Los Angeles, where the aficionados got caught up talking about 1950s Darmstadt and couldn't get off the subject even after audience members begged them to.

Serialist music is fun for experts to talk about, partly because it makes no sense. There was no discernible point in writing a dry, unrewarding, unmemorable piece like Boulez's *Le Marteau sans maître,* and that's exactly what's fascinating about it. Unlike the music of any other era, 20th-century music, which for most people is still identified with high modernism and nothing else, has always been a Cause—a Worthy Cause at times, a Lost Cause quite often, a Noble Cause, a Hopeless Cause. As a cause it never achieved the big public triumph it sought for decades, and so still seems unfulfilled. It never had the opportunity to become so ubiquitously popular that it overplayed its hand, fell into complacent excess, and made even its advocates finally glad to see it depart. Might as well expect the Irish to just drop their interest in independence from British rule without achieving it as expect musicians who spent their lives fighting for the cause of 20th-century music to move on to something else.

And so, just at the moment when one would expect all kinds of hype about the new music of the 21st century, we get—nothing. The turn of the millennium occasions no focus on the new, just attempts to keep the old alive. Newspapers and press releases trumpet the same names that were in the air when I was an undergrad 25 years ago. You wait for all those composers born in the 1920s and 1930s to be replaced in the critical dialogue by the names of those born in the 1940s and '50s. But it never happens. Finally, in the *Times* a few weeks ago, Paul Griffiths, noticing their absence, wrote an article titled "Where Are America's Young Composers?"

Well, I know where they are, I've been to their apartments, they leave messages on my answering machine. But you're not going to hear about them, because there's a moratorium on discussing them except to dismiss them. Young composers are not allowed to climb the ladder that the generation before last climbed.

I have three explanations for this neglect—explanations not mutually exclusive, but that kind of go hand-in-hand. The first is admittedly a little mystical: it's that an end-of-the-millennium feeling prevents us from looking ahead. There's no point in investing our time and enthusiasm, I imagine people thinking deep down, in whatever's going on musically at the moment, because when the calendar changes it'll be a whole new game anyway. We won't allow ourselves to perceive what's new now, with this mammoth deadline just ahead.

The second, more pragmatic explanation is based on hard evidence relayed by those working in the field. Arts organizations are reforming themselves after a corporate model. They have become more bottom-line-conscious, which means that they try to make money by programming artists you've already heard of. No one who is not famous yet will be allowed to become famous, because those who are not famous do not bring in a guaranteed audience. Presenters have quit putting their money into artists' fees and have directed it into marketing and advertising, for which they need recognizable names. The strategy has a foreseeable crash point, because some of those famous names—Boulez, for example, is 71—ain't going to be around for much of the new millennium.

There's a well-known syndrome in the prize-giving world, known as the Matthew Effect after the Bible verse Matthew 13:12: "For whosoever hath, to him shall be given, and he shall have more abundance; but whosoever hath not, from him shall be taken away even that which he hath." According to the Matthew Effect, recognition tends to accrue to those who already have it. For instance, an organization can bring prestige and attention to itself by giving Charles Wuorinen a prize because he's already won the Pulitzer and MacArthur awards, whereas if they give an award to some far better but less acclaimed figure, no one may notice. So Carnegie Hall takes no risk by bringing in Boulez, even though he's a quantity so known that you can't imagine anything exciting coming from the choice.

Times of economic insecurity exacerbate the Matthew Effect. In the publishing business, I watch it grow worse every year. As the print media get more panicked about corporate bottom-line pressures and Internet competition, placing articles and books about rising young artists becomes impossible. People will only buy a book or newspaper, publishers are convinced, to read about people they already know about. In hard times, only those who have plenty of recognition will get more of it. The money people may be right in the short run, but they're courting cultural catastrophe.

The third explanation seems so obvious, and is so meticulously avoided by every other writer, that it feels like a breach of manners to bring it up. Griffiths complains that the young composers he's discovered aren't nearly as exciting as the modernist masters because their music is based on pastiche, and on reworking the more audience-friendly styles of early modernism. Well, of course it is: The young hotshots he gets to review up there at the *Times* are those who write in conventional classical genres, orchestra pieces, chamber music. Those composers are desperately trying to make careers by catering to an orchestral establishment for whom 12-tone music was a PR disaster and Romanticism a fail-proof standby. For them to try to advance the musical language in any interesting direction would be professional suicide.

Griffiths is absolutely right: Pastiche is not a theoretical idea that critics and aficionados can get passionate about. If you're determined to limit your sights to composers writing within that orchestral establishment, *of course* you can't progress any further than Boulez and Stockhausen. That's as far out as that tradition went.

But there's an equally obvious rejoinder. If you'll look at composers working in new media, computers, unconventional ensembles and formats, the 1990s have been boiling over with new ideas, new energy, new and more seasoned assimilations of technology. Classical critics and administrators dearly yearn for the music world to continue in its familiar form, and therefore dismiss any composers who color outside the lines as, "Well, you know, not really picking up the inheritance, now, are they?" But the music world of Y2K emerges from a vastly different sociology than that of 1950, and the best music around reflects the changes. For young composers today to reinvent the world with the same contempt for nostalgia that Boulez's generation enjoyed, they have to work in media over which they have complete creative control, not kowtow to commissioning ensembles who have rigid European standards locked in their heads.

The pretense that today's young composers can't rival their grandfathers requires ignoring the most patent facts. They won't write complex music, runs the woeful lament. Are you kidding? Michael Gordon's *Four Kings Fight Five* climaxes at eleven different tempos at once. Mikel Rouse is writing operas in which different scenes in different meters and keys overlap simultaneously. Larry Polansky's *Lonesome Road Variations* for piano is longer, more massive, and more intricate than Ives's *Concord Sonata,* and far more than any Boulez sonata. Paul Dolden is making sampler pieces with 200 orchestral lines going at once. We got complexity out the wazoo. It's just not the *atonal* and *arrhythmic* complexity of the serialists. You can hear deeper into the complexity than you can with your average Boulez or Carter tone poem. And it's actually more exciting to hear how the complexity works than it is to be assured by a learned treatise that *Le Marteau sans maître* is a seminal work.

I can make one ironclad prediction for the coming century: As long as institutions and critics continue to define "composer" as "one who writes in conventional notation for conventional European-style ensembles," the young composers who get lukewarmly lauded in the newspapers will never have the magnetism of the modernist giants. The Aaron Jay Kernises and Michael Torkes and Augusta Read Thomases of the world, doing their damnedest to ingratiate themselves with the little old ladies on the orchestra boards, do not offer a creative energy for intellectual discussion to crystallize around. On that we're all agreed, right? Let's all take the next step together—quick. "The present-day composer refuses to die," said Frank Zappa, and he was right—but the 20th-century composer will be dead in nine more months. Let us not enter the 21st century looking backward.

ding! dong! the witch is dead

modernism loses its grip as the odometer turns over

JANUARY 25, 2000

May I be the only classical music critic in town to welcome the new century with open arms? Hurrah! Hurrah! Twentieth-century music is dead.

Uh-oh: I've just denounced what I'm supposed to pledge allegiance to. Of course, there were actually two 20th centuries. The first, symbolized by Stravinsky, Bartók, and Ives, was a dramatic irruption of violent, irrational energy, as music abruptly claimed all those sonic phenomena that earlier centuries had prohibited. The second 20th century, which began as World War II ended, was quite the opposite, a worship of technical devices by people who, in any other generation, would have likely become lab technicians rather than composers. Yet by a quirk of inadequate terminology, both 20th centuries—the lion's roar and the ferret's jargon-blurred murmur—became yoked together under the term "modernism." And by another ironic inadequacy that made no difference until this month, "20th-century" and "modernist" were synonymous in music.

It's not that the late 20th century didn't produce great music. Any era that can boast Nancarrow, Feldman, Ashley, and Scelsi can hold its head up with the best. But while bad 17th-century music is merely dull and bad 19th-century music is tediously grandiose, the late 20th century's bad music was pervasively ugly, pretentious, and meaningless, yet backed up by a technical apparatus that justified it and even earned it prestigious awards. Twelve-tone technique—the South Sea Bubble of music history, to which hundreds and perhaps thousands of well-intended composers sacrificed their careers like lemmings, and all for nothing—brought music to the lowest point in the history of mankind. Twelve-tone music is now dead, everyone grudgingly admits, yet its pitch-set-manipulating habits survive in far-flung corners of our musical technique like residual viruses.

The effect of the rolling over of the Christian-historical odometer is purely psychological, but nevertheless potent: postmodern 21st-century music has been around for years, and the last argument for denying its existence has just collapsed. Treating "20th-century" and "modernist" as synonymous was a critical ploy for keeping modernism alive and current-seeming long after the aesthetic had begun to erode in the 1970s. Attendant to that ploy, the Uptown critics have pounced on every young composer, no matter how mediocre, who promised to extend the lease on modernism a few more years; John Zorn, Tan Dun, and Aaron Kernis all benefited from that psychology, which now devolves on Britain's young Thomas Ades, whose music is hailed as "serious" for being merely confused. While early modernism was an honest blow struck for freedom of expression, late modernism deteriorated into a web of pretensions and syllogisms, an insider's game of careerist one-upmanship.

At the start of this new, still-promising century, let us reiterate some eternal musical truths that the 20th century lost sight of:

There is nothing wrong with simplicity. It is easier to write complicated music than simple music; Beethoven's sketchbooks show how hard he struggled to achieve simplicity. It occasionally happens that profound music is difficult to understand, but it does not follow from this that music that is difficult to understand is therefore profound. Most difficult-to-understand music is simply unclear. The value of music is not proportional to the quantity or intricacy of its technical apparatus. Like many great composers throughout the ages, Mozart believed in an "artless art" in which the effort of composing is hidden beneath an effortless surface; this is as it should be. The audience wants to be delighted, inspired, entertained, not reassured that the composer is highly educated and worked hard. There is nothing wrong with occasionally writing an ostentatiously technical piece for the delectation of one's colleagues, but to do nothing but that is to pretend that composers have no obligation to society, and by extension that neither do doctors, politicians, generals, or any other profession. A piece of music is not good just because it is popular, nor is it bad just because it is popular. The music profession has many incentives to bestow fame and honor on certain of its members; the quality of their music is only one of those incentives and never an essential one.

Let's keep these truths in mind and see if we can create a 21st century less burdened by boring, ugly, pretentious music than the 20th was.

aesthetics

let x = x

minimalism versus serialism

FEBRUARY 24, 1987

Donal Henahan of the *Times* once wrote that, for the listener, the advent of minimalism after two decades of serialism was like asking for a little dessert after a heavy meal and getting a pie in the face. It was a typically unsympathetic comment, but it did obliquely recognize an aspect of new music that has gone virtually without comment: that minimalism and serialism are but opposite sides of the same coin, as notable for their similarities as for their differences. One can imagine some 22nd-century musicologist lumping them together as part of the same phenomenon, one that I currently call "the objectivist mindset."

Consider the seminal works of each movement: Boulez's *Structures* and Reich's early tape loop and process pieces. Both had as their raison d'être the desire to remove human personality from the creation of music, to allow mathematics in one case and nature in the other (as though there were any difference) to speak for themselves without the ego's intervention. Both stemmed, after a long history, from the West's newfound distrust of subjectivity, which in late-19th-century music had reached an excess still unpalatable to many musicians today.

In tracing this argument to the more recent past, I will be accused of oversimplification. Every 12-tone composer in America will insist that subjectivity plays a large part in his or her music, while the minimalists will claim that the initial choice of their simple materials is their own arena of subjectivity. But the fact is, regardless of such unavoidable personal touches (for complete objectivity, as Boulez and Robbe-Grillet realized, is an asymptotic impossibility), the single intuitive choice between one note and another is presently considered suspect. Most composers feel at ease when they can point to a structure that justifies the notes, and will at least appeal to perceptual or aesthetic theory when logic fails them. Heaven forbid a "professional" composer should be caught explaining a particular passage as an expression of some instinctive, emotional, or—even worse—spiritual feeling. Once common, that practice is now smugly derided in the music journals.

What we do have today (omitting for now what Morton Feldman refers to as "the jokers in the deck") are two schools of objectivists: those who feel that a piece of music's objective structure should be hidden from the ear of the average listener, and those who believe in exposing it honestly. It's likely that such a distinction will someday seem as inessential as the stylistic differences between Brahms and Wagner, or between the neoclassicism of Schoenberg and Stravinsky, do now.

Undoubtedly our musical situation is fragmented. But the overriding duality that pertains is not minimalism vs. serialism, but minimalism/serialism vs. X, with many of the more thoughtful composers trying to figure out what X is. It has something to do with intuition, with the choice of a note or rhythm simply because one likes it, or has something emotional or spiritual to express; it has to do with the transcendence of *technique,* which from our habitual science-worship Americans presently overvalue. The challenge is to rescue subjectivity from bad faith, to learn to rely once again on taste, feeling, inspiration, and the right brain.

Please note, I make no value judgments. It's not that the subjectivity of X is any more desirable per se than the present objectivity. In the dialectic of human imagination, subjectivity and objectivity imply each other, and each is unthinkable without its opposite. The great numerical structures of 14th- and 15th-century music came closer to God, or god, in their way than anything has since. But the present picture is distorted and out of balance, as much so as the subjective hysteria of the early 1900s. The toll this overemphasis takes on the human spirit is counted in the number of young composers who learn early to squelch their musical impulses and compose according to academically approved patterns.

So I get excited when I hear a composer begin to escape the Scylla and Charybdis of minimalism/serialism and redefine X. Elodie Lauten approaches X when she pushes the minimalist style towards a sense of liquid, atmospheric improvisation. John Adams looks for X in a sort of old-fashioned orchestral rhetoric. George Perle finds it by liquidating his technique until it disappears in the whimsicality of his imagination. Harold Budd has reduced minimalism to so few notes that nothing is left but the X that was in it to begin with. Ben Johnston has tapped the X in Southern hymnody. Perhaps the one major figure who's pursued X most aggressively is Frederick Rzewski, whose recent music, I'm convinced, is stranger and freer than anybody's realized. Then, of course, the ultimate joker in the deck is Feldman himself, whose music has never been anything but X, X, X.

But the more immediate reality, the one that critics, teachers, and young composers have to wrestle with, is a petty, bitter, political fight between the structure-hiders and the structure-revealers, Uptown and Downtown, those whose objectivity requires 12 pitches vs. those who can do the job with five or seven. Like the U.S. and the USSR, we argue scholastic points of doctrine, with no awareness of our own relativity, no hint that a contrasting way of life is offered by the Third World, the American Indian, the intuition. Also as with those Tweedledum and Tweedledee superstates, the real issue is power: the fact that the structure hiders still have a near monopoly on the academic job, the big funding, the more glamorous venue, which creates defensiveness on one side and resentment on the other. Even Cage, for all his anarchic freedom, uses the most objective musical methods possible, and if there is a difference between Cage and Babbitt, it's that Cage writes better English. Criticizing Cage, Earle Brown once pointed out that the purpose in writing music is to charm the ego, not merely to bypass it. Our musical situation, I submit, is not nearly as fragmented as we think; but it will require that revolution in thought before we learn to see it without blinders.

a tale of two sohos

plato/aristotle

JANUARY 26, 1988

Music history, if I may alter Whitehead's phrase, is a series of footnotes to not only Plato, but Aristotle. I was reminded of this, oddly enough, by John Zorn's liner notes to *Spillane* (Nonesuch).

Plato insisted that art reflect reality with absolute accuracy, and he banned painters from the Republic because they didn't know enough about carpentry to paint a bed. By contrast, Aristotle's *Poetics* insisted on a beginning, middle, and end for each work of art, and allowed artists to depart from Truth for the sake of a more aesthetically pleasing form. That raised the banner of artistic license, and the ensuing fight has never ceased. Every time an Aristotelian movement pushes music toward concessions for the sake of intelligibility, a Platonic jolt of reality bursts onto the scene and demands satisfaction. When Schumann's aestheticism softened the edges of classical form, Wagner invented atonality in an attempt to capture a truer psychological reality.

Zorn's *Spillane*, in both its sounds and liner notes, is the latest jolt. In this case, it represents a hectic, urban, computer-age reality, since "speed is taking over the world. Look at the kids growing up with computers and video games, which are ten times faster than the pinball machines we used to play." It's a reality perfectly reflected in the music, which lurches among sound worlds like the soundtrack to an action movie we can't see. As Zorn notes, "My works often move from one block to another such that the average person can hear no development whatsoever. But I always have a unifying concept that ties all the sections together." It's nice to have that assurance, but one tenet of today's realism is that order doesn't emerge from the music any more than it does from life; one has to *read it in,* or else submit to the fact that it has none.

Against this superrealism the present scene throws postminimalism. Minimalism has its origins in the explicit process, a desire to have the listener follow every move. Postminimalism deals with reality too, of course, but it arranges it, if not in Aristotle's beginning, middle, and end, in an order that can be followed; it does so not only for the sake of pleasing form, but in order to communicate truths that the composer has perceived. It acts as a filter for experience: understand this little bit, then this, then this, and perhaps afterward you'll have a better insight into reality. After all, some things about being human don't change, video games notwithstanding.

But what is reality? (I'll answer this question in a future column.) Nelson Goodman muddied things by pointing out that our reality depends to a great extent on how we're used to seeing it depicted. "That a picture looks like nature," he wrote in *Languages of Art,* "often means only that it looks like the way nature is usually painted." In ordering reality, the minimalists do not falsify it, since "there is no such thing as *the* way the world is." Rather, they allow music to communicate insights implicit to a particular reality. The superrealists, on the other hand, may be indulging a self-fulfilling prophecy: the more they portray the world as chaotic and formless, the more chaotic the world becomes. There is no such thing as ontologically neutral art. The artist cannot escape responsibility: no matter how innocently he "paints what he sees," he is toying with our perceptions.

But given that he's toying, should he do so purposefully or let it happen unconsciously? Have the postminimalists, in carefully ordering our perceptions, emasculated the richness of life? Given human psychology, what are the ethics involved? The *Goldberg Variations* are the epitome of order;

did they help make Bach's era more orderly, or did they only provide a comforting (read: bourgeois) *illusion* of orderliness, one that let the reigning powers squelch an embarrassing reality? Marxist aesthetics have made us forever suspicious of soothing sounds in a troubled society. It's a too-easy transition from "logical" and "entertaining" to "mindlessly relaxing," and no one feels queasier about the proximity of New Age music than the postminimalists, some of whom have taken to greater dissonance in an effort to dissociate themselves.

Should music explain itself, entertain, and provide insights into life, or should it throw the world at us and leave us to our own devices? I've found myself on both sides. If Plato and Aristotle couldn't settle the matter, I doubt that Zorn and Daniel Goode (one of the best new tonal composers) will come up with a more satisfying answer. But these are the battle lines I see being drawn for music of the 1990s; utopian versus superrealist, interpretation versus anti-interpretation, communication versus chaos, postminimalism versus what Europeans call "New York noise." (It's not solely a New York phenomenon, but only New Yorkers have taken it to Europe.)

There are two Downtowns now, as diametrically opposed as Uptown and Downtown were a dozen years ago: one side builds on the foundation laid by the first Soho school—Reich, Glass, Laurie Anderson, and Meredith Monk—the other scorns a "purified tonality" as insufficiently gritty to reflect life. Deep down, it's the old Brahms/Wagner debate that music seems unable to escape, both sides descended from Beethoven, music's original Dr. Jekyll. Zorn is staking out his claim as the latest Wagner. Anybody want to be Brahms?

a secret manifesto

fred lerdahl

JULY 26, 1988

A friend once called me with the exciting news that, for the first time, a philosopher had dared to assert that Wittgenstein was *wrong* about something. I have to call him back, because now, in one of those infinitesimal shifts that mark the glacial pace of academic thought, a university composer has suggested that Schoenberg, too, was wrong.

Under the thick title "Cognitive Constraints on Compositional Systems" (in *Generative Processes in Music,* edited by John A. Sloboda,

Clarendon Press, Oxford), Fred Lerdahl, composer and professor at the University of Michigan, Ann Arbor, has written what appears to be the first official complaint, in fluent academese, that serial music is, as he delicately puts it, "perceptually opaque." In other words, it's hard to listen to, and doesn't mean much to the listener. In 1981 Lerdahl worked with Pierre Boulez at IRCAM developing algorithms to compose music, and his argument stands on the insights gained from that experience. For decades, crackpots have written books condemning atonality as inferior to tonality, usually citing the sanctity of the overtone series (by which argument even minor keys shouldn't exist). But when a respected theorist/composer publishes a theoretical demonstration that Schoenberg miscalculated, that's news.

Pierre Boulez once called Schoenberg wrong, of course, but he meant the old man hadn't gone far enough. In his roundabout way, Lerdahl implies that he was on the wrong track to begin with. I'll try to break down the argument, for few readers are likely to shell out the stiff sticker price ($75) for the privilege of wading through this abstruse collection. Lerdahl begins with a work he obviously admires, Boulez's *Le Marteau sans maître*, but admits that even experienced listeners fail to "assign to it a detailed mental representation." That's a nicely precise way of saying the damn thing can't be remembered. Because its details have only a statistical quality, he argues, *Le Marteau* sounds *complicated*, but not *complex*; complexity means richness of structure *perceived* by the listener, even if only subconsciously. "The best music," he claims, "utilizes the full potential of our cognitive resources," and *Le Marteau*, in trying to use too much, doesn't use enough.

Like Boulez, Lerdahl dreams of a common musical language, a desire that, for many composers, the celebrated banner of "pluralism" has failed to stamp out. As Pound put it, artists who inherit a common style "don't have to start by reforming anything." Lerdahl distinguishes between natural compositional grammars—like the standard tonalities of folksongs, jazz, and jingles—and artificial ones, the latter unavoidable in a self-conscious society that splits musical activity into composing, performing, and listening. These days, he complains, nonserial composers either revert parasitically to earlier natural styles (the New Romanticism) or rely solely on ear and intuition. "But composing is too difficult for such a solution," he astutely notes; a significant level of musical complexity can't be reached by intuition alone (nontraditional improvisers take note). Large-scale complexity needs structure; midrange depth requires a compositional grammar. Scorning New Romanticists, Lerdahl insists that, if our compositional grammar is to be artificial and nonparasitic, it has to take into account the way people actually listen.

Lerdahl lists 17 constraints on possible musical languages. The musical surface must be separated into discrete events; enough repetition, parallelism, and symmetry must be present to allow the perception of hierarchies; enough regularity should be present to distinguish among stable sections and transitions, and so on. (I'm reminded of Twain's rules for the novel: "The personages in a tale shall be alive, except in the case of corpses, and the reader shall be able to tell the corpses from the others.") Then, in a reversal of Boulez's expansion of musical materials in *On Music Today*, Lerdahl sets *limiting* guidelines for pitch and rhythms that seem unnecessarily timid: octaves must be present in the tuning, they must be divided into equal parts to reduce memory load; triads turn out to be the best octave-dividers, and all irregular rhythms are bound to be perceptually reduced to twos and threes. He's sacrificing surface complexity for grammatical depth, a move that many microtonal and ethnic-influenced composers aren't likely to follow.

But the more important point is how Lerdahl uses these guidelines to criticize serial music. His basic argument is that most natural listening grammars are *elaborational*—filling out a path, say, from B through E to F-sharp with any of several similar contours. Language itself is elaborational. Twelve-tone music, however, is *permutational*—B, E, and F-sharp are systematically flipped into different orders—and since hardly any other human activity involves permutation, serial music is at its core nearly impossible to remember. Another powerful argument, equally applicable to stochastic music and the latest fractal geometry fad, is that serial music fails to hierarchically organize pitch space, so that the ear has no reference for measuring melodic skips and steps. Despite its constant use of high and low notes, most serial music is perceived within a vaguely moving middle. That's an elegant argument, and far more effective than the old we need triads-because-of-the-overtone series shtick.

So 12-tone music is hard to listen to, you're saying. Do tell. My Aunt Rita could have told 'em *that*, and no one's throwing her an honorary doctorate. True, but I'm not going to criticize the academics for sticking to their blowguns. We have enough musicians who float in the breeze of public opinion. Their crime is ignoring evidence, not only the evidence of their ears, but the info they could have cadged from other disciplines. Where Lerdahl finally runs aground is in his evaluative assumptions, for this is a manifesto cleverly disguised as a research paper (the only way a manifesto can survive in 1980s academic America). He insists that his observations have no bearing on the artistic quality of particular serial pieces; they obviously do, but hey, Lerdahl wants to keep working. In closing, though, he poses a rhetorical question: "If a piece cannot be understood, how can it be good? Most would agree that comprehensibility is a necessary if not sufficient condition for value."

Boy, there's the rub. Who told the academy that music must be understood to be enjoyed, and on whose authority did they elevate that half-truth to scripture? Find me a mass by Dufay or Ockeghem that lends itself to "detailed mental representation" (and remember that Ockeghem was called "cerebral" by the square-rhythmed 19th century). Comprehensibility was not a high priority in the Middle Ages. That music, like much ethnic art and post-Cage music, was written not to be picked apart by the analytical left brain, but to "quiet the mind, rendering it susceptible to divine influences" (a definition Cage found in both medieval and Indian treatises). Lerdahl relates everything back to *cognition,* but cognition is only one aspect of musical experience, and not always an essential one. Many of us are attracted to certain music *because* it resists cognition, shuts up the left brain, and lets us revel in irreducible terms. Music that makes its logic explicit to the ear is a relatively short-lived aberration in music's history, one nascent in the 16th-century madrigal, full-fledged in Haydn, ill in Scriabin, and nearly dead by 1950.

Still, Lerdahl's theory is flexible enough to support more nonrationalist music than most. His broad definition of comprehensibility as the hierarchical proportioning of pitch and rhythm includes simply being aware of movement along a scale, accent within a meter. Ockeghem's music fights *structural* comprehension, but in terms of melodic and metrical *motion* it's perfectly graspable—as is, indeed, the atonal music of Ruggles, Dallapiccola, Wolpe, and a few others. Perceptually meaningful use of pitch space is exactly what separates George Perle's music from the serialists, and the few great atonal composers have always made short work of serialism's flaws.

More importantly, Lerdahl's relativism makes sense in context. His constraints are based on the way tonal music is perceived (which is psychologically fundamental according to Lerdahl's earlier book with R. Jackendoff, *A Generative Theory of Tonal Music*), and Lerdahl assumes that atonal music aspires to the same *type* of listening that tonal music does; he assumes, in a way, what he wants to prove. To the extent that his generalizations apply to early serial, Cage-influenced, and pretonal music, he's wrong, but he's right insofar as the 12-tone language was originally intended to be analogous to tonality. (Schoenberg set up "tonic" and "dominant" transpositions of the 12-tone row, though no one's ever heard them that way.) *Le Marteau,* coming from a similar intellectual milieu to *Waiting for Godot*'s, is an exception; Boulez didn't *want* listeners to form a mental representation of *Le Marteau,* he wanted to create something outside the bounds of prediction and memory, without past or future. Lerdahl knows that, but times have changed. Memorability is now a positive value with composers as well as listeners.

There's a large body of music today, however, that is neither comprehensible nor "mind-quieting" music that indulges in conventionally expressive contrasts, but whose expressed content seems arbitrary. *That's* the repertoire that has not yet found a convincing apologist, and that's where Lerdahl's critique is powerfully effective. The American serialists have, in essence, taken Boulez's explosive, referentless language and tried to create sonata forms with it, with ludicrous results. This music, never held to account aesthetically, gets discussed in only two ways: (1) analyzed by colleagues and younger composers with charts and diagrams and a nodding admission that "these structures may not be consciously audible," or (2) vaguely praised by critics intimidated by its intellectual reputation. (As you glance through the *Times* and *New Yorker,* note how many academic composers have built a reputation on critical insecurity.) Lerdahl's article, limited as it is, at least calls for a reexamination of American atonal music's premises, to see where it diverges from auditory perception, and to find out why such a large body of music can be so horribly unsatisfying.

I could wish that Lerdahl had absorbed enough of the European mindset to concede that music need not always be the fruit of rationalism; that art is ultimately a mystery, and in the century of Sartre, we need not compose according to Hume. But he's the first theorist to point out, with IRCAM-granted authority, that much contemporary music is racked over a desperate incongruity of ends and means, that entire schools of composition are producing musical effects unrelated to what they intend. Two thousand newspaper critics could say the same thing, and it would have no impact whatever; only blows struck from inside the walls hit their target. And, since Lerdahl's constraints support a language isomorphic to tonality (if not actually tonal), the writing of tonal music may soon lose the stigma it's carried in the university for almost three decades. It's too soon to claim that Lerdahl's leading a revolution in the musical academy parallel to that of Richard Rorty in philosophy. But he's started a line of questioning that can only improve our musical health, and it's worth a cheer.

the modernist dance

war in the brain

JULY 18, 1989

Thy beauty, if it lack the fire
Which drives me mad with sweet desire,
What boots it?

RALPH WALDO EMERSON

To many . . . criticism must seem like an attempt to tattoo soap bubbles.

JOHN MASON BROWN

The Fibonacci series is the series of numbers in which each is the sum of the two before it: 1, 1, 2, 3, 5, 8, 13, 21, and so on. As the numbers increase, each pair nears the Golden Ratio, a proportion found in plant growth patterns and considered artistically pleasing since ancient times. Much of Béla Bartók's later music is patterned around the series, from the placement of a movement's climax within its total length to the division of rhythmic motives as 5 plus 3, even 3 plus 2. So consistent a system couldn't have happened by accident; it was a left-brain logical control Bartók placed on his music in order to free him from the square, Germanic rhythmic conventions that preceded him. Don't think of Bartók as a pointy-headed note-counter, do you? That's because he dissolved the system into voluptuous waves of melody, a compelling fusion of intellect and emotion.

Bartók's Fibonacci two-step epitomizes the modernist dance: deploy a technique from the logical, analytical, verbal left brain to find new musical territory; then induce the intuitive, holistic, spatial right brain to landscape that territory in musical terms. Until recently, logic was the "progressive" element in avant-garde music, the means of conceptual advance. Intuition was the "conservative" element, the means of turning logic into breathing, "feelable" music. The stuff we call academic is a one-foot dance: composers became so enamored of the first step that they forgot to take the second. You could say that modernism started dying when it realized that if you lead every step with your left, you eventually hit a wall. Consequently, our culture is gradually reversing its polarity: right brain is hip.

It's no accident that classical music is the left brain among Western traditions. The tendency's been strongest since the arrival of the symphony and its co-invention, the admission-charged public concert. At that point, composers began to assume that you weren't going to listen to music while swigging Rolling Rock and sticking your nose in your lover's ear; you're going to sit there, upright, in a reasonably uncomfortable chair, with your limbs still and your trap shut. It's a godawful way to listen to music. *Unless*—unless unless unless—the composer is willing to keep the left brain occupied as *well* as the right, i.e., tell a "story" via the music's logic (or lyrics). The left is the hemisphere that tracks time, and if you're not going to let it gab with pals or grab some nookie, you'd better entertain it or it's going to start looking at its watch.

In other words, there's a link between music's left brain and the concert hall. If you're making music to dance, drink, undergo root canal, or meditate to, different conditions apply.

No other aspect of listening is as subjective as hemisphere orientation. To *comprehend* the simplest Mozart sonata movement, you've got to have a little left-brain development (sure, you can enjoy it as just pretty sounds, but you're missing something). Considerably more left-brain sophistication is needed to catch the drift of Schoenberg's First Quartet, and to follow most American serial music you need a left lobe that looks like those aliens with huge foreheads on *The Twilight Zone*. This music takes pride in the way it's extended to the *n*th degree a musical logic (originally intuitive) abstracted from classical voice-leading. Some of that music is understandable only on paper, not in performance, though groups like Speculum Musicae keep it viable by playing it with an élan that compensates for its dearth of inherent energy.

More recently we've heard the antipodal rebellion, a type of free improvisation that eschews whatever stinks of the left brain: structure, process, repetition, pattern, form. This music takes pride in leaving the left brain to float without moorings, in pushing the listener into a timeless, right-brain mode. It's daring; people who want aural landmarks to figure out what the performers are trying to do, so the mythology goes, are timid, afraid to abandon themselves. A recent improv record has this classic right-brain slogan emblazoned across its cover: "Music begins when definitions are silenced." In the other camp, a popular left-think saying goes: "Structure is the most expressive part of music." Which statement you feel closer to says something deep about what you want out of music. (If "Boogie till you puke" was your choice, you're so far right that you're on the wrong page.)

Left- and right-brain listening leads to polarized criticism, too. The right-brain pronouncement par excellence is "It don't mean a thing if it ain't got that swing." A quicker gloss on the Emerson quotation above, it's led jazz critics into endless argument about what has "that swing" and what doesn't because, as a right-brain quality, "that swing" isn't available to measurement or definition. (Wittgenstein, who said, "What we cannot speak about we must pass over in silence," would have made a lousy jazz critic.) I used to think most jazzers were curiously inarticulate, until it dawned on me that verbalizable (left-brain) concepts in jazz are few, trivial, and in the background, while jazz's network of right-brain ideas (Roscoe Mitchell's "Nonaah," for instance) can only be picked up by listening, not by talking.

Contrariwise, it can be difficult to convince jazzers and rockers that classical musicians really like listening for structure, form, and process. The left-brain notions I sometimes cover in this column (this is, after all, a leftist newspaper) have occasionally incited indignant letters from right-brainy musicians who are offended that I would tattoo soap bubbles, try to pitch concepts and categories on sacred, nonverbal ground. But writing about music's left-brain logic can be exciting because it's susceptible to precise discourse; to a surprising extent, words capture and clarify it. To refer to ineffable qualities, language must use metaphor, and metaphors assume the audience's familiarity with what's being referred to. Right-crit has difficulty preaching to the unconverted.

Well, in this century we've explored both extremes, and the interesting things we've learned are (1) how easily the listening process can be manipulated and (2) how few people are willing to let you manipulate it. Suppress your left brain and you can listen to your friend's description of her landlord problems as a string of random sounds. Suppress your right and you can listen to traffic noises as though each were a comment on the one before it. Thousands of new music fans have become "virtuoso listeners," able at the drop of a cymbal to jettison any set of expectations you can isolate. It's called progress. The problem with *other* people is that they're conditioned by the vernacular music they hear on commercials and in the grocery store, which appeals, on however primitive a level, to their entire heads. The most naive music we know has lyrics, repetitions, and song forms for the left brain to latch onto, and smooth, natural-sounding melodies and harmonies to soothe the right. That saccharine rendition of "Girl from Ipanema" that makes you want to retch has more intuition than Babbitt's Piano Concerto, and more structure than some downtown improvs.

Avid music lovers, God bless 'em, develop their heads far past the naive level, classical fans perhaps more on the left (if they're into form and not just tone quality), jazz fans on the right (unless they delight in analyzing Thelonious Monk's harmonies). That's why "serious" music can go further in one direction or the other (or both) than the glop you hear while standing in frozen foods. But when music goes *less* far in one direction than naive music does, your average listener misses something. Even diehard jazz fans start saying "that ain't jazz" when you subtract the left-brain elements, the meter, the song forms, the harmonic bass; they think it's lost "that swing," but what it's really lost is the grid against which swing is perceived. The swing is still there—critics hear it—but it has no friction to make it spark. Likewise, a sterile 12-tone construction sounds *unlogical* because it contains no natural line to play its intricate structure off of. This is why so much free improv sounds "too intellectual" and why so much serial music sounds made up. It's hard to perceive either logic or intuition without the other as background.

Jonathan Kramer's book *The Time of Music* does a great job of demonstrating how music creates dissonance between right- and left-brain perception. For instance, the right brain recognizes the gestalt of a musical gesture as having a beginning, ending, or transitional character, but the left brain keeps track of where a gesture occurs in a piece. When a composer *opens* a piece with a *closing* gesture (as happens in Haydn's String Quartet Op. 50 No. 1, his Symphony No. 100, and Beethoven's Quartet Op. 135), he creates a dissonance between hemispherical meanings that makes you wonder what's going to happen. (To read Kramer, you'd think Haydn was one of the wildest experimentalists ever. And he was.) Closer to home, listen to Ornette Coleman's *Free Jazz:* the centripetal force of its subtle background structure enlivens the profusion of soaring lines. Listen to Boulez's *Pli selon pli:* the panache, the sonorous ferocity make the calculated form sound impassioned.

Kramer's book isn't the only evidence of a slowly shifting panorama. The total left-brain music I've described doesn't really exist now except at Elliott Carter birthday bashes; people don't write that crap anymore, though many composers still don't listen to their music enough. The total right-brain stuff has been considered unutterably hip these last few years, but Anthony Coleman, John Zorn, Patrick Brennan, and plenty of others have shown they're acutely aware of the limitations on that end. We've worked hard on the left foot, we're practicing the right, and lots of composers are trying to put them together again. In the 1990s, if we get the hang of it, music is going to dance, sing, leap, break hearts, and clap its hands with its right brain, while, with its left, it shouts insights of incredible, life-changing significance. Either that, or the concert-hall ritual will be tossed in history's dumpster.

it's only as good as it sounds

richard rorty

FEBRUARY 6, 1990

Suppose for a moment that liberalism is true. This being the *Village Voice*, we assume that every week, but just this time let's grab the idea and trail it to its lair in the modest realm of music criticism. In the first place, *true* doesn't mean "corresponding to reality": it means "suppose that liberalism is for us an ultimate value, something to which we're determined to cling." Because to believe that there *is* some "essential reality" to which sentences could correspond, some "nature of things" we ultimately have to conform to, to assume that Truth is *found* rather than *created* is by definition a conservative notion. By way of example, to argue that heterosexuality is natural is conservative, to argue that sexuality is whatever we make it is liberal.

This is the Wittgensteinian premise of Richard Rorty's new book *Contingency, Irony, and Solidarity* (Cambridge University Press): that truth is a property of language, not a quality found in the world. I don't want to get lost in the philosophical implications of Rorty's theses, and I'm not concerned with defending them—that's an academic job. I want to fire Rorty's ideas into a few music camps and see them scatter. Music, too, has its conservative and liberal parallels.

The conservatives are easy to spot, for they rail against music that turns its back on a sacred pattern. The ultraconservatives are the Schenkerian theorists, who assert that every (good) piece of music has underneath it a descending scale segment *(Urlinie)* expressed by the keys it moves through. (The more hip Schenkerites bend over backward finding *Urlinies* in Thelonious Monk's music so they won't feel guilty listening to him.) It's an idealist, essentialist conservatism, intended to apply to music of all eras. Boulez's famous 1955 pronouncement—that every composer who doesn't realize the inevitability of the 12-tone language is "useless"—applied only to a certain point in music's development. That's a historicist conservatism.

In this century, we've wrested music away from its culturally agreed-upon foundation. In self-justification, liberals have asked over and over, what kind of music *should* we write? The inquiry has taken two directions, one inward, one outward. The inward path is that of John Cage, La Monte Young, and the serialists, who framed the question, How do we find music's fundamental essence? Cage reduced sounds to the random operations of nature, Young to overtones of a basic hum, serialism to algorithms. The outward path is that of Charles Ives, John Alden Carpenter, the Italian futurists, and John Zorn. Their question is: what kind of music reflects the world we live in? Ives depicted distant Connecticut hills and marching bands out of sync, Carpenter skyscrapers and the hustle and bustle of 1920s Chicago, Zorn the speed of video games and the discontinuity of TV channel-switching. Each follows the same impulse, modernism's catch-up-with-the-world thesis. The inward path imagines an essentialist mandate, the outward path a historicist one.

But the truth is, either mandate requires a little self-deception, a thumb on the scale. There's no reason music *should* reflect the world. If a chaotic world needs chaotic music (Downtown neoexpressionism's article of faith), the terrifying 14th century wouldn't have produced the orderly isorhythmic motet. One might easily argue, citing Jung, that music is *compensatory*. It could act as society's *shadow*, providing an outlet for what is denied, ignored, repressed. (Sometimes that's my capsule definition of the music I like.) Since I don't believe we live in an unusually chaotic period, my theory about neoexpressionism is that it provides an illusion of freedom, chaos, heroic survival, in a world that, when you really look at it, seems even more rigidly controlled by corporate machinations.

The inward path requires brainwashing because music reduced to its essence is boring. What fascinates about Cage's and Young's music is not how natural it sounds (how many people do you think find Cage's aleatory works or a five-hour piano etude "natural"?), but, beneath the pose of "getting back to nature," how weird it makes nature seem. Despite their aims, both Cage and Young *interpret* reality. Asking which comes closer is like asking which is the *real* table, the one I pound my fist on, or the physicist's field of swirling molecules? The discrepancy abandons us to Stravinsky's slogan, "All art is artificial."

And that slogan leaves us without the mandates that have fueled most 20th-century revolutions. Cage, Young, Boulez turn out to be what Rorty says Nietzsche and Heidegger are, rungs on the ladder we climbed to find ourselves, but which must now be thrown away. Theories, systems, and beliefs about the world may add bonus points to good music, but they can't make it any better than it sounds. Audiences have known that for ages. They never bought any of those theories for why music "should" be written this way or that, because, unlike composers and theorists, they never confused music with science. (Science is no "accurate" world picture either, as Rorty notes, but that's somebody else's funeral.) Audiences don't want a photo of the world; they don't care what the "essence" of music is. They want to hear something that sounds good and/or makes them feel good, keeping in mind that that can vary from pretty chords to a well-constructed fugue.

That's how Downtown music got started—minimalism's sound was better than its theory. But metaphysics, to use Rorty's term for the "truth is discovered" idea, creeps back in devious ways. No one spouts manifestos anymore because their inherent conservatism has become almost transparent, but unspoken mandates reassert the composer's obligation to theory and rob her of her subjectivity. According to one social theory, "art music" *must* incorporate ethnic musics (i.e., reflect New York). By analogy with political liberalism, music *must* synthesize classical music and jazz. The most advanced technology *must* be used because it's there. Improvisation is "better" than other music because it is more "risk-taking," so composers of good notated music throw in improv sections the way neoclassicals used to flirt with 12-tone rows—just in case. A mandate is a macho thing. It lets you claim that your music is more important than someone else's even though it doesn't sound as attractive.

Much of what Rorty has to say about the way vocabularies succeed each other could be applied to music. His bugbear, that of recent philosophy, is the impossibility of synthesizing European with analytical thought: the two areas of discourse don't assume the same distinctions, they don't play in the same ballpark. That's all Carnap proved when he pretended to set up truth criteria for Heidegger's statement "The Nothing nothings," though he thought he was destroying existentialism. For Rorty, to *synthesize* the two vocabularies would imply that they are both partial views of a deeper truth, when in reality they are simply language games with different rules. He wants to replace those vocabularies with one of his own in which they can both be discussed, not because his vocabulary is *truer,* but simply because it avoids the knots the others are tied up in. A new vocabulary is no more than (he borrows the term from philosopher of science Mary Hesse) a "metaphoric redescription."

In asides, he takes the principle outside philosophy. "Revolutionary achievements in the arts," he writes, ". . . typically occur when somebody realizes that two or more of our vocabularies are interfering with each other, and proceeds to invent a new vocabulary to replace both." Any downtown musician immediately thinks of the conflict faced by those trained in both classical music and jazz. For more than 30 years, ever since the old "Third Stream" experiments, hundreds of composers have tried to synthesize those two vocabularies with only isolated successes. Both involve rules, and the rules conflict: expressively individual jazz licks poked into a cold, classical structure generally come off as nonsensically as Carnap's parsing of Heidegger.

In Rorty's model, the failure may stem from a metaphysical conviction that both classical music and jazz have discovered innate musical "truths," that "in essence" they have something in common, therefore a common denominator is possible, a broad enough vocabulary could encompass both. To assert that (and I'm not denying it, I'm only trying to show that it doesn't follow from a liberal position) is to deny the createdness and contextuality of classical music's and jazz's truths, the fact that both developed rules in response to particular and different performance situations. In other words, they aren't *natural*. They're language games we created, and fusing them can be like crossing baseball with Monopoly. According to Rorty's model, a third vocabulary will eventually emerge, but it will have to be a true third stream, a vocabulary that will replace them without pretending to synthesize them.

For his own part, Rorty is trying to avoid the trap of claiming that his vocabulary is "truer" or more fundamental than the existentialist and analytic vocabularies he's bridging. Instead, he tries to make his vocabulary more appealing, more suited to what people want a philosophical vocabulary to do right now. If he's "lucky," as he puts it, a younger generation of philosophers will find their thoughts so well expressed in his vocabulary that they'll adopt it as their own. The same goes for a new artistic vocabulary. "We call something 'fantasy' rather than 'poetry' or 'philosophy,'" he claims, "when it revolves around metaphors which do not catch on with other people: that is, around ways of speaking or acting which the rest of us cannot find a use for. . . . Conversely, when some private obsession produces a metaphor which we *can* find a use for, we speak of genius rather than of eccentricity or perversity. . . . It is the difference between idiosyncrasies which just happen to catch on with other people."

Rorty doesn't argue for pluralism in the sense that musicians often use the word. He quotes Joseph Schumpeter—"To realise the *relative* validity of one's convictions and yet stand for them unflinchingly, is what distinguishes a civilised man from a barbarian" (emphasis mine). He knows that internal conviction, the "Here I stand, I can do no other" attitude, is as essential to making compelling art as it is to writing persuasive philosophy. The wishy-washy inclusionism of much "world music" will find no theoretical basis here. What could get a shot in the arm is the mandate-free attitude so central to, if sometimes forgotten by, Downtown music. Liberal musicians don't evoke imperatives. They justify the music they make by saying, "I like it, this is important to me. This says something I want to say. I like the way this sounds. This is the music I wanted to hear. It's my obsession. I've polished and defined it as much as I could, and I hope you'll resonate with it." To claim more than that is conservative.

noises of fate

you don't need a sampler to recontextualize

JULY 24, 1990

Recontextualization.

My editor discourages me from using words that big in the first half of a column, but don't turn the page yet. It's only a newspaper article.

Musically, recontextualization simply means that you hear something, and then later you hear it again, and the two experiences are not the same. Either it's changed, what's around it has changed, or you've changed. There's always a change, because the sheer fact of having heard it before alters your perception. "I love you" has a different force the second time. People who find repetition inherently uninteresting have blocked out a vital aspect of life.

Recontextualization became a Thing in Europe in the '60s. Stockhausen's Klavierstück XI (1956) contains 19 segments of music, playable and repeatable in any order. With each repetition of a segment, the tempo and dynamics are supposed to change depending on what came before. You hear what you heard a few moments ago, only now it's, say, slower and louder. But Stockhausen, worshipping at the 12-tone altar, miscalculated. Nobody recognizes those segments when they come back.

Collage was the next step. Recontextualization *within* a piece of music wasn't coming off, but you could make it happen to things *outside* the piece. The big success was Berio's *Sinfonia,* which buried a movement from the Mahler Second in extraneous material. Pousseur included Schubert lieder and long passages from *Tristan* in his partly aleatory opera *Votre Faust.* This was long before quotation became a jazz fad. In the '60s, anticipating Mike Bidlo, who now makes his living faking Picassos, composer Paul Ignace submitted Berlioz's *Symphonie Fantastique* to an orchestra and had it performed under his own name (entirely legally, since the copyright had expired) as *Symphonie Fantastique No. 2. That's* recontextualization.

The sampler has made recontextualization a whole new ball game. Mere stealing is too easy. The sampler is to collage what the camera was to painting. *Again,* realism has become outdated. Now people *interpret* sounds from the real world to make a point. Linda Fisher quotes cartoons and turns them into dark symptoms of psychosis. John Oswald takes *Le Sacre du Printemps* apart (digital) bit by bit and reconstructs it as a stylized state of strangely familiar angst. Carl Stone takes a speck of

Schubert so small we can't recognize it and magnifies it until we hear it for the first time.

You don't need a sampler to recontextualize. In *Travelogue,* Joshua Fried has a singer sing back "Surfin' U.S.A." as she hears it on tape. You don't know what she's hearing. You only hear the way she recontextualizes it under the frantic discipline of the performance situation.

But when recontextualization takes place *within* a piece, we call it form.

Take sonata form. Beethoven works his first theme into a crisis, takes it apart motive by motive, has an "aha!" of insight, then puts it back together in the recapitulation. A multi-movement work is a miniseries that attacks the problem in stages. Like the *Hammerklavier* Sonata: B-flat runs up against B-natural over and over in every movement, and each movement contributes to a solution. The main theme at the end of a movement is supposed to sound purer, more consonant, more triumphant than it did at the beginning. Lead into gold.

The sampler: the machine that replaced sonata form.

Why does Beethoven bring the theme back? Because that's life. Recontextualization = karma. You tend to get involved with married, inappropriate, or unavailable men or women. You alienate people close to you, and always think it's their fault. Or you're the cranky kid who grows up to be a critic. By age 30, everyone can find recurring patterns in their life too consistent for coincidence. You have a life crisis, a few years later you have it again. Is it the same this time, or different?

Recontextualization is the background against which fate becomes visible.

The Jungian line is, if you're dealing with your life creatively, it'll be different. If you project it onto other people—"I didn't bring that on myself" or "I'm just the victim"—you won't see how your karma works, and it'll come back in the same form until you understand. Lead turns into gold in stages.

Sonata form works on its karma. Collage and strict minimalism don't; they repeat recognizable musical objects but without reinterpreting them. Serialism reinterpreted, but its musical objects weren't recognizable when repeated.

Recontextualization isn't the only thread that ties Western, post-Renaissance music together, but it's the thread that, so to speak, distinguishes Western music. Western music depicts the life of the conscious ego. As Beethoven pointed out, Western music goes somewhere, because the ego develops and changes. Other cultures have attuned their music to a broader concept, the Self. "The Self," as Robert Ashley sang it, "the one and only Self is ageless / Without age and without aging." Eastern music often exists without moving far from center. Ditto for a lot of avant-garde music.

Music relinquished form in the face of the fact that Asian and African musics don't use form in the sense that Europeans have. Form became European music's fetish, and got in the way of hearing sounds. But the recent return to form is enlightened. In fact, that's the ultimate recontextualization, the meaning of "classical music" in the '90s. We can use form now with a recognition of its contingency. It's a part of Western inheritance that some of us missed listening for, because we connect music with the ego. And now, instead of applying form with unconscious ethnocentrism, we can use it consciously—conscious that we don't need it, that we could do something else. Western music spent its time on the analyst's couch, and the breakthrough came. Music's ego connected with its Self.

The concept of form has itself been recontextualized.

(Those ivy-covered academics who never acknowledged the temporary necessity of minimalism, of drone music, of nonform: they missed the breakthrough, and still use form in a deaf, archaic manner.)

So what's wrong with sonata form now? Its optimism: it *means* hypothesis, experimentation, and conclusion. No matter how conscious we become about our motivations, problems are never really solved, they just come back on higher levels. Bruckner's symphonies draw to a close, but today our music simply stops. From exhaustion. How many lifetimes on one problem? Living after Freud, we can't trust the final cadence. It rings false to our psychology.

Very few Americans can even *hear* Beethoven's music in such a way as to grasp what Beethoven *meant*. We don't realize that we disagree with what Beethoven is saying. Young people with no upper-class pretensions turn off instinctively. Our official classical music culture is largely a sham.

The good young composers know that. That's why they invent new forms of recontextualization, used in a way that postelectronic ears from a heterogeneous society can hear it, *must* hear it. Examples:

In Brenda Hutchinson's *Eee-yah!*, she sings a loud, grating Thai pig call. Next she rings a bell and chants the names and relationships of people she was close to who died. Then, softly and on tape, the sampled pig call comes back. This time it sounds like goodbye. Recontextualization.

In Nicolas Collins's *Tobabo Fonio* and *It Was a Dark and Stormy Night*, some sampled Peruvian band music is taken apart and reconstructed so that we come to it two different ways, first through its physical qualities as revealed in the electronics, then imaginatively through the instrumental recomposition.

In *Eee-yah!*, the pig call returns unchanged; what's changed is its *feeling*, because of what we've been through in the meantime. *Stormy Night* is based in logic, and is easy to recreate in words. For *Eee-yah!*, you had to be there to understand.

Collins's case shows that recontextualization can occur *between* two pieces. There's a breakdown in the concept of "the work," or rather, the rebuildup is not yet complete. The problem isn't solved in one lifetime. "Blue" Gene Tyranny, sans sampler, takes the phrases from his song *Somewhere in Arizona 1970* and recontextualizes them in his piano improv *The Intermediary*. You hear again the tunes you just heard, but they're no longer linearly arranged.

In Stone's *Shing Kee*, that Schubert phrase is recontextualized both from its original context *and* within the piece. When the sample is repeated with a few more milliseconds added each time, the quantitative change in duration effects a quantitative change in the perception of timbre. We learn not to judge something on too little information.

In Diana Meckley's *Strange Attractors*, you hear this 21-against-22 rhythm over and over in the string quartet. At first, you can't make anything out. Then the texture gets thinner and thinner. You almost get it. It thickens again. Then tapes of the sampled sound bring the quartet back garbled. By the end of the piece, you think you finally know what you heard. You're listening backward to figure it out. It's like living.

This is a movement. These people don't need to be associated with each other to be playing the same games with our brains. Something is "in the air." Or, forget the air: you can buy that something at Sam Ash.

We can only make the art we feel. Life imitates art: we learn that from Oscar Wilde in literature, Nelson Goodman in philosophy, Jung in psychology. The world has no form—not even chaos—until we impose form on it. Until we project on it a form already present in our unconscious. And once it's projected, Webern said, "To live is to defend a form."

In music, form simply means that you hear something, and then later you hear it again, and the two experiences are not the same. Either it's changed or you've changed. There's always a change because the mere fact of having heard it before alters your perception. "I love you" doesn't mean the same thing the 2,000th time that it did the 12th. People who find repetition inherently uninteresting have blocked out a vital aspect of life. Recontextualization is the background against which fate becomes visible—or audible.

And baby, fate is what it's all about.

sounding the image

FEBRUARY 4, 1992

Now that we hear Inuit throat songs and Balinese gamelan on the radio, the chestnut about music being the universal language has dropped silent from embarrassment. But that music *is* a language remains an overly literal 20th-century metaphor. Music is a language to the extent that it has syntax, rules that govern its continuation, a level of predictability with which events happen. But that's the formulaic, yang side of music. Rules don't govern everything, and some passages take even the composer by surprise. In the hullabaloo about language, music's less describable side—*image*—has suffered neglect, in both composition and discourse.

Language and image began to split in the 19th century with the Brahms/Wagner dichotomy. Wagner's images sometimes had barely enough connective tissue to hold them together. In this century, Stravinsky is the great image maker, Schoenberg the language inventor. Morton Feldman frequently remarked how unfortunate it is that composers neglect Stravinsky these days. Every Stravinsky piece, even when 12-tone, contains arresting measures that bore into the memory: the ambiguous, off-balance major triad in *Symphony of Psalms,* the unbelievable cadenzas doubled by tuba and timpani in the Concerto for Piano and Winds. *Requiem Canticles* (to purposely pick the most abstract example) keeps converging on a chord for four flutes, horns, and timpani that could have inspired Feldman's entire output.

Now imagine picking out your favorite sonority from Schoenberg's Third String Quartet or Piano Concerto: the idea is ridiculous. A language (Romantic tonality, impressionism, serialism) is easy to describe, but not to remember in the inner ear. Consequently, strong language composers get their syntaxes dissected in a billion dissertations. I could review a new book laying out the language of music almost every week, but the other side isn't alluded to in professional literature. The distinction will never penetrate academia's stone walls, because you can't pick up a score and prove that images exist. They emerge in listening, and their proof is in pointing them out.

Even as you read this, the balance is changing in a healthy direction. Feldman wrought irresistibly seductive images and floated them at you so unremittingly that even American ears couldn't miss them. That's his importance for young composers; the Feldman-influenced generation is already image-obsessed. Another gorgeous image maker is Messiaen. As Messiaen's and Feldman's followers have shown, the danger of image composers is that imitations of them are too recognizable. Strong Stravinsky, Feldman, and Messiaen influences bring charges of plagiarism, to which imitators of Schoenberg, Hindemith, and Babbitt are immune. You have to come up with your own images, but language is a safe territory. An image is a gift, and not knowing whether you're going to get a gift or not is what keeps *good* composers awake at night. Retreat into language hides the insecurity that one may not be original. That's why it's become popular in a century that makes originality a source of anxiety.

Minimalism was an image/language confusion. It sprang from an intuition that something was missing, but because the minimalists were trapped in a linguistic framework, they each tried to stretch images into a language, and the images usually evaporated. (The dissonantly connected triads from *Einstein on the Beach*'s magnificent "Bed" scene are an exception.) The power of images is that they *appear*, yet continue to occupy you after they've passed because somehow they were there all along. Perhaps that's a Western perspective, but I find the same thing true in listening to Balinese gamelan, Japanese gagaku, even American Indian songs. Minimalism, its refreshing virtues aside, preserved images in formaldehyde.

Conlon Nancarrow's career has moved from language to image. Canon, an intense form of counterpoint, has always been part of language. But in his Study No. 24, the player piano revealed to Nancarrow that canon could generate images, that voices working together by rule (language) could coalesce into spellbinding moments (images). That's the great achievement of the late Nancarrow canons: solidly grounded in a language, they give us unforgettable images.

Someone will object that you can't separate image from language. Fair enough; creating images requires language, and any use of language will result in images. But 20th-century music's language preoccupation has tended to let images happen in an archaic, unconscious manner, and they've often turned out ugly. Twelve-tone composers remain obstinately oblivious to the fact that audiences find their music anxiety-stricken and violent. They either deny that music expresses emotions (you laugh, but they really do) or say, "Well, these are anxious and violent times, so I guess that's how music has to come out." But that's not how music "has to come out." It's only how it comes out when the brain is working harder than the ear, and images emerge haphazardly.

I don't mean to make image sound like some spooky, mysterious attribute of genius. Composers who produce images claim to *feel* how they do it, but the process isn't conducive to verbalization. Production of visual images has been shown to be a function of the right side of the brain, and it seems reasonable to assume that the same is true for sonic images. Babbitt demands that every aspect of language become conscious, but image can't be brought under control of the analytical brain. A psychologist friend of mine likes to say that just beneath the surface of consciousness is a state in which time doesn't exist; your math teacher humiliated you 20 years ago, but on some gut level it happened yesterday. Image is the part of music that exists outside the time coordinates of the piece. Neglect to penetrate beneath the conscious surface, and the music doesn't do for us what it's supposed to do psychically. And now, after a long dry spell, music's doing it again.

waiting for monteverdi

minimalism

JULY 21, 1992

"I'm sick of people saying that minimalism is dead!" Glenn Branca shouted during our discussion about a recent *Times* pronouncement. "Minimalism hasn't gotten started yet," I countered. "Exactly!" the guitarist/composer replied.

Reports of minimalism's death are greatly exaggerated, especially in the trendy *Times* arts section, which can't hear a sneeze without reporting an epidemic. Anyone who thinks the movement could expire at this early stage hasn't a clue what minimalism meant to those of us who got excited about it in the '70s.

The clues were there to read. In 1967, as minimalism cooed its first duh-dee-duh-dees, a seminal book appeared, Leonard Meyer's *Music, the Arts, and Ideas* (University of Chicago, out of print, as important music books usually are). Every musician I knew read it. A curmudgeonly empiricist, Meyer boldly attempted to sum up 20th-century music, though his view of post-Cage currents was the usual academic caricature. He provided, however, a valuable model of how musical eras develop. A new music begins, he claimed, with the "preclassic" phase of maximum redundancy and low information. It moves into the classic phase in which information and redundancy are optimally balanced, then gets tired and lapses into the mannerist phase of ornate complexity and difficult comprehension, whereupon a new preclassic style takes over. The process takes, oh, 150, 200 years.

The cycle's turned several times. Renaissance polyphony blossomed into the florid overperfection of Palestrina, then gave way to the boring recitative improvisation of Jacopo Peri and Giulio Caccini, the inventors of opera, who ushered in the Baroque era's preclassic phase. A century and a half later, J. S. Bach's chromatically saturated counterpoint yielded to the dippy, preclassic symphonies of Sammartini and the Mannheim school. Each time a new era revs up, the academics and culture vultures are sure the barbarians are at the gates. They enshrine the beautiful but exhausted old style and lampoon the new one as simplistic and illiterate. Their evaluations are correct; in its experimental decades, the new style is undeniably monotonous. But the naysayers are shortsighted.

What happens is, once the new style has been collectively developed, "geniuses" appear who not only make something brilliant with it, but integrate into it the virtues of the old style. In the early Baroque case, it was Monteverdi who came along and brought the subtlety of a master contrapuntalist to Peri's and Caccini's experiments. Among early symphonists, it was Haydn and Mozart who imbued Sammartini's frail forms with harmonic power.

The condescension that has greeted minimalism for 20 years is the ignorance of those who don't understand history. When I first heard Steve Reich's *Drumming* and Philip Glass's *Music in Fifths* in 1974, I thought they were too easy, but those monotonous little note patterns contained the germ of a new era. They brought names to mind: Peri, Caccini, Sammartini. The music was in a textbook preclassic phase, redundant, unsubtle, and one-dimensional. Now, in what I call the postminimal music heard every year at the Bang on a Can festival, minimalism is growing inexorably toward its classic phase. It hasn't arrived yet, but it's moving audibly.

There's an unacknowledged principle that I call the Allure of the Undeveloped Language. It is, in times of great historical change, the best young composers—those who would rather be leaders than clones—who abandon their training and join the amateurs. Say you're starting out in 1592. You have a choice: try to beat Palestrina at his own game, writing ever more florid motets (you'll never succeed), or go over to the new figured-bass recitative camp and improve on what they're doing. The *career*-ambitious composers, following their teachers, stick with the old style. The *artistically* ambitious ones, taking the risk, flock to an arena in which they can make a personal mark. Monteverdi took the dare, declared his music the *seconda prattica*, and said that the old rules no longer applied.

This was the psychology of the '70s. You're going to write a more elaborate 12-tone piece than Babbitt's *Reflections?* You're going to out-serialize Boulez's *Pli selon pli?* In your dreams. You can't outdo Babbitt, you can only become a watered-down imitation. Although they won't admit it,

Boulez and Babbitt closed the book on that period as surely as Palestrina and Bach closed theirs. And the New Romantics are going back to compete with Mahler? Good luck. But the smart composers were listening to Reich's *Piano Phase* and saying, "Gee, I could do better than that." And it doesn't diminish Reich's stature that a lot of them—Branca, William Duckworth, Peter Gena, Michael Gordon, Lois V. Vierk, Mikel Rouse, Janice Giteck, Carl Stone, Peter Garland, Paul Epstein—*have* done better.

This has been my take on minimalism for 18 years, and Bang on a Can clinches it. The switch from an overelaborate style to a new simplicity has happened often enough that we ought to be used to it, able to get through it without a lot of name-calling. Charges by Wuorinen and Babbitt that minimalism encourages musical illiteracy exactly parallel complaints by Zarlino and Artusi about the early Baroque: equally true, equally irrelevant. Technology can't speed up the fact that a new musical language takes generations to find its expressive power. Minimalism, or postminimalism, or the New Tonality, or Bang Music, hasn't died. It's waiting for its Monteverdi.

dads versus shadows

james hillman

MARCH 16, 1993

In the '80s trendoids claimed distinctions between Uptown and Downtown were melting. There was a superficial truth to that: Uptown, it became hip to feign nonchalance and toss in token pop references, and Downtown half-assedly picked up on fractals and the Fibonacci series. But while surface differences blurred a little, battles still raged on a deeper level. Those trying to fathom these politics should read James Hillman's *The Myth of Analysis* (1972, Harper Perennial). Long before Hillman gained notoriety in the Iron John men's movement, he was the John Cage of psychology, brilliantly defusing unconscious assumptions.

In the book's first part, "On Psychological Creativity," Hillman outlines our internal myths of how the creative process works. The instinct to create (which everyone possesses, he and Jung claim, though Americans are champs at squelching theirs) gets modified by the psyche and takes on coloration from whatever psychic archetype is dominant. Thus different people experience creativity completely differently, and Hillman draws the possibilities into six categories.

The first one Hillman describes is God the Creator, filtered through the father archetype. The Father-God creates through method, hierarchy, structure. The composer creates masterpieces for posterity via an ordered system, and expects descendants to carry on his tradition. Hillman mentions Bach, but I think of Schoenberg, who wrote that his 12-tone row would "ensure the supremacy of German music for the next hundred years." Hillman states the attitude Schoenberg imparted to his followers: "[T]here is only one God, only one right way, one truth." Exaggerated, the archetype hardens into the *senex*, the sterile old man who can no longer create but wages war against the irrationality of youthful imagination. Some of our most celebrated professors, warped by this identification, are less known for their arid music than for the bile they heap on those who compose without system or tradition.

Second is creation *ex nihilo*, which takes art as always unique, new, unprecedented, projected through the *puer aeternus* (divine child). True art constantly moves on, tracing the trail of the zeitgeist. Originality is the cardinal virtue, and since "one can make nothing endure without killing the spark that is not meant to last, there must be continual . . . inspiration from the divine." Maturity and tradition are enemies of this eternal novelty. Example: Charles Ives, who disdained structure and method, and whose torrential inspiration dried up early in middle age.

Third, creativity projects itself through the shadow: "Iconoclasm, rebellion in the name of liberation, the creative process as protest." The creative urge merges with sexuality, and "is supposed to be kept in the irrational dark so that its primal power will not be inhibited." Drugs, drink, and magic help bring this image to the brink of death, whence it draws inspiration, and whatever threatens to curb its power—bourgeois morality, for instance—must be antagonized. Gee, you don't know any Downtown art that fits this pattern, do you? No wonder those *senex* professors hate us.

Prometheus, the fourth type, embodies the creative urge understood through the ego. Through the fire he stole from the gods, man "can convert nature's mystery into a problem to solve, thereby extending the realm of conscious control." This is a utilitarian view of creativity, the process as self-imposed puzzle, and the theft from the gods must be paid for with hard work. This type's hero used to be Hindemith, who theorized his own rules of harmony, invented *Gebrauchsmusik* (functional music), and could write a viola sonata during a train ride. Its motto is the chestnut that "art is 10 percent inspiration and 90 percent perspiration."

More in pop music than in art, the instinct can project through the persona, the fifth type, resulting in the indistinguishable merging of creativity and celebrity. "One becomes one's image," and then "the individual who wears the mask can no longer put it down because the mask itself has become the psychic carrier of the creative instinct, sometimes sacrificing the person in suicide and personal tragedy." Details of the artist's life take on mythical importance for the masses. Madonna, or the Kronos Quartet.

Last and less recognized is the notion of creativity via the great mother archetype: "The creative is an external source, a mothering unconsciousness, . . . naturally subject to periodic barrenness, like the seasons." The artist paints what she sees, receives what she is given, and accepts that at times nothing comes. Stereotypically but aptly, I think of the first great woman composer, Ruth Crawford: taking ideas of men like Cowell, Rudhyar, Seeger, she gave them more perfect expression than they could themselves, then endured a barren spell between 1932 and '41.

The categories aren't ironclad. Crisis can force a switch from one image to another; Hindemith, for example, was a shadow composer before his conversion to the ego. Others get caught between conflicting archetypes. Father types control our universities, shadow composers sell more records. You can make a party game assigning artists to the various categories. The point is that none of these archetypes is inherently privileged, none more right than another. Most artists feel so possessed by their operative archetype that they deny the validity of others, but there is no *essence* of creativity. Each has its excesses, but you can't dismiss an entire psychological complex because it can go too far: they all do. It's OK to feel there's only one way to compose, but it's not OK to attack someone for disagreeing.

Uptowners have to learn that irrationality has its place. Downtowners can learn that art isn't antithetical to tradition and structure. Everyone needs to learn to express these archetypes consciously, not with intolerant ignorance. Until we adopt an attitude that sees all creative modes as equally natural and fruitful, each with its place in the psychic spectrum, music will continue to be oppressively politicized.

vexing the purists

vexations

JUNE 8, 1993

Sometime circa 1893 Erik Satie penned two lines of chromatic piano music, eerily strung with diminished triads. Over them he wrote, in his curiously archaic French, "To play this motif for oneself 840 times in a row, it will be good to prepare oneself beforehand, and in the greatest silence, through serious immobilities." Joke? Idle musing? Or performance instructions? John Cage decided the last, and organized the first complete performance of *Vexations*, 19 hours long, on September 10, 1963. That feat, which Gavin Bryars has called "a poor man's *Ring of the Nibelungs,*" has been repeated many times since, most recently May 15 at Roulette, where, in honor of the 100th anniversary, it was performed by 21 pianists. I was one of them, and, in the same spirit of participatory journalism with which Tom Johnson once wrote about singing in *Einstein on the Beach,* I thought I'd write about what playing *Vexations* taught me.

When I arrived, Joshua Pierce had just begun, playing the four lines of music straight, elegantly pedaled. After 55 minutes (the time allotted each pianist), Kirk Nurock took over. Suddenly, Satie sounded like a Stockhausen Klavierstück. Nurock played the right notes, but accented different chords from one repetition to another, blurred sonorities with the sustain pedal, varied between legato and staccato. After all, Satie's manuscript prescribes no dynamics, pedaling, or articulation. Next, Lois Svard varied the music by crossing her hands, playing the right hand lower than the left, sometimes doubling the left in octaves. Such techniques had a brooding effect, like a cello transcription of a violin sonata, and extended the invertible counterpoint already inherent in Satie's score. I was told that earlier in the day Grete Sultan, a Cage associate and the only pianist here who had also played in 1963, had also experimented with octave doublings and transpositions.

Nurock is a professional jazzer, Svard a fine classical pianist. I knew I couldn't duplicate their feats, but I felt the same obligation to draw the audience into the music. I decided that the pitches, being precisely notated, were sacrosanct (a principle that meshed well with cowardice, since I was afraid I'd screw up if I strayed from the notes I'd practiced). The thing that I thought made paying attention difficult was metronomic regularity. Rubato (stretching of tempo) isn't generally associated with Satie performance, but it was pervasive in late-19th-century piano playing. So I bent the established tempo and flowed with the swell and ebb of each phrase.

Then I got a lucky break: a car alarm went off outside the window, a slow, steady beep. Here (I thought with all the lucidity I could muster while playing the piano in front of 20 people) was a chance to abide by the Cagean promise of allowing the accidental sounds surrounding a performance to become part of it. So I clicked with the alarm's tempo, using it as a metronome, then shifting an eighth note so that the alarm was playing the offbeats.

I marked the end of the experimental section of this performance, for none of the pianists who followed—David Shea, Anthony Coleman, Norman Yamada, William Duckworth—departed from the general tempo or dynamics. Duckworth, who's been doing *Vexations* performances since 1968, was Nurock's antipode, playing at an arrow-straight lento of 28 beats per minute, without the slightest digression in phrasing or volume. If I'd had to listen to 19 hours of an uninflected *Vexations*, I'd want it to exhibit it the serene blankness of Duckworth's limpid, monochromatic purity.

What Nurock made me realize, though, was how little sympathy I now have for the kind of purism that disdains to meet the audience even halfway. At previous *Vexations* performances I've been involved in (1975 in Austin and 1987 in Chicago), I was a purist myself; I demanded strict, ornamentless playing, and disciplined myself to avoid extraneous thoughts and listen for every note. A thousand or so new-music concerts later, my patience isn't what it used to be, though it may be approaching that of the average audience member. Pierce's lyrical phrases encouraged my mind to wander, and I let it. Nurock and Svard made me listen despite myself, and I felt as though I suddenly heard *Vexations*'s undulating counterpoint for the first time in years. Perhaps, as Satie's ambiguous reflexive pronouns suggest, *Vexations* is supposed to be played "for oneself"; I was amazed at how quickly time passed while playing, how slowly while listening.

The 20th century has been a grand experiment in purism, from Schoenberg's first 12-tone row through Cage's late works. Cage studied with Schoenberg, who said, "Those who compose because they want to please others, and have audiences in mind, are not real artists." But Satie was a friend of Stravinsky's, from a different tradition, not a Germanic purist but a nose-thumbing bohemian. Schoenberg accused Stravinsky of equating art with neckties and "merely trying to satisfy the customers."

Would Satie, the authority-defying eccentric who formed his own Metropolitan Church of the Art of Jesus the Conductor with a membership of one, have excommunicated me for not submitting to the tyranny of his enigmatic notations? Or, had he performed, would he have pulled his own practical jokes? Through the tradition he started, Cage is as much the author of what we know as *Vexations* as Satie is, and Cage is dead now; this was presumably the first performance since that sad August afternoon. We are at liberty to remove Satie from '60s New York and return him to his place in fin-de-siècle Montmartre. In so doing, we may find ourselves freed from Schoenberg's austere ultimata and turning toward the customer-pleasing Stravinsky.

musical amnesia cured!

imagism

FEBRUARY 15, 1994

The opening gesture of Michael Gordon's *Thou Shalt!/Thou Shalt Not!*
repeats 24 times before anything else happens. The piece clearly isn't minimalist, however. Twelve of the repetitions are literal, the other 12, inter-
mingled, are varied by the addition of a beat here or there or a shift of
tempo. Nothing that happens is gradual or predictable. Awkward, mis-
shapen, defying you to tap your foot to its brake-pedaled pulse, that gesture brilliantly trumpets the *reemergence,* in 1983, of imagism.

Oh criminy, another -ism? Nah, at ease. Imagism is less a movement
than a tendency that music periodically flirts with, traceable virtually to
the medieval era. An *image* is a memorable, idiosyncratic entity on the surface of music, perceived as a separable whole. The *language* of music is the
context in which images are woven together, the logical construct that
makes them plausible. Memorable images dot the history of music, from
the weeping descents of Josquin's *Absalon, fili mii,* to the spine-chilling
trombone chords of *Don Giovanni,* to Wagner's eyebrow-raising leitmo-
tifs, to Walden Pond's gorgeously pure G major in Ives's "Thoreau" movement. In Romantic music, image is nearly synonymous with theme.
Nineteenth-century music struck such a deep chord not because it hit a
perfect balance between image and language (though that's close), but
because the logic of its language made its images seem fated, self-evident.
The only style that doesn't support images well is 12-tone music, and even
that produced a couple of imagists: Luigi Dallapiccola and, in certain moods,
Roger Sessions.

After tonality collapsed, composers obsessed about creating a new language. They knew it was Romantic music's logic that made it so potent, but
they forgot that images were the agent needed for that power to connect.
As a result, for over four decades they gave us works full of elegant, seamless language, but no images. What does that sound like? Convincing but
unmemorable. Hundreds of compositions by Babbitt, Carter, Kirchner,
Berger, Perle, and so on, made you think, *while* you listened, "Wow, this is
really well-crafted"; then, 10 minutes into intermission, you couldn't
remember a note. Those works proved the composer was brilliant but gave
the listener nothing to take home. I've gone back to recordings of them
countless times, trying to recall why my first impression was positive, then
forgetting again.

That was Uptown (and still is). Downtown ran parallel, but craftsman-ship wasn't the point. We spent the '60s and '70s drawing quasi-languages from circuitry and gradual processes. It's easy to remember the overall qualities of those pieces by Wolff, Brown, Lucier, Berhman, Mumma, Goode, Tom Johnson, and others, but rarely anything specific within them. The '80s tried to turn free improv into a viable language: images arose hap-hazardly, but were not nurtured.

During this rather dry period, the image was sustained by three remark-able figures whose similarity has never been noted, one Uptown, one Downtown, one European. The first was that French oddball Olivier Messiaen: listen to the succession of bird calls in his *Oiseaux Exotiques* and you'll hear a feat of pure imagism, without logic or even connective tissue. The other two were friends of the abstract expressionist painters, though they are now relegated to separate worlds: Ralph Shapey and Morton Feldman. Shapey's aesthetic statements make an imagist manifesto: he eschews development, composes "graven images," and works, he claims, "with the 'It is,' not the 'It becomes.'" His music deploys images (the gran-ite opening chords of the *Fromm Variations*, the timpani motive of *Three for Six*) like blocks, recombining them in myriad forms. Feldman's images repeat with tentative irregularity, and, in his superlong works, reappear in ghostly quiet every half-hour or so.

Partly due to Feldman's influence, even more to the can of identical worms minimalism opened up, downtown is now awash in images. The music often doesn't seem crafted at all, just a series of insistently repeated, varied, and contrasted patterns like *Thou Shalt!*, but it embeds itself in the memory on first hearing. Every other piece hits you with unforgettable, irreducible, unexplainable, repeated moments: individual notes held from a descending chord series in "Blue" Gene Tyranny's *Nocturne With and Without Memory*; the circling-in-place "Om shanti" chant from Janice Giteck's work of the same name; three notes from Beethoven's *Missa Solemnis* stolen for Neil Rolnick's sampler piece *Sanctus*; the refrain "Yellow like a sunflower, taller than Jesus" in Mikel Rouse's *In Cold Blood* opera; the poignantly descending chord progression in Todd Levin's *Prayer*; the two alternating chords, one dissonant and one consonant, from Glenn Branca's Third Symphony; the jazz cadence in Stravinskian rhythms on "precepts doubtful" in William Duckworth's *Southern Harmony*.

Totalism is a special case of imagism: using complex rhythmic struc-tures drawn from world musics, it weaves an underlying web for your attention to stick to while the images float by. Neither postminimalism nor totalism has quite developed enough syntactic finesse to make its images seem natural, predestined, carved in stone. Only Duckworth, with his sly blues formulas and numerical processes pushed deep into the background, has found a smooth fusion of image and logic. For now that's just fine, even though it means the classical critics still won't get it. Halfway through the 21st century, though, the philosophic differences that separate Babbitt from Cage will not sound as obvious, I suspect, as this tremendous swing between opposite poles, from a totally linguistic music in the '50s to the imagism of the '90s. And since I'd rather listen to music that's individualistic and memorable than anonymous, no matter how well-crafted, I'm tickled to be around for the '90s.

end of the paper trail

scores

JULY 25, 1995

Way back when I was a teenage Cage fanatic eager to up the ante on avant-gardism, I collected, as everyone did, records. At the time, Deutsche Grammophon sold the best possible recording for four dollars, unsurpassed by today's $18 CDs. But more important, I collected scores. I felt a recording would give me superficial familiarity with a work, a live performance some intimacy, but if I wanted to know the piece in the biblical sense I had to study it on the printed page. Music is more multidimensional and full of technical detail than a novel or a painting, and often, the more dazzling the master-piece, the more you need a score to figure out how the composer did it.

Then I moved to Manhattan, and scores pretty much ceased to be part of my life. For one thing, after 1970 publishers lapsed into utter ignorance of new music, publishing only those Americans who write in the most con-ventional European genres. Even then they barely distribute the music, using modern works primarily as tax write-offs, so that many composers refuse to deal with them. Boosey & Hawkes got hip (or venal) enough to sign up Steve Reich, but aside from that one exception it is laughable to imagine going into venerable Patelson's Music to catch up on recent trends, as one might easily have done 30 years ago. I don't own a single score for a work written after 1980 that wasn't self-published and given to me by the composer. Aside from a few artist-run mail-order concerns like Frog Peak Music and Deep Listening, that's the only meaningful way today's scores circulate.

On top of that, Downtown composers don't always make scores, at least not ones suitable for public consumption. As busy, practical, and unconcerned for posterity as Mozart was, they write parts for their players, or simply computer-sequence the music, punching it in to be played on MIDI synthesizers without ever touching paper. When I need hard copy from them, as when I lecture or write analytical articles for academic journals, I have a hell of a time getting it. One prominent composer gave me xeroxes of his players' parts so I could assemble my own score; no one had ever asked him for one before. I have sometimes transcribed music from recordings, taping it for half-speed playback when it's too complex.

Granted, the decline of music's paper culture has a bigger upside than down. A kind of religious faith in the score as being more essential than the sound was responsible for the cerebral dead end that 12-tone music brought us to. When I first became a critic, I would follow the score at performances, as I often had before and as Uptown critics routinely do. But I soon found that while I ended up with lots of technical trivia to write about, I had nothing to say about how the piece sounded, how it worked psychologically, what impression it created on the audience. What looks wimpy on the page can sound spectacular, and vice versa. I think the basis for the reputation of stuffed shirts like Elliott Carter and Mario Davidovsky is that Uptown critics follow their scores during concerts and find impressive devices, whereas if they relied on their ears they would draw a blank like everyone else. In the 10 years since I learned that, I have never followed a score at a live performance unless I was already familiar with the music. One Downtown composer sends me his scores before concerts, and I ignore them until afterward.

The disappearance of the score accompanies a drastic upswing in the quality of new music over the last seven years, particularly among the young. Now that composers computer-sequence their music, the time lag between writing a passage and hearing it played has narrowed from several months to a few minutes. Revising a melody or rhythmic device that didn't work the way you thought it would is a quick, private transaction with no paper trail. By the time a composer goes public with a work, she's heard it 750 times instead of twice, and the wrinkles have been ironed out. As a result, 22-year-old technonerds routinely turn out pieces more sophisticated and engaging than those of your average 50-ish pencil pusher. Afterward, they have little incentive to write down what they did.

I wouldn't go back to the bad old days for love or liquor, but I miss scores anyway. For while new music's listenability is way up, the quality and density of intellectual discourse have hit bottom. You don't need printed notes to enjoy new music, but you sometimes need them to communicate, critic to critic, how intricate and radically new the music's methods are. What sounds like a vigorous and unrepeatable free-for-all onstage may be a well-contrived 27-against-32 polyrhythm with structural implications for the rest of the piece. I can play CDs at lectures and vaguely impress musicians, but if I can show them *how* Eve Beglarian weaves vocal improv into her music, *how* Nick Didkovsky creates his rhythmic structures, or *how* La Monte Young tunes his piano, they get excited. The beautiful effects in the music have become theirs to re-create. Hard copy by itself is sterile, music can be mystifying, but when you put the two together, sparks fly in between.

After one talk I participated in, composer Roger Reynolds lamented to me, "Students no longer know how music is made." The scarcity of paper means scarcity of community, of mutual development of ideas, since no one's quite sure what anyone else is doing. The problem is keeping a healthy balance of means and ends. Let us have print, but never again delude ourselves that an interestingly made score can ever justify music that doesn't sound good. As Peter Gena says, "Analysis is the cigarette after"; meaning, first you fall in love with a work, and then, only because it fascinates you, you look underneath the hood and figure out how it works. Without a score, there's no hood to open.

reflections on books, figures, and events

no shortcuts

john cage

MAY 10, 1988

A critic devoted to the work of John Cage faces an inherent conflict. No composer has a soft spot in his heart for critics, but the premises of Cage's music seem, at times, to render analysis impossible. In an early interview, Cage said, "I find myself more and more questioning the professional function of the critic." His stated aim in all his activities is to free himself, the listener, and the reader from likes and dislikes; he refuses to harbor preferences. An incredulous critic once pressed him to admit he'd choose a fresh banana over a rotten one. At 16, I was so enwrapped in Cage's ideas that I began to feel guilty listening to records when I could be outside listening to traffic.

The conflict is not only the critic's but Cage's. Cage himself began as a critic—in 1941 and '42 he covered the Chicago new music scene for the journal *Modern Music*—and in many respects he's never quit being one. Not always capable of Cage's bodhisattva-like detachment, I've taken a perverse pleasure in keeping track of the things he doesn't like: vibraphones, dominant seventh chords, and radios, for example, which he's incorporated into his music in an effort to accept them. Other judgments are more permanent. New York, Chicago, and Los Angeles have "bad orchestras," the first "a group of gangsters." Always conscious of the social metaphor in music, Cage objects to jazz for enslaving one player to the beat while freeing another from it. Haydn cadences too often. Improvisers (this is also Boulez's and the general avant-garde criticism) invariably fall back on taste, habit, and "favorite licks."

Nevertheless, Cage has been both hailed and excoriated as the *anything goes* composer, the granter of freedom to whom "any sound can be music." That's half the story, and two recent events have filled in the rest. One was the Cage festival/symposium at Wesleyan University (February 22 to 27), handsomely organized by Neely Bruce in honor of Cage's 75th birthday.

The other is the publication of Richard Kostelanetz's second Cage monograph, *Conversing with Cage* (Limelight Editions), made up of fragments from unpublished or obscure interviews. At the symposium, theorists analyzed his music, drew charts, and derived systems. Early concerts were recreated with an eye and ear for authenticity, including the 1965 Rose Art Museum premier of Cage's *Rozart Mix*, Alvin Lucier's first brain-wave piece, and Christian Wolff's *For 1, 2, or 3 People*. Both book and symposium suggested that Cage's agenda has been misunderstood.

For some, that realization has been growing for years. My understanding of Cage deepened in 1975 at "June in Buffalo," the symposium in which Morton Feldman attempted to turn SUNY into Darmstadt-on-the-Niagara. Faced with 50-odd composers eager to impress him, Cage assigned each a number and, characteristically, let the *I Ching* determine who would speak. One woman grew belligerent, periodically shouting that the system was stupid, and that those who wanted to talk should do so. Everyone wished she would shut up, while Cage gently reasoned with her. Then, on the third day, he came in and said, "I've been thinking it over, and Mary's right. We'll forget the *I Ching*, and those who want to speak may do so as they wish." Jaws dropped.

That day I realized that, above his writings, even above his music, it's Cage's *personal example* that we should treasure. No composer has had better reason to become bitter than Cage (years after *Life* magazine had done a spread on him, he supported himself by washing dishes), and his freedom from rancor makes the bitterness of others seem petty and self-defeating. How many more performances might Babbitt, Feldman, Shapey, and Young have had if they had shown as much respect for those who disagree with them as Cage has? That's a lesson for young composers to mull over, far more practical than any advice about software or self-promotion.

That same week, I became aware of what Cage means by freedom. In a performance of Cage's theater piece *Songbooks*, Julius Eastman (a fine composer/performer and a gay activist) used the direction "Give a lecture" as a pretext to undress a male student onstage and gesture sexually. Cage's reaction was inscrutable, but the next day, the man whom no one could imagine even swatting a fly fumed, in impressively subdued tones, about the difference between *liberty* and *license*. Unbelievably, he banged his fist on the piano and shouted (or perhaps only paraphrased) the too-little-famous words that appear in caps in his book *A Year from Monday:* "PERMISSION GRANTED. BUT NOT TO DO WHATEVER YOU WANT."

The Wesleyan festival was the first official sign I'd seen that the last sentence is sinking in. In a brilliant lecture, Kostelanetz put Cage's random operations in a new perspective. "Chance," he proclaimed, "isn't important in Cage's music." Random procedures aren't perceptible as such; they're merely a compositional tool for achieving Cage's real aim, which is "uninflected nonhierarchical structure." As proof, Kostelanetz pointed out that such structure is what Cage's early scores and subsequent chance pieces have in common. It was critics and performers who jumped on the notion of chance: the former in order to brand him a sloppy composer, the latter to grab at an excuse for self-indulgence. Kostelanetz reminded us that Cage isn't a '60s composer but "a '30s lefty" with a conviction that art must benefit society.

If this be revisionism, let us make the most of it. Cage has too long taken the rap for the shoddy, casual randomness of so many downtown performances. His image problem parallels Schoenberg's; denying the charge that the 12-tone method made composing *easier,* Schoenberg insisted the opposite was true and warned that only those who had mastered tonal composition should attempt it. Similarly, Cage's formula, "Everything is permitted only if zero is taken as the basis," makes composing more difficult, for how many can discipline themselves to reach zero? At Wesleyan, composer William Duckworth reminded us of Cage's complaint, "Just because my name comes up doesn't make a failure a success." I haven't seen him quote it, but I think Cage would like Jung's definition of freedom: "The willingness to do what one *must* do."

Though most of the material in *Conversing with Cage* is familiar, myriad small cracks are filled in to complete our picture of Cage's unconventional thought, sometimes making it seem more conventional. Some of the views are pure common sense, stated only because wrong conclusions have been drawn. Cage denies that musically untrained people are likely to have fresher musical inspirations, "because when people don't know anything about music and improvise it, . . . you get something that . . . begins at a kindergarten level. . . . That's what happens with a good deal of electronic music now. Because the people who use electronics for the most part skip the business of studying music and so . . . do things that are not really interesting musically." When an interviewer says of a performance, "They should have done it well or not at all," Cage responds: "I couldn't be in greater agreement. If there are intentions, then there should be every effort made to realize those intentions. Otherwise carelessness takes over."

Elsewhere, he admits he is "an elitist. I always have been. I didn't study music with just anybody; I studied with Schoenberg. I didn't study Zen with just anybody; I studied with Suzuki. I've always gone, insofar as I could, to the president of the company." Nor does Cage consider his music immune to criticism; in fact, he offers advice: "What can be analyzed in my work, or criticized, are the questions that I ask. But most of the critics don't find out what those questions were. And that would make the difference between one composition made with chance operations and another." He then provides a deft example of self-criticism with regard to the trouble he had applying the *I Ching* to the music of William Billings as part of *Apartment House 1776.*

From these comments an enormous set of Cagean criteria could be constructed. Does the music have intentions? (The answer is rarely *no;* David Tudor and Petr Kotik have inherited Cage's uninflected, nonhierarchical structure, but I dare you to name a third.) If so, is every effort made to realize them? If a climax is attempted, does every element contribute to it? If ambiguity is intended, is it carefully drawn? Is the music *clear?* Does the imposition of the performer's ego overshadow his sounds? Is she trying to impress us, or compel us to accept a particular opinion, political or otherwise? Is the composer in a rut, acting out of habit? Has he or she asked the right questions? Is there sufficient variety? Could greater variety be achieved, given more preparation or attention to aspects that were unthinkingly ignored? All of these questions arise, directly or obliquely, in Cage's books.

Near the recent symposium's end came a wonderful panel in which Wolff, Lucier, Earle Brown, and Gordon Mumma, with Cage in the audience, reminisced modestly about the days in which they got together and, essentially, invented a totally new conception of music. Speaking on the panel for a younger generation, Duckworth listed some criteria by which Cage-influenced music could be judged: "Intention, method, commitment, discipline, attitude, and ultimately . . . the development of moral character." He added, "There are no shortcuts for those who would be influenced by John Cage."

It was a good note to end on. The Wesleyan symposium opens chapter three of Cage's reputation: after the *clown* composer, then the *freedom* composer, we are at last given Cage the *discipline* composer, the man who spent a year of his life making thousands of splices for his four-minute tape piece *Williams Mix.* (One of the quarter-inches of tape contained 1,097 fragments.) How many musicians who cite Cage as a predecessor put a sliver of as much care into their work? If Downtown performances are sloppy today, if people blow into saxophones, wiggle their fingers on the keys, and call it "new music," it's not because Cage has had too much influence. He's had too little.

After Duckworth spoke, someone rose to comment that though everyone was calling Cage a father figure, his horoscope has Cancer rising: he's actually a mother figure. The panel agreed that Cage is a nurturing presence. But the father image also holds and is too little acknowledged. Many of us, encouraged by Cage, sense him looking over our shoulders, a constant reminder not to become satisfied with our levels of consciousness. Over two decades, I've reluctantly come to disagree with Cage on many points, but if I thought the act of criticism was precluded by his philosophy, I'd have a crisis of conscience about continuing. As it is, I'll go on, wincing when I like things he objects to and vice versa, trying continually to discipline myself, to keep my ego out of my work, to encourage variety, to learn to like things I don't, and—in his words—to get myself out of whatever cage I find myself in.

e.t., go home

tuning

JUNE 29, 1993

It is mathematically impossible to tune a 12-pitch keyboard so that you can play consonantly in every key. Keyboard tuners have struggled with that intransigent fact for over 600 years. Their solutions are now amassed in a two-and-a-half-inches-thick, six-pound encyclopedia, written by Owen H. Jorgensen, RPT (Registered Piano Technician). Its jaw-breaking title is *Tuning: The Perfection of Eighteenth-Century Temperament, the Lost Art of Nineteenth-Century Temperament, and the Science of Equal Temperament, Complete with Instructions for Aural and Electronic Tuning* (Michigan State University Press, 1991, $80; I'm indebted to pianist Philip Bush for introducing me to it after his concert of alternative tunings). Between charts for tunings dating back to 1373 runs Jorgensen's agenda: to subvert the unquestioned hegemony of equal temperament—E.T.—the practice of tuning the 12 steps equidistantly without regard for consonance.

Terse, energetic, and precise, Jorgensen turns our conceptions of tuning "progress" inside out. He obliterates the myth that J. S. Bach invented E.T. and wrote *The Well-Tempered Clavier* to demonstrate it (an error he pinpoints in the 1893 *Grove's Dictionary*). In fact, Jorgensen proves with abundant documentation, E.T. wasn't used on pianos until 1917. Nineteenth-century tuners considered it unrealizable on keyboard instruments that had to be tuned by ear (as opposed to fretted lutes or organ pipes, which could be measured manually), and not terribly desirable. Early tuners caused confusion by calling tunings "equal" that were merely unrestric-tive, meaning that all keys were usable, though not identical in interval size.

Throughout the 19th century, Jorgensen demonstrates, pianos contin-ued to be tuned in well temperament: the keys most closely related to C major (such as F and G) had the purest triads and sweetest (flattest) major thirds, while those closer to F-sharp were brighter and sharper. Romantic accounts that linked keys to colors were based in tuning. Because of its dis-mally flat third, B-flat minor was described as "preparation for suicide" in 1784; Chopin clearly had something similar in mind when he pitched the Funeral March from his Second Sonata in B-flat minor, but we lose that quality on an E.T. piano. If, in playing older music, "you take the specific eccentricities of a temperament away . . . it's like removing the color from a painting." Our ears have been systematically desensitized to accept not only imperfection, but monochromaticism. Jorgensen aptly explains why, in their original tuning, the fugues from Bach's *W.T.C.* go limp when trans-posed to the wrong keys.

What interest could historical tunings have for an inveterate avant-gardist like myself? The first practical method for equal temperament, Jorgensen writes, appeared in W. B. White's *Modern Piano Tuning* textbook of 1917, synchronistically coinciding with the invention of the 12-tone row. Atonality, Jorgensen never tires of reminding us, is the only idiom E.T. supports. In other words, unconsciously and in the long run, tuning deter-mines what kind of harmonies composers write. "The degree of tempering to be done on the just intonation intervals," he muses, "has always been a philosophic question." If we stick with E.T.'s bland evenness, we're stuck with an atonal *framework* to compose in, even when we write tonally. Who tunes the instruments guides the future of music.

A return to more highly inflected tunings could offer an impetus toward richer tonalities than minimalism has provided. When E.T. became a real-ity, Jorgensen says, tuning ceased to be an art and became a science, and now that 12-tone music is moribund, he predicts the return of more artis-tic tunings. "It is possible that in the future well temperament could again become the common tuning while equal temperament could become a his-torical temperament reserved for the old twentieth-century piano music of Debussy, Prokofieff, Barber, etc., that requires it." Don't slam the door on your way out, 20th century, and don't hurry back.

The book convinced me to take the plunge: my grand piano is now tuned to Thomas Young's well temperament of 1799, which Jorgensen calls "the most perfect ever published" in some respects. "Another person lost to historical accuracy," my piano tuner, Tom Patten, sighed when I told him what I wanted, but he didn't charge me a cent more than equal temperament. Result? The piano sounds more alive overall, with subtle and unpredictable variation among the chords, for while some fifths are purely consonant, others (four to six cents narrow) buzz busily. Since Young's temperament was prevalent in Beethoven's day, and since Beethoven's harmonic form contrasts keys to excellent advantage, I've been playing his sonatas as test cases.

The *Appassionata* Sonata's Andante in D-flat major is unexpectedly cheery due to a buzz in the tonic triad that disappears when transposed up or down a half-step. Playing through the *Hammerklavier* (which I can do if I adjust the metronome marking down to about five beats per minute), the Allegro's B-flat blares brilliantly; then the Adagio's F-sharp minor, a markedly muted key, retreats into shadowy solitude. And where Beethoven melts his F-sharp theme into G-major non sequiturs, the whole character changes, for while the fifth on F-sharp is perfect, that on G is narrow and the major third unusually sweet, giving G major an ethereal, almost attackless mellowness. And to make sure I hadn't ruined my piano for dissonance, I played through Webern's Variations and Ives's "Alcotts" and "Thoreau." Sounded great.

Only downside was, since my piano had been accustomed to E.T. for 22 years, my octaves soured in three weeks, and needed retouching. Still, I'm hearing key contrasts the way Beethoven intended them and picking up a 19th-century sense of key colors that our era has needlessly forfeited as a resource. Equal temperament and I have parted ways.

composing the lingo

harry partch, american inventor

MAY 7, 1996

Harry Partch was the central figure of American music. I can't think of another statement more guaranteed to elicit contempt from the academic establishment, reproving looks from jazz critics, even raised eyebrows from Cage fans. Ten years ago I would have demurred myself. But I'm more and more drawn to that conclusion as I hear Downtown composers struggle to divest themselves of layer after layer of European brainwashing. The Kerouac of music, Partch molded his aesthetic around the slang of the hoboes he traveled among, and if his music doesn't sound like second nature, it's because we still listen through a German filter. In reality the above opinion says less about Partch than about what constitutes Americanness in music; where we put Partch depends on where we decide to put Europe. My vote is, on the other side of the ocean.

The incredibly well-organized American Composers Forum (formerly the Minnesota Composers Forum) has just released a welcome slew of new Partch materials through the Innova label. *Enclosure 1: Harry Partch*, as they've titled it, is a video of four films, long rumored but rarely seen, that Partch made in the late '50s–early '60s with Chicago filmmaker Madeline Tourtelot. *Enclosure 2* is a whopping four-CD set of Partch memorabilia, including early performances, interviews, public statements, tuning demonstrations, dramatized extracts from his memoir *Bitter Music*, and even 46 minutes of friends reminiscing at his wake.

Enclosure 3, yet to come, will be a tome subtitled *A Partch Scrapbook*. The materials contained in these sets are rough, quirky, unpolished, often recorded under adverse conditions. They will not impress anyone who didn't take Partch seriously in the first place; don't listen to them unless you've heard his masterpieces *Delusion of the Fury, The Bewitched, U.S. Highball, Castor and Pollux*. But for those of us converted long ago, the lot is a treasure trove of early sketches and intimate moments that invite us to rethink Partch's significance.

And it needs rethinking. Because Partch built his own Dr. Seuss world of flamboyant instruments, invented his own 43-tones-to-the-octave scale, and devised his own notation, his music now rests in the hands of specialists and has spawned a cottage industry jealously guarded by those who performed with him. Scores, except for *Barstow* and *On the Seventh Day Petals Fell in Petaluma* (both published in *Source*, the 1960s journal of avant-garde music), are nearly impossible to come by. Those who can get access to them have a hell of a time figuring out what pitches are intended. Each instrument—the Spoils of War, the Quadrangularis Reversum, the Diamond Marimba—has its own tablature-like notation, and the info Partch provided in his book *Genesis of a Music* is not always sufficient for transcription. Despite the fine recordings available, Partch's methods remain hidden from outsiders who would like to study them, and the priests of his cult are in no hurry to change the situation.

The priests swear by the 43-tone scale, but *Enclosure 2* allows Partch to make abundantly clear that tuning was only a secondary issue. What he was passionate about was the concept he called corporeality: the "essentially vocal and verbal music of the individual," the ability of music to be "vital to a time and place, a here and now," the exact dead opposite of

German classical abstraction. *Genesis of a Music*'s magnificent opening essay, "From Emperor Chun to the Vacant Lot," mentions tuning only in passing as it explores in depth the history of the musically communicating human voice. For Partch, the Christian church wiped out the corporeality of ancient Greek music by insisting on hymns in which the God-praising words were already known and distorted by many notes to each syllable, encouraging a passive, uninvolved listening attitude.

Partch scorned abstract music, devoid of words, dance, or drama. Like so many young people who avoid sitting in concert halls today, he found passive listening a denial of the body. (In one telling story of his childhood, he heaps resentment on the girl who called him naughty for unselfconsciously drawing a male horse as he had seen it, with phallus proudly erect.) Aside from purity of tuning, he devised his scale at least partly to capture the exact inflections of spoken English. He may have written operas, but he was closer to Bob Dylan than to Verdi, and also to the Balinese Monkey Chant, the Korean P'ansori epic, ancient Greek drama, early Florentine opera, the blues—any genre which uses music to enhance, not dominate, a story. He saw his reputation veering toward that of a tuning theoretician, and he tried to head this off at the pass. In the only segment of *Enclosure 2* that deals with tuning—a demonstration with musical examples called "A Quarter-Saw Section of Motivations and Intonations"—he attempts, in an impatient preface, to put tuning in its place:

"The experiential, ritualistic, dramatic area has constituted a very large part of my belief and work. . . . I have easily given as much time to this endeavor as to intonation, which is basically the content of this tape. . . . I shall pass over, with compelling sadness and with no further comment, easily two-thirds of my life's work to discuss and demonstrate intonation. . . . News stories and even reviews have almost consistently latched onto the number 43 as though this were the touchstone of my life. It is not. It is, in fact, about the one-half truth of the one-fourth factor. It is totally misleading." The examples are invaluable, though, as apparently the only surviving aural document of how Partch thought about harmony, especially for his fascinating concept of tonal flux, in which chords mutate into each other through tiny pitch slides.

The rest of the CD set is obsessed with corporeality, and the early music Partch wrote to advance that concept can be pretty weird. His 1943 setting of Psalm 137 wails dismally, and in a 1947 recording of his Li Po songs (self-accompanied on Adapted Viola), his energy is so astonishing he sounds a little crazy. Put those recordings together with the photo of an amazingly clean-cut young Partch on the cover and you can't imagine how this music could have meant anything to anybody in the context of the 1940s. Use of normal flute and oboe in *Y.D. Fantasy* (from 1944) shows that he wasn't reluctant to employ conventional tuning, and in Philip Blackburn's rendition of a 1929 pop song (published under the pen name Paul Pirate), we get a rare glimpse of a pre-just-intonation Partch writing for good old badly tuned piano.

What clashes with Partch's reputation is the desire for correct and natural English declamation he speaks of so eloquently in one interview after another. Partly this is the natural result of overspecialization; most composers spend their time among similarly educated colleagues, not among street people, too far from the pulse of America to pick up the lingo. They write music about music theory for the same reason English professors write novels about university life. And so the tuning specialists involved in extending Partch's work show little concern for corporeality. There are a couple of exceptions in Ben Johnston's output: *Visions and Spels* and *Letter from Calamity Jane*. Dean Drummond, caretaker for several of Partch's original instruments, has commissioned new works for the Partch ensemble, a noble effort. The results, however, have been as abstract as any Darmstadt serial piece, usually without even a feelable beat.

Today's corporealists don't come from the world of microtones. Robert Ashley and Mikel Rouse wed vernacular phrases to music in ways that I think would have tickled Partch. Otherwise, corporeality has primarily become a woman's movement. Laurie Anderson, Meredith Monk, Laetitia de Compiegne Sonami, Brenda Hutchinson, Eve Beglarian, Elise Kermani, Pamela Z, Maria de Alvear, Susan Parenti—all these women who use their voices in a direct, communicative way come closer to the effect Partch was seeking than any of the tuning purists. Abstraction remains the favored realm of the ambitious male who would rather get in the history books than connect with the audience in front of him. Even guitarist-composers working with rock, that great fortissimo outburst of corporeality, are turning it toward wordless abstraction. Looked at from that angle, the question becomes not "Is Partch the greatest American composer?" but "Aside from Partch and a few others, does American music exist at all?"

sin more!

"I have never heard anyone play Chopin as well as I do!" crows an audibly drunk Harry Partch after playing a few bars on the piano in 1966, and suddenly, you have to remember that one of the works he burned in an iron stove at age 28 was a piano concerto he had worked on for four years. These CDs fill out our picture of Partch into a life of tremendous complexity. We finally hear Partch's settings of "The Jabberwocky" and passages from *Finnegans Wake*, plus an overdue recording of *U.S. Highball*, his unparalleled homage to hobo life. In an early version of *Barstow*, the rhythmic momentum is oddly submerged beneath the pitch-bending surface of strings and chromelodeon (43-pitch reed organ); the most infectious aspect of Partch's music, his dancelike percussion momentum, seems to have entered his aesthetic later.

The Tourtelot films of *Enclosure 1*, 70 minutes worth in all, don't date as well. They include an abstract film of gymnasts shot from odd angles to an oompah-pahing band accompaniment; a documentary of a pipe-smoking, uptight-looking Partch playing his instruments in his Chicago studio, and the film *Windsong*, for which Partch wrote the score, an updating of the Apollo and Daphne myth with the protagonists on the beach in shorts. The music survives and the personal glimpses are curious, but there is no hint of the gleeful, nose-thumbing Partch of later documentaries such as *The Dreamer That Remains* (1972), made after his elevation to a cult figure in the '60s. He seems uneasy that his music will be dismissed as not serious if he so much as cracks a smile.

In audio, though, Partch emerges as a whole human, full of demons and self-contradictions. He praises Mussorgsky as the only Western composer he likes, the John Field Piano Concerto as the best ever written, and the overdubbed boy's voice in Stockhausen's *Gesang der Jünglinge* as a brilliant idea. A musician who fell afoul of Partch while staying with him recounts finding an ice pick driven through his pillow. And another friend remembers what Partch called the five most evil words in the English language: "Go and sin no more!"

morton feldman's abstract expressions

JULY 23, 1996

Every Bible-thumping evangelist is certain that *he* will recognize Christ when the Savior returns. Likewise, every orchestra conductor and music professor is poised to champion the Next Great Composer, if only he or she would appear. They're all so mistaken. If and when Jesus vacations in this dump again, he'll be some radical, bum-befriending left-winger who'll look a lot more like Abbie Hoffman than Ralph Reed, and the preachers will call the cops to kick him off the church steps. And the Next Great Composer is always so deficient in social graces, so oblivious to the mandates of European tradition, that the classical musicians write him off as an amateur. Never fitting the official pattern, genius always takes the world by surprise.

And thus Morton Feldman, ignored by the classical establishment during his life (1926–1987), takes his place at Lincoln Center Festival 96 this August 2 through 4 as quite possibly the greatest composer of the late 20th century. Once known only as John Cage's quiet, heavy sidekick, the composer who made "as soft as possible" his trademark has come into his posthumous moment of glory. Among other works, the Chamber Music Society of Lincoln Center will play *The Viola in My Life 1* and *Why Patterns?*, Aki Takahashi will perform the delicately off-balance and 75-minute-long *Triadic Memories*, Joan LaBarbara will sing *Three Voices*, the Kronos Quartet will wind through six hours of the Second String Quartet, and John Kennedy will conduct Feldman's late, shimmering masterpiece, *For Samuel Beckett*. And, in an inspired move, the festival has de facto paired Feldman with Beckett, the playwright whose sense of bleak yet richly textured motionlessness is so perfectly parallel to Feldman's own. A Downtown composer occupying a Lincoln Center pedestal next to the century's greatest playwright? The times, they are a-changing indeed.

I knew Feldman slightly. I was only a grad student, and while he certainly paid attention to students, he favored the women. The irreverent caricatured him as a frog, with his large bulk, immensely thick glasses, preternaturally low hairline, and long, oily black hair. Convinced of his historical importance, he put people off with his arrogance, and yet he conferred attention on young composers so magnanimously that newcomers spontaneously called him "Uncle Morty" behind his back. He was famous for his bons mots. In one lecture I heard, he stated that it was impossible to teach composition in a university—even though that's what he did, at SUNY at Buffalo. One student became livid (Feldman always infuriated someone) and shouted, "How can you spend your life doing something you don't believe in?" Morty looked perplexed for a moment before replying, in his nasal, curvilinear Brooklynese, "That's a definition of mat*yoo*rity."

Thanks in part to such maturity, Feldmania has swept college music departments from the students upward, and the academics can no more stem the tide than they can ban nose piercing. No composer in decades has had such a widespread influence. Long decays and uniform dynamics are in fashion. Youngsters who write 12-tone music now specify *pianissimo* throughout. The noisy British improv group AMM has taken to soft and sustained playing. Even the music Cage wrote after Feldman died sounds like Feldman.

Perhaps what makes Feldman the composer of the moment is that he's the only Downtowner who beat the academics at their own game, the only one the establishment can embrace without dropping their European expectations. On the surface, his music meets most modernist criteria. It is atonal. It is highly chromatic, rippling with dissonant intervals. It rarely articulates a steady beat. Its rhythms are complexly notated, even if they don't sound complex when played.

What sticks in the classical-music craw is the stasis of Feldman's music, its absence of drama, direction, or virtuosity. What it has instead, and what sparks its influence, is its *mood,* a subtle and intricately etched melancholy found (as Feldman noted) in Kierkegaard, Van Gogh, Beckett, Rothko—but almost never in music. (When an interviewer traced this moodiness to Feldman's Jewishness and sorrow over Auschwitz, Feldman admitted that "I do think about the fact that I want to be the first great composer who is Jewish." Mendelssohn and Schoenberg, OK, but what about Mahler?) Because his pieces usually have one dynamic marking throughout, Feldman has been called a minimalist, and even, in an implied slap at Glass and Reich, the *real* minimalist. But how can a work as bristlingly complex, as difficult to grasp or even follow its score, as *For Samuel Beckett* be considered minimalist? The idea is absurd. All Feldman's music shares with the minimalists' is its flatness of surface, and his pensive moods, nuanced via reminiscences and slightly varied repetitions, couldn't be more foreign to the mass-produced impersonality of minimalist music and art.

The moods do come from painting, though. Feldman's milieu in the '50s was the art world, hanging out at the Cedar Bar with the abstract expressionists: de Kooning, Pollock, Guston, Kline. And while music was paralyzed at the time by the either/or of Schoenberg versus Stravinsky, painting was exploding in all directions. "There were luminaries," Feldman later said, "but the feeling that I had was that there really weren't issues."

Many composers, I think, envy painters and novelists because they aren't held hostage to a highly technical German tradition, and their arts don't seem split into a pair of artificial dichotomies (serialism versus minimalism, structure versus intuition). But only Feldman lived so much among painters that he absorbed a non-composerly attitude. For him, ideas became the enemy of music. Ideas are weapons in the war of careers, and their end result is ideology, not art. "There was a deity in my life," Feldman said, "and that was sound." "Those 88 notes are my Walden." He chided his students for trying to make their music *interesting;* he wanted to make his *beautiful.*

For Feldman, the image replaced the idea. The pairs of rocking, chromatic chords in *Why Patterns?*, the dense and slowly modulating thicket of *For Samuel Beckett,* the 12-tone row from Webern that makes sporadic appearances in the String Quartet II, the reappearing languorous arpeggio in *The Viola in My Life*—these irreducible images that can't be analyzed, only listened to, were partly suggested by the slowly shifting shapes in Alexander Calder's mobiles. Other qualities come straight from the canvas: the painterly application of touches of sound to an ineluctably flat aural plane. The length of his late works, two to six hours nonstop, intended to entice you to live with the music the way you live with a painting on your wall, slowly acclimatizing yourself to its implied universe. The obsession with minute choices of tone color, so intense that when Earle Brown once remonstrated, "But Morty, just because you've chosen the instruments, that doesn't mean the piece is finished," Feldman replied, "For me it is."

This isn't to say that Feldman tried to compose like a painter, for the reliance on images also comes from Stravinsky. Even if Feldman resisted taking sides in that debate, he appreciated Stravinsky's receptivity to sound, and he was certainly familiar with Stravinsky's *Requiem Canticles* (1966), whose muted chords for timpani and quadruple flutes sound stolen from Feldman's late music. Schoenberg concentrated on method, but for Stravinsky, just as for the abstract expressionists, "material reigns supreme," as Feldman wrote. "Construction is kept at a minimum. The material is always 'on camera.'"

But we miss Feldman's significance altogether if we don't see that the most important thing he brought back from painting was the artist's attitude of subjective immediacy in an era in which composers had become theorists and technicians. "Music is not painting," he observed, "but it can learn from this more perceptive temperament that waits and observes the inherent mystery of its materials, as opposed to the composer's vested interest in his craft." What Feldman particularly loved about abstract expressionism was that it wasn't polemical; it was a reaction not to history, but to the direct, in-the-studio experience of manipulating paint. Watching Pollock and Guston on one hand, and his Europe-certified composer colleagues on the other, he came to contrast the dangerous and vulnerable life of the artist with the safe, justifiable career of the professional composer. "[T]he real tradition of twentieth-century America," he wrote, "a tradition evolving from the empiricism of Ives, Varèse, and Cage, has been passed over as 'iconoclastic'—another word for unprofessional. In music, when you do something new, something original, you're an amateur. Your imitators—these are the professionals. It is these imitators who are interested not in what the artist did, but the means he used to do it. . . . The 'freedom' of the artist is boring to [the imitator] because in freedom he cannot reenact the *role* of the artist."

Feldman became the Great One by imprinting young composers with the attitude of the artist, while everyone else was role-playing. As gorgeously seductive as his music is—"sometimes too beautiful," Cage pointed out in *Silence*—the painterly listening mode it requests can challenge a concert audience. Paradoxically lush and austere at once, *For Samuel Beckett* contains an overload of detail, but nothing to focus on; hearing Kennedy conduct it at the Spoleto Festival in June was like seeing Monet's *Water Lilies* from two inches away, scintillating but mystifying. Yet this Lincoln Center retrospective will undoubtedly draw an international audience of Feldman devotees, like pilgrims to Mecca, proving that this contentious "amateur"'s instincts were right all along.

one-note wonder

a new york retrospective for italy's saintly mystic, giacinto scelsi

FEBRUARY 25, 1997

There are no known photographs of Giacinto Scelsi. "He didn't," as Frances-Marie Uitti puts it, "want his body photographed"—that is to say, his corporeal form. She describes him, though, as a short man, 5'6" or 7", stocky but not fat, powerfully built, with a mischievous smile and bright blue eyes that were absolutely clear into his seventies; and he loved to wear Tibetan caps over his head of thick Italian hair. Uitti, one of new music's most expert and adventurous cellists, worked closely with Scelsi (pronounced Shell-see) from 1975 until his death in 1988. She is the impetus behind this upcoming week's remarkably diverse retrospective of Scelsi's music at Merkin Hall, the Kitchen, Greenwich House, and elsewhere. And as she describes this reclusive, mysterious hero, this veritable saint of recent European music, it dawns on me that I have never had a visual image to connect with his growling, sliding, writhing, meditative, formless, melodyless, harmonyless music, so unlike anything else in European history. It's no small feat that the man remained even more elusive than his music.

Morton Feldman, in an off-the-cuff comment, dubbed Scelsi "the Charles Ives of Italy," and for lack of any firmer image to grasp, the title has stuck. The resemblances are superficial, but compelling as far as they go. Just as Ives was born to a successful Connecticut business family who looked down on musicians, Scelsi was born to Neapolitan nobility and scandalized his family by becoming an artist. Both were independently wealthy, neither lived ostentatiously, and neither relied on their music for income. Both composed by improvising, and both relied heavily on other musicians to prepare their scores for performance. Both suffered from nerves so sensitive that going out in public, even to hear their own works, was a torturous ordeal. Both remained unknown to the public until late in life; when I heard my first Scelsi work in 1973, he was 68 and still almost totally obscure. (I was at Oberlin the year the orchestra there recorded his incredible *Anahit* for violin and ensemble—his first disc available here, I think—so I got a prime seat on that bandwagon.)

Yet how could any two artists differ more in personality, temperament, and significance? Ives was deeply attached to his 19th-century New England roots, and in expressing them created an American aesthetic where none had existed before. Scelsi, steeped in inherited culture, rejected his European heritage lock, stock, and barrel, turning to Persian Sufi and Egyptian musics, absorbing Tibetan and Indian thought. Ives was a conservative Protestant who quoted hymn tunes; Scelsi was a devotee of the occult who immersed himself in Madame Blavatsky, Sri Aurobindo, Krishnamurti, Tibetan practices, and secret doctrines. At bottom, the comparison seems to spring mainly from our surprise that a European composer could work in isolation; we Americans thought we had a monopoly on that condition.

Like that other recluse, Conlon Nancarrow, however, Scelsi has become an excuse for a parade in the last 10 years, and his works are now staples of the European avant-garde circuit. If his music sounds like it came from Mars, his origins explain at least his early work. Italy has always produced two musical archetypes in tandem: the facile, lyrical melodist (Verdi, Puccini, Berio) and the introverted intellectual whose music appeals only to specialist tastes (Busoni, Dallapiccola, Maderna). Scelsi is clearly one of the latter. He is also part of a European generation born between Schoenberg and Ligeti (K. A. Hartmann, Wolfgang Fortner, and Boris Blacher are others) who got knocked out of circulation by a double punch, first World War II and then the implacable ascendancy of serialism. Scelsi, Uitti says, sat out the first punch in Switzerland in a depression so deep that 300 doctors failed to cure him. He studied composition with a Schoenberg student, Walter Klein, and then, having been the first Italian to write 12-tone music, was also the first to abandon it as a dead end.

The cures for Scelsi's psychic and musical malaises both arrived through Eastern meditation. One day he passed by a piano, Uitti explains, and "started to play one note over and over, and became absorbed. He began to improvise, to tape his improvisations and rework them onto the page, receiving music in a deeply inspired state. His whole view of composing and proper use of sound had changed." In a widely quoted statement from the early '50s, Scelsi wrote, "Sound is spherical. When we listen to it, however, it seems to have just two dimensions, pitch and duration. We know there is a third—depth—but depth in a certain sense escapes us. Painting long ago discovered perspective. . . . Yet music . . . has not succeeded in going beyond two dimensions."

To achieve perspective, Scelsi narrowed his other dimensions. His breakthrough work, a kind of paradigm for his later music, was his *Quattro pezzi su una nota sola*—*Four Pieces on One Note*—of 1959. They aren't really on one note, but slither, crescendo, and slowly glissando around a central pitch with the drama of a Mahler symphony and the intensity of focus of an Indian raga. This was the inception of what Scelsi called his "one-note" music, a microtonal idiom in which tunings squirm restlessly. In later works with Sanskrit, Assyrian, Latin, and mythologically inspired titles like *Anahit, Konx-Om-Pax*, and the ecstatically glowing *Uaxuctum* for four vocalists, Ondes Martenot, and orchestra, the one-note aesthetic expanded to symphonic proportions, with huge, moaning, microtonal gestures that leave the scales and metric grids of European music far behind. Paradoxically, it takes tremendous nuance of notation to make Scelsi's music sound like it isn't notated at all. His music for strings is so detailed, so attuned to the exact sound and technique of the instrument, that he often notated a violin part on four staves, one for each string.

Scelsi's manner of composing was unusual, especially for a European: he would improvise into a tape recorder and then either notate the results or have an assistant do it under his direction. Soon after his death, the practice spawned an intercontinental controversy. Vieri Tosati, Scelsi's main assistant for the last 10 years of his life, was interviewed for the *Giordinale de la Musica* and told the interviewer, more or less, that he had basically written Scelsi's music for him. Word spread like wildfire that the great man was a rich fake who had been able to afford to pay others to write his music.

Unhappily for those of us who live to report on musical controversies, this one seemed pretty thin in content and died out quickly. First of all, Tosati clammed up and refused to speak another word on the subject. Second, according to Uitti, Tosati's own music is conservatively Wagnerian, and while Scelsi had had several other assistants in preceding decades who helped notate his music, there was never any corresponding change in his inimitable style. Uitti suggests that the controversy was fanned by enemies who resented Scelsi for his apostasy against the 12-tone tradition.

Perhaps all that survives from that flare-up is what it revealed about the European attitude toward improvisation. Liszt and Beethoven composed by improvising at times, but the option wasn't available for any self-respecting 20th-century European; it flouted current European ideas of method and structure, of the paradigmatic making of a musical artifact from the outside in. Scelsi was a worshipper of sound, a believer in the immediacy of undefinable auditory experience. As such, his more relevant American analogues are the Indian music–studying La Monte Young (though without Young's theoretical interests) or, perhaps most appropriately, Feldman himself. He was also the only European composer to date whose interest in Asian aesthetics seems more than anecdotal, the only European to totally break free of the limits of Western rationalism and achieve a true spirituality in sound akin to non-Western traditions. Next to him, Pärt and Górecki seem like mere dabblers. And his posthumous presence in New York this week promises the most intense and enlightening musical experience New York has been offered in years.

father of us all

the critic as composer

JULY 8, 1997

Virgil Thomson: Composer on the Aisle
By Anthony Tommasini
W. W. Norton & Company, 605 pp., $30

Perhaps no one has ever erected a statue to a critic, as Sibelius said—though I hear there's one of J. S. Dwight in Boston—but biographies of critics are beginning to appear, and none can be more important than Anthony

Tommasini's *Virgil Thomson: Composer on the Aisle.* Thomson was the best music critic in the English language since Shaw—and better than Shaw if concision, career duration, and consequentiality of subject matter are your criteria. At the same time, Thomson was a leading composer in the Americanist movement of the '20s and '30s, too neglected today partly because of the continuing resonance of his criticism. Among other things, he wrote what Andrew Porter, late of the *New Yorker,* considered the greatest American opera: *The Mother of Us All.* I agree with Porter. It is the only opinion we hold in common. It must be true.

Given Thomson's iconic status as a critic, then, you have to wonder why composer-critics have become so uncommon, and Tommasini provides a few answers. Interestingly, though he had written occasional reviews since 1922, Thomson himself was reluctant to become a full-time critic. He had seen his composer friend Theodor Chanler peremptorily fired from the *Boston Herald* for criticizing the Boston Symphony Orchestra and infuriating the conductor Serge Koussevitzky. But the *Tribune's* visionary chief editorial writer Geoffrey Parsons saw possibilities in Thomson, and, hiring him, whipped him into shape and sanded off his pugnacious style in memos as entertaining as Thomson's reviews. "[A] cult is a cult and must be approached patiently and calmly—the way you would a nervous horse," he wrote after one of Thomson's attacks on Sibelius.

Thomson needed smoothing out. He was blunt. Asked by the wife of the *Tribune's* owner why he wanted to be a critic, he replied that "the general standard of music reviewing in New York had sunk so far that almost any change might bring improvement. Also I thought that perhaps my presence in a post so prominent might stimulate performance of my works." Of Aaron Copland's book *What to Listen for in Music,* Thomson wrote the author—a supportive friend—"Your book I read through twice and I still find it a bore." Copland responded with astonishing good humor: "I was about to think that so much praise must be deserved when your letter arrived. Thought I: we can always depend on Virgil." Invited to vacation on the Greek island of Corfu by new-music patron Betty Freeman, Thomson insulted her cooking. Behind the charming public image, Tommasini shows us a churlish and petty man.

Equally disillusioning is the pettiness competition Thomson carried on with Gertrude Stein in their operatic collaborations, a relationship I had pictured as idyllic. They were no longer on speaking terms even before the first opera *Four Saints in Three Acts* was produced, Stein sending him a card that read, "MISS GERTRUDE STEIN declines further acquaintance with Mr. Virgil Thomson." Thomson felt he should get two-thirds of the royalties for *Four Saints* because Stein had opportunities to make additional money publishing the libretto; Stein responded that her well-known name was more crucial to the success of the venture than his music, whereupon Thomson attacked as ludicrous the idea that her impenetrable texts had any commercial value. Thus the squabbles and vanities of genius.

Ultimately, Tommasini credits Thomson's self-serving behavior to his perception that his music was never taken seriously enough, and he charts Thomson's struggles against a classical-academic establishment that looked down its nose at his melodic simplicity and use of the American vernacular. As usual, Roger Sessions comes off as the Boris Badenov of American music, only with no sense of humor: he bullied Chanler, who was initially enthusiastic about *Four Saints,* into writing a nasty review. The history of great American music has struggled forward against the wind of sustained protest from Sessions and his ilk. And while Thomson could usually count on positive reviews from his own paper, he endured a lifetime of haughty put-downs from Eurocentric Uptowners at the *Times* (a paper that, interestingly, Tommasini is currently a stringer for). Thomson was a Downtown composer before Downtown existed.

He justified his music's simplicity as partly the result of being a critic. In his famous essay "Why Composers Write How," he wrote, "[T]he composer who has written criticism with some regularity—who has faced frequently the deplorable reality that a desired audience effect cannot be produced by wishful thinking—. . . cannot help learning a good deal that is practical to know about clarity, coherence, and emphasis." He might have added, but didn't, that a critic-composer's relation to his own style must perforce become somewhat artificial. He is not allowed to believe, as other composers so often do, that his own compositional idiom is the only valid one. Faced with the entire panoply of current styles, and obliged to spend some time inside the head of every composer he hears, he has hammered home on a weekly basis the contingency and relativity of his compositional choices.

As a result, the composer-critic tends to retreat and distance himself equally from all the styles he encounters in his weekly rounds, writing a music not closely attuned to the current scene. He seeks refuge in a private idiom safe from his own criticisms of others. The late 20th century's other best-known composer-critic, my predecessor at this paper, Tom Johnson, aimed in his music for maximum objectivity, writing music according to strict compositional logics that allowed him to say, "I want to *find* the music, not compose it." By seeking total objectivity, Johnson attempted an uncriticizable music, for how can you criticize something merely "found"? Thomson's solution was to combine a radical objectivity of source material—the hymns, folk tunes, dances, and parlor-song idiom of American vernacular—with radically subjective disjunctions in key, tempo, and melody. Critics who disparaged his music were both too highbrow and too hidebound to catch his sense of humor and Dada-inspired streams of consciousness.

The fear about practitioner-critics, of course, is that they can't be objective. And today, having passed through grad school and picked up a superstitious penchant for speciously precise technical jargon, the vast majority of composers are no longer able or willing to write clearly and colorfully. Composer-critics are rare. What do we have instead? In recent years at the *Times*, Donal Henahan and Edward Rothstein undertook one-man campaigns to destroy contemporary music, with the Downtown variety a high-priority target. This is what's called objectivity: the fact that their vicious, prejudiced vendettas had no *obvious* personal motivation. And because they didn't write or perform music and meticulously avoided knowing composers personally, their blasts weren't backed up by professional insight. How much better it would have been to have another Virgil Thomson in that position, passionate and partisan, but admittedly so and surgically accurate. The critic as keeper at the gates of culture is a function that long ago outlived its usefulness, if indeed it ever had any. A critic-composer never sees himself as a gatekeeper, because he's afraid of being left outside himself.

With Thomson's own pristine writing as constant example, Tommasini has written a clear, engrossing biography attentive to the overriding themes of Thomson's life. He has a mania for including extensive biographical background on everyone Thomson ever met, and you have to be entranced by the entire scene to savor every paragraph. Thomson's homosexual life, which he was extremely private about (he was arrested at a gay bordello in 1942), makes up a large part of the book; refreshingly, however—given current trends in musicology—Tommasini does not try to reduce or even relate the simplicity and aimlessness of Thomson's music to his sexual proclivities. Thomson would be embarrassed to see his private life so exposed, but he would surely concede that Tommasini has been meticulously fair and even-handed throughout. The book is a good starting point for a fresh look at the relation of criticism to music, a subject everyone complains about and no one analyzes.

minimalism isn't pretty

tony conrad makes a truculent comeback

APRIL 28, 1998

By the time minimalism emerged as a public phenomenon in 1973, it was squeaky clean and spruced up for company. And as the audience for minimalism grew, it became known as a music of pretty harmonies, hard-edged melodies, and motoric rhythms, made by the tightly knit ensembles of two highly visible figures, Steve Reich and Philip Glass.

Before its emergence, however, minimalism was a nameless, cantankerous Downtown movement of many composers and musicians. It was not so much audience-accessible and "classical" (as it would be from 1973 on) as often gritty, demanding, writhing, rebellious, austere. Minimalist concerts went on for hours nonstop, sometimes all night, often at deafening decibel levels. So many minds collaborated that it was not always possible to tell who introduced what innovation. In fact, the original minimalist scene so bristled with tension that it virtually exploded, and when the smoke cleared, newcomers Reich and Glass just happened to be the only ones left standing.

Step aside, pretty guys: Early Minimalism is back. Composers we haven't heard from in decades, their names barely known to aficionados, are suddenly concertizing and swelling our CD cabinets with new discs.

Consider the fates of the first minimalists:

- Electronics pioneer Richard Maxfield, his mind blown on drugs, ended his life by jumping out of a window at 42.
- Terry Jennings, child prodigy and composer of some of the first extremely long instrumental works, was killed at 41 in a drug deal gone sour.
- Angus MacLise, a reputedly phenomenal drummer, died, in a possibly drug-related death, in Kathmandu in 1979.
- Tony Conrad, who introduced drones and mathematically pure tuning into minimalism, got out of music and made groundbreaking structuralist films, the best known being *Flicker*.
- Charlemagne Palestine, a legend for his night-long performances frenetically strumming pianos and organs, likewise disappeared into the visual art world.

- Dennis Johnson, whose lengthy piano works anticipated La Monte Young's *The Well-Tuned Piano,* couldn't stomach the music business, and turned his number interests toward computer science.

- John Cale veered off into rock and did a nice business with a little group called the Velvet Underground.

Out of the original New York minimalists of the early '6os, only La Monte Young and Terry Riley went on to new-music careers. Until 1987, Young was independently well-funded enough to maintain a shadowy presence, unrecorded and unheard except by those who sought him out at his Church Street loft. Riley bailed out of a meteoric rise by not recording a note during the '70s, and the variety of his recent musics baffles listeners who were enchanted by his early modal improvisation. No wonder Glass and Reich were able to pick up the remnants of the movement and walk away with it.

Today, however, after years of scorn from other musicians, minimalism has entered history, and is being rediscovered by two crowds. One is the academics, who have misdubbed it The Last Official Movement in Western Music and declared it fair game for Ph.D. dissertations. The other is the ambient DJ crowd, who have appropriated rough-edged early minimalism with a more accurate ear: not just as a source of new structures and languages, but as a radical, looser approach to the experience of time. With all this attention, it makes sense for the early minimalists who aren't dead to attempt comebacks, and two are under way.

The more audacious is by Tony Conrad, who, after 20 years of silence, has suddenly unleashed an apparently limitless barrage of CDs of his new and old music, culminating in a four-CD set self-consciously titled *Early Minimalism: Volume One.* Conrad started out as a violinist, and as a teenager became interested in alternative tunings via a surprising route: his violin teacher assigned him the *Mystery* (or *Rosary*) *Sonatas* of Heinrich Ignaz Franz von Biber (1644–1704), a curious set of Baroque variations in which each movement requires a different tuning of the violin. Fascinated by the different sonorities available with each retuning of the open strings, Conrad got hooked on the acoustics of pitch, and his mathematical bent led him to explore the overtone series.

So when Conrad met La Monte Young in 1959, Young was the man with the concept and Conrad the man with the know-how to make it sing. Young had already been making extremely slow pieces of music in which notes were held for minutes at a time. Conrad introduced Young to the arithmetic of the harmonic series, and—according to the argumentative, 96-page booklet included in *Early Minimalism*—also introduced the idea of a drone. With MacLise, Riley, Cale, and Young's eventual wife Marian Zazeela, the group performed as the Theater of Eternal Music, singing and playing exotically tuned strings and saxes over drones loud enough to be heard—as Glass and others have remembered—outside the building and way down the block.

What we should have on disc today are those amazing Theater of Eternal Music performances. Sadly, those have been caught in a copyright dispute and frozen by threats of litigation for almost 30 years now. Young claims that since he determined the frequency ratio progressions, he should rightfully be listed as sole composer. Conrad and Cale claim that since the pieces were improvisatory, all participants share credit equally. Young possesses the tapes but can't release them, and Conrad has occasionally picketed Young's performances with signs reading, "La Monte Young wants me to die without hearing my music." The fight goes to the heart of what constitutes an improvisatory work; neither side will be generous, and no solution seems imminent.

Deprived of the Eternal Music tapes, Conrad has released in *Early Minimalism* the one solo recording he made in the mid '60s outside the confines of what he calls the "Dream Syndicate" (a term so catchy it was taken over by an L.A. postpunk band). Titled *Four Violins*, it's a 32-minute, overdubbed, rough-hewn continuum of amplified violin drones touching on various harmonics. Also, since 1987, Conrad has been recreating the spirit of the Eternal Music improvs as closely as he can in a series of pieces he calls *Early Minimalism*, all for amplified strings.

A fluent postmodern theorist and scintillating wordsmith, Conrad has written garrulous liner notes casting Young as a modern Pythagoras, not only for deriving harmony from number relationships but for creating a cult with himself as high priest. "The nascent idealism of the early 60s," Conrad writes, "made it easy to fall for Pythagorean number mysticism without having a clear perception of the anti-democratic legacy which Pythagoreanism brings with it." And so, ironically, Conrad the math genius takes a "more democratic" and less strict approach to tuning, seeing the harmonic series only as an ideal to be approximated. The *Early Minimalism* pieces grind restlessly around variably consonant overtone complexes for about an hour each.

Such austere drone landscapes don't make for comfortable listening; you have to surrender yourself to Conrad's bristling harmonics, with no tempo or melodic landmarks to hold onto. I still prefer his newer, livelier, drum-driven work, *Slapping Pythagoras*. Perhaps *Early Minimalism*'s inadvertently biggest selling point, however, is the CD video footage included with the "enhanced" CD of *Four Violins*. Interviews give vivid glimpses of Conrad's eccentric personality and incisive monologue style. "Life should be abundant enough," he muses in a defense of minimalism likely to gratify both its friends and enemies, "for everyone to find their greatest pleasure in wasting time." If past behavior is any indication, Young is unlikely to rise to Conrad's bait, but I sure wouldn't want someone this blessed by the Blarney Stone barreling down on *my* reputation.

The other, less truculent comeback is that of Charlemagne Palestine. Once known for his Cognac-fueled but ecstatic attacks on the keys of a Bösendorfer grand piano, surrounded by stuffed animals, he reportedly reached a point in the '70s at which his concerts consisted of insulting audience members. Now, after more than a decade of silence, he has started performing in Europe occasionally, and in February he made his American re-debut playing an all-night concert in Santa Monica.

I had long despaired of hearing his legendary strumming techniques, but since 1995 three CDs have been released. Of these, *Strumming Music* comes closest to what I'd heard of his reputation: simple tone-complexes drummed so insistently that the clash of overtones (even in equal-tempered tuning) begins to create sparkly illusions. *Four Manifestations on Six Elements* features both piano and organ, the latter in sonorities remarkably pretty as Palestine seeks his "sonic alchemy."

Both those discs document performances of the '70s. Now his first post-hiatus disc (recorded in 1987) has appeared, *Godbear,* with his trademark teddy bear on the cover. Unlike the shimmering early stuff, this is a growly attack on thick bass chords. That seems a well-calculated ploy given today's tough-eared new minimalism fans. Reich's and Glass's reputations for easy-listening prettiness and simplicity for easy-listening prettiness and simplicity have never sat well with the underground music scene, but Conrad's raspy violin drones and Palestine's fervent hammering conjure a disturbing energy that hip-hop fans and collage-spinning DJs can respect.

There's a tremendous vein of early minimalism still to be mined: in addition to the output of Terry Jennings and Dennis Johnson's amazing piano works such as *November*, Barbara Benary's music deserves major attention, and the scores of Julius Eastman—once thrown out on the street by the sheriff—await painstaking reconstruction. After three decades, minimalism is returning to its roots, and they turn out to have a refreshingly gritty authenticity.

Additional research: Joel Hunt and Dan Hirsch.

grand old youngster

turning the century at lincoln center

JULY 20, 1999

In honoring Steve Reich as the featured composer for this year's festival, Lincoln Center performs a very different service than in past years. Morton Feldman, featured in 1996, was an underground figure whose reputation had swelled to the point that public recognition could wait no longer. Ornette Coleman, honored the next year, had been famous for decades, but the facets of his work had rarely been brought together in such a way, filling him out in several dimensions. Reich, on the other hand, has been retrospected to death. The concerts that take place this week—including *The Cave* performed Thursday, *Drumming* and a new work for the Kronos Quartet Saturday, and *The Desert Music* and *Tehillim* Tuesday—are a nod of the head to an artist who may now be considered, by general acclamation, America's greatest living composer.

It seems odd to end this noisy, high-tech century with Reich, music's sweet-sounding eternal youngster, as the leading available Grand Old Man. And yet there are enough parallels with Aaron Copland to suggest a ready-made slot for his reputation to fall into. Both New Yorkers, they started out in the avant-gardes of their generations before undergoing highly public reactions against modernist complexity and discovering their own crowd-pleasing diatonic idioms. Each remains loved not for his entire output, but for a handful of works written in his thirties and forties that captured the public imagination: *Drumming* versus *Fanfare for the Common Man, Music for Eighteen Musicians* versus *Appalachian Spring*. Both are technically competent enough to please musical experts; neither is thought of as a primarily technical composer. Both . . . well, you can play this game yourself.

I never heard Copland called the best living composer, but Reich has less European competition. A nonmusician recently asked me point-blank to name the greatest, and with Feldman, Cage, Messiaen, and Nancarrow now dead, I couldn't blurt out a credible candidate. Robert Ashley flashed to mind, but he is too sui generis in his approach to compare, and too far outside the mainstream for the view to find resonance; similarly with La Monte Young (who was actually once considered as a Lincoln Center Festival dedicatee). A few years ago, Mark Swed threw Lou Harrison's hat in the ring—he's certainly a composer of masterly and often accessible works, though perhaps too variable in style and quality, and too tied to Javanese gamelan, to achieve sufficient general acclaim. The most popular European names since Reich—Arvo Pärt and Louis Andriessen—seem indebted to him. Of course, musicians Uptown have no end of names to suggest—Boulez, Carter, Babbitt—all of whom would swim against the tide of waning tolerance for serialist complexity. I can't imagine any of these names drawing as many people to Lincoln Center as Reich will.

More objective data come from William Duckworth's new book, *20/20: 20 New Sounds of the 20th Century* (Schirmer Books). Duckworth polled his colleagues for lists of the 20 20th-century works that mattered most to them personally, and boiled the list down to 20 finalists; the resulting book, laced with Duckworth's reader-friendly historical/philosophical commentary, is an exemplary amateur's introduction to new music. The short list, though—which includes "O Superman," *I Am Sitting in a Room*, and Pärt's *Miserere* as well as *Le Sacre du Printemps* and *Rhapsody in Blue*—is less informative than what Duckworth calls "the long list," the original 86 pieces his friends' overlapping lists provided.

Of the 29 still-living composers on the list, nine appear for more than one work (surely a strong criterion for considering someone one of the greats): Stockhausen, Ligeti, Terry Riley, Xenakis, Meredith Monk, Pärt, and Ashley each twice, and Reich and Philip Glass tied at three works each. Glass as the world's greatest composer? Well, cognoscenti of all stripes would shout that one down, a little unfairly in my opinion. Most often heard, perhaps, but not for the best reasons. One could argue, and should, that this specific-composition-based poll handicaps composers whose life's work is more of a continuing process, like Young and Pauline Oliveros; but the public clings to products, and has difficulty perceiving process.

If music were a merito-democracy in which musicians' votes counted for a little more than nonmusicians', Reich might well be elected the greatest at the turn of the century. What's lacking about this week's tribute is a sense of excitement, an anticipation that his recent music may have burst through to a new level of profundity (as has been so true of Feldman, Nancarrow, and Ashley). Copland, in his late years, found his populist middle style unsustainable and timidly crept onto the 12-tone bandwagon; I feel Reich has sometimes failed via an opposite response, clinging too stubbornly to an early style that seemed perfect only for its historical moment. Hopefully, Reich's new *Triple Quartet* for the live and prerecorded Kronos Quartet will make us feel like we're celebrating a master entering his last, greatest phase, rather than thanking a once-young revolutionary for the breakaway he made 30 years ago. But the best thing about a Reich tribute is that he fits perfectly the criterion Duckworth asked for: his music matters to us personally.

concert reviews

maximal spirit

la monte young

JUNE 9, 1987

The following passage appeared in 1977 in a book called *Culture, Crisis, and Creativity*, although the ideas were formulated by 1926. They are by Dane Rudhyar, astrologer, composer, and philosopher, but they could stand as program notes for La Monte Young's mammoth masterwork *The Well-Tuned Piano*:

> A piano is thus a microcosm of tones . . . the sounds produced by striking, touching, caressing the keys . . . can be made to participate in the complex resonance of the whole sounding board. One can [experience] them as modes of vibrations and centers of activity *interpenetrating* in a higher dimension of the sound space. The composer-pianist pressing the keys can act somewhat as does a sculptor when he deals with the clay. . . . The piano [becomes], if handled in a truly "magical" manner and not as a pretext for finger dexterity, a collection of gongs and even a miniaturized symphony orchestra. . . . What I have called *orchestral pianism* then replaces the dreary type of classical or neoclassical pianism . . . in which mechanized fingers . . . uniformly strike insensitized keys.

There's no question of influence. Rudhyar never realized the compositional ideals he clearly foresaw, and he seems to have been only vaguely aware of Young: his description of Young's music in *The Magic of Tone and the Art of Music* quotes a secondhand account. *The Well-Tuned Piano*, which Young recently played over seven Sunday nights at his Dia Art Foundation Performance Space, has been in development since 1964. Though Young has only heard one Rudhyar work, the startling unanimity of their thinking points to a common spiritual source.

The recent reemergence of avant-garde guru Young, whose influence has widely spread through an underground network, invites a reexamination of his significance, though little has emerged aside from the clichés that have followed him for two decades. "Father of minimalism" is Young's

currently advantageous PR moniker, but I'd like to think his real significance lies elsewhere. Not for inspiring the Ravelian glitz of John Adams's
The Chairman Dances or the simplistic neo-Baroquisms of Glass's *In the
Upper Room* is La Monte Young assured a place in history. In using sound
as a spiritual medium, Young travels a road paved by Scriabin, Rudhyar,
and Cage; minimalism took the Hollywood exit long ago (c. 1973).

"Around 1960 I became interested in yoga," Young recently said, "in
which the emphasis is on concentration and focus on the sounds inside
your head. Zen meditation allows ideas to come and go as they will, which
corresponds to Cage's music; he and I are like opposites which help define
each other." Differences between Young and the minimalists run even
deeper. From Pandit Pran Nath, Young learned that "in singing, when the
tone becomes perfectly in tune with a drone, it takes so much concentration to keep it in tune that it drives out all other thoughts. You become one
with the drone and one with the Creator. It's a very, very strong experience
for the performer, but it happens with the listener, too." That oneness with
sound and existence, sought by yogic meditation, is a highly alert state,
very different from the semiconscious, hypnotic trance that was so long
assumed to be the aim of minimalism that it became self-fulfilling. The
music press, lacking acquaintance with Eastern spirituality, has confused
the issue for decades, to the extent that the public is hardly able to distinguish between Young's awareness-heightening tone ratios and Glass's
mind-numbing repetitions.

My personal experience with *The Well-Tuned Piano* was one of just
such heightened concentration, despite an alarming tendency for other
people to fall asleep and snore. (Then, I never drink before concerts, and
never refrain afterwards.) Played on a Bösendorfer Imperial grand piano
tuned to Young's special brand of just intonation, *The Well-Tuned Piano* is
an unparalleled Western exercise in attunement to sound. Its underlying
metaphor is so simple as to almost escape detection: rain. "Imitating nature
in her manner of operation," each large section builds up from sparse,
melodic notes to dense, stochastic "clouds" (Xenakis's word *and* Young's)
with such gradualness that intense listening is needed to catch the process
in motion. Here, form followed acoustic necessity: the flow of momentum
marshaled the vibrations of air in the room, slowly making the ear aware
of sounds that weren't actually being played. The play of combination and
difference tones created astounding aural illusions. More than once I
became convinced Young was singing (he wasn't); the sound source would
seem to suddenly shift location; I thought I heard foghorns, the roar of
machinery, wood blocks, a didgeridoo, and most powerfully, the low, low

vibration of the 18-cycles-per-minute E-flat that the ear supplied as the "missing fundamental" of the piano's overtones.

As fantastically well-produced as Gramavision's five-LP boxed set is, the nature of microphones allows only a faint suggestion of such effects. The advantages of the recording are that (1) its wide dynamic range clarifies the piece's contours, and (2) the liner notes contain a second-by-second account of the music's form. That form is uniquely fluid, and not as haphazard as a casual listener might think; interestingly, while both minimalism and serialism aim for a music devoid of memory or anticipation, Young plays Wagner-like, with constant suggestions of themes past and present. The tuning specifications can make the piano sound like a gamelan or bells, an aspect captured by the recording. Since the progression from idea to idea depends somewhat on the whim of the moment, the piece is unnotatable in principle, and, like any spiritual art form, Young is passing it on orally: his composer/tuner Michael Harrison has learned the piece Eastern-style, from observation. Young's achievement represents the first successful implantation of an Eastern heart into a Western body (a grand piano). It relates less to minimalism, though, than to Rudhyar's concept of *tone*, an organic, site-specific, sonic symbol, as distinct from the abstract *notes* of the classical tradition.

The three concerts of Young's early music, May 16, 18, and 20 (I heard the latter two), evoked another surprising distinction between Young and minimalism. His music from the late '50s, as represented by *For Brass, For Guitar,* and the String Trio, had its roots in 12-tone technique. The String Trio—played by Ben Hudson, John Graham, and Charles Curtis—expanded Webern's tri-chord aphorisms into multi-minute values, though hearing the piece through the distracting pulse of bow changes required an aural squint. The meditative values that sound natural and intuitive in the music of Morton Feldman and Pauline Oliveros were here mechanical; 12-tone rows do not lend themselves to magnification, though one can guess how the piece might have stirred Stockhausen's imagination when he saw it in 1959. Young must have found himself between '58 and '62, for in *The Second Dream of the High-Tension Line Stepdown Transformer* (one of the century's great titles) his meditative lines began to flow. In this ethereal realization by eight excellent trumpet players, only four pitches were used (in frequency ratios of 12:16:17:18), their combinations carefully circumscribed to give an impression of purposeful freedom.

What the retrospective revealed, though, is that Young is the last American avatar of what I call the Darmstadt mindset: the conviction that music must exhibit a theoretical consistency with the composer's conception of reality. It's clear that, through the 12-tone pieces, jazz improv, drone installations, conceptual pieces, and the labyrinthine fantasia of *The Well-Tuned Piano*, Young considers his music unified in personality, intention, and philosophy. His early distaste for intervals of a third, due to their overuse in classical music and the cowboy songs of his native Idaho, is now justified a posteriori by treatises on the superiority of ratios derived from three and sevens (thirds derive from fives). As with Boulez and Stockhausen, there is a compulsive need to justify every step, to make explicit in afterthought the revelations of intuition. By contrast, in conversation and lecture, Glass gives no impression of having thought deeply about the principles of his music, and John Adams has no compunction about rifling the past for ideas; Steve Reich seems caught in the middle, torn between his metaphysics and the criterion of applause. I'm old-fashioned enough to admire Young's theoretical drive, which lends his output a coherence that should be envied by the academics who most underrate him.

And yet there is a dark side to the Darmstadt mindset. A pussy-cat next to Boulez and Stockhausen, Young is not guilty of what Dutilleux called "aesthetic terrorism," the use of analysis as intimidation by the serialists of the '50s. But many are put off by Young's obsessive self-documentation, and by the litany in his program notes of claimed historic achievements and indebted musicians. Given that Young has earned an unshakable position in the history of music, there are those who would prefer he leave it to others to point out the fact. Arguably, though, his underground position is special. Having exercised a major influence for more than two decades before his first record on a commercial American label, he may underrate the extent to which his music is popularly regarded. Too, Jung has detailed the frequent confusion, in those who have had profoundly spiritual experiences, of the ego with the Self from which creativity flows. I don't object to the self-importance as long as it doesn't appear in the music, and I don't hear it in *The Well-Tuned Piano*. Considering the work's harmonic, thematic, and timbral complexity, my gut feeling was that five and a half hours was not a minute too long.

As I see it, Young's reputation is popularly premised on an unhelpful connection. If the minimalists took their impetus from Young's drone pieces, they absorbed only the letter of his music and not its spirit; minimalism is the most materialistic (in two senses of the word) music since Strauss. At least Babbitt's musical atomism concentrates on abstract relationships, rather than on prettiness and the money to be gained thereby. Except in the music of Terry Riley (who, though only a year younger, calls Young a "mentor"), Young's *real* influence has not yet begun to be heard.

When it is, I suspect it will manifest on the same level as that of the music of Scriabin, Rudhyar, and Ives, in terms less of technique than of a spiritual attitude toward sound. And if he has as many surprises left in store after his 30-year-retrospective as Cage has had since his 25-year one (1955), we've got a lot left to learn from La Monte Young.

big machines, little issues

the 1987 international computer music conference

SEPTEMBER 29, 1987

URBANA, ILLINOIS—The International Computer Music Conference has had more enticing locations (Paris, Vancouver, and The Hague) in the last three years, but Urbana's a great place. U. of I. undergrads are all blond. The guys have shoulders like bookcases, the girls have fluffy, shampoo-commercial hair and tanned legs. Cornfields and haylofts are ten minutes away. In the midst of this real-life teen-sex movie, about 320 academics—many bearded, one black, perhaps a dozen women—met August 22 through 26 to discuss the future of music.

Whose music was an untouched question. Two composers, well known in new-music circles, complained in the Music Building lobby that a certain software program was geared toward the pop market. "But there *is* no market for our music," one shrugged. "Ah," grinned the other, "but in 200 years people will pronounce your name and say—'The Master.'" They were satirizing the profession's platitudes, while granting bitter recognition to their impotence outside the ivory tower. The music played here was produced in a rarefied atmosphere by composers who have now been insulated from audiences and critics for three decades. As one participant, Jean-Baptiste Barriere, put it in an incredulous review of the 1986 conference, "Life is elsewhere! The most interesting music today using the computer is . . . inaudible in the noise of the conference. It is somewhere else, and it does not claim to be computer music; it desires simply to be music."

Still, given my expectations I was surprised the music was as good as it was; that is, only a small majority of the works were boring, hideous, or both. Everyone agreed on the percentage, though there was some dispute about which works fit those categories. This was a trade show, only second-arily for public consumption. The participants came from Western Europe, Canada, and across the U.S., but the selection of pieces exhibited a healthy

Midwestern bias. Oh, there were a couple of serial works, a smattering of minimalism. But most of the music fell into two genres, "wall-of-sound" pieces (as I heard people call them) and gesture pieces.

Gesture pieces are a Midwestern peculiarity, mistaken by New Yorkers for watered-down serialism. Unlike serial music, gesture music relies not on pitch discrimination, but on the overall emotional flow of a succession of quasi-theatrical musical motions. Greek composer Iannis Xenakis was the conference's honored guest, and his four works fit in so smoothly with this aesthetic that he began to sound like the "Midwest composer of Europe." He lectured on his new UPIC computer music setup, a screen-operated system that converts, with a sweep of the hand, drawn visual images into sound. Its musical results, as manifested in his noisy tape piece *Mycenes Alpha,* were flatly unsubtle but gave new meaning to the term "gesture music."

Accustomed to Downtown DX-7 performances, I thought that listening to tape pieces in a darkened hall had vanished with love beads, but I was reminded that these boys, all institutionally supported, were working with the Big Machines, supercomputers too large to transport. (Max Mathews, who invented computer music in 1955, noted of one synthesizer, "It's mobile; it moves on money.") Of the few live electronics pieces, one was sensational. Richard Boulanger (Berklee College, Boston) brought with him an invention called the daton (drum and baton), and performed on it the duet *Shadows* with violinist Dorothy Martirano. Boulanger played by expressively tapping a membrane, which added rhythms and dynamics to a "score" of pitches and timbres prestored in the computer. Not only did it beat listening to a tape recorder, it allowed the piece to flow with the performer's inspiration.

Nor did déjà vu end with the tape pieces. What we collegiate wits used to eloquently term "squeakfart music" is still around, despite myriad demonstrations that the old "space sounds" need no longer be tolerated. There were moments when it seemed that the only effect of 30 years of digital synthesis research was the elimination of tape hiss. If the conference established anything, it was that digital technology has shot ahead by seeming decades in the last three years, while aesthetic thinking continues to plod. Even the most hackneyed works exhibited a striking timbral sophistication. *Beams!* by James Mobberley (U. of Missouri), for trombone and tape, sounded like 5,000 other gesture pieces, but the derivation of all of its taped sounds from trombone samples—like mouthpiece noises or flicking the bell—lent it a slick, metallic unity that such pieces never had before.

Wall-of-sound pieces, bands of noise whose texture is modulated from within, date back to Xenakis's musique concrète and Ligeti's instrumental continuums, but the computer has given them new life and greater definition. The best of these was *Riverrun* by Barry Truax (Simon Fraser U., Vancouver), a gritty continuum built up through the addition of tiny burbling sounds. The others were more or less deft imitations, but it was significant that one of the most effective textural continuums was created with only a piano. *Dulcimer Dream* by North Texas State composer Phil Winsor used computer probabilities to select a progression of virtuosically Chopinesque chords whose subdued fury, in Adam Wodnicki's hands, was quite different from the cold violence that electronic sounds most easily express. The program notes slyly commented that the resonant drone made by repeated piano notes was a texture not reproducible by electronic means.

Winsor wasn't the only minimalist. *Music for Signals* by New York composer Laurie Spiegel was in her usual modal/pentatonic vein, and Brian Evans's *Marie Sets,* based on algorithms, was tonal without being repetitive. Scott Wyatt's (U. of I.) Terry Rileyish *Circulation* bordered on commercialism, but it was more refreshing than mindless. John Cage's spirit, too, hovered for a wonderful moment during *Algorithms III* for ensemble by Cage's associate Lejaren Hiller. Hiller had programmed his computer, among other things, to select quotes from popular symphonies, producing a happy cacophony that sounded as though P. D. Q. Bach had discovered the *I Ching.* The academic community greeted these unscholastic offerings with surprisingly benign countenances. Whether such tolerance stemmed from a new openness, apathy, or weariness of fighting against a winning cause, I couldn't discern, but several welcomed the diversity. Whether it indicates that minimalists are now eligible for teaching jobs remains to be seen.

One bracing whiff of nostalgia dispelled the déjà vu. U. of I. composer Salvatore Martirano restaged his *L's G.A.* (Lincoln's Gettysburg Address), the film/theater/tape piece that most epitomized the wild state of avant-garde experimentation in the 1960s Midwest. While Martirano's jarring films repunched 1967 into our consciousness, Michael Holloway read Lincoln's reinterpreted words while breathing helium through a gas mask. The rest of the conference paled as it came home that '67 could have decked '87 with one blow. As proof, a more recent theater piece barraged the audience with noise, choral shrieks, and a heavy-handed text meant to force us to understand the horror of war. Had an unknown composer been responsible, I would have strangled the culprit, but it was by Xenakis.

The papers, arguably the meat of the conference, were dauntingly technical, but at one I heard an astounding statement from David Cope, well-known for his flawed but ground-breaking book *New Directions in Music*. Once while suffering a creative block, Cope explained, he devised a program that could simulate his style. It was full of mathematical rules about what intervals he was most likely to use in what configurations. He had used it to create "dictionaries" of typical motifs of Bach, Beethoven, Brahms, and Bartók, and he played computer-composed examples of opening measures in each of their styles; they were plausible, even daring. "If I go to my studio in the morning with no ideas," Cope continued, "I turn on my computer, and by noon it can produce four or five string quartets in my style." So much for the tortured-creator stereotype.

Cope was surely exaggerating and possibly kidding, but no eyebrows were raised. Seemingly implicit to the academic conception of music is the assumption that it is not only rational and ultimately explainable, but reducible to algorithms, as long as the algorithms are complex enough to allow for perceptually unexpected occurrences. (It's easy to see why they're threatened by composers like Satie, Cage, and Feldman, whose irrationality throws those premises into question.) Theorists have long analyzed music according to a linguistic analogy that relegates every note and group of notes into higher-order sections. Many of the papers spoke of "tree descriptions" and "event structures," and diagrammed notes and phrases the way your English teacher used to diagram sentences. The "50 Accepted Masterworks" have been squeezed into that framework for so long that it's only natural to assume that the process can be turned around, that the formula can be abstracted in order to generate works that analyze well and—theoretically—sound as good.

This masterwork generation was explicitly referred to by Brooklyn College professor Charles Dodge, one of computer music's guiding lights. He's working with "1/f noise," a type of randomness whose probabilities become more determined as they continue. He admitted that, while analyses of many classics fall into a pattern generally resembling 1/f noise, it's a big step between knowing that and being able to generate the *Jupiter* Symphony from it. Dodge's *Rondeley* for choir and tape (flat, vague, and dull) made the point succinctly. Queen's College professor David Keane, by contrast, urged attention to the phenomenology of listening; his tape and dance piece *La Aurora Estrellada* went overboard in the other direction, leading the ear through simple patterns with exaggerated caution. Even he, though, spoke in terms of information processing, as though a piece of music were just a pattern to be assimilated and understood. Given all the duds the academy churns out every year, you'd think it would occur to someone that their most fundamental assumptions might be in error.

But these are Big Issues, and Big Issues weren't on the agenda. They arouse antagonism, and there's no room for that in this crowd. Every time one of these professors is denied tenure, 300 people line up for his job, and with those odds, making enemies and contradicting the prevailing wisdom aren't worth the risk. (Sociologists predict that the situation won't lighten up in the liberal arts for at least 15 years.) The upshot is that the university has become the opposite of what we, in the 60s, thought it should be: rather than a forum for self-questioning, it's a bastion of conformity, of timid acquiescence to hidebound hypotheses.

The closest thing to a protest came at the tail end of the conference, when, after a piece that sounded like Ping-Pong balls bouncing on a vibraphone for 17 solid minutes, somebody shouted, "Encore!"

first flight

john adams

DECEMBER 29, 1987

There are small birds that build their nests in holes in the precipitous banks of Wyoming's Snake River. Each baby bird, when he leaves the nest, is forced to shoot 60 feet straight out to the opposite bank on *his first flight ever*, or else crash and drown. John Adams, who wrote his first opera under unprecedented media pressure, must know how those fledglings feel. When was the last time a musical reputation so hung on one work?

Let no criticism that follows detract from the fact that Adam's maiden theatrical flight is a triumph. *Nixon in China* is a profound puzzle and—here's the trick—a solid evening's entertainment. It may miss being the Great American Opera, but not since *The Mother of Us All* has an opera come so close to one's fondest hopes for what American Opera could be. Leighton Kerner detailed Nixon's dramatic aspects in his November 17 review of the Houston Grand Opera production, which BAM imported. It would be redundant for me to echo his praise of the cast, sets, and direction, but Adams's insights into minimalist opera invite further comment. I'm sure he doesn't feel like it, but Adams comes off looking like the naïf who sheepishly wonders, under the startled stare of 20,000 eyes, why everyone thought it was so difficult to write an opera.

First, credit where due. The night I attended (December 6), Adams didn't run onstage for his applause (good for him, it's an awkward, pointless ritual), but perhaps Philip Glass should have taken a small bow. If Monteverdi stood on the shoulders of Peri and Caccini to invent opera, Adams isn't shy about his equal indebtedness. The arpeggiated chords and harmonic changes over a pivot note can be traced to any Glasswork after *Einstein on the Beach,* and the final scene, in which Chou En-lai remains upright as the rest of the cast dozes off and the music dies away, is a clean lift from Gandhi's final solo in *Satyagraha.* Handel himself couldn't have engineered a more dexterous theft, though Adams's syncopations and dotted notes reveal that he is as bored with Glass's rhythms as anyone.

Adams's ingenuity shows in what he does with Glass's devices. The danger with minimalist textures (as the narrated parts of the new *Akhnaten* recording evince) is that they can sound like background to a melody that won't show up. Fine, says Adams. Put that pedestal in the pit where it belongs, bring the bust back onstage; the sung libretto will be the melody minimalism has been waiting for. Scales rise, the chorus starts singing, and before you can say "phase shifting," what the '60s glorified as *process* is relegated to the more modest (and thoroughly defensible) role of *accompaniment.* Why hadn't anyone thought of it before?

Adams makes the style work for him in many ways. He bends Alice Goodman's ravishingly poetic libretto to the music by fragmenting it into Gertrude Steinish enigmas. Treatment of the English language, disgracefully handled in most American operas, is here the focal point that unites musical and textual ideas. Overcome by the historicality of his meeting with Chou, an excited Nixon stutters, "News, news, news, news, has a, has a, has a, has a mystery, a mystery!" and minimalism's hiccups and reiterations seem created for this moment. As if to drive home the Chinese emphasis on collectivity, the most stunning music is given to the chorus: one soft, hypnotic chant—"The people are the heroes now / Behemoth pulls the peasant's plow"—sets the tone and reverberates until the final curtain. At once bold and cautious, Adams backs off from the free-form romanticism of *Harmonielehre,* but he does edge toward nonminimal styles, and the closing scene's sultry foxtrot evokes a summit dissipated in disillusion.

If *Nixon* has a conspicuous flaw, it's that the text is more subtle than the subtext the music shoves under it. The orchestra's incessant momentum implies that these characters, powerful yet at the mercy of their appetites, are caught up in world events they can nuance, but not control; their vocal lines color the harmony, but the rhythm grinds on willy-nilly. During the Nixon-Kissinger-Mao meeting, one wishes the music would pause and give Goodman's attempt at an "opera of ideas" some breathing room, time to provoke thought. How potent, how stupefying an effect it would have been if Mao, unlike Nixon, had been able to stop the music in its tracks with a single, unfathomable word! The text pointed that way, and someone as close to Mozart as to Glass might have taken the hint.

But such "what ifs?" have the benefit of hindsight, and Adams's perceptions of minimalism's potential are sufficiently astounding. The debt to Glass isn't kindly repaid; *Nixon* makes one suddenly realize that minimalist opera can be fun. It's one thing to piously marvel at what a swell guy Gandhi was, another to see Mao humor Nixon as you would a precocious teenager, muttering, "*Six Crises* isn't a bad book." Not worried about his modernist credentials, Adams has relaxed into a *human* opera, full of characters one admires, laughs at, fears, and pities, and this wealth of alternate readings keeps the imagination active. Aside from Beethoven, Berg, and Debussy, how many composers have written a *debut* opera this absorbing? Adams may have found his groove. We look forward to *Gorbachev in Washington*.

admiring the waterfall

david garland

JANUARY 5, 1988

"The literature of expostulation, of Catastrophe," wrote author Marilynne Robinson in a brilliant think piece in the October 13, 1985, *New York Times Book Review*, "is taken to be very serious. But among people carried along in a canoe toward a waterfall, the one who stands up and screams is not the one who has the keenest sense of the situation. We are in a place so difficult that perhaps alarm is an indulgence, and a harder thing—composure—is required of us."

Composure: that's the key to David Garland's music. His "control songs" are about the world's problems, but instead of throwing them at us in unmediated confusion like so much Downtown art, he rearranges them so they'll mean something to the perceiver. Like a smooth pop performer, Garland seems less interested in impressing the audience than in making contact, but the buttons he pushes aren't worn with use. He slips in high-tech and avant-garde techniques when he needs them, but if a nursery tune will serve his purpose better, he has no artsy pretensions to defend. When

Garland drones, "I write the songs no one else bothers to write," it's no self-effacing joke, it's nicely ironic music criticism. His music is deliberately out of kilter with the rest of intellectual life because of its attempt to say something about, not art, but day-to-day existence. But if no one else *would* write these songs, no one else *could*, either, for no other new music figure is so sincere, so urgently comforting, as David Garland.

Like many natural phenomena, Garland's performances are complex only in description. He's calm, yet uninhibited; unassuming, but a hypnotic presence. He can rock quietly, using (in "Very Popular") a piece of Styrofoam instead of a trap set. On *Control Songs* (Review), with John Zorn and Christian Marclay, his songs take on an acidic, industrial intensity; performing with accordionist Guy Klucevsek, they become sweetly pastoral; when solo, as at the Knitting Factory December 9, they are naked but warm. Afraid, he says, that some of his concerts have been "too solemn," Garland pushed this performance in a cabaret direction, adding new, more upbeat songs, including an untitled one ("I really want Frank Sinatra to sing this song, or maybe Charles Aznavour"). All these facets arise without contradiction, in a spontaneous persona. Even the "Solomon Song" from Weill's *Three-Penny Opera* became, in Garland's sepulchral tones, another warning about the gap between public and private perceptions.

What impresses me most is the consistency of Garland's inspiration. His melodies (the perky, descending triads of "Keep in Touch," the charming symmetry of "This Is Love") are Schubertian in their simplicity; they stick in the mind, bringing the words home over and over. The lyrics often read well ("Bright, my herd of buffalo / Dark, my quarrelsome me"), and yet there's no academic sense that these are "poems set to music." His hand and body movements—playing an imaginary Theremin, conducting little squiggles of electronic sound—are built into the music, and when listening to *Control Songs* it's hard not to join in.

Gregory Sandow's recent Chuck Berry piece quoted Robert Pattison's theory that Romantic music was about joy, whereas rock and roll is about fun. Garland tosses a small wrench into the argument, because while his concerts are always fun, his songs—hardly Romantic, arguably rock—are very much about joy. "Keep in Touch" is a sprightly ballad about how good even flawed relationships are:

> I think I'll probably be
> Here for you when you need me.
> Just give me the word, I'll come right away
> Unless I guess I'm busy or something.

"TV Can Teach Me" documents the bewildering world shoved into our faces by the nightly news; after hearing about another domestic murder/suicide, this phenomenological Tom Lehrer admits:

> I can't help but wonder
> What good this news does me.
> I watch it all nightly
> But still I don't get it.

But such feelings elicit musing, not despair. We're still human, we still have our daily routine, we're still selfish, and we're still in love. Ain't it great?

Garland's probably grimacing under such analysis, because for him, everyday heroism means resisting abstraction. One of my favorite Garland songs, "Forest Fractures" (*not* performed at the Knitting Factory), includes a warning against "artistic" intentions:

> Are they here to chop the woods down,
> Stripping bare the forest floor . . . ?
> No, it's worse, they come as poets,
> To interpret what is here.

Perhaps it's best just to say that Garland is the only composer under 40 whose music I go around humming; who can perform for over an hour (as he did at the Knitting Factory) and still be greeted with shouts of "Too short!" In a music scene where standing in the canoe and screaming is still considered hip, Garland remarks on the beauty of the approaching waterfall. Enjoy him at storefront spaces while you can, for soon he'll be faced with the inevitable problem: how to get such intimate, communicative music to a wider audience.

yawn

r. i. p. hayman

FEBRUARY 16, 1988

As instructed, I had my sleeping bag with me when I arrived before midnight at Penine Hart Gallery January 30. I rarely take a sleeping bag to a performance, but this was R. I. P. Hayman's *Dreamsound*, no ordinary concert. For most composers, boredom is merely a byproduct, but for Hayman it's a sine qua non. About 25 other adventurers showed up, some in nightgowns or pajamas. Incense burned. A humidifier spewed steam, spiked, as we later learned, with essence of lavender, a soporific. Two TVs shone silently, one with *Benny Hill,* the other with a video of a roaring fireplace. Bach's *Goldberg Variations*—originally written to help Bach's patron sleep—played softly, and pastoral slides illuminated the ceiling in elongated distortion. As I picked a corner in the warmth of the video fire, I asked myself whether I really wanted to be put to sleep by a guy named R. I. P.

Hayman's been doing sleep-music experiments around the country for 10 years. He's serious, but he presents them with humor; during his somnolent introductory speech he removed his tux to reveal a nightgown and nightcap. His assistant Barbara Pollitt served herb tea, warm milk, and cookies, as Hayman explained the procedure of this "event for sleeping audience." The chanting we now heard on tape, he said, was the dream-singing of the Temier people of Malaysia, who sing together in their sleep to the accompaniment of a shaman's drum. Hayman gave us pens and paper to write down anything that came to us in the night, and then had us each repeat a phrase into a tape recorder, something we wanted to hear subliminally as we slept. I recited the words "sunset in the Chihuahuan Desert," hoping to evoke my favorite place and time of day.

As the TVs went blank, Hayman and Pollitt played delicate, static music on wooden flute and harp. This segued into an almost inaudible tape of beautiful, wave-patterned organ music. The influence of a roomful of sleepers is irresistibly contagious, Hayman said, and so it almost proved, for within minutes the room was filled with contented snores—except for my corner. I never could sleep away from home. I tossed and turned, admiring the organ's continual ritardando, for a couple of hours.

At last, the event suddenly became a relay race, and we were all wearing Three Stooges masks. I stepped through a screen door onto a balcony, and saw that we were in Colorado, surrounded by woods and mountains. Leaving, I hurried to my job at the police station, where I was the librarian for recovered stolen videotapes. Hayman had promised pleasant dreams, and he delivered: I felt great, and had become the Nicest Guy in the World. Hookers, looking for tapes overdue to video rental places, heaped verbal abuse on me, but I continued my tasks with a smile. I went to lunch and was taunted by a street person, but I just nodded sympathetically; the pine trees smelled like health itself, and nothing was going to upset my well-being.

I woke up and grabbed in the dark for my watch, to check the time; after a moment's reflection, I realized that I was listening to a tape of a ticking clock. I went to the bathroom and coming back I remembered having heard the sound of pouring water earlier. Evidently, my subconscious was now Hayman's oyster. An uncomfortable notion, but I drifted back to sleep.

Hayman twice came by to play my recorded message, and I woke up both times. I never did dream about the Chihuahuan Desert, but I ended the morning dreaming about the chihuahua my brother and I had as kids.

I was first up, and in time to see Hayman apply his nightcap tassel to a snorer's nose, which made her roll over and breathe quietly. (Severe snorers, he said, get a squirt of water in the armpit.) I looked around; occasionally someone would open their eyes, hastily scrawl down a dream, and then snuggle back in. Hayman and Pollitt were in an adjoining room, preparing breakfast and awaiting the results of their experiment. I learned that, in addition to performing on an intimate Chinese lute during the night, he had dropped rosebuds near our faces and played tapes of ocean waves, birds, and crickets. He interviewed me, and taped my dream account. Among Hayman's dreams, his waking ones, is to put sensors on the eardrum to be able to amplify the sounds we imagine while sleeping. Another is to have a group of people sleep together regularly in an attempt to start having communal visions, as some cultures do. For the time being, these *Dreamsound* evenings are the most ambitious projects he can realize.

One by one, his drowsy subjects wandered in. Some remembered nothing, but most recounted fantasies suggested by the environmental sounds. One woman admitted only that her dream involved "Mick Jagger and a lot of water." (Sorry I missed that one.) Another recalled a full-length epic, beginning with her waking up and being embarrassed because everyone had dreamed but her, and ending with a friend eating rats to train for a horror film part. At 11 A.M., I gave up waiting for those who were still snoring and writing, and stepped out into the quiet of a Manhattan Sunday morning, a little awed by the power of someone who could make a music critic dream of being a nice guy.

searching for the plague

diamanda galas

AUGUST 15, 1989

Out of a cloud of smoke, illuminated by colored lights, Diamanda Galas appears and disappears, clutching a microphone that seems to grow out of her hand. Behind her, overdubbed voices babble in Greek, then a drum pounds out an austere beat. She points in accusation, genuflects obsessively, snarls like an old crone, beams smugly like a TV preacher, and chatters like the Javanese monkey chant. "When any man hath an issue out of his flesh, because of that issue he is unclean," Diamanda booms. (Can she be called by other than that demanding, diamondlike, diabolical first name? There's nothing gala about this performance.) "This is the law of the plague: to teach when it is clean and when it is unclean." The words are by God, via Moses, from that most severe chapter of the Bible's severer testament, Leviticus.

I'm describing "The Divine Punishment," part one of Diamanda's *Masque of the Red Death,* her "plague mass," performed in its near entirety July 25 at Alice Tully Hall. It was the musical climax this year of that sadly titled series "Serious Fun!" Diamanda's *Masque* is a heroic, one-woman assault on AIDS, and more specifically on the sanctimony that sees the plague as divine retribution for sin. Her formidable weapon is Kierkegaardian irony, an attack on "Christian society" accomplished through pretended identification with its oppressive element. Her starting point is Leviticus, the book most often quoted in condemnation of homosexuality (though not the quotation itself). The effect she creates is that of Meredith Monk's evil twin or Laurie Anderson's sinister shadow, although, like any Jungian shadow, this one, difficult to face, is ultimately beneficial. Diamanda shows us the ugly underside of the West's religious foundation, not to condemn, but to heal.

Masque is divided into three cogent phases; the division is clear on the two CDs (Restless), but was less so in performance, since Diamanda omitted a few numbers and made the finale the performance's centerpiece. Like a medieval logician, "Divine Punishment" uses scripture to relocate our thinking, for the Bible provides not only the judge's, but the victim's point of view in psalms and lamentations: "Deliver me from mine enemies, oh my God. . . . The mighty are gathered against me; not for my transgressions, not for my sin." Switching to her own text, she showed the progression by which those apparently singled out for affliction become considered enemies by society: "I am the sign. / I am the plague. / I am the Antichrist."

Diamanda followed this at Alice Tully with part three, "You Must Be Certain of the Devil"—perhaps because it's the rock-oriented section, and she might have lost her rock audience with too ascetic a first hour. "Welcome welcome welcome, welcome to the holy day," she crooned with game-show-host insincerity, switching dramatically from an antiliturgical tone to a down-to-earth perspective (her own text):

> In Kentucky Harry buys a round of beer
> to celebrate the death of Billy Smith, the queer,
> whose mother still must hide her face in fear.
> Let's not chat about despair.

Crescendoing out of her irony, she preached against skinheads and Nazis, mixed desperate psalms into sarcastic gospel numbers, and finally shouted, "Don't believe the lies! Acquired immune deficiency is homicide!" Showing off an impressive piano technique that I forgot she possesses, Diamanda included only one number from "Saint of the Pit" (part two), though it is in some ways the darkest section of the trilogy, with its plague verse from Baudelaire and Gerard Nerval.

This gig was advertised as "vocal pyrotechnics at the edge of sanity"; that might have sufficed for her earlier works like *Wild Women with Steak Knives,* but here that tag threw the wrong spin. New musicians like Julius Eastman and "Blue" Gene Tyranny have written pieces protesting the treatment of gays, but Diamanda's the first I know of to make a powerful AIDS statement, and the political relevance and insight she has achieved rival Mozart's Beaumarchais operas. To slough off her histrionics as quasi-madness, as though she were just another nihilistic, East Village taboo-breaker trying to bug the establishment, is to relegate her to the harmlessness of mere art. Rather, she represents the very center of sanity in its gut reaction to a tragic insanity.

No part of her surgery on the cultural psyche is more delicate than her acerbic appropriation of the Old Testament, a strategy likely to scatter listeners in every direction. To one crowd, it must be even more reprehensible than stomping on the flag; others of my acquaintance were put off by the intrusion of the unpopular old Book in a new-music performance. Raised a Southern Baptist, I was hit in a different spot. Diamanda fiddles like a virtuoso on the smarmy subtext that generally accompanies declaimed scripture: never doubt who the clean and unclean are, God's on *our* side, his vengeance is against *them,* and *we* know without specifying who *they* are. (Coming from this background, the Taoist notion that God doesn't take sides was tremendously liberating.) Through her fiddling, though, she washes the familiar words clean of reflexive sanctimony; she hears in Leviticus not an innocent hygiene lecture, but the beginnings of a divisive ontology, and she's brilliantly discovered how to present scripture in such a way as to cut through millennia of accumulated, subversive mis-interpretation. Has any composer since Haydn made better use of the Bible than that?

The Devil, so the preachers say, quotes scripture too. What *is* the subtext when those words come from an apparent demon, enveloped not in a white polyester suit but in smoke? The worst thing that could happen (and I bet it did among some audience members) would be for the us/them identification to switch polarity to an equally repugnant anti-Christian ressentiment—one hate balances another. Diamanda's text, however, points in another direction, toward a Jungian world in which each of us is both us *and* them, both victim and hypocritical, unfeeling oppressor. The best words came last, not sung (that *I* could hear), but as an epilogue in the program:

> LISTEN, MAN
> IT MAY SOON BE TIME
> FOR YOU TO GUARD A DYING MAN
> UNTIL THE ANGELS COME
> LET'S NOT CHAT ABOUT DESPAIR
> IF YOU ARE A MAN (AND NOT A COWARD)
> YOU WILL GRASP THE HAND OF HIM DENIED BY MERCY
> UNTIL HIS BREATH BECOMES YOUR OWN.

In a way, Diamanda's always been a performer in search of a plague. Her reputation as a vocalist originated with performances of pieces by Xenakis and Globokar, and, just as her earlier music shares the noisy, undifferentiated quality of that branch of the European avant-garde, its histrionic political approach seems left over from the European '60s. *Masque of the Red Death*'s urgent focus makes it more individual, and its unity of purpose underpaints several vernacular and avant-garde styles with a single hue. The vocal techniques are reduced in number, sharpened in intensity: a chanting style reminiscent of Hebrew cantillation (its microtonal inflections repeated with perfect control), her trademark high chattering, and, at the end, a sexily husky French cabaret style. Noise, though, is still the stratum that unifies the backgrounds of the different parts, as though the factory sounds, the rock beat, the overdubbed babbling, even the garish, TV jazz that accompanies "You Must Be Certain of the Devil" are variously articulated forms of primal noise.

The extremely unfortunate aspect of this otherwise gripping concert was the sound quality, a problem that's shot a lot of Fun! out from under this Serious series. Pointlessly excessive volume drove a few dozen listeners from the hall, and the reverberation was so muddy that, from the right aisle, I made out less than 10 percent of the words (best percentage I heard of from other seats was 50, still too little for so message-heavy a work; lucky I've now got the text in front of me). For that reason I urge every audience member even slightly intrigued to buy the two new CDs between which the work is divided, "The Divine Punishment" and "Saint of the Pit" on one, "You Must Be Certain of the Devil" on the other. The CDs contain about 10 numbers omitted from the concert, including (in "You Must Be Certain") a torturously slow, seething version of "Swing Low, Sweet

Chariot," and some effective, Dies Irae–quoting numbers from "Saint of the Pit." On disc, as in performance, it's compelling music.

Even so, one has to ask after listening, even *while* listening, whether *Masque* transcends its own entertainment value, whether it justifies its confrontational energy. "Can music," as Ives queried in a parallel argument, "*do* this?" The disturbing-theater-piece genre has gone through perceptual changes in the last 20 years that are difficult to ignore. In concert, it seemed inevitable that Diamanda's virtuosity, her commanding energy, drowned out the message she was using them to get across; nothing in the piece itself was as politically eye-opening as the AIDS statistics that came with the press kit. Ultimately, *Masque* was less a thought-provoker than a series of impotent symbols for realities that we already know would be disturbing if we had to confront them. (What did the piece mean to PWAs in the audience? Comfort? Acceptance? Or was this lesson meant to change the lives of the not-yet-sick?)

The movie *My Dinner with Andre* tosses out an acute diagnosis of the way audiences have come to find depressing, apocalyptic messages in art *reassuring*, since they reinforce the platitudes we've come to believe anyway. (Andre's challenge was for art to present alternate, feasible, more beautiful realities to convince people that the world can change for the better: a profound prescription for the 1990s.) Right now, to make any vision of torment stand out over the general, anguish-saturated din requires supernatural magnetism, sonic energy, and stage presence. Diamanda, bless her adamantine conscience, has all three. But after she gasped out her final cry of despair, the majority of the capacity crowd leaped to their feet and cheered. If her bleak jeremiad disturbed them, they sure seemed happy about it.

oceans without walls

laurie anderson

OCTOBER 17, 1989

"Tonight's topics," announced Laurie Anderson at the beginning of *Empty Places*, "are politics and music. There are those who say that politics and music just don't mix." *Empty Places* is Anderson's new 90-minute solo show at the Brooklyn Academy of Music through October 15 (I attended opening night, October 3). The announcement was a little disingenuous, for music never became an issue in the work. Anderson is the avant-garde's emissary to the real world, and her art is no longer about art. It *is* about politics: personal, relational, national, and global. Music—along with gags, stories, and an oversized halo of video and slide screens—was the pretext, the arsenal, the piece of meat brought along to keep the dog quiet.

It was a change for Anderson, a gradual and apparently difficult one, though in hindsight you could see it coming. In 1980, her music was so centered that you had to wonder where it was going to go. Her technotricks couldn't get any more clever, her appropriation of Massenet for a pop song came from the foul line of left field, her glosses on New York art life were photorealist. How can you be any more Laurie Anderson-ish than "O Superman," her fluke hit single, and what do you follow it with? I bet she asked herself that question. Her concert last year at Serious Fun! was jarring, unintegrated. Clearly a sketch for *Empty Places,* that gig was similar in tone and used some of the same material. But last year, the contrasts of light and dark humor grated, frustration ripped the seams, her control over the audience wavered. I thought, uh-oh, here begins the slow slide.

I thought too soon. *Empty Places* is the *real* Anderson. The warmly reverbed violin double-stop she started with riveted you with its sense of purpose. Her stand-up routines no longer broke the mood; they explained the songs, and the songs explained the jokes. She modulated her humor from Pee-Wee Herman happy to Dostoyevskian crisis in an irresistible curve. Her video and audio illusions entertained, but they underlined rather than dazzled. She's never been so slick, her surreality has never touched so close to home. Used to be you'd chuckle, soak up a couple of insights, hum the tune later. Now she's so penetrating I spent the following morning wrapped in the mood she had set.

Revolt, in the meantime, has moved from background to surface. Walls were the archetypal image here, both the ones we build around ourselves and those erected by others. Outside those walls are the military mind, the national debt, rules left over from grade school, everything rigid, mechanical, logical, imposed, everything that squelches us inside the dismal consistency of our personalities. Inside is everything organic, spontaneous, intuitive, the urge to leap into a fountain on the way to work, the Caribbean of the mind. She reviewed the musical qualities of Hitler, Mussolini, and Reagan, and deconstructed "The Star-Spangled Banner" to show us how soft the realities are that we're afraid to bang our heads against. She's always enjoyed exposing illusions, but there's a new urgency in the way she warns us about what those illusions represent. (It's difficult to give many examples without spoiling punchlines.)

Digression being the better part of charm, she didn't sing that cantus firmus alone. Surrounded by slide and video images of trains, walking crowds, and bathroom tiles, she fiddled in silhouette, a ghostly gypsy; accompanied herself with sampled bird songs, sometimes slowed to low chirps; engineered her own echo by projecting her delayed voice from distant speakers. Most of the effects, though, played argumentative roles. Using three mikes wired to harmonizers, she split her persona three ways: an obnoxious bass played the explanatory corporate male role, a three-soprano chorus added teenybopper commentary, and her warm, inviting alto offered the more serious moments, the dream images, wishes, and confessions.

Overall, *Empty Places* occupied a literary genre, presented with a musician's nonlinear sense of theater. The actual music was a subterfuge. She sang a dozen times, but she only had two songs, and one was a fast version of the other. The slow songs sat motionless in space, rocking between two chords, trying to forestall time. The lilt of a grace note in her song about the capricious Rio Grande, the tiny fermatas and pauses, were delaying tactics, holding back until the message sank in. Waaaait, can't start that next thought till the D chord resolves . . . there, new idea, a non sequitur—hold chord for the subconscious to work out the connection. Those chords intensified the words, made them seem larger and truer than if she had only said them, made you remember them; which is to say, she used music exactly the way Handel did in the *Messiah*. The fast songs released tension, gave you a blank wall of activity to stare at while the slow ones soaked in.

No shell-game hustler on Broadway could have calculated the audience psychology better. Distract the left brain with a twisted-logic joke, then ease into the right with sung clichés—"Keep those cards and letters coming / And please don't come again"—that don't mean anything until they accumulate. It was the best solution I've seen to the problem of how to convince a jaded 1980s audience that you MEAN what you're saying and it's IMPORTANT. You can't shock anyone anymore, audiences no longer pay to be berated, preaching is indulged and then quickly forgotten, you can't sugarcoat the truth and keep your self-respect. But you can attack on two fronts at once: get *within* the left-brain defenses of people who have heard every saner-world argument in the book and dismissed them all, then rub the right brain until they *feel* that things can and must change. The music's cool, minimalist facade commanded attention while she slipped you the idea that commanding has to end somewhere. Without that facade, she'd be another Pauline Oliveros, sincere, right, but disadvantaged by a skeptical audience.

Future shock notwithstanding, we live in a sluggish culture when it comes to translating philosophical ideas into political action. (Compare China.) Anderson's concerns are essentially romantic, because before romanticism came to popularly stand for emotionalism and impracticality, it stood for asserting the claims of nature against industrial society, for making allowance for individual freedom, for protesting the reduction of experience to rationality. There's a direct line from Emerson's chafing against foolish consistency, from Thoreau's self-emancipation—"Wait not till slaves pronounce the word / To set the captive free / Be free yourselves"— through Kerouac and Cage to Anderson's "Sometimes I wish I hadn't gotten that tattoo."

But to invoke romanticism in this context is to hand out a pen with which to write her off. It's been 70 years since Wittgenstein ran logic to its tautological dead end, 58 since Gödel proved that, even in mathematics, truth is a wider concept than provability. Rationality's limits have been drawn in a dozen odd disciplines, but Western politics and business blunder on as though Locke's word had been the last. How do you defuse the macho corporate mentality when philosophy, art, and science have failed? Cage's greatest contribution to our culture may be that he converted thousands of art-world types (myself included) to the romantic, irrationalist mindset, the doctrine of unprovable truths. What Cage is for artists, Anderson is trying to be for the rest of the country. It's not enough for the avant-garde to go to the front; somebody's got to bring Truth back.

I like having Anderson in that job. Her stories of the misery she saw at the hospital when she fell in a manhole and hurt her legs, of the NASA scientists who spent a fortune studying how insects walk, her calculations that the national debt would rise $36,000,000 during her concert and how much you'll have to make in 2030 to pay your share cast a wide net that catches everyone somewhere. Someday there will have to be a book, *The Philosophy of Laurie Anderson*, and it's going to make a lot more sense than Andy Warhol's did. I hope it includes the story about the biophysicist John C. Lilly and the whale he raised in a large tank. (I'll ruin one punchline, since humor wasn't its point and it summed up what I got out of the concert.) Lilly claimed the whale was communicating with him telepathically, and finally he realized what it was asking: "Do all oceans have walls?"

You want to answer, and this is the point of *Empty Places*, to make you want to say it: No, big guy. Some oceans don't have walls. Some are vast and wide and more boundless than any imagination has yet dared to be. We'll play in one of those oceans when we get rid of the walls we've built; the militaristic thinking; the continual division into mine and yours; the accounting of all value in dollars; the judgment of everything male, dexter, and yang as good and of everything female, sinister, and yin as bad or at least inferior; the obsession with imposing on the universe instead of receiving from it. Sounds like it'll be a great place. Lead us there, Laurie.

insiders, outsiders, and old boys

new music america '89

DECEMBER 5, 1989

Put quickly, New Music America '89 was creatively organized, too often deafening, overly ambitious, marginally too commercial, argument-provoking, mostly SRO, and better than I expected. (This week I'm reviewing the festival as festival; next week I'll discuss the music.) Members of the New Music Alliance, the festival's toothless watchdogs, had expressed two fears: one, BAM's Next Wave advertising might swallow the festival and undermine its individuality, and, two, the festival would duplicate what can be heard in New York any time. The first fear proved justified in September, when everyone was saying, "So, I see New Music America begins next week." (Next Wave started October 3, the festival November 10.) The second challenge was the one BAM and this year's NMA director Yale Evelev handled brilliantly.

That finesse alienated much of the new music community. John Zorn, for example, used his page in the New Music America catalogue to explain why he's always hated NMA:

> I am sick of seeing the same tired names over and over again and pompous, overblown projects put together because the names look good on grant applications. . . . Typically, younger artists who need the exposure are begrudgingly given short spots in satellite venues while major names are headlining the large theaters on their own. Less than an actual music festival, New Music America is a one sided overview that's more about politics, marketing, and sales than about the music it pretends to support. . . . It's no more than a convention for people in the music business who try to "outhip" each other in the manipulation of artists. This postmodern yuppie tendency of business people dictating creative policy to artists is a very real danger that I intend to avoid at all costs.

As far as he goes, Zorn's given us a succinct history of the festival. (Forget for now that Zorn *didn't* avoid the danger at all costs, but rather accepted the festival's $10,000 orchestra commission.) Writing an "outsider" diatribe in the program, however, betrayed forgetfulness of the first premise of Mus. Crit. 101: concerts are for audiences, not for satisfying the vanity of composers. What looks like the "same tired old names" to insiders may not have sunk in yet to audiences. William Duckworth recently surveyed jazz musicians at Birdland and found that not one had ever heard of Zorn; in his composition class at Bucknell University, no one had heard of Laurie Anderson. There's no reason why politics, marketing, and sales should make NMA *less* than an "actual" music festival, because that's what real-world music festivals tend to be about. The only festivals that pretend to support music (as opposed to attracting and entertaining audiences) are academic conferences.

New Music New York (the festival's first year, 1979) happened because a group of composers realized that their music was not well described in the prevailing critical vocabulary of pitch, method, and form; it required a post-Cagean vocabulary of sound, process, and structure. The Zen-influenced, downtown composers were aesthetically "homeless," and NMNY was a shelter. That gave the first festival a composer-defined focus, but its premise was that enjoyable music had been squelched by the reigning discourse, and that if people only had a chance to hear it for themselves in a neutral environment, a new, more sympathetic vocabulary would arise. They were right. NMNY created a public perception that music can break out of set categories and define new genres.

NMA festivals since, this year more than ever, have diversified to a point that even a critic with three or four working vocabularies might be at a loss. Over the years, the festival organizers have increasingly refrained from drawing distinctions, in the theoretically plausible conviction that to draw a line is to make a judgment, inevitably leaving someone on the wrong side. The tendency reached a kind of climax in the mid-'80s, when it was magnanimously suggested that what rock 'n' roller Patti Smith was doing was new music too, ergo she should be admitted to the festival. (Crowds back then numbered in the dozens and honoraria in the $200 range, but whoever raised the proposal seemed to think Smith would be thrilled to have NMA on her resume.) It was like building a shelter for the homeless and leaving the definition of "homeless" so loose that you end up inviting Donald Trump.

How little the rock world cares about skinning new music's small potatoes was graphically affirmed this year by the World, whom NMA had contacted a year ago about presenting one of the festival concerts. Two weeks before the festival, the World booked Deborah Harry for that night and bumped NMA downstairs. (I had to talk my way past three bouncers and when I got upstairs thought, "Big deal, this is rock, and the singer looks like Deborah Harry." Luckily I ran into Evelev as I was leaving, and he steered me into the tacky disco where Miniature was playing.)

NMA '89 had an Oedipal complex. It allegedly celebrated its 10-year anniversary, but seemed more concerned with dissociating itself from past festivals. Laurie Anderson's touching recollection at the opening night benefit of what New Music New York meant to Soho composers was the only moment of tribute. Midcareer composers were nearly absent, or else (like the Downtown Ensemble) tucked away into obscure corners at afternoon, weekday concerts. Context was prohibited; the only composers well known outside New York were so distant either chronologically (Nancarrow and Moondog) or geographically (Rzewski) as to preclude connections. NMA '89 wanted you to think new music had sprung full-blown from the head of—well, not Zorn, but someone no older. If you'd made a continuing contribution to new music in this town over the last 15, 20 years, you were probably excluded.

Still, I was often proud of the festival's achievements. They didn't happen at BAM; most of the big, well-hyped productions were disappointments. As always in New York, you had to search for the exciting new stuff, but it was there. Allowing the whole circle of New York's new music spaces—the Kitchen, Roulette, P.S. 122, Merkin Hall, Experimental Intermedia, Dance Theater Workshop, and others—to each devise its own series was a smart strategy (borrowed and institutionalized from past NMA alternative festivals) that promoted a system of checks and balances. P.S. 122, for example, had a program of 14 artists, 12 of whom I had never heard of before. Here I especially appreciated discovering Henry Gwiazda, whose sampler collages of birdsongs, babies crying, and car horns had a good-humored momentum. This concert was packed elbow to elbow, and a dozen unknowns got some good exposure. (Crowds all week were tremendous, and, though it seemed otherwise, a few of the ticketholders weren't foreign journalists.)

The festival's one major sin was its neglect of women composers (by my rough calculation 12 percent of the total acts, a fourth of them women who worked with men, and almost half sloughed off on P.S. 122's afternoon concert). Reports were that more women were accepted into the festival than finally appeared, because they weren't picked up by the various spaces; which merely devolves the blame onto the new-music good ol' boy network and dramatizes the underground fact that this decade's scene has always had a misogynist bias. The attitude is related to, though hardly identical with, BAM's and the Kitchen's cynical assumption of recent years that only macho, "kickass" music can attract an audience. One of the most popular attractions (at the Kitchen) was Heiner Goebbel's jazz-theater collage *The Man in the Elevator,* whose stiff, unrelenting histrionics made me feel as though a kickass version of "Deutschland über Alles" had been pounded on the side of my head. Kickass generates more cheers, but that doesn't mean it leaves a deeper impression. At Merkin Hall, Mark Waldrep's *Piano Maps* brought deserved bravos by encircling soft piano sonorities with hints of synthesized sound. The most common complaint I heard all week was that too much music was painfully overamplified.

In NMA's early years, there was controversy about programming music that had acquired any hint of commercial viability, in keeping with the idea that a nonprofit, government-supported festival should be leading, not following, public taste. Philip Glass and Laurie Anderson were admitted because they had originally come from the alternative scene, and the strategy was always to use big names to lure people to the little ones. This year's emphasis on vernacular could have been made without commercializing the festival, but it generated a double standard: the jazz admitted was allowed to be far more conventional than the "classical" music. Edward Wilkerson's band Shadow Vignettes wasn't at all "outside" by usual AACM standards, nor would Lester Bowie's gleaming showband have raised eyebrows at a conventional jazz festival. If these are "new music," then there's no good rationale not to include 12-tone music or the latest David Diamond symphony.

As an entertainingly controversial spectacle, NMA was more successful this year that it has often been. Its failures mainly reflected the increasing sharpness of the festival's self-definition crisis. For composers, when NMA ceases to be a shelter for the aesthetically homeless, it starts to be redundant and unrelated to creative music's struggle for acceptance. Nevertheless, Zorn takes the festival too seriously when he asks it to be "the last cry of freedom in the wilderness," something that "has nothing to do with ticket sales." NMA has never been a true reflection of new music's writhing vitality, never will be, wasn't meant to be. It is a *symbol* in the corporate, publicly visible world that a new music scene exists. Its significance for composers is collective, not individual. Dilute that symbol, and it becomes all the more difficult to explain to outsiders that composers are involved in a valid, useful project.

From the audience's point of view (which is also, I try never to forget for a moment, the critic's) the festival loses curiosity value when its focus blurs. Under pressure to represent every possible type of disenfranchised music, NMA is always structured through a system of interlocked compromises, and is never as coherent (nor, for me, as enjoyable) as any festival put together to satisfy a vision that owes nobody anything. The attempt to do too much with too little became obvious in embarrassing technical glitches at Merkin Hall, the World, and Trimpin's eviscerated mechanical music concert. But that says little more than that America doesn't have enough arts funding to be Europe. The disturbing issue this year was that the festival welcomed so much music that couldn't call itself disenfranchised. It was disconcerting to attend a festival advertised as perception-stretching, and find an opener like Kip Hanrahan's pretentiously sentimental cocktail music. A festival celebrating American music's diversity is a pleasant, liberal idea, but not many people will want to sit through much of it. What we need is a festival devoted to experimental, alternative musics, music that will stretch our ears until we need a new vocabulary to talk about it. Something like, say, New Music New York.

dark stormy night

nicolas collins

MARCH 13, 1990

It was a dark and stormy night—February 23, to be exact. We were all huddled together at the Kitchen, facing the performance area. "Play us a piece, Nick," someone might have said. And so, Nicolas Collins proceeded as follows: "It was a dark and stormy night. We were all sitting around the camp fire. I turned to Ben and said, 'Ben, tell us a story.' So Ben proceeded: 'It was a dark and stormy night.'"

This kind of nested self-reference was only one of the ways in which Collins's *It Was a Dark and Stormy Night* kept us entertained. Collins is a whiz at both computer and low-tech electronics, and his music has heretofore emphasized technology. He's built this amazing computer/trombone that does sound manipulations at the touch of a finger, and he uses it to wreak havoc with tapes, radio signals, and other people's improvisations. Until now, the quality of the result was fairly dependent on the expertise of whomever Collins worked with. But *Stormy Night* felt like a breakthrough: his conceptual insight expanded from the gizmo level to that of musical form.

Stormy Night is one of those formal/logical coups that begs for verbal analysis. First (necessary flashback), Collins plays a solo work called *Tobabo*

Fonio. He points his trombone at the audience, and it buzzes. He clicks buttons, and the buzz changes timbre. Suddenly, the sound crescendos and spreads to the loudspeakers on either side. Collins breaks the noise into a rhythm and loops it into an additive process, a new noise entering every few repetitions. The noises give way to flashes of trumpet, and, somewhere, a snare drum begins to crack. Gradually, they turn into raucous Peruvian band music, which has apparently been in the loop all along. The second you realize what's happened, the music vanishes from the speakers back into the trombone, and quickly fades out. It's a straight linear process, but full of dramatic surprises and pulled off with impeccable showmanship.

Hey, that's a cute trick. Everyone's mildly pleased. Then the other performers come out: accordionist Guy Klucevsek, vocalist/percussionist David Moss, guitarist Robert Poss, trumpeter Ben Neill running electronics, and the Soldier String Quartet. Moss launches into this story-within-a-story-within-a-story-within-a-story, each new fictional protagonist beginning with that same old moonless, inclement late evening. As the tales develop, they center around the idea of copying: for example, one's about a painter whose Vermeer forgeries become so popular that other artists start forging them. This is another level of self-reference, for Collins's music, *Stormy Night* included (though this isn't apparent yet), is parasitically based on found recordings.

Moss's characterization, switching personas to enter each new level as though trapped in a literary computer game, is antic and brilliantly real. Beyond his inherent theatricality, though, he drives a battery of voice-activated percussion, so that his speech-rhythms become an irregular accompaniment of cymbals, drums, bells. Meanwhile, a drone's begun in the instruments, spreading from guitar to accordion to strings. (I suspect that this, too, is initially in response to Moss's voice, fed backward into Neill's resonating electric guitar.) The instruments draw frills around the drone's overtones, making a sporadic, thrashing—but pretty—melody. As the crescendo continues, the strings and accordion begin punching out vibrant staccato chords (accurate, though sans conductor, and cued, I later learn, by certain words in Moss's text). Rests between chords grow shorter and shorter as a familiar outline begins to appear.

Punchline: once all the instruments are playing all their notes, they're grinding out the same wild Peruvian melody from *Tobabo Fonio*. Besides Moss's words, that five-note tune was all we had really heard all night.

With the text outlining a labyrinth that Umberto Eco would be proud of, and the melody pursuing its own, less distinct self-reference, you were challenged to follow with both verbal and nonverbal sides of your brain at once. I couldn't keep it up, but, going back and forth, either level was sufficiently engaging. The two works had drawn parallel processes, and during *Stormy Night,* you *felt* them converge on a more and more concrete level.

It provided the same kind of pleasure you get from Ives's Second Symphony, where little, barely recognizable bits of "Columbia, the Gem of the Ocean" finally add up to the whole tune. Or from hearing Ockeghem's "Ma Maistresse" chanson, then hearing fragments of its melody recontextualized and threaded through his *Missa ma Maitresse.* Or from reading the first and second halves of Beckett's novel *Molloy* and finding just enough similarities that you begin to suspect that the same events are being described from two points of view. And yet, Collins approached the idea via a technology unknown when those works were made, and manifested a very old pleasure on a brand new level.

It was like traveling from point A to point C, jumping to point B, and arriving mysteriously at point C again. Many serial and conceptual pieces from the '60s *tried* to pull off this kind of perceptual trick, but very few succeeded in making it audible (no winners come to mind, though Stockhausen's Klavierstück XI strikes me as the beginning of the trend). It took serialism's conceptual parallels, *filtered* through minimalism's clarity, to make it possible. And Collins pulled it off.

let there be noise

david rosenboom/trichy sankaran

MAY 8, 1990

Avant-garde music has never gotten credit for an advantage it has over virtually every other type: freed from the demands of stylistic coherency, it's the perfect vehicle for sonic archetypes, a channel for the unconscious. Perhaps that's its ultimate meaning. In illustration, David Rosenboom's *Systems of Judgment,* excerpted April 19 at Merkin Hall, began with thunder. Not a boom, but a resonant, pulsating drone, a divine force whose recurring forward thrust created an air of expectancy that anything might happen. Let there be noise.

And there was noise. Rosenboom, who teaches at Mills College (please don't confuse him with guitarist/composer David Rosen*bloom*), performed his orchestral epic by himself, with piano, violin, and a tableful of digital gizmos. Talk about power trips. The drone's harmonics flipped restlessly between major and minor, yin and yang. Part two started, the drone gave birth to stochastic, rain-thickets, filter-swept winds, and a "Theme of Wonderment" on the violin. This theme—the image of the Subjective Self—played against a marvelously real computerized string section, as calm amid creational chaos as the "contented river" of Ives's "Housatonic at Stockbridge." River: there's another archetype Rosenboom caught vividly, the *stream* of consciousness.

The program notes braced me for musical gobbledygook, but they turned out to be worth the effort: "There is a conceptual paradigm which guided the creation of the musical form. It attempts to elucidate parallel views of evolution by examining and speculating about processes which we, any organism, or any system must use to learn to make differentiations, be self-reflexive, and arrive at judgments from which language may be formulated. The counterpoint of the form is conceived in a multidimensional *concept space* linking three views of evolution. The first focuses on an ontogenetic view, the evolution of the individual of a species. Its imagery involves using the idea of the drone, a sonic singularity, to represent birth or the beginning of self-consciousness."

Rosenboom studied at the University of Illinois; I was educated in the Midwest too, a few years later, so I've read tomes of similar chin music. Until Rosenboom's concert, I had never heard it in the actual music. I attended Rosenboom's lecture at Studio PASS (Public Access Synthesizer Studio) the evening after the concert, and though I was hard put to negotiate his software mazes, he had clearly come up with some multidimensional ways of characterizing musical processes that make it easy to move between diverse listening experiences. If the satirical [THE] duo exposes the hocus-pocus in '70s conceptualism, *Systems of Judgment* is the payload it was searching for.

Unfortunately, at the concert Rosenboom played only three parts of his seven-movement, 64-minute work, and you could feel that stages were missing. So it's a good thing that the entire piece has come out on a Centaur CD. In a live hearing, the noisily climactic seventh movement finally lost me, but on the CD the piece gains impressive magnitude with clarity. Rosenboom conceptually bridges La Monte Young's primeval tone and the stochastic noise textures of Xenakis. In between, you encounter Scriabinesque piano harmonies, Ivesian layering, African rhythmic articulation, tensely minimalist stasis, joyously wild Messaien-like melody, drizzle, storms, limpid pools, mountain climbs, all audibly referring back to that opening thunder. And yet the framework wraps these into a unified, uncultivated landscape, each terrain just a logical footstep away from the others. The piece sums up the 20th century, and sounds ravishing in the process. Finally there's a CD your whole family can enjoy: the minimalist, the aleatorist, the improviser, the just-intonationist, even that hard-to-please serialist.

Rosenboom shared the Merkin program, part of the World Music Institute's American Music Series, with ·South Indian *mrdangam* (two-headed, barrel-shaped drum made out of jackwood) virtuoso Trichy Sankaran. Sankaran played two hot solos of progressive rhythmic variation on his drum, one of them accompanied by drones it triggered from Rosenboom's computerized tamboura. Then Sankaran and Rosenboom collaborated on *Layagnanam,* in which the latter's computer echoed and transformed the drum patterns. I couldn't quite hear that this lived up to its program-note claim of analyzing the *mrdangam* patterns well enough to really accompany them. Computer-improv systems range between two extremes: one at which the electronics echo the instrument in a Mickey Mouse manner, the other at which the computer's transformations long ago lost any audible relation to the instrument. For now, anything well in the middle must be counted success, and *Layagnanam,* occupying that middle, was fun enough to listen to.

And another Rosenboom conceptual improv, *Is Art Is* played on piano and *mrdangam,* spun jazzy circles on superfast irregular rhythmic patterns, Sankaran outlining Rosenboom's ostinatos in cliff-hanging unison. It brought the house down, and showed that Rosenboom has more tricks up his sleeve (including dazzling finger technique) than a small sampling of his work would suggest. But it was *Systems of Judgment* that seemed to fulfill a dozen 20th-century promises at once, the most *intellectual*—in all good senses of the word—new work I've heard in a long, long time.

music in time of war

the composer-to-composer symposium

AUGUST 7, 1990

TELLURIDE—The mountains that surround this 9,000-foot-high Colorado town form a physical barrier to the larger world, but not a psychological one. The censorship of 2 Live Crew became the focus of the Telluride Institute's Composer-to-Composer symposium (July 8 to 15), even though only one of the participants—Laurie Anderson—had pop-music connections. The festival, directed by composers Charles Amirkhanian and

John Lifton, is a think tank at which, for three years now, composers from diverse countries and aesthetic camps have met to chew over each other's philosophies. The first year, the big issue was intonation. Nobody cried. This year, things got more emotional, and this sleepy ski retreat became, for one week, the hottest political music scene in America.

Two issues provided the impetus: 2 Live Crew's recent legal troubles over the raunchy, women-demeaning lyrics of their album *As Nasty as They Wanna Be* and the NEA's inclusion of the "obscenity clause" in their grant acceptance letters, requiring each funded artist to promise that grant money will not be used for that oxymoron "obscene art." During the week, before the public was invited, the composers—Anderson, Gerri Allen, Leo Smith, Ge Gan-ru, Pauline Oliveros (all New Yorkers), Amirkhanian, Lifton, Henry Brant, Roger Reynolds, Larry Polansky, Robert Morris (all Americans), Germany's Gerhard Staebler, England's Hugh Davies, Canada's James Tenney, and I Wayan Sadra from Java—issued a brief, vague manifesto condemning censorship, which was carried by some of the AP wires. In part, it read:

> We affirm the obligation of all artists to make the art they believe in,
>   whatever its style,
>   whatever its message.
> Therefore we abhor censorship in all forms. . . .
> In articulating the sensibilities of a battered world, artists require
>   complete freedom.

Hoping to take more potent action, they also opened the Telluride Composer's Defense Fund at the Telluride Bank, money designated to aid oppressed and silenced composers anywhere in the world. These were symbolic measures. But the festival's focus was the heated discussion generated at the censorship panel.

It began much as the private sessions had, with the playing of one and a half cuts from *As Nasty as They Wanna Be.* Laurie Anderson's initial response seemed to speak for the entire crowd: "For me this isn't a First Amendment issue whatsoever. These guys have absolutely every right to sing whatever they want. And I have absolutely every right to make their lives as miserable as I can." Asked by an audience member whether she thought there might be more sociological meaning to the words than appeared on the surface, she said, "To me, it's stretching it to think that 'Make that pussy splat' is code for anything." She added, though, "On another level this is a song about incredible anger. And I think if we don't listen to that aspect of the song we're really missing it."

It was a highly politicized group. Anderson had the pop perspective, but others had had face-to-face experience with censorship. Polansky is a former chairman of the Oakland ACLU; Staebler has been barred from East Germany for his musicopolitical activities. Entering the U.S. under a Third World passport, I Wayan Sadra (Indonesia's leading composer) was detained at Los Angeles Airport for five hours, where authorities wouldn't allow him to get to his bag containing the Telluride Institute poster, which showed that he was an invited artist. It wasn't his first run-in with higher-ups; in 1979, a theater production in Java for which he wrote the music was delayed when tanks and soldiers surrounded the theater. The production indeed criticized the government, but in such veiled terms that the military didn't catch on, and eventually left. In Java, Sadra explained, an artist who creates a work that offends the government can be put in jail with no legal process. Nevertheless, he talked about censorship more as a challenge than an evil. "As artists," he said, "we have to know what to do to not be caught by the censors. This takes far more creativity than just thinking about what we would do if we were free."

For Sadra, the 2 Live Crew issue seemed simple. "If you're worried about wanting to talk about sex and it's forbidden, and that upsets you, why don't you just take a different path? Why don't you get involved with people who are economically disadvantaged? How can artists help the situation of poor and disadvantaged people? This is what's important. We agree that there's a problem of censorship, but sometimes it's important to have some limits." The answer didn't go over well. As one audience member responded, "My limits may be different from your limits, and your government's limits are very different from your own. If every time you get stomped on one side you have to choose a new path, don't you end up running a maze rather than being direct?"

Ge Gan-ru, who escaped China to become a music faculty member at Columbia University, spoke in stronger terms. Following the Cultural Revolution, he had been interned in a state farm on an island north of Shanghai, working in the fields 14 hours a day, along with 40,000 other young people, to "reform his thoughts through manual labor." In China, he said, "they not only control your thoughts, but everything: where you should live, how you should eat, what kind of job you're going to do." Gan-ru studied violin secretly, by candlelight, with a mute, in a barn with the windows closed. Had he been heard practicing scales, he recalled, he would have gotten in trouble with the authorities, for the major scale was a foreign, Western influence. Finally allowed to study at Shanghai Conservatory, he began composing, and said he was asked, "'Why do you write this kind of music? This kind of music is not understood by the audience.' We have a slogan: Art is for people. You are supported by the people. So if you write something they don't like, they have no reason to support you. If you want to express your own feeling, they don't allow you."

Via the NEA's obscenity clause, that same argument is now coming from the U.S. government. Because several highly visible arts figures— Leonard Bernstein, Joseph Papp, Bella Lowitsky—have returned NEA checks rather than sign the obscenity clause, Pauline Oliveros was called upon to explain why she accepted $25,000 for what she termed "a potentially offensive project": "I called all my advisers. They begged me to take the money, and asked me to consider what the issues really were here. First of all, the NEA itself is under attack. The right wing has had an agenda for some time to destroy it, to take control of art and culture to use it for their own purposes. Howard Fine asked me, what was the effective action? Was it *effective* to send the money back? The answer to that seems to be 'no.' It doesn't help the NEA, it doesn't help the artist either. They said, take the money and do your art. You've worked for it, you deserve it. But what *is* the effective action? Write to your senator, call the White House. On the basis of the information I collected, I signed the check, and sent a letter to Frohnmeyer expressing my terror at the fact that I had signed a contract with the obscenity clause in it." For context, consider that the years Oliveros sat on the NEA Music Panel, 1975–79, were the only years in which that panel was friendly to new music.

According to Oliveros, artists who returned the money fell for the right wing's trap. "I think the clause is a virus shrewdly calculated to cause confusion," she said. "It caught the arts community off-balance." Anderson agreed. "This [2 Live Crew issue] has nothing to do with pornography. It has to do with power. It's a smokescreen so we don't look to see how much suffering there is in this country, and at how much spiritual and emotional upheaval is in process. Jesse Helms says this is to protect women and children. As a woman I deeply resent this. I can protect myself. We have many laws in this country about child abuse, rape, racism, and even homophobia. These laws are quite hard to enforce. It's not working. It's easier to attack artists who are making images of this kind of suffering."

Obscenity has become an issue, so the discussion led, because the right is losing control. "Those who are in power in this country," continued Anderson, "are the same people who were in power when John Jay, the first Supreme Court justice, said, 'Those who own this country ought to rule it.' Those who own this country now are the same people as they were then: white men." Gan-ru backed up the opinion with his homeland experience.

"In China, the political movement is a circle. You have depression, then you have bad times. Whenever the government feels like it's losing control, they start some political campaign. Just like here. If it weren't the flag issue, or 2 Live Crew, they'd pick somebody else."

Peter Yarrow of Peter, Paul, and Mary wasn't an invited participant, but he stood from the audience to remind us that "Puff the Magic Dragon" was forbidden in the '60s because of fears that its lyrics were about drugs. He was told by the FCC, in conjunction with Spiro Agnew and the FBI, that if a radio station played his songs along with other songs that *might* be interpreted as drug songs, those stations could lose their licenses. "It's like saying you'll be arrested for going over the speed limit and we're not going to tell you what the limit is. What is frightening is the leap from this 'protection' of society from drugs, in a completely fallacious fashion, to the potential protection of society from ideas that might potentially be inimical to the power of the government. We are living in an era in which the arts have become the cutting edge of a call to sanity and another kind of dream. If we cut that language off, we have lost the control of the most powerful force for real change in this country."

By now the panel had taken on the emotional momentum of a Baptist revival service, and Yarrow led a song. Over and over, with a few people crying, a few dozen composers and new-music fans sang:

Don't ever take away our freedom.
Don't ever take it away.
We must cherish and keep that one part of our lives.
And the rest we're going to find one of these days.

Anderson closed with a call to arms. "Jesse Helms and others have taken on this job of being judges of paintings, pieces of music, etc. No one gave them the right to take this. They took it. And I think that, in this time of war, we're being very stupid if we don't think we can take it back." But the final warning came from Gan-ru. "From my experience in China: Keep your eyes open. Be careful."

don't worry, be hopi

AUGUST 21, 1990

WALPI—Every winter solstice the kachina spirits leave their home in the San Francisco Mountains north of Flagstaff to live among the Hopi mesas in northeastern Arizona. They stay until the first corn harvest, in the post-summer-solstice lunar month of *Kyaamuya*—"the moon of great power"—and then return. Their return is marked by the *Nimån*, or Home Dance (sometimes Going-Home Dance). I had seen other Hopi dances, but I had never observed the *Niman* until July 24. And I had never before been to the Hopi reservation at a time when *pahaanas* (whites) were allowed into the ancient village of Walpi.

Walpi is connected to First Mesa by a strip of rock, buttressed by logs on both sides, just wide enough to drive a pickup across. The village is crowded with houses built onto and carved out of the sandstone, and surrounded by a cliff with a 400- or 500-foot drop that Hopi children sported near with breathtaking fearlessness. The *Niman* is a Christmas-like celebration: the kachinas present the village with the first corn harvest, and the dancers give every child a cornstalk tied to a toy, bows and arrows for boys, kachina dolls for girls. (Between dances the kids, wearing Batman and Dick Tracy T-shirts, shouted about Nintendo and Ninja Turtles.) The *Niman* also honors young women married during the past year, but there were no brides at Walpi this time. A Hopi grandmother told me, "They got tired of having Indian weddings. Too much work."

The *Niman* was performed eight times in the day, lasting some 40 minutes with more or less an hour in between. About 17 of the village's elder men emerged dressed as the Hemis kachina, the ripened-corn kachina in Jemez Indian style: shirtless, backs smeared with black, fox pelts hanging from the waist, pine garlands around the neck, and on each head a large mask with decorated *tableta*. Accompanying them were a couple of clowns and several *rugan*, female kachinas impersonated by men. Unlike the social dances, these included no drums. Percussion was provided by hand-held rattles, by turtle-shell rattles strapped behind the dancers' knees, and, in one of the repeated songs, by notched sticks held against resonating pots that the *rugan* rasped with a ferocious roar.

This wasn't new music, though some Hopi music is. The steps and melody of the Butterfly Dance, which I heard in 1983, are composed anew every year, necessitating six months of daily rehearsal. But that's a social dance, and the kachina dances are less elaborate, more traditional. The *Niman* comprised only two songs, using four pitches between them: A, C, D, and E-flat (intonation varied with the heat). Listening to long, minimalist permutations of a few notes from voices muffled by masks, it took a long time to make musical discriminations. The first time through, I was lost. At the second dance, I began to classify the various rhythms, and by the third I could locate myself within the cycle at a given moment. By the fifth I was finally able to notate snatches of melody.

Within a song each melody was repeated five times, and at the end of each second song the first recurred once as a closing stanza. Two types of rhythmic deviation ornamented the steady beat. The first was a simple change from a beat of two subdivisions to one of three: BUM-bum-BUM-bum-BUM-bum-(rest)-BUM-bum-(rest). The other was a more complex shift from the main tempo to another tempo *about* one and a half times as fast, distinguished by the fact that the subdivisions changed tempo as well. The first device is characteristic of San Juan pueblo music, the second is most conspicuous in Zuni music; the Hopi use both. In the second, the exact relation between tempos was obscured by the haphazard rebound of the rattles, as well as by the fact that the kachina dancers seemed to disagree about what that tempo was.

These shifts between tempo, which immediately distinguish Pueblo music from all other Native American traditions, are clearly body rhythms—any quantitative notation would falsify them—but the *Niman* changed my sense of what that means. In the Butterfly Dance I had noticed that different tempos were connected with different body movements; for example, turning may require a slower beat than a mere shuffling of feet does. In the *Niman*, however, body gestures were limited, and the rhythms fell in place from melodic rather than choreographic necessity. Some of the more energetic dancers altered their foot pattern on the slower tempo, but it wasn't unanimous. Nevertheless, the music arrested the ear with a flexible attitude toward tempo that urban new music, omnivorous with regard to most cultures, has yet to experiment with.

The Hopis don't commercialize their rituals; few tribes are so difficult to find good, recent recordings of. (There are great older recordings; one of my prized possessions is a 1940s disc of Hopis singing their own streamlined version of "Dixie.") I missed the *Niman*'s final ceremony, in which the priests blessed the kachinas, because the official at Punsi Hall asked us not to go past the central plaza where the earlier dances occurred. In fact, my wife and I were among the few *pahaanas* who observed the rules given us. The Hopis are threatening to close off more dances (as they recently closed off the Snake Dance at Hotevilla) because tourists take up so many of the best seats, crowd the adobe roofs of pueblos, and ignorantly plop themselves in the locals' private lawn chairs. The Hopis dance not for aesthetic or recreational reasons as we do, but to preserve the universal harmony. If we non-Hopis want to keep studying their music, we have to learn to preserve it, too.

enough of nothing

postminimalism

APRIL 30, 1991

There is a widespread misperception among critics, and presumably among music lovers in general, that postminimalism aspires to the condition of classical music—and fails. You could date the movement, and the misunderstanding, to 1979, the year of William Duckworth's *Time Curve Preludes:* that was the first major work that sounded minimalist but refused to satisfy minimalist expectations. Since then, postminimalism has become the lingua franca of under-50 composers across the continent, including even a few in noise-happy New York. And yet, the music still gets, not bad press exactly, but condescending and misdirected reviews, reflecting disappointed conditions that no postminimalist ever wanted to fulfill. The history of musical discourse is littered with "ars nova" treatises, and it's time for another.

First, what postminimalism (PM below) is not. It isn't watered-down minimalism, Steve Reich minus the rigor. Its connection to minimalism, which barely justifies hanging onto an unfortunate term for now, is its tendency toward diatonic tonality (common to lots of musics) and its inheritance of numerical, often additive, rhythmic structures from Reich's and Glass's early works. Nor is it, as *EAR* "Stuck-in-the-'60s" magazine would have it, a reactionary movement. There's the rub: PM contains enough conventional scales and harmonies that classical critics hear it as ineptly imitating sonata form. And it's found so little use for noise and discontinuity, discarded elements of the '60s avant-garde, that the free jazz and art-rock crowds don't grasp its central experimentalist impulse, which has to do with form rather than materials. PM may be the first avant-garde movement blasted by its opponents for a supposed conservatism.

Nor is PM one of those collectively anonymous movements (like, say, '70s 12-tone music) easily described by outward characteristics. PM can be political, as in the additively reconstructed worker songs of Peter Gena's *Mother Jones* and *McKinley*. It can use noise, like Arthur Jarvinen's spray-can-hissing *Egyptian Two Step;* it can be sharply dissonant, as in Michael Gordon's *Thou Shalt!/Thou Shalt Not!;* and it can use bizarre instrumental techniques, like Stephen Scott's bowed piano music. For some composers, notably Peter Garland, it's closer in spirit to the American ultramodernism of the '30s than to the Euro-contaminated '60s. PM's unity comes from the problems it attacks, not from the solutions found or the way it strikes the ear.

So, what is it? If you heard the March 20 Merkin Hall concert of Philadelphia's Relache ensemble, either live or on WNYC 10 days later, you got an overview, for at least four of the five works were prime suspects. Relache is postminimalism's unofficial specialist ensemble. Oh, they've dabbled in jazz and improv, they have good 12-tone chops, and I'm sure they'd rather not be pigeonholed. ("Music without Boundaries" is their recent hip slogan.) But their woodwind-heavy sound and silken ensemble technique are a postminimalist's wet dream, and PM is the music they've shown most affection for; their new, first CD on Mode contains luscious examples by Paul Epstein and Thomas Albert. And what they made clear was that postminimalism—though hardly a style John Cage would have envisioned—is the language Cage called for in *Silence,* a new language freed from dialectical antithesis, and founded on rhythm rather than pitch.

"There is not enough of nothing in it," complained Cage about 12-tone music, and that applied to any pitch-based music's inability to theoretically integrate silence. The phrase came to mind during *Om Shanti* by Seattle composer Janice Giteck: here was a work in which some of the movements bounced jazz-syncopated lines in vibrant, Lou Harrison–like gamelan textures, and in which violin and cello vied in a passionate duo. Yet it was also a piece that soprano Barbara Noska (in thrilling voice, singing the style she does perfectly) could bring to a halt by chanting "Om santih santih santih santih santih" over and over and over. Time stopped, time started again, without the jolt you'd feel if your needle got stuck in a Brahms symphony. All the resources of earlier music—jazz rhythms, Hebrew modes, European chamber music gestures, even the big M's repetitions—coexisted in a fluid medium in which no element created expectations that conflicted with the others. This was the synthesis collage music has pointed to for 35 years.

You heard how pervasively PM switches the roles of rhythm and harmony in Lois V. Vierk's *Timberline,* commissioned for this concert (we'll return to this analysis after a word from our sponsor) by Taittinger Champagne. In classical music, harmony shaped the piece through tension and release, while rhythm played a supporting role. But Vierk (composer of the *Attack Cat Polka*) wrapped her form in harmonies of Sibelian gloom that repeated again and again, and it was the rhythm that changed to shape the piece. When, as here, PM uses conventional harmonies, it excises their karma, their tendency to resolve in predictable directions. Too, PM generally avoids melody as such, since melodies impose formal contrasts antithetical to PM's continuous-textural-evolution methodology; but Vierk threw in a pretty filigree of 32nd-notes in the piano to distract those not used to listening on a formal level. Good idea.

Vierk's music seethes with glissandos, but in *Timberline* she took them out of the foreground and buried them in the bass for a striking effect. Mary Ellen Childs's *Carte Blanche,* the other Taittinger commission, also grew from glissandos, and from a repeated sigh of closely spaced pitches. From here the texture expanded through the accretion of repeated motives, not in a mechanical way, but at varying rhythmic intervals. The phasing that began in Reich's *Piano Phase* has passed into PM as a basic technique, no longer to create perceptual illusions, but to give the style a flexible rhythmic-level structure. Austere and riddled with dissonances, *Carte Blanche* wasn't as charming as *Parterre,* the other Childs opus Relache has played (and recorded on the Minnesota Composers Forum label), but its shape was clearer and more compelling.

Tina Davidson's music hasn't always showed postminimal tendencies, and harmonic tension played a larger part in her *Blue Dawn (The Promise Fruit)* than it did elsewhere. But the piece took its time building from reiterated Ds in several octaves up to A and beyond, and its continuous evolution of a texture to climax and back was a PM touch. As in Vierk's piece, the intricately constructed rhythms were articulated by harmony, and the latter expanded in dissonance so smoothly that they made *Blue Dawn* the best Davidson piece I'd heard yet. The work whose PM roots were dubious was Eleanor Hovda's *Ariadnemusic,* even though its shape was similar to that of the Childs and Davidson pieces. Hovda's music seems more related to an earlier, continuum aesthetic derived from the '60s Polish school, a style whose most characteristic gesture is to float in and out of audibility like tentative breathing. *Ariadnemusic*'s bowed cymbals, expressive flute solos (by Laurel Wyckoff), and *sotto voce* violin trills merged in haunting timbres, but the similarities to PM seemed coincidental.

The works by Vierk, Childs, Davidson, and Hovda, you noticed, all opened with long crescendos drawn from repeated licks—if that doesn't indicate a new style has congealed, what would? If PM exhibits a cliché, it's the tent-shaped, single-climax piece, the form organized around an epiphany toward which everything builds and from which it recedes. Cage wanted to rid music of climaxes because they implied hierarchy, one part of a piece being more important than another. More cogent from a critical standpoint, climaxes are tricky, and PM, with its medieval-level harmonic technology, hasn't yet revved up the technique to clinch them. Climaxes resolve dissonance, and in the West we haven't cultivated rhythmic dissonance to the point that we can create convincing climaxes unsupported by harmony (or at least volume). That may be PM's PR problem: the climax is integral to music's entertainment side, something concert-hall audiences may never relinquish without grumbling. There's a type of listener for whom a climaxless piece is inherently "unemotional" (think of all the people who've never caught on to Satie's *Socrate*), and I suspect lots of classical critics, weaned on the Romantics, fall into that category.

The climax of Childs's *Carte Blanche* depended on pitch in a manner strikingly reminiscent of the first movement of Bartók's *Music for Strings, Percussion, and Celesta:* a high point reached via slow, upward expansion of the pitch range (with celesta patterns, no less), quickly evaporating into a few final, sliding gestures taken from the opening. Still, Childs's most overall successful pieces came four days later at an Experimental Intermedia concert, and the best ones eschewed climax altogether. For example: *Click*, a fiendishly complex game of patty-cake played with three sets of claves, and *A Chording To*, which echoed chords between live and taped accordion (Guy Klucevsek) at varying rhythms with the naturalness of breathing.

Vierk's music has always been ambiguous with respect to climaxes; her pieces typically metamorphose between a quiescent texture and a frenetic one, with the frenetic end conveniently placed last, so that the "climax" is really just the endpoint of a process. It's a cool solution to the problem of climax without a tonal framework, and how she inflects that design seems to be the main point of each piece. *Timberline* took a more circuitous path than her other works, and she ventured a step further by widening her harmonic vocabulary in the final minutes to increase the crescendo's emotional force.

But the Relache concert's only piece that truly transported me was Giteck's *Om Shanti*, because it skipped the formal problem and achieved sensuous passion without straining after cathartic moments; it had "enough of nothing" in it. (For a similarly gorgeous example of Giteck's artistry, listen to her Cabalah-inspired *Breathing Songs from a Turning Sky* recorded on Mode.) The other works I admired less for their ultimate effect than for the insightful attacks they waged on well-defined problems. PM is a style still under construction, though it's racked up a greater number of smashing successes in its first 12 years than many movements have in a similar period. If the '60s taught a lesson, it was that avant-gardeness depends not on what materials music uses, how shocking it sounds to suburbanites, or even on its attitude toward society, but on the direction of its dialogue with history, and on whether what it tries to achieve has been done before. In that respect, Giteck, Vierk, Childs, Davidson, Hovda, and Relache are leading into new territory.

voltage high

ron kuivila

DECEMBER 10, 1991

A spark, Ron Kuivila likes to say, is the visual analogue of a sound. It happens with a certain duration and intensity, then disappears, leaving a sensory memory with a spatial location. When you stand in front of *Dolci Mura*, Kuivila's sound installation currently exhibited at Generator, sparks fly all around you. They sing, too.

As you approach *Dolci Mura* (Sweet Walls), you're stopped by three parallel wires. The top one is part of a "Spark Harp"; strung an inch above it is a looser, thinner wire through which 12,000 volts of electricity shoot, every 35 seconds or so. The current makes the wires snap together, rattling and emitting a field of tiny sparks. Touch the wires, and you get a jolt significantly sharper than a nine-volt battery against your tongue. (Kuivila promised it was safe, but I found three experiments sufficient.) On the wall behind the Spark Harp are two Spark Harmonicas that operate on the same principle, though with the thicker wire replaced by a pipe. All three produce a periodic *ts-ts-ts-ts-ts* of soft sparks.

Between the Harp and Harmonicas are three diagonally mounted, rotating antennas tipped with flint, which strike emery cloths to give off horizontal spark lines. A fourth antenna jingles a set of keys in five-beat patterns at varying tempos. Not much racket there, except that all this activity is picked up by an ultrasonic microphone that converts the upper harmonics, via amplitude modulation, into a heavy metal rattling. The real shockers are the "Conjugal Pairs" on each side, whose wires, separated by a quarter-inch gap, jerk with a 12,000-volt spark shooting across the gap every 30 seconds with a raucous *ztztztzt!* The installation's one mute icon, "Distressed Music," is a compact disc that's been baked to a crinkly orange in a microwave. Generator oughta post a warning, kids, don't try this at home.

Kuivila has been active in Holland, Belgium, Switzerland, and Italy these last few years, but *Dolci Mura* is his first New York installation since 1987. It represents the start of a new phase in his work. He's long made individual, autonomous, sound-producing objects; now he's combining them, and his challenge, he explains with nonstop enthusiasm, is "orchestration. I'm interested in what I call temporal tessitura. Each object has a time domain, so a larger temporal structure can be imposed on the materials in the same way that you locate things in a gallery. Everything can be heard, but still overlaps with everything else."

Dolci Mura certainly succeeds in that respect. Within its mostly gentle but impersonal clanging, it takes a while for the softer sounds to appear in isolation and reveal how much is really going on. It also takes time to link each amplified ultrasonic noise with its source, a fun bit of audiovisual detective work. For me the most wonderful moments are the unexpected drops into silence; the whole conglomeration fades to a tentative halt as if taking a breath, then zaps back into activity. Kuivila appreciates the effect: "There's this musical experience of recognizing a sound the moment it disappears, like when the fan turns off. I think of those as very beautiful moments."

Those moments don't happen by accident, and the brilliant simplicity of their organization is typical of the thinking that's put Kuivila at the top of the installation heap. *Dolci Mura*'s antennas and wires are coordinated by a MIDI-controlled Yamaha DMP7 mixer run by computer. The strategy is to phase events over a large time scale; for example, the Spark Harp and Harmonicas together stretch out a rhythm of five-against-six-against-seven over several minutes. Kuivila has moved away from Cage's indeterminacy (so influential in sound-installation work) and returned to the rhythmic grids Cage used in the '40s. "Going back to those rhythmic structures admits that there's an indeterminate relation between the sound material's unfolding and the audience. In fact, that's where indeterminacy resides. You don't have any sense for what kind of attention you're going to receive.

"I'm also interested in the Nancarrow idea of complex tempo counterpoint, and in mapping that at a much slower tempo. It's the compositional version of the radio programming problem, which is to have in a 15-minute interval some representation of what's going on. The amount of time someone will stand in the gallery is relatively brief. You want a structure that reveals as much of the sonic material as possible in a short window of time, but continues to unfold in a fashion that invites extended listening."

For Kuivila, sound-installation art is caught in a bind between sensuousness and conceptualism, "between the 'mindless sound' of Cage and the 'soundless mind' of Marcel Duchamp. In a gallery, if you have something running autonomously, you immediately have the problem of it becoming simply a wind chime—a craft, rather than an art form. Part of the reason for that, I think, is the context that's been set by Duchamp. We think of Cage and Duchamp being creatively similar: one challenged the frame by including noise, the other by including the found object, the ready-made. The crucial difference is, with Cage, sound has a substantive, sensual existence. With Duchamp, it's a system of interrogation, of questions being asked of different systems. This piece is a negotiation between these two spaces, the space of Duchamp's interrogation and the space of sound as noise, or silence, even at the same time."

Fifteen minutes is the minimum you should allow to soak up *Dolci Mura* if you want to get beyond the fun of being surrounded by high voltage. Experienced at length, it's a delightfully theatrical conglomeration of metal and wires; Kuivila admits that he's "trying to recall opera in its original form, which is, of course, the theater of machines."

isn't that spatial?

henry brant

SEPTEMBER 15, 1992

Driving I-81 through Virginia recently, I stopped at Luray Caverns. This gave me a chance to hear the world's most spatially extended instrument, the "Great Stalacpipe Organ" built in 1954 by Leland W. Sprinkle. Across more than three acres of once-pristine underground majesty, Sprinkle, an engineer with a musical bent, combined "Man's genius and the Hand of God" by grinding down selected stalactites to ring at equal-tempered pitches. He then installed rubber-tipped plungers to strike them, remote-controlled by a four-manual keyboard. Such a monument to art's priority over nature should have inspired me with pride, but I was glad Sprinkle didn't live near Carlsbad. Upon questioning, our tour guide swore that no stalactites had ever broken off from the vibration of daily tappings. Well, thus the official line; the mechanical version of "America, the Beautiful" she had the organ play was suspiciously deficient in several pitch areas.

What the Stalacpipe Organ did provide, as "America"'s harmonies thinned and thickened with Cagean randomness, was the chance to hear music from inside, to have my sense of sound location screwed up by notes pinging from widely scattered areas. And as coincidence would have it, at that very moment a New York audience was having a similar experience at Lincoln Center's North Plaza, where Henry Brant's *500: Hidden Hemisphere* for three wind ensembles and steel-drum band received its world premiere. I heard the second performance the following day, August 23. Brant, 79 this month, is the pioneer of music written for spatially separated ensembles, an idea he drew from Charles Ives. (Ives was inspired by the multileveled landscapes of Connecticut and upstate New York.) Brant remains little known because his mammoth works are difficult to organize, but he's an original with an impressive underground reputation. (A musician I bumped into in Luray Caverns admired him.)

Four orchestras grouped around the reflecting pool at the North Plaza, 165 musicians in all, attracted a huge, curious crowd. On the north, across from Juilliard, Lieutenant Commander Lewis J. Buckley conducted the United States Coast Guard Band. On the east, crammed against Avery Fisher Hall, was the Goldman Memorial Band, conducted by composer Brant. On the south, next to the Metropolitan Opera, was the U.S. Military Academy Band, led by Lieutenant Colonel Frank G. Dubuy. And on the west, conducted by composer and Brant expert Neely Bruce, stood Pandemonium, the Wesleyan University Steel Band. One passerby asked, "Is this a contest?"

According to the program, *500: Hidden Hemisphere*, written for the Columbus quincentennial, was divided into 16 continuous sections with titles like "Conclaves," "Citadels," "Incantations," and so on; with a little imagination, they were easily discerned. Picture a gargantuan, musical bridge game. West opened, as Bruce's steel drums beat out a few syncopated jazz motives. South responded with a flurry of chimes, echoed in the west by glockenspiels, and on the north by timpani. Fanfares flared with a Roy Harris–like flavor of mournfully modulating harmony. It was classic Brant, jazzy with ambiguous 1940s tonalities, yet also smoothly eclectic. Two sections titled "Bazaar" I and II clashed marches, quasi-show tunes, and jumpy pop styles against each other at once. Still, Brant's been at this spatial thing for decades, and his effects were moving, imaginative, but rarely spectacular.

Virgil Thomson called Brant the best American orchestrator, and the instrumental concept of *Hemisphere* was brilliantly suited to its venue. Each ensemble was conceived as a single, multicolored organism, and every element calculated for utmost audibility. The steel drums, undulating in tense chromatic scales, formed the rhythm section over whose syncopated chorales the other three groups alternated their lines. Brasses and wood-winds melodicized in octaves and unisons, making a spatial counterpoint separated not in range, but by hundreds of feet. Percussion provided pointillistic sparkle; East had no fewer than three glockenspiels, South rang two sets of chimes, and North's three drummers blasted nine timpani between them. Contrary to the essentially chamber-music conception of most 20th-century orchestra works, *Hemisphere* was truly symphonic, its elements streamlined for maximum collective effect.

As in Conlon Nancarrow's player-piano music, Brant's static textures continued as others played against them in various permutations. In fact, Brant and Nancarrow grappled with similar problems; if you're the first in history to attempt various tempos played against each other, or musics played at great distances, you clarify your forms to isolate the idea. Other multiple orchestra pieces, like Stockhausen's *Gruppen* (I heard the American premiere in Chicago), use the ensembles only to differentiate syntactic levels and create a few echoes. *Hemisphere* was like living inside the music, twisting your neck around constantly to follow the tunes. Most remarkable was the way distance and open spaces softened the brassy melodies. The music pierced an ambience that never ceased to overwhelm it. Such sonorities are impervious to recording, though perhaps Brant's most successfully characteristic disc is *Western Springs* on CRI. If you skipped the concert, you can't hear what you missed, without a quadraphonic system and a football field.

I left exhilarated at my first live experience with Brant's orchestral antiphonies. Then, walking home through Central Park, I was startled to find the effect duplicated by the various competing rock and jazz groups scattered around. They weren't as well coordinated as Brant's ensembles, admittedly, but then, they weren't destroying natural wonders to play "O beautiful, for spacious skies" either.

the limits of craft

frederic rzewski/philip glass

DECEMBER 8, 1992

Frederic Rzewski's music is neither Uptown nor Down, European nor American, conservative nor avant-garde. His most characteristic work is introverted, mercurial, structural yet highly emotional, and untied to any school or theory. He writes in two categories, stunning and enigmatic. The difference is, the stunners make his astounding compositional technique audible. November 13 at the Kitchen, he played two of each. *Bumps,* enigma number one, was an intuitive approach to the old "moment form" (as in Stockhausen), a collage of short motives, interrupted ostinatos, rhythms tapped on the piano lid, and half-pedaled after-rings. Similarly, *The Turtle and the Crane* connected Satie-esque passages with repeated notes.

The first stunner was *De Profundis*, a theater piece in which Rzewski spoke and chanted a searing letter from prison written by Oscar Wilde about the life of an artist. Unfettered by pianistic convention, Rzewski breathed audibly between notes, whistled along with a romantic virtuoso moment, slapped his face and chest for sounds, honked a bicycle horn, and yelled nonsense syllables like a madman. The piece was as touchingly exposed as Wilde's letter. "People who want self-realization can't know where they are going," Rzewski intoned while playing. "The final mystery is oneself."

Andante con moto revealed Rzewski's incredible compositional chops and chutzpah. It was, believe it or not, a set of variations on the second-movement theme of Beethoven's *Appassionata* sonata. The theme rarely became obvious: instead, Rzewski jumped between registers, as in the *Appassionata*'s final variation, and the tritone resolutions, off-rhythms, and phrases that hung expectantly in the air were haunted by Beethoven's ghost. (Sophisticated audiences are fun. During a pause, Rzewski drew appreciative guffaws by suddenly hitting the diminished-seventh chord that leads to the *Appassionata*'s third movement.) *Andante con moto* proved that Rzewski has technique up the wazoo. The other pieces showed that he doesn't use it when aiming for levels of meaning that technique can't reach.

Philip Glass's music at Brooklyn Academy of Music the next evening made a fascinating contrast, for his relation to technique is entirely different. If Rzewski's imagination is on 24-hour call, Glass's has only to make a brief appearance in each piece, and technique does the rest. And it works. It works the way it worked for Stravinsky, which is to say, not equally well in every piece. Glass's choral piece *Itaipu*, with its incessant short isorhythms, its "BA-bum, bum, baah" in measure after measure after measure, sounded like an accompaniment to a film or theater piece that just wasn't there. Like many of Stravinsky's smaller works, *Itaipu* revealed too much about the emptiness of mere technique.

That wasn't true of Glass's new *Low Symphony*, based on themes from the David Bowie–Brian Eno *Low* album. Intelligentsia of a decade ago might have dismissed the symphony's impressionist harmonies, its noble film-music melodies, its repeating, exotically rhythmed cycles, as a rehash of *Iberia* or *The Planets*, but it wouldn't have been fair. Despite the structural repetitions, the *Low* symphony's surface was constantly fresh and varied. In recent music, Glass keeps you from noticing his repetitions through a lavishly applied layer of compositional technique. That layer makes the music comprehensible, entertaining, linear, and communicative. It's obvious *how* the music is composed.

Rzewski, on the other hand, when he hid his technique, left me wondering, for all my admiration, what he was driving at. Yet he also put more of himself into the music than Glass did because he wasn't hiding behind his chops. Rzewski's music is a frank tour of the composer's mental workshop, while Glass only allows you in the drawing room, all spruced up for company.

Schoenberg's anatomy of technique is classic: "Evenness, regularity, symmetry, subdivision, repetition, unity, relationship in rhythm and harmony and even logic—none of these elements produces or even contributes to beauty. But all of them contribute to an organization which makes the presentation of the musical idea intelligible." Glass fluffs out a little beauty with lots of regularity and symmetry, Rzewski tosses symmetry aside and packs in as much beauty as he can. Charles Ives would have said that Glass represents manner, Rzewski substance, but that's too pat; it's a Euro-Romantic view, and fails to take account of the Indian music Glass studied, the change in focus and expectations wrought by Cage and world musics. I might have agreed with Ives had I not reversed an allegiance a few years ago after realizing Stravinsky's music is better than Schoenberg's.

The question might be recast: does a composer satisfy the demands of the craft, or the needs of the listener? Why do these differ? Is that our cultural neurosis, or the nature of craft? If Bach satisfied one set of demands with his cantatas and the other with *The Art of Fugue*, why don't recent composers similarly divide their efforts? Isn't Craft a god who *must* be propitiated, and won't an *occasional* offering do the job? Stravinsky-Glass and Schoenberg-Rzewski is a metaphor of limited fruitfulness, for Rzewski, like Glass and unlike Schoenberg, is often more concerned with images (fragmented ones) than with pitch syntax. But there's a pathological beauty to the way the two enact a distinctly 20th-century paradox: Glass writes the better music, but Rzewski is the better composer.

opera is relative

einstein on the beach

DECEMBER 15, 1992

It did not last: the Devil, howling, "Ho!
Let Einstein be!" restored the status quo.

J.C. SQUIRE

What happened to opera? Or rather, what *didn't* happen to it? In 1976 it was poised to break out of Heldentenorland, drop centuries of accreted flab, and move to the Nevada of the mind: a sparser, drier location, but one with plenty of air, fewer people, looser laws, room to move around. Opera was no longer going to require opera houses, narrative, coloratura sopranos, declamatory singing, vocal cadenzas, period costumes, sextets, climaxes, denouements, all those cast-iron vestiges of 19th-century Europe. It could be American, postmodern, clean, flat, intelligent, open-ended, abrupt, visual, multilayered, ambiguous. All that was promised by one incendiary, inconsistent work: *Einstein on the Beach.*

I've worn down my four-record set of *Einstein* to slick vinyl wafers, but I hadn't actually seen Philip Glass's seminal opera until November 20 at the Brooklyn Academy of Music. The music has a few dull, thin stretches, which I hoped Robert Wilson's stage action would flesh out. It didn't. What's tedious on the record was more so in the theater, though beautiful passages became more compelling as well. The "Night Train" scene with its interminable la-si-do-si pattern tires me, and its pretty but nearly immobile staging edged me toward wrist-slitting mode. The texts, so elegantly read by dancers Lucinda Childs and Sheryl Sutton, now have the charm of familiarity, but have become no more transparent through repetition. I never felt *Einstein* quite fused all the wonderful elements it brought together.

But such faults didn't matter. *Einstein* is less important than the liberating paradigm it suggested. When the "Bed" scene's celebrated white bar tipped from horizontal to vertical (a six-minute process) and then lifted into space, it reminded you of the vertical white bar in the opening "Train" scene; that showed you how an opera's unity could be visual as well as musical, and how visual and musical unities could operate on the same level. When the "Trial" scene's courtroom attendants opened their bag lunches, you saw how opera could incorporate daily life, not only tragic grandeur. When Gregory Fulkerson (Einstein) emerged to play the violin repertoire's most devilish solo—hours of lightning-fast sawing in which he missed, by my count, one note—you saw how Harry Partch's dream of integrating the instrumentalists into stage action could be fulfilled in a natural way.

Lots of fat-lady standards don't have as many beautiful sections as *Einstein.* The "Bed" scene, my quiet favorite, opened a new era in harmony. The "Spaceship" scene was as thrilling for its staging—horizontal and vertical elevators crisscrossing a web of lights—as it's always been for its electrifying ensemble technique. And part of the beauty of such sections was the way your mind could roam around in them, rather than diligently follow the obligatory dramatic thread. Wilson's stage processes prevent close attention so that you'll suddenly realize that things have changed without noticing how. Opera has rarely made narrative sense, and in *Einstein* it quit pretending to. Instead, it made musical sense, visual sense, choreographic sense.

So what happened? The *Einstein* era and the Carter era were equally abbreviated. With Glass's *Satyagraha*, the Reagan-Bush cultural hiatus began: libretto in Sanskrit, refreshingly, but in 4/4 meter and back in the old opera house. Musically as well as politically, we retreated from goals within our grasp. In the '80s, with far less hoopla, only Robert Ashley went on writing revolutionary, nonanachronistic operas that fulfilled, in their television-info-overload way, the *Einstein* promise. And Ashley has yet to get his operas produced in their intended form, or aired on American TV.

Einstein smashed a hole in the prison wall. Glass sang so joyfully, if incoherently, in the fresh air outside that he was invited back in. And he accepted. He wrote *Akhnaten*, which was OK. Then he wrote *The Fall of the House of Usher*, the only opera I've ever seen worse than *The Death of Klinghoffer*. And now he's written *The Voyage*, a beautiful, complexly melodic work that held my attention throughout. But seeing *Einstein* reminded me how irrelevant the *Voyage*'s achievements are to *Einstein*'s promises. I couldn't sit out *Einstein* as patiently as I did *The Voyage*, yet every scene in *Einstein* provoked more thought than the entire later opera. Ashley's *Improvement (Don Leaves Linda)*, recently released on a Nonesuch CD, is a true 1990s opera, but *The Voyage* is a 19th-century opera written in 1990s style. All it showed was how to bring a new idea into the Met without upsetting the status quo. *Einstein* said, to hell with the status quo.

Long before 1976, the only way for opera to go was OUT. The opera world has little place for musical brain. Within that world, *Wozzeck*'s taut expressionism will forever be forced to compete with *Traviata*'s tawdry blandness, and *Traviata* will always, always win. There's no honest way for new, intelligent, relevant opera to survive in a milieu that is more than half devoted to nonentities like Donizetti and Bellini, composers who couldn't write the sharp in a secondary dominant chord without exhausting their compositional muscle. Boulez said, "Burn the opera houses"; I say, "Let vocal-sports fans place bets on high C's in their moldy halls, and let's start something new somewhere else." That something new could have begun with *Einstein*. Now that the climate's freeing up again, can we pick up where we left off?

well-tuned blues

the forever bad blues band

FEBRUARY 2, 1993

If you've never been in La Monte Young's Tribeca loft, it smells the way the Kitchen smelled January 9 at the American premiere of Young's Forever Bad Blues Band. Young's incense served two functions: to create the right vibes and to track the time. An assistant showed Young each new stick, lighting it as a signal of how far along the performance was. Good thing, for Young can play forever, and his musicians were pushed to their limits. The Forever Bad Band—what a title for an old Idaho hillbilly who became a world-famous music guru—toured Germany, Austria, and Holland in 1992, and this was their first American appearance. Young, earthily humorous beneath his mystic facade, developed an Idaho-tinged persona for his quartet, wearing a purple bandanna tied behind his head, a denim jacket with the sleeves ripped off, and leather gloves. He could have completed the effect by roaring in on a Harley.

Now known for his mathematical sine-tone installations, his fanatically pure tuning, his knotted beard, and his five-hour improvisation *The Well-Tuned Piano*, Young started out in jazz and blues. In 1953 he beat Eric Dolphy for a sax chair in the Los Angeles City College Dance Band. ("Best dance band in the U.S.," Young recalls; "I was lucky, because Eric played beautifully at the audition.") The tapes that survive of Young playing sax in the early '60s reveal incredible stamina, an ability to reel off thousands of notes for half-hours at a time with no lapses of technique or inspiration. (Those tapes, if they make it to disc someday, will rewrite our history of early minimalism.) But while his improv style in the *W.-T. P.* owes much to sax figurations, today Young plays only the keyboard.

I heard the FBBB twice, on the 9th and 15th. Each performance began at 8:54 and ended promptly at 10:54. (Young carefully records his every note, and his tapes run two hours.) His leisurely time-sense a legend, Young opened with a few "clouds," the harmonic flurries that constitute much of the *W.-T. P.* It took 15 minutes to ease into 12/8 meter, and the group didn't stray from the opening chord until around 9:25. Young's Korg synthesizer is tunable to within one cent (1/100th of a half-step), and his quiet, opening four notes gave away his septimal scale, for the B-flat in *Young's Dorian Blues in G* made a 7/6 interval, a third of a half-step flatter than on the conventional piano. (Tuning aficionados might note that the E in the IV chord was a 5/4 major third above the C, despite

Young's famous avoidance of 5-based intervals in his other works.) Like many tuning theorists, Young believes that blues singers instinctively aim for flat, seven-related intervals, and this narrow tuning had a bite no other piano blues could have provided.

Once the swing began, Young kept a remarkably low profile, playing mainly a 3-against-2 pattern with occasional breaks into quick, high-register fingerwork. The stars, guitarists Jon and Brad Catler (on bass) and drummer Jonathan Kane, were tirelessly entertaining and inventive. The Catlers, who also play in the Microtones, had been tuning freaks long before they worked with Young. Jon switched between fretless and just-intonation fingerboards for his guitar, dropped the melody to strum his higher strings harp-like, and, in both gigs, snuck in a justly-tuned version of "Summertime." Kane made Young grin by throwing the beat into duple and 3-against-2 rhythms, and his relentless energy matched that of Young's early tapes. He took to wearing gloves in the final performances, and one concern about repeat gigs was whether his hands could take the abuse.

There were few landmarks, but the variety was unending. By 50 minutes in, the band fell into a more traditional 12-bar pattern, with chord progression I-IV-I-V-IV-I. Young, fond of parallels between blues and Indian music, compares the effect to raga performance, in which the second composition is more regularly rhythmic. The 12-bar period dominated on January 9, but by the 15th the group had slowed the chord changes into a more static, meditative continuum. At both gigs, dynamics ebbed and swelled with extreme gradualness into slo-mo Wagnerian climaxes. Volume hovered between 100 and 110 dB on my decibel meter (which I bought especially for Kitchen concerts), reaching 114 at the end (I leave at 120), but instead of being pounded by racket, we were massaged by pure harmonies. It made a difference.

"The problem with equal temperament," Young told me, "is that nothing reinforces anything else. You go for a big sound and you get a big noise." More are beginning to agree. Microtonal pioneer Ben Johnston claims that one cause of society's problems is that people grow up bathed in loud rock in the usual equal-tempered tuning, and that the irrational intervals of that tuning create an unconsciously disturbing disharmony in the ear. If that's true, the SRO crowds that flocked to the six Kitchen FBBB performances went home blessed by a blasting dose of in-tuneness. The Kitchen had to turn so many people away from the door that they held the show over one night, but the remaining, tentatively planned performances have been canceled due to scheduling problems. The Kitchen's looking to cosponsor the FBBB at a larger venue, and, for those who want their Idaho frequency-bath at home, a CD should be out within months.

voice of the unutterable

the s.e.m. ensemble

DECEMBER 28, 1993

Many centuries before Descartes articulated the mind/body problem, personhood was considered divisible into three parts: body, spirit, soul. In 787 A.D., as psychologist James Hillman dopes it out in the *Puer Papers*, the priests of the Catholic church met in Nicaea and dethroned the soul, setting the stage for a soulless Western culture that now must look to Asia and Africa to regain what it lost. How did they dethrone it? They decreed that images could be used in the church only if they were interpreted as illustrations or allegories of the ideas of church doctrine. Images themselves, which had been adored throughout the ancient world, could no longer be venerated. Statues were shattered. Ideas won. Ideas feed the spirit, but images, taken in their irreducible complexity as manifestations of the psyche, nurture the soul. The church bartered away our soul for political power. (A millennium later, science would attempt to knock off the spirit as well.)

How could music nurture the soul? The S.E.M. Ensemble offered an amazing demonstration December 4 at Alice Tully Hall. The ensemble's Czech-born composer-conductor Petr Kotik has been stubbornly determined to live the life of a European-style genius in godforsaken America, and, against all odds, he's succeeding. Like Boulez, he's making a career conducting large ensembles in the music you need to hear to understand his own. His latest coup was to bring back the legend David Tudor for his first orchestral performance since 1958 of Cage's *Concert for Piano and Orchestra*. Wind players blew isolated notes, violinists waved little glissandos, and Tudor, frail as he now is, smashed forearm clusters on the keyboard. (Tudor's protégé Joseph Kubera soloed on a second piano.) Adding his own touches, Tudor drew electronic squeaks by scraping his prepared, amplified strings, and sparked loud burbles from what looked like plastic Slinkys suspended from a bar.

You know how I love Cage's music, but I find a dry spell in his output of the late '50s and early '60s, a period in which he accepted the "parametrical" sound definitions of European atomism. (He recovered in the mid '60s with *Variations IV.*) Cage used gorgeous images in his early music, but *Concert* falls at the historical low point of the musical image, at which logic obliterated concern for sonic resonance. After about an hour, following the splintered course of Cage's temporary surrender began to seem a high price to pay for a slice of history.

How could music nurture the soul? By providing us with images. More than the other mid-century masters of sonic complexity, Edgard Varèse knew how to sculpt them, as Kotik proved in a clean, sonically vivid reading of *Déserts*. Sonorities in brass and winds bounced back and forth, while five percussionists struck up a wildly cavorting interplay of motives behind them. Though the piece never repeated, it seemed to hover in air, every motive and chord poised to reappear at any moment. What makes Varèse's music so much more bracingly memorable than, say, the ephemeral, ever-in-transition logic of an Elliott Carter piece is that Varèse valued sonorities over ideas, and burned them onto our eardrums.

How could music nurture the soul? By providing us with images. And because it is the nature of sound to die away within seconds, musical images require repetition. An icon cannot flash by and be venerated, it must be held in the mind. *Da-da-da-*DUH would mean nothing if Beethoven had only played it once. After decades in which repetition was specifically prohibited (Babbitt, Boulez) as insufficiently macho for the linear-information-processing brain of Superlistener, it is now the crucial device of our time, reintroduced not only in the mechanical manner of minimalism (though that was a step in the right direction), but it its *imagistic* form by Morton Feldman. Within white culture, perhaps only a Jewish composer could have pulled off such a feat; not a hyperrationalist Jew like Babbitt, but a Talmudic mystic with respect for the unutterable. What did the rabbis care what happened at Nicaea?

S.E.M. gave the American premiere of Feldman's *The Turfan Fragments,* a piece preceded by its luminous European reputation. As the soft pulse of pizzicato basses alternated with the confident peeps of woodwinds, pinpricks of timbre poked against squirming scale segments, building up organlike sonorities note by note. And every configuration happened seven, 13, 20 times in a row. "OK, OK, I got the point," the intellect would say, and the soul, beginning to stir, answered, "Yes, this is the point—listen." In this piece more than any other, Feldman proved that a semi-dissonant, multitimbral chord repeated over and over, not in a steady pulse but irregularly every few seconds, becomes the voice of the unutterable. Even if you analyze it by ear, it dissolves your analysis by simply returning, resonating the same nodal points of the hall again and again. The piece worshiped sound, and elicited such worship from the listener.

Feldman knew exactly what he was doing. "Unfortunately for most people who pursue art," he said in an interview, "ideas become their opium." And another time, when a student shouted, "You're full of shit!" Feldman retorted, "What're you full of, ideas?" He knew what academics and many experimentalists have denied: that ideas will never save a piece of music that fails to provide images. S.E.M. had given a preview performance of *Turfan Fragments* last summer that impressed me, but by December 4 they had polished their playing until its chords and squiggles sparkled with loving precision. The Cage grew tiresome, the Varèse was thornily seductive, but the Feldman was commanding, mystic, and ultimately, through its repetitions, psychically enveloping. Few other recent New York premieres have been so exquisitely played, none so hauntingly soulful.

how peculiar?

the american eccentrics

JUNE 14, 1994

My favorite story from Berlioz's *Memoires* concerns the composer's attempted revenge when, studying in Rome, he learned that his fiancée in Paris had become engaged to someone else. Berlioz bought two pistols, a woman's dress as a disguise, and vials of laudanum and strychnine to poison himself after shooting the woman and her betrothed. However, he accidentally put the box with the dress on the wrong stagecoach, and, after a few days' travel, felt so much better he sold the pistols and abandoned the plan. Equally screwy, Beethoven used his manuscripts to cover his chamber pot, leaving a smelly legacy for future musicologists. Wagner wore silk clothes and made all of his friends sit around while he sang his operas in their entirety. Yep, a pretty eccentric bunch.

Every week those guys get played at Lincoln Center without ever being referred to as "The European Eccentrics." But when the New York Philharmonic offered a weeklong festival of Pauline Oliveros, Terry Riley, Henry Brant, Conlon Nancarrow, Charles Ives, Trimpin, John Cage, Alvin Lucier, Henry Cowell, and others May 23 to 31, it felt a need to call them "The American Eccentrics." Cowell's widow was reportedly horrified (Cowell had enough trouble in life with charges of deviance), and Yoko Sugiura-Nancarrow wondered aloud how someone whose work habits were as disciplined as Conlon's could be called eccentric. The event sparked an entertaining week in which Downtown musicians suddenly tried to look at themselves through the eyes of the classical mainstream.

Maybe *eccentric* was meant to describe the music, not the personalities. But Berlioz used a cloth bag to mute a clarinet and wrote for four brass choirs surrounding the hall; Beethoven added a chorus to his Ninth Symphony, which was unusual for the time; and writing a four-night-long opera for a specially built hall hardly put Wagner in the mainstream. No, I get it: Nancarrow, Cowell, et al. were eccentric because they didn't work within the *European* tradition. In that case, "centric" equals "European," and "American eccentric" collapses into redundancy. In the classical music world, simply to compose in an American way is to be off-center.

On the other hand, perhaps *eccentric* was someone's desperate and heroic stratagem to safeguard a musical category from the academic composers, who've already infiltrated the Pulitzer, the MacArthur award, and everything else. If Lincoln Center had just tagged the festival Great American Music, within hours Charles Wuorinen and Mario Davidovsky would have banged on the door, screaming, "You can't do that! All the great music is 12-tone, and uses accepted European genres." But now Lincoln Center can reply, "Sorry, Mr. Wuorinen, you're just not eccentric enough. Even male *lawyers* wear ponytails these days. Tie your beard in a knot like La Monte Young, and we'll talk." Other terms could have served the same function: Gunther Schuller calls Cage et al. "the kook composers," Roger Sessions called them "tinkerers," and Milton Babbitt and others refer to them as simply "amateurs." *Professional* composers, by implication, live not by performing, recording, and commissions as Meredith Monk, Philip Glass, and Steve Reich do, but by teaching theory to graduate students. Or, as Morton Feldman defined it, "an amateur is someone who doesn't shove his ideas down your throat."

Eccentric in this case says less about the composers (many of whom feel very much at the center of their tradition) than about America's incurable phobia regarding artistic creativity. That phobia leads us to ascribe "normalcy" to composers in suits and ties who can justify their music with diagrams, like CPAs. For me, the epicenter of American music is Harry Partch, a realist so practical he did his own carpentry; the most eccentric composers of all are those living anachronisms who still try to graft themselves onto the 19th-century European tradition. If Lincoln Center wants to focus next year's fest on Schuller, Babbitt, and Sessions, they could call it "The American Anal Retentives": just as accurate and even more evocative.

I'm giving Lincoln Center a hard time only to make them aware how odd it is for living composers to be certified as peculiar by a major institution, especially those who have spent their lives merely responding to immediate artistic necessity. There was nothing eccentric about the fest's performances, many of which were superb, and little strange (aside from Brant's poker-player's visor and refusal to sit) about the Merkin Hall panel featuring Trimpin, Oliveros, Lucier, Brant, Tania León, and NY Phil bassist Jon Deak. How warmly audiences respond to alleged eccentricity became apparent in the lengthy standing ovation that overwhelmed the 82-year-old Nancarrow, frail but momentarily present, after Ursula Oppens's fiery playing of his *Two Canons for Ursula*. It was even gratifying to see NY Phil musicians learn that minimalist music is harder than it sounds. Poor dears, used to following either a conductor's stick or the fluid body language of chamber music, they couldn't click into a minimalist beat to save their lives, with the result that Cage's Second Construction went limp and Riley's *In C* slogged along pathetically. (You can't taper minimalism's clean, flat phrases.) Eccentric music has its own performance tradition, and if you can't hear that, of course you won't take the music seriously.

No matter: whatever the event portends for the future, it gave evidence that at least a few minds in the NY Phil—including artistic administrator Elizabeth Ostrow, who conceived the fest, and Deak, who enthusiastically led the panel—realize that the intellectually bankrupt classical establishment could draw new vitality from a vibrant tradition only 80 years old that the orchestra has hitherto ignored. I disagree with my friends who labeled the fest too-little-too-late tokenism. Whatever marketing ploy it took to get these concerts across, they revealed a heart centered in the right place.

flutes and flying branches

the taos pueblo powwow

AUGUST 16, 1994

TAOS—Surrounded by mountains on three sides, framed by majestic clouds out of a painting by Bierstadt, the powwow field bathes in a capricious breeze aggressive enough to blow cedar branches off of the audience shelter. Whatever else Euramericans stole from the Indians, they left the Taos people a natural amphitheater next to which Lincoln Center is a storefront cubbyhole with folding chairs. Everything that enters this holy space— Indian singers and dancers from all over, kids, dogs, honest jewelry vendors, shyster trinket salesmen, white powwow groupies in all stages of frontier-hippie chic—absorbs the well-being that seems to bubble up out of the ground. "Make me one with everything," you find yourself saying, and that's just at the hot-dog stand.

This powwow (July 8 to 10) is a dance contest. I ought to be jotting down descriptions of the brilliant costumes, but instead I'm running around the huge circle from one drum group to another, trying to unravel secrets of Indian rhythmic ensemble. The Plains singing style (in three varieties—Southern, Northern, and "crackerjack soup") is the lingua franca of such gatherings. Less rhythmically bizarre than Hopi or Zuni music, it is even more difficult to transcribe into notation because of the elaborate vocal technique. The singers sit circled around a large drum, striking it in unison. The songs repeat in cycles difficult for the Euro-ear to catch, and some verses are set off by more emphatic accents. I once knew a Zuni head drummer in Chicago, and asked him why he would accent some parts of the melody and not others: he couldn't comprehend such a question, or pretended not to.

These powwows have something peculiar in common with New York: here you can mention "composers," and no one wonders what you mean. A Poncha family from Oklahoma has composed a special prayer song for the occasion, and the announcer notes that "the Poncha tribe is known for their ability in composing songs." Unlike in white society, a talent for writing songs is prized, and not unusual. The songs follow strict formulas, each starting on a high note and descending through several phrases to a low chanting tone (bringing the gods down to earth, as Dane Rudhyar explained it). To isolate the differences between song types takes acute listening and lots of experience. Northern style starts on a higher, more strident pitch than Southern, but I don't know crackerjack soup from chicken scratch (an Indian rock genre).

One of the worst mistakes a dancer can make is to fail to stop dancing on the final beat of a song. And yet Plains songs, like Philip Glass's early music, stop suddenly and unpredictably, as if by magic. Theoretically, that's up to the lead singer; if he jumps in with his opening phrase as a verse ends, the music keeps going, and if he doesn't, all the drummers and dancers miraculously know to quit in one final, precise drumbeat. And yet, the lead singer is allowed a few tricks. The one in the group Bad Medicine enjoyed starting up again after a false stop, faking out both dancers and singers.

Occasionally a dancer comes over and accompanies a song with a few dissonant flute notes, and for a few delicious minutes two groups rehearse at once, in aleatoric polyphony. Good sportsmanship is even more highly prized than knowing the rules. One dancer who voluntarily excused himself from the field after a disqualifying mistake received a round of applause.

What's a critic doing here? The Indians don't want me writing about their music. When I ask a girl at the judges' stand for a list of the drum groups performing, she stares at me as if I had asked for the key to her apartment. Not only are the Indians tired of being ignorantly misrepresented in the white press, they don't see any point to our omnivorous publicity machine. Lots of friendly competition goes on between these groups, but any kind of fame or stardom, any emphasis on personality, talent, or technique over the musical process, would upset the balance that keeps music central to this society.

I'm here for perspective, for this music embodies everything that musical art in urban culture lacks. Although the songs are too complex and minutely nuanced to capture in notation, mistakes in timing and intonation are virtually unknown. And most of the groups contain kids as young as 10 years old, who must be immersed in this music from infancy. One song divided the beat something like three plus two, or seven plus five, and the younger kids had no trouble drumming in time. The simplest song exhibited the ensemble virtuosity of eight people playing a Coltrane solo in unison. To enjoy this level of sophistication with every member of the community participating bespeaks a profoundly musical way of life.

With our need for individuality and personal expression, there may not be much about American Indian music we can assimilate. It's entirely at the service of a religious way of life. Every time a dancer dropped an eagle feather, the dances paused for a ceremony in which a patriarch blessed the sacred feather, commending it to north, south, east, and west, sometimes accompanied by a sun dance song. One prayer song was sung for someone who had been injured by one of those treacherous flying cedar branches. There was no line to be drawn between social life, music, and religion, and such unanimity of artistic culture seemed unthinkable without the fundamental conservatism that supported it. And yet, a white musician disturbed by his own culture's unbridgeable gulf between the average person and any decent level of musical expertise may be forgiven for watching the performances at Taos with unabashed awe and envy.

the tingle of p × m^n − 1

la monte young and marian zazeela

OCTOBER 4, 1994

Math phobes can get lost this week. God, I love numbers. My high school math teachers thought I should go into math. Come to think of it, so did my music teachers. And when La Monte Young sets up one of his vibrating sine-tone sculptures such as the one that's running Thursdays and Saturdays from two to 12 at the Mela Foundation, 275 Church Street, I get to use music as an excuse to bathe in the algebra I left behind. Let others get their ears massaged by the pulsating drones; I like to gaze at the tuning diagrams and let my mind slither naked through the mysterious clusters of luscious integers.

And what integers there are: large prime numbers, octaves of primes, whole classes of primes newly categorized for musical purposes. Having captured another octave of the overtone series, Young has strung his aural hammock between the 1792nd and 2304th overtones, where he's basking peacefully. The installation, whose 107-word title begins *The Base 9:7:4 Symmetry in Prime Time* . . . (I save more space by not completing it than I waste with this parenthesis), consists of 35 sine tones stretched across 10 octaves, 20 of them squeezed into a small band in the seventh octave, some separated by only 1/14 of a half-step.

Young likes the effect of large prime-numbered ratios, including Mersenne Primes (primes that conform to the formula $2^p − 1$, such as 31) and what he calls twin primes (primes separated by only 2, such as 59 and 61). He's even invented a new type: Young's Primes, expressible by the formula $p × m^n − 1$, where p is a prime, m is a positive integer that isn't a power of 2, and n is an integer greater than 1. Example: 71.

"This is over my head," you're saying, but listen. The point of all those "minus ones" is that Young uses tones that *approximate* the most consonant overtones, but are far more complex in their resulting combined wave forms. His math gives him a variety of sizes of seventh and ninth intervals, all closing in on the octaves over a fundamental B (actually a quarter-tone flat). In each octave, all the pitches are within the major third between A and C sharp. Imagine a ladder of 10 octaves of the same pitch. Now imagine the rungs bent and diffracted into lots of different tones, the lower rungs slightly lowered, the upper rungs raised. And because even these exotic overtones of a single low pitch are theoretically more harmonious than the scientifically irrational tuning of a modern piano, you're hearing a wild frontier of tonality that has never been explored, the outer edge of consonance.

Walk into *The Base 9:7:4 Symmetry* and you'll hear a whirlwind of pitches swirl around you. Stand still, and the tones suddenly freeze in place. Within the room, every pitch finds its own little niche where it resonates, and with all those close-but-no-cigar intervals competing in one space (not to mention their elegantly calculated sum- and difference-tones), you can alter the harmony you perceive simply by pulling on your earlobe. If you visited Young's installation *The Romantic Symmetry (over a 60 cycle base)* at Dia Art Foundation back in '89, you remember the effect. But while *Romantic Symmetry* was more "melodic" in a sense, since its overtones were more evenly spread through the range, *The Base 9:7:4 Symmetry* is more textural. Moving your head makes those tones leap from high to low and back, while that cluster in the seventh octave, with its wild prime ratios like $269:271$, fizzes in and out.

Marian Zazeela's light sculptures in the same space are the perfect visual analogue. Her *Ruine Window 1992*, for example, is a simple geometric construction of white boards illuminated with magenta light from one side, blue from the other. Since she's working with colored shadows instead of colored surfaces, and light behaves differently from pigment, the colors combine opposite to the way we expect. (You only learn light-color theory in art school, Zazeela says, if you go into television.) Stand in front of *Ruine Window 1992* for a while, and let your eyes move up and down the verticals: not only will the colors take on a deep intensity, creating an illusion of two-dimensionality, but the edges will flicker in your peripheral vision. As the shimmering of Young's overtones resists being recorded, Zazeela's shadows fall flat when photographed, one reason she's never been sufficiently celebrated in the art world for the originality of her minimalist constructions.

Both the sound and light sculptures are static entities that move wildly within your eyes and ears, proving with pure wave forms how subjective perception is. Since we're more sophisticated visually than aurally, I figured out an exercise that, if you can hum, will help you hear more precisely what Young's sculpture is about. If you can isolate one of the lower drones (not easy), slowly hum a major scale up, from that pitch. (The beginning of "Row, Row, Row Your Boat" will do.) By the time you reach the third, fourth, and fifth steps, you'll be humming pitches that find no resonance among the other drones—you'll be in the empty spaces. Hearing a gap within an articulated pitch space, as some European works of the '50s and '60s, like Xenakis's *Pithoprakta*, asked us to do, is usually a task beyond mortal ears. But here, in these sustained sine waves, even earthlings can make out the negative musical spaces between the rungs of Young's overtone ladder.

Why would you want to do that? Because it's there. Because music isn't always just background, or something familiar. Because you've never heard so complex a chord so pure. Because music that refuses to change subverts capitalism. Because you'll never get any closer to the music of the spheres this side of enlightenment. And because there are more numbers in the musical universe than I IV V I.

the british don't have oral sex

now eleanor's idea

DECEMBER 13, 1994

Why not? Because nobody there takes a bath! Jane Austen didn't take a bath! She wrote her ass off, but she didn't take a bath! Disraeli never took a bath! Charles Dickens never took a bath until he met Mark Twain, who kidded him so bad about stinking that he took a bath! He hadn't seen his own legs in 15 years! The fucker almost drowned! And as for banks, there is no excuse anyone can see for banks! The bank is not a safe place if you have something of value! The bank is geometry! We need a place to feel the feelings we feel in the bank! Among the different degrees of deadness found in rocks, deadest are the rocks from which we build our banks! A vibrant bank is no bank at all! There is no wind in the bank! Nor speed! Nor velocity! There is only alignment!

Whoa, wait a minute. Where am I? Sorry about that, I'm . . . I'm just returning from the parallel universe that was at BAM November 16 through 19. There were white rocks and white yucca plants and a white highway onstage, and white chairs with big flowing backs. And Robert Ashley, the great poet of our time, such a throwback to the ancient past that he makes the music that goes with his epics just as poets will do again in the distant future, was telling it like it is. As the rest of us timidly dig our toes in the hot sand, fretting about what kind of music to make in these 1990s, Ashley's out in A.D. 2075, striding into the great beyond.

> Baby's off the magic powders
> Positive opinion hungers
> Nothing getting done for me!

he moaned over and over, and his chorus answered, every time, "VERY GREAT HIP BOOK I KEEP IT BY MY BED." It was church—not some Protestant, rationalist church with a feel-good message, but Catholic or Muslim or Neptunian, with a liturgy to which the people responded, a liturgy you've heard a thousand times before but must have forgotten. Only it wasn't about the peace of God and all that bullshit, it was the *real* stuff: the mathematical explanation for premonitions, and why pasta is the perfect food, and how the approach-of-the-end-of-the-world-feeling happens to men every 14 years but to women every 10 years, and how cursing slows down the connections in the brain, turning language into music.

Of course orientation to a new universe takes time. The onslaught of words was frustrating and confusing and too much to take in, and you'd look at your watch. But if you left too early, before the big moment came, you were damned, or rather, fucked. You had to sit there until Jacqueline Humbert's silken voice dissolved into melody, "This is as high as I can go / How do you know that you know it?" over and over, and then you understood. You had to listen to Joan La Barbara explain the miracle of cars until the melee of English and Spanish voices became too thick to follow, swelling into a slow-motion whirlwind of vocal glissandos that made your skin writhe. Then, suddenly, that old universe you came from, the one where you imagined that the British, at least Mick Jagger though admittedly not Margaret Thatcher, probably do have oral sex, didn't make sense anymore. This new universe was suprapersonal, Buddhist, without causality as we know it, and so your watch-watching ego dissolved. You were converted. You were in love.

Then it made sense that Linda, heroine of *Improvement* (very great hip CD I keep it by my stereo), felt complimented that her husband, Don, had abandoned her in a bathroom in a rest stop because it showed such faith in her resourcefulness. You understood the truths from *Foreign Experiences* paraphrased in the opening paragraph above. You saw why Don had to learn to swear, shocking as it still sounds in sung opera, in order to quit talking to himself. (*Foreign Experiences* may become the first avant-garde opera CD to carry a parental advisory warning.) But all that still didn't prepare you for the high climax of *Now Eleanor's Idea*, the ultimate song that explains all existence: how probability is self-knowledge, and logic is the study of coincidences, and intuition doesn't recognize coincidences, and religion is the practice of feelings. The universe revealed here was the same one as in all of Ashley's works, for *Improvement* talked about *Atalanta*, *Now Eleanor* retold the story of *Perfect Lives*, and *Foreign Experiences* quoted an old Ashley piece, also about oral sex, called *Purposeful Lady*

Slow Afternoon. The singers were merely a receptacle for an electrical charge sparking around the stage in constant motion, magnetizing the audience. Arias turned into duets and duets into sextets in midsentence, one song sung by seven heads. Days later, you can still hear them on that radio in your mind: Humbert's an amazing singer, brilliant acting standing still, Ashley tells it like it is! Thomas Buckner smoothly croons, exuding calm though cruelly questioned, Ashley tells it like it is! Eerie Joan La Barbara sends glissandos ringing through the ether, Ashley tells it like it is! Frantic son Sam Ashley, raving, waves his fists at fucking assholes, Ashley tells it like it is! Chanting Amy X Neuburg, expressive, gestures like an angel, Ashley tells it like it is! Fierce low-rider Marghreta Cordero singing loud, aggressive, Ashley tells it like it is! Because an opera isn't a line! It's a field! We don't need a story, we need a place to feel all those feelings not recognized in our ordinary universe! A place to store all those truths we mistakenly think our rationalism disproves! Opera's not a mirror of life! It's geography! It's architecture! It's . . . It's . . .

view from the gap

emerging voices

MARCH 21, 1995

We live on the fault line between two generations. If the fact is obvious in student/teacher relations at any music school, it is especially poignant at a high-powered department like the University of California at San Diego, which invited me out for a festival aptly called "Emerging Voices," February 22 through March 1. As the only intrepidly avant-garde department from the '70s to have preserved its reputation, UCSD attracts an exciting level of students, alert and focused on the changes society is going through. At the same time, the department is centered around two towering figures of modernist tradition: Roger Reynolds, the only Pulitzer-winning experimentalist since Charles Ives, and Brian Ferneyhough, the British-born guiding light (and only listenable composer) of the "new complexity" movement. Via the Bang on a Can All-Stars and San Francisco's Paul Dresher Ensemble, the fest brought New York–style new music into an atmosphere already tensed between academic rigor and postmodern sensitivity to diverse cultural voices. Sparks flew in spectacular trajectories.

Heard from the hinterlands, New York sounds shocking and stodgy at the same time. The BoaC and Dresher ensembles played particularly rock-oriented programs, much of which the students perceived as ersatz: classical musicians playing rock written by classical composers. A common complaint was that rock licks sound stiff and lifeless when notated by structure-conscious postgraduates. Ph.D. candidate David C. Meckler, in a paper titled "'Tis a Gift to Be Simple, but It Takes Courage to Be Painfully Obvious," pointed out that new-music composers avoid dialogues with living pop figures and plunder only the dead, as in the Kronos Quartet's arrangement of "Purple Haze." As if on cue, the All-Stars played a Nirvana tune as an encore, with Maya Beiser wailing the vocal line on cello. Meckler further complained that fans who take Hendrix and Nirvana seriously feel insulted by new-music groups that marginalize rock songs as "fun pieces" for encores.

Fair enough: some new musicians need to learn to treat rock with as much respect as they would Indian classical or Balinese music. And yet part of UCSD's dour view of New York and San Francisco stemmed, I suspected, from an inability to see beyond the split personality that new music rebels against. Vividly and at length, both ensembles made the point that we are not hopelessly stuck with a binary choice between cerebral abstraction and cliché-ridden vernacular: we are free to inhabit the vast, rich terrain in between. If many works failed, some were inspiring, either because the composers had enough sense not to imitate vernaculars they weren't trained in, or because they came from rock to begin with. My favorites included Dresher's *Double Ikat* and John Luther Adam's *Coyote Builds North America* played by the Dresher ensemble, and Steve Martland's *Horses of Instruction*, Nick Didkovsky's *Amalia's Secret*, and David Lang's *Press Release* played by BoaC. Not a bad haul.

Meanwhile, the student music we heard, none of it embarrassing and almost all expertly performed, tended toward the modernist, atonal abstraction nurtured by the faculty, though made fresher in several cases by strong dashes of Morton Feldman's quieting influence. (One delightful exception was Stephen Parkinson's *Paradise Canyon* for piano, played delicately with paint rollers.) But if students buy their teachers' modernist spiel, why did one of the largest and most enthusiastic crowds show up for a spellbindingly energetic performance, by Professor Steve Schick and his assistants, of Steve Reich's *Drumming*? And, given the usual time lag before experimental music becomes eligible for academic treatment, why did Meckler undertake his discriminating analysis of passages by Martland, Michael Gordon, and other young New Yorkers decades ahead of schedule? It is rumored that many UCSD students write one body of music to show their teachers and another, more vernacular and personal, for private distribution.

Totalism was the opening panel's hot topic, defined by UCSD composer Rand Steiger as "using all the influences you have available." Totalism's belief that complexity and accessibility can coexist, urged most loudly by Gordon, Dresher, and myself, ran up against a network of hallowed assumptions. Virtuoso bassist-composer Bertram Turetzky, Mexican composer Hilda Paredes, and others insisted that playing to the audience inevitably watered down your music. This side shuddered at the idea of forming your own ensemble or record company and marketing your music effectively; such commercialism was beneath the true artist, who should merely do his best and wait to be discovered. Yet all Dresher and Gordon advocated was taking responsibility for one's own music, including making it comprehensible to nonmusicians.

I believe it's perfectly true for the older generation that the better they made their music, the further it soared away from potential audiences. But professorial skepticism notwithstanding, the totalist generation too is motivated by an ideal: that of a society in robust musical health, where composers lead satisfying careers making audiences feel addressed, enchanted, and included. The older generation, insufficiently recognized for their austere achievements, feel betrayed and envious because their juniors have seemingly abandoned intellectual rigor to make a cheap bid at popularity—and are succeeding. The younger generation feel unsupported and resentful because their elders refuse to concede validity to minimalist, rock, or vernacular styles, and have closed off their grant and award structures to those who don't toe the modernist line. Politeness and due respect kept this rift thinly veiled for the week of "Emerging Voices." But the view the students had, from inside the gap, must have been a doozie.

bang! crunch! who's on first?

twisted tutu

OCTOBER 29, 1996

Recently a friend e-mailed to ask if I'd write an article about pieces that are based on, and deconstruct, earlier pieces of music, like Berio's *Sinfonia* or Stravinsky's *Pulcinella*. I replied, a little self-righteously, that Downtowners don't pay much attention to earlier music, that they prefer to escape the weight of history and reinvent music from scratch. The next day, I heard Twisted Tutu at Roulette. In pieces performed there, composer Eve Beglarian reworked music chosen from the 12th through 20th centuries. So, let me revise my distinction: Europeans and Uptowners tend to rework recent music as a way to pay homage to a teacher, or to align themselves with a tradition they want to be seen as belonging to. When Downtowners use quotation, the original music is usually from such a distant source that it has the character of a random found object. Except, of course, for some of the free-jazz guys, who play postmodern covers of jazz standards to align themselves with greats like Thelonious Monk. Come to think of it, may I opt out of this argument?

What I can say is that when Beglarian uses songs by the 14th-century master Guillaume de Machaut, it's not to make herself cool by showing what tradition she belongs to; it's to make people realize how cool Machaut is by bringing him up to date. She gives back to her source as much as she gets from it.

Beglarian is also an apostate Uptowner. She went to Princeton and Columbia, and knew Babbitt pitch sets and Wuorinen time-point systems inside and out. To the despair of her profs, though, her music got more and more consonant, rock-influenced, and audience-friendly. During the '80s she was president of the academically stodgy International Society for Contemporary Music, a day job that had no more to do with her compos-ing life than being a short-order cook would have. For years her music went unheard, and when heard was condescended to by her Europhilic associates. Then in 1993 Kitty Brazelton and David First discovered Beglarian and started programming her on various Downtown series. And so she exploded on the new-music scene as a kind of full-grown miracle, sprung from the head of Zeus.

In flat contradiction to the old cliché about women artists not being innovators, Beglarian has been innovating at a pace that some of us have trouble keeping up with. For example, lately she and her pianist partner Kathleen Supové—who perform together as Twisted Tutu—have been monkeying with their concert format by dovetailing their pieces so that they run continuously, and you can't tell where one ends and another begins. It makes for an agreeably disconcerting experience, sort of like ambient, but it plays hell with critics who are trying to keep track of what goes where. In particular, at this gig they played a piece by Randall Woolf (Supové's husband), segueing directly into some Senegalese and Vietnamese folk songs, fading into a Beglarian song sharply interrupted by a disco sound mix. Since I don't know much of Woolf's music, I thought for a while the whole thing was his piece and that his sense of form had gone haywire. When I realized my mistake, I knew I was going to have to talk to Beglarian to find out where the lines were.

The evening's first piece was clear enough: *Hildegurls,* a setting of Latin chants by Hildegard von Bingen, the 12th-century mystic composer and poet who has skyrocketed to faddish popularity in recent years at the hands of feminist musicologists. Beglarian and Supové sang the chants in a reverently literal setting. On the taped background, the chant (played on violin) was surrounded by a halo of shimmering sounds, which had been orchestrated in great detail, Beglarian told me, from recorded samples of a harp, ukulele, blown glass, a rattlesnake, and viola harmonics: an effect amazing in its textured complexity. Next, Supové spoke Woolf's *One Tough Lama* over resonant synthesized chords, reciting into a harmonizer that made her sound like an obnoxious little boy. The text was from a peculiar interview with a 13-year-old Tibetan lama living in Wyoming:

"The Dalai Lama . . . has got 12 bodyguards around him when he travels. What do you think would happen if some butthead pulled a gun on His Holiness? Do you think those bodyguards would practice nonviolence? No way, man. Some dweeb with a gun shows up, he's gonna pop a cap in his ass."

I hadn't digested that insight before two taped folk songs began simultaneously, sung by women Beglarian had worked with this summer: Treva Offutt of Senegal and Thi Hong Ngat Nguyen of Vietnam. Beglarian had recorded the songs separately, then later realized that they were in the same key and worked together in touchingly beautiful counterpoint. This bled into the most emotionally exposed song of Beglarian's I've heard, *My Feelings Now.* Over slow, bittersweet jazz piano chords, Beglarian sang a "found" text she had heard from an Indonesian friend, a kind of association game that, in her friend's fractured English, ruminated on the words "Makes me thinking of . . ." The subdued liveliness of the taped-drone background, it turned out, was due to Indonesian flute and vocal music subliminally mixed within the electronic sound.

Then, Bang! the quiet was shattered by a bunch of disco songs in a collage called *Spontaneous Combustion 1.* Beglarian had made this mix for her brother Spencer's performance-art piece about AIDS activist David Feinberg. The mix was full of late-'70s gay-culture icons, such as Gloria Gaynor's "Don't Leave Me This Way" and Thelma Houston's "Never Can Say Goodbye." In an inspired technological gambit, Beglarian had computer-altered the tempos and keys of all the songs until they were identical, merging into a seamless texture, a ghostly effect, like five bands playing at once, each fading in and out. What intrigued her, she said, was that "all these songs, which came out before anyone knew anything about AIDS, were weirdly prescient, all with lyrics about death and loss and absence."

Crunch! went Supové's sampler as this was ending, and *No Man's Land* began, a gritty homage (with text by art critic Janet Malcolm) to the intersection of Church Street, White Street, and Sixth Avenue that we had all crossed to get to the concert: "An unpleasantly wide expanse of street to cross, interrupted by a wedge-shaped island on which a commercial plant nursery has taken up forlorn and edgy residence, surrounding itself with a high-wire fence and keeping truculently irregular hours." All these pieces being run together gave a lot of information in a short time. Luckily, the concert's second half was more leisurely, with pieces separated by pauses: a perky theme and variations on Machaut's "Douce dame joli," an electronically tampered recording of a personals ad recorded off the phone, and Beglarian's *Buncacan Song*.

The climax was the last piece, a Twisted Tutu arrangement of Beglarian's *Wonder Counselor*. It was originally a commission for pipe organ and tape, based on the Bible verse "His name shall be called Wonderful, Counselor. . . ." With typical joie de vivre, though, she filled the tape part with samples of a snake hissing, birds croaking, waves splashing, and a woman having an orgasm, the last of which rendered the result somewhat questionable for liturgical use. The core was a thick taped drone in which higher overtones ebbed and flowed, as Beglarian and Supové tossed off flurries of rhythmically complex counterpoint derived from a 13th-century chant sequence, "Res est admirabilis"—"It is a wondrous thing." In so doing they tapped some element of medieval mysticism, and a stream of ecstasy shot in from the ancient world to give us a spiritual high. Stravinsky said, "The great composer does not borrow—he steals." But Beglarian does more than steal; she hooks into some weird things and always brings the energy back alive and kicking.

regarding henry

the world's first multicultural modernist conservative patron saint of outsiders

APRIL 1, 1997

At Henry Cowell's Musical Worlds, a centennial festival that took place March 12 through 18 at Bruno Walter Auditorium, the New School for Social Research, and Symphony Space, a number of Henry Cowells emerged:

Henry Cowell No. 1—Theorist of Modernism. Between 1916 and 1919, while still a teenager, he wrote a book that would be published in 1930 as *New Musical Resources.* In it he outlined a new theory of rhythm capable of bringing to Western notated music the same level of complexity found in Indian, Arabic, and African musics. Among his suggestions: dividing a measure into five, seven, nine, and so on equal notes to imply different tempos; constructing a scale of 12 tempos analogous to the 12 pitches of the scale; using lines on a graph to indicate exact acceleration and ritardando. The book, an invigorating influence on several generations of American composers, was naturally a major focus of Brooklyn College's Henry Cowell symposium. (And, though out of print for most of its existence, *New Musical Resources* has just been republished by Cambridge University Press.)

Surprise! In 1955 in Germany, Karlheinz Stockhausen writes an influential article in the Darmstadt journal *Die Reihe* outlining Cowell's exact ideas, but without mentioning Cowell's name. In his three-orchestra piece *Gruppen,* Stockhausen uses a scale of 12 tempos, and in his Klavierstück XI, lines on a graph to indicate acceleration. Oddly enough, Cowell's student John Cage had visited Darmstadt in 1952. Did Cage pass on Cowell's ideas to Stockhausen? The only hard evidence is a 1959 *Die Reihe* article by Mauricio Kagel, who raves about Cowell's book and its potential importance for European serialist music. Kagel then promises to give a complete outline of Cowell's systems in a future *Die Reihe* article. That article never appears.

Is it possible, asked Keele University musicologist David Nicholls in one of the symposium's most electric moments, that *Die Reihe*'s coeditor—Stockhausen—killed Kagel's promised article because he didn't want the world to know that his revolutionary rhythmic ideas came from Cowell? If so, a delightful irony ensues: all those Americans who imitated the latest ideas from Darmstadt in the '50s and '60s to gain the prestige of a European pedigree may well have been stealing ideas from a German who had stolen them from an American. One thing the Cowell symposium suggested is that it is time to rewrite the history of modernist music with greater credit given to its American roots.

Henry Cowell No. 2—"The world's first multicultural composer." The quote is from festival producer Richard Teitelbaum, and it was backed up by a Symphony Space marathon pairing Cowell's works with examples of the world music he incorporated. A jovial performance by the Thunderbird American Indian Dancers was followed up with Cowell's *Trickster Coyote* (complete with choreography by Erick Hawkins, for whom it was written in 1941), and traditional Persian music with his *Persian Set.* If Cowell's works naturally lacked the texture and authenticity of the traditional musics, he compensated as much as a Western composer can through invention and formal ingenuity, and did not suffer in comparison.

Of course no one called Cowell what he would be called today: another colonialist white male appropriating the indigenous musics of people of color. A panel on world music skirted around the sensitive issue, and it's easy to see why they would have felt guilty confronting it: no one seriously believes that poor Cowell, a prolific and generous promoter of world musics who made so little money from his own, benefited from "ripping off" musics of Iran, China, Native America, and so on, at the expense of native musicians. He had a vision of a world in which every composer could choose any materials that spoke to him from all the world's traditions. What would have been fruitful would have been a panel on why that vision seems so politically incorrect today, and on whether Cowell's music possibly offers a much-needed rebuke to the current paranoid and sanctimonious climate.

Henry Cowell No. 3—Radical Composer of Conservative Music. Musicologist Steven Johnson struck a sobering note by showing how often Cowell used only one idea in a piece, how square his rhythmic conceptions were, and how often this grandfather of American radicals wrote music that was downright academic. Amid the euphoria, it was a needed, if unsettling, dose of reality. Various heated objections were raised: that complaining of Cowell's lack of development imposed a Eurocentric standard, that his flat structures concealed an extremely subtle variety. But they failed to dispel the widespread perception even among his closest colleagues, John Cage included, that Cowell never lived up to his potential as a composer. The old cliché about Cage—that he is more important for his ideas than for his music—is far more true of Cowell.

·Yet the festival's concerts paradoxically both reinforced and shattered that dim view. There were long stretches, during the Musicians Accord concert of Cowell's late chamber music and Mary Ann Hart's recital of his songs, when you couldn't help but wonder why so many diehard avantgardists were assembled to listen to so much timid, cutely melodic, neoBaroque music, no matter how charmingly crafted. But occasionally a breathtaking piece would dart up from the surrounding plains like Devil's Tower: the rhythmically impossible *Quartet Romantic* of 1917 (which Musicians Accord heroically played sans clicktrack or conductor—I couldn't see how); the smoothly Arabic *United Quartet* that the Composers Quartet performed so passionately; *High Color* for piano, which required Sarah Cahill to play an Irish tune while athletically alternating huge cluster chords with both forearms, a feat she managed with the grace of an Olympic gymnast.

The real puzzler was Cowell's bizarre inconsistency, and only seminal Americanist musicologist Wiley Hitchcock ventured a viable answer: "Cowell was a complex individual."

Henry Cowell No. 4—Patron Saint of Outsiders. Like last summer's Morton Feldman tribute at Lincoln Center, Cowell's "rehabilitation," as composer Peter Garland kept calling it, seemed to mark a landmark in the recognized legitimacy of an indigenous American classical tradition. In an angry talk that brought forth a sustained fountain of applause, Garland compared Cowell's *New Music Editions* to his own now-defunct *Soundings* journal, both of which kept experimental American music alive in their respective eras with hardly a cent of institutional support. American funding organizations, Garland charged, are set up to support composers who stick to European traditions, not those "Downtowners" and "Experimentalists" who grounded their tradition in *New Musical Resources.*

"I used to be amused," Garland fumed quietly, "at how people would gush over composers . . . who had suffered under Stalinism. . . . Those composers who suffered under cultural Reaganism were, and continue to be, grossly unfashionable." The real problem, he continued, is that since Cowell's experimental followers are outnumbered by the conservative Europhiles turned out by the universities, "how can our rights be protected in a supposedly democratic system, where the majority rules?" The crucial step, I suppose, is to make the public and cultural organizations realize that Cowell was the beginning of a legitimate, indigenous American classical music tradition passed down through Cage, Harrison, Partch, and others to present-day Downtown music. Whether this Cowell centennial conference achieved that or not, it felt good to try.

what our pulses say

david garland

JUNE 22, 1999

He calls his songs "control songs," though they generally tell us how little control we have over our lives. His new CD is called *Togetherness,* though its lyrics suggest that he doesn't believe such a state exists. David Garland's persona is a core of unrelievable pain hidden beneath a layer of naive optimism covered by a veneer of bemused cynicism. He acts so simple, but the clues about that inner complexity fall thick and fast. And finally in the last few months, as on June 4 at Tonic, he's back concertizing again after a hiatus of several years, during which we've only heard him as that DJ on WNYC who loves science fiction music, space-age bachelor pad music, and anything else peculiar. The return is long overdue.

Take "This Is Love," one of his best songs. It's an ode to dating, set to a tune of nursery-rhyme simplicity:

> What's your name? What's your number?
> Is it Sue? Is it five?

But he's not as accommodating as he pretends:

> You just looked at your wristwatch,
> Never mind, I've got time.

Finally he mentions casually, despite the ominously biblical language,

> They will smite you down
> But then I will come by
> And I'll pick you up.

From his chipper tone you don't know whether he's picking you up to comfort you, or just to take you on a date likely to be a further ordeal. He's caring and considerate, he's selfish and self-absorbed. In short, he's just like all of us. Well, I shouldn't speak for *you.*

But this Everyman knows that love is far from the only thing we're motivated by. In "Play within a Play," an actor and actress begin a conventional dialogue of troubled passion over a seething tango, then switch direction in mid-gush:

> HE: My family wants, my job wants, and you . . .
> SHE: I want to be best at whatever I do . . .
> HE: My personal past forms my point of view.
> Then they look at each other:
> This is no love scene!
> The pulse in our wrists has much more to say.

Much more to say, indeed—Garland's genius is for filling in with music what the lyrics leave unsaid. Who else would underlay the following poignant story of faded love:

> He wears his wristwatch
> She wears her jacket.

Under the blanket.
They're never naked
They've almost forgotten how.

with chords luminous in their sense of mystery and potential discovery? Or with singing over and over again the phrase "Hey, watch my pony— he's falling down," to an accordion-and-toy-piano refrain not a bit sad or ironic or cutesy, just calm and comforting. Of *course* his pony is falling down. How could it be otherwise?

That's why Garland has done for the pop song what Robert Ashley has done for opera. The lyrics are often too oblique to make sense—"Seeing my surface I witness the contours / each imperfection is structured just right"—but they distract your attention, feeding you partial truths, while the music circles back behind your unconscious and zaps you with the Real Truth, the ineffable inevitabilities of being human. It can do that because Garland has a superb melodic sensibility. Listen to "Happy Ending"—it's a silly enough rock song on first hearing, but the way the harmony pirouettes around the tonic key, slipping back in at the right moment, reveals a sophistication that he's scrupulous about never showing off.

His voice itself is the same way: so warm, untrained-seeming, and conversational you don't notice its exquisite control. Just the guy next door singing to you about his job until he leaps gracefully into a high register or idly wanders down to a low B-flat below the bass clef. The CD (on Ergodic) sports quite a cast of electro-gizmos and Downtowners (Guy Klucevsek, John Zorn, Bobby Previte, and others among the latter), but for this lite gig at Tonic he stripped down his arrangements for trio. Will Holshouser did an expert job on accordion, and Brian Dewan (also a superb songwriter, Garland tells me) brought a sturdy virtuosity to an electric zither, an instrument I wasn't prepared to be nearly so impressed by.

Garland's trio was followed by Billy Martin, who opened with an athletic and impressively punchy solo piece for two thumb pianos. Martin then brought out the Komodo Whirligig Orchestra, actually five people each playing a gourd or wood block with a mallet. For half an hour those mallets tapped out Martin's *Stridulation for the Good Luck Feast* in 13 movements, each movement marked by subtly different rhythmic strategies. Not very high in entertainment value, but within his breathtakingly austere limits Martin showed considerable rhythmic ingenuity, and, to my pleasant surprise, the full-house audience in this rock bar listened as quietly as rabbits. Yet another young American composer stripping music down to start over from zero: watch out.

mistaken memories

tony conrad: one-idea composer or late bloomer?

FEBRUARY 13, 2001

I ran into my old friend Al Niente at Tony Conrad's January 18 gig at Tonic. Conrad was droning away raspily on his violin, seeking out obscure overtones above thick drones emanating from a compact disc. Al mentioned that Conrad's music sounded much like it did back in the 1960s. Then he added, "I never trust these people who base their entire life's work on one idea. It seems careerist, rather than artistic." "I could never find an idea interesting enough to base my entire life on," I joked. "That's just my point," he shot back. "Neither has anyone else."

Al had me stumped. I admit to a prejudice that the composers who turn out to be truly great are those who transcend the trajectory of their early careers in their midforties, and who take some left turn into new vistas. (Having recently turned 45, this is a matter of some urgent personal concern.) Like Robert Ashley leaving conceptualism behind at 48 and inventing the unprecedented continuity of *Perfect Lives*. Like John Cage abandoning modalism and rhythmic structure at age 40 to begin chance composition. Like a 44-year-old Morton Feldman beginning to write eccentrically notated works ranging from 90 minutes long to six hours.

And it's not just American experimentalists. My hero Claudio Monteverdi jettisoned his Renaissance contrapuntal training at 40 to join the new Baroque "amateurs" with his *Orfeo* of 1607. Beethoven, at 42, stopped composing and eventually emerged with a new style so avant-garde no one's caught up with it to this day. Wagner (b. 1813) transported himself from the stolid German forests of *Lohengrin* (1848) to the chromatic quicksands of *Tristan und Isolde* (1858). Coleman Hawkins switched from swing to bebop at around 40, and Miles Davis—having spearheaded cool jazz and hard bop in his 20s—made a critic-exasperating jump to fusion in his early 40s.

Counterexamples would be cruel to enumerate, but there are plenty of older composers around still making basically the same music they did in their youth, and wondering why no one makes a big deal about them anymore. It seems like there's some psychological barrier an artist has to break through in his or her 40s in order to go beyond what is merely a product of one's time into something bizarre, supremely personal, and, ultimately, unexpectedly universal.

But it's not clear how this tenuous paradigm applies to Tony Conrad. After all, despite some early innovative conceptualist works, Conrad didn't have much of an independent early career back in the 1960s, but was known for being part of the Theatre of Eternal Music alongside (or under, depending on whom you're arguing with) La Monte Young. By 1966, the then 26-year-old Conrad had opened a separate career in underground film with his classic piece of stroboscopic minimalism, *The Flicker*. When he returned in the mid 1980s with his *Early Minimalism* series, a group of raucously droning violin pieces based on a rough, fluctuating approach to pure tunings, he had pretty much been forgotten by the music world for over a decade.

And now we have this unique career based on re-creating a music remembered from 35 years ago that never really existed. At Tonic, Conrad played a lusher, denser sound continuum than one hears in his single surviving solo recording from the '60s, *Four Violins*. With a rough tone constantly in flux yet hitting precise points of crystallization, he played around a seventh harmonic over the drones, eventually moving to clearly defined 11th and 13th harmonics: phenomena made memorable by their rarity. Toward the end of the first hour, he was joined onstage by an ensemble including Arnold Dreyblatt on bass, Mark Stewart on cello, Jim O'Rourke on hurdy-gurdy, and others, magnifying the density of the drone texture. At last Conrad put down his violin and plucked deep glissandos on a large, horizontal stringed instrument, a new device but hardly a radical change.

So is Conrad a one-idea composer? Did that idea take a detour through other media before it could blossom into a full conception? Or is the new idea of his late career a remembrance of tone structures that never really existed? Such questions may be impossible to decide. But while superficially Conrad did about what I expected, he also led me through obscure regions of the harmonic spectrum I had never experienced before, feeling too pleasantly lost to care whether he had been there before or not.

passings

legacy of the quiet touch
morton feldman, 1926–1987

OCTOBER 6, 1987

"The authentic poet," wrote Wordsworth, "must create the taste by which he is to be enjoyed." Morton Feldman was an authentic poet. "Uncle Morty"— as he was called by dozens of young musicians—died September 3 at 61, of pancreatic cancer. He was not so intimate with musical society that his death feels like the end of an era; by choice and temperament Feldman stood on the periphery. It's more as if a rare species of small, velvet-throated bird has become extinct. Like his conversation (he was deliciously quotable), his ethereally sustained music was a sharply critical conscience of his time. His music's roots go deep into the spirit of Jewish mysticism ("Certain intervals," he said of his *Rothko Chapel,* "have the ring of the synagogue"), and his unmitigated subjectivity was fundamentally at odds with all other 20th-century music; not only neo-Romanticism and its structuralist nemeses serialism and minimalism, but even the aleatoric tradition that claimed him. "Those 88 notes," he loved to say, "are my Walden."

I met Feldman only a few times. The impenetrable Brooklyn accent in which he quoted Spinoza, Bergson, and Adorno gave him the endearing air of an earthy philosopher. Avuncular without being particularly personable, he was not the type to warm up to young unknowns and admirers. But I have been lucky enough to get to know some stunning unrecorded Feldman pieces: *The Swallows of Salangan, Why Patterns,* the Oboe Concerto. It's frustrating trying to find his music. His pages of isolated durationless notes give a false impression that the music is easy to play, and it falls flat in the hands of anyone so deceived. (A good, taut Feldman performance should put you on edge.) His unconscionably scarce recordings are equally difficult, because the music is too quiet to record well.

As a result of his insufficient recognition and ahistoric viewpoint, Feldman's music is widely misunderstood. The obits all mentioned his 1950s association with John Cage, Earle Brown, Christian Wolff, and the abstract expressionist painters from whom he drew his aesthetic. But it was afterwards, in the late '60s and '70s, that Feldman transcended the American aleatoric movement and began to write a music timeless in its devotion. One can imagine his ghost blinking in mute incomprehension at the AP obituary's oxymoronic reference to his "expressionist, minimalist style."

Feldman's music is not universally admired. He's been charged with repeating himself since the '50s, and I've seen him described as "mining a barren vein over and over." Presumably the people who've said so also dislike the paintings of Rothko and Pollock for the same reason. Once, listening to Feldman talk about composition, Earle Brown remonstrated, "But Morty, once you've chosen the instruments, that doesn't mean the piece is finished." Feldman said quietly, "For me it is." He would later say that was "a facile remark," but one could also say that a late Rothko was finished once the painter had chosen the colors; it's *knowing what colors to put together* that counts. In music, color includes pitch, and choosing was Feldman's genius. In his Oboe Concerto, he knew whether he wanted five or six contrabasses on a given pizzicato.

Also, those who think Feldman repeated himself don't understand his contribution to rhythm. He invented at least five types that I know of: fermata rhythm (free, no beat), rhythm of extremely slow beats, the physical pulse of notes dying away, precisely measured long durations, and, in his 90-plus minute works, the megarhythm that fades into *scale;* not to mention the myriad types that result from those rhythms in polyphony. Listen to his works, play them, and you begin to feel how subtle but sharp these distinctions are. When he combines two in the same work, you hear a rhythmic shading absolutely unknown elsewhere.

Feldman complained that though Leinsdorf and Munch had complimented his music, no one wanted to play it because it wouldn't get them good reviews. Luckily, students are a more important legacy than prestigious performances, recordings, writings, or reviews, and Feldman's students will render his critics irrelevant. Look at their scores: they may sound like Mozart, Stockhausen, or hell, but they reveal their origin. (Even physically: Feldman was a very nearsighted chain-smoker, and a generation of composers sport cigarette burns on their early manuscripts.)

Take Peter Gena, once so under the Feldman influence that he wrote an almost immobile waltz; now he's into a kind of postminimal structuralism, but he still has that unique sense of orchestration that came from the man to whom instrumentation was everything. Listen to the interplay of slow durations in *des Sondages* by Bernadette Speach, or the thoughtful chord permutations of Steven Swartz, or even the Feldmanesque sonorities in the hectic, Nuyorican music of William Ortiz, whose pop-flavored style is otherwise further from Feldman's than anything you could imagine. A "Feldman school" is unthinkable, because he espoused no theory, but the "Feldman touch"—a careful, ear-determined weighting of intervals and timbres—is a permanent contribution. Through his students Feldman has bent, however gently, the future of music in his direction, and created the taste needed to enjoy him.

In one of the last reviews of his life, I called Feldman "perhaps the greatest composer living." I hope he saw it, because reaching listeners was important to him, and reviewers rarely gave him his due. I hate to have to replace the last word of that description.

the antidote to publicity

virgil thomson, 1896–1989

OCTOBER 17, 1989

Surely no classical critic can resist marking the September 30 passing, at 92, of Virgil Thomson, the finest music critic of the English language. Shaw, the only other candidate, was less succinct and so mired in the details of London performance that he has to be drastically edited to match Thomson's timelessness. (Still, I named my son Bernard when my wife objected to Virgil.) Thomson's criticism was a model of clarity, forbearance, and courage. Whenever my prose sags, I read him for a lift. A self-described "stormy petrel" on the *New York Herald Tribune* from 1940 to 1954, he coined the motto "Intellectual distinction is news" and later claimed, "Musical polemics were my intent, not aiding careers or teaching Appreciation." Declaring himself "sales resistant to reputations," he enraged the managements of the New York Philharmonic and Metropolitan Opera. He was capable of great egotism (if always graciously expressed), he heaped scorn on Charles Ives's best works, and he was hard on John Cage despite personal debts. But his musical insights were catholic and surgically precise, and generations of musicians too young to feel the sting of his comments have idealized him as the composer/critic par excellence. Posterity seems to be granting him that rare status, a critic remembered for his wisdom, not his misjudgments.

I spent an evening with him at his Chelsea Hotel apartment in 1988. A considerate and cantankerous host, he chastised me for a poor memory and showed impatience with any comment I shouted into his hearing aid that struck him as deferential. I couldn't help deferring; as a composer he was a favorite, as a critic a hero. With Gertrude Stein he wrote what I consider the best American opera, *The Mother of Us All,* certainly the *most* American. A compelling feminist statement as well, it's never quite been recognized as such, partly because of the enemies Thomson's essays earned him. His definitions of criticism can hardly be sharpened: "The function of criticism is to aid the public in digesting musical works. Not for nothing is it so often compared to bile." And, in a letter to an angry opera matron, he justified his profession in a few crisp strokes: "Music criticism may be unnecessary. It is certainly inefficient. But it is the only antidote we have to paid publicity."

that which is fundamental

julius eastman, 1940–1990

JANUARY 22, 1991

It's January 1980. Place: myopically conservative Northwestern University in Evanston, Illinois. Julius Eastman, in motorcycle boots and dreadlocks, stomps on stage and introduces three multiple-piano works: *Evil Nigger, Gay Guerrilla,* and *Crazy Nigger.* "There was a little problem with the titles of the pieces," he tells us without a trace of irony in his deep, distinctly articulated voice. "A few students and one faculty member felt that the titles were somehow derogatory. There is a whole series of these pieces which I call the 'Nigger' series."

This column is a ridiculously belated obituary. Julius Eastman died May 28, alone, at Millard Fillmore Hospital in Buffalo. He was 49. According to the death certificate, he died of cardiac arrest. Depending on who you talked to, it was brought on by insomnia and possible tuberculosis, dehydration, starvation, exhaustion, or depression (supposedly not AIDS). According to his brother, his body was cremated, and there was a family memorial service in Annapolis, Maryland.

I found out last week, and most of his closest associates, when I called them for confirmation, had heard nothing about it. Those who had were dubious, for rumors of Eastman's death had circulated before. Eastman pretty much dropped out of the music scene around 1983, started drinking heavily and smoking crack (though the last friends who saw him insisted he was drug-free in the weeks before his death). He had been living some-times with his mother in Ithaca, sometimes with his brother in Brooklyn, with friends in New Jersey, at Catholic Charities in Buffalo, and often in or around Tompkins Square Park. He was a brilliant, honest, original, and influential musician.

"The reason," he said at Northwestern, in smoothly modulated tones, "I use that particular word is, for me, it has what I call a *basicness* about it. The first niggers were, of course, field niggers. Upon that is the basis of the American economic system. Without field niggers, you wouldn't have the great and grand economy that we have. That is what I call the *first* and *great* nigger. What I mean by niggers is, that thing which is *fundamental;* that person or thing that attains to a basicness or a fundamentalness, and eschews that which is superficial or, could we say, elegant. A nigger attains *[sic]* himself or herself to the *ground* of anything. There are many niggers, many kinds of niggers. There are 99 names of Allah, and there are 52 niggers. We are playing two of these niggers."

One of the least-recognized and most imaginative minimalists, Eastman was a pioneer. His *Stay on It* (1973), performed across Europe by SUNY Buffalo's Creative Associates, was one of the first pieces to introduce pop tonal progressions in an art context, and the middle section was an early use of free improvisation. He was also a remarkable singer with a dark, ver-satile, sepulchral timbre that, once you heard it, you never forgot. That voice brought him 15 minutes of fame in 1973: Nonesuch recorded *Eight Songs for a Mad King,* which British composer Peter Maxwell Davies had written expressly for Eastman's growl. Eastman's moment of infamy came in 1975, when, at Morton Feldman's annual June in Buffalo symposium, he performed in John Cage's *Songbooks,* and fulfilled the instruction "Give a lecture" by talking about sex and undressing a young man onstage. The next day an angry Cage pounded on the piano and fumed that the freedom in his music did not mean the freedom to be irresponsible.

Disorganized Eastman manifestly was, but he wasn't irresponsible in his art. His music had a beautiful directness, a common sense that cut through all the bullshit of modern-music rationalizations. His tonal logic was clear and grippingly cumulative. "These pieces," he explained, "are an attempt to make organic music. That is to say, the third part of any part has to contain all the information of the first two parts, and then go on from there. Therefore, unlike Romantic music and Classical music in which you have contrasting sections, these pieces' sections contain all the information of previous sections, or else the information is taken out at a gradual and logical rate."

Though tonal and repetitive, his music seethes with tension, hatred, triumph. *Evil Nigger* hammers repeated tones so insistently that the piano is sure to be out of tune afterward. *Gay Guerrilla* builds up searing discords with slow, propulsive momentum—BUM baba BUM baba BUM—before breaking, one piano after another, into "A Mighty Fortress Is Our God," reinterpreted as a powerful, wordless gay manifesto.

"These names, either I glorify them, or they glorify me, and in the case of *Gay Guerrilla*, that glorifies 'gay.' There aren't many gay guerrillas. I don't feel that gaydom does have that strength. Therefore I use that word in the hope that they will. At this point gay guerrillas can't match Afghani guerrillas, or PLO guerrillas. A guerrilla is anyone who is sacrificing his life for a point of view. If there is a cause, and it is a great cause, those who belong to that cause will sacrifice their lives. Without blood there is no cause. I use *Gay Guerrilla* in hopes that *I* might be one, if called upon to be one."

What Eastman sacrificed his life for remains unclear. For his younger brother Gerry, a guitarist for the Count Basie Orchestra, Julius died of "mental stress causing physical deterioration. . . . Racism within the classical world prevented him from doing the things he was doing. The system was rigged against him. It's the same old Scott Joplin/Charlie Parker story, only with a different person. Julius is just another in the line of black geniuses who get squashed in this particular hemisphere."

And yet others disagree, pointing out that Eastman had had enviable opportunities. After graduating from the prestigious Curtis Institute in composition, he was discovered by Lukas Foss, who conducted some of his music with the Brooklyn Philharmonic, and brought him into SUNY at Buffalo's Creative Associates beginning in 1968; the group toured Eastman's music in Europe and continued to perform it through '79. Eastman also had a brief theory-instructor stint at SUNY, reputedly a disaster because he couldn't adjust to the rigors of teaching. He was twice featured on New Music America, 1980 in Minneapolis (a performance I participated in) and 1981 in San Francisco. In between, he toured Europe, sponsored by the Kitchen, and also worked with Meredith Monk. As late as 1986, the Brooklyn Academy of Music's "Next Wave" series featured his music in a dance collaboration called *Geologic Moments*, with Molissa Fenley. A black fraternity and black faculty members protested the Northwestern concert mentioned above, saying that the titles, if taken out of context, could exacerbate campus racial tensions. As a concession, concert organizer Peter Gena didn't print the titles in the program.

Explanations of Eastman's downward spin vary widely in chronology and nuance. Arts consultant Renee Levine, co-director of the Creative Associates during Eastman's tenure there, says, "He was terribly conflicted about success. I'd call to offer him a gig and he'd say, 'Sure I'll come, if you can give me a thousand dollars a week.' He torpedoed an invitation from the French Conservatoire by insisting on a far larger fee than they had offered anyone else." Eastman's mother thinks he let his life go to waste in 1983, after a promised job at Cornell failed to come through. Despite working as a vocal coach and dance accompanist, he never landed the permanent academic position he looked for, but then, in the status-conscious '80s nobody without a doctorate got a teaching job. One thing everyone agrees on is that he was a brilliant enough composer, pianist, singer, dancer, even choreographer, with promising connections that should have guaranteed him a successful career—by American composer standards.

Summing up the general reaction, composer Peter Gena said, "It's a sad commentary that someone so talented could fall through the cracks." Others saw Eastman's end as inevitable and self-inflicted. "He was terribly undisciplined," said one colleague. "He had an unbelievable voice, and so much talent he didn't know what to do with it. He didn't realize what a gift he had." Foss echoed, "He was a very talented musician in every respect: as a composer, a singer, a pianist. He could have had it so good, if only he hadn't had the personality problems." Renee Levine painted a vivid picture: "He was so charismatic, so . . . *arresting,* so charming. He was a Renaissance man. He had a lot of tickets written to him. But he lacked discipline. He became increasingly unreliable. And sometimes he was just damned outrageous. But I loved him, and it breaks my heart."

More pertinent than figuring where Eastman's life took its wrong turn is starting a project to collect and revive his gorgeous body of work. There are no commercial recordings, but the Creative Associates archives at SUNY Buffalo have tapes and manuscript scores of some pre-1980 major works, including *Throughway, Macle, Stay on It,* and *If You're So Smart, Why Aren't You Rich?.* Eastman lost some scores and most of his tapes in the early '80s when he was kicked out of his apartment at 4th Street and Second Avenue. (They were confiscated, his brother recalls, by the sheriff's office.) His mother has a few scores he kept under his bed at her house, but she has no idea where the symphony is that he wrote in his last years. Other works are in his brother's possession, and pianist Edmund Niemann has a piano sonata that Eastman wrote in '86. Where the *Nigger* pieces, or *The Holy Presence, Jeanne d'Arc* for 10 cellos, are, no one I talked to knew. His scores were sketchy, and even once they're collected, reconstruction will depend on the memories of musicians who played them.

"The Julius we knew and loved died long ago"—that resigned sentiment cropped up in various wordings. Yet some thought that, in the last few months, he was getting his act together. I last saw Julius at a BAM concert in the fall of '89. He looked great, thin and muscular as usual, cleanly dressed. He was in good spirits. He seemed ready to make a comeback. I remember hoping that I would finally get a chance to write about his music, which had meant so much to me, in the *Voice*.

philosopher no more

john cage (1912–1992) quietly started a spiritual revolution

AUGUST 25, 1992

At the 1991 Bang on a Can festival John Cage looked awfully frail, and I started wondering, What will happen to the new-music community when he dies? My hunch is the center won't hold. Improvisation is moving back toward jazz, rockers are returning to clubs, new music is reclaiming classical turf. Cage was the river that dozens of avant-garde tributaries flowed into and from. Without him, what figure will be left whom *every* adventurous musician claims as inspiration?

On August 11, 25 days short of his 80th birthday, Cage suffered a stroke. Dancer-choreographer Merce Cunningham, his companion of 50 years, found him around 6 P.M. when he returned to their apartment at 18th Street and Sixth Avenue. Cage was taken to St. Vincent's, where he died the next afternoon at 2:40 without regaining consciousness. (Imagine how many close brushes with mushroom poisoning, including a couple stomach pumpings, he survived to live this long.)

Please, reader, observe four minutes and 33 seconds of silence.

The new-music scene feels parentless, the guiding spirit gone. The 20th century itself has unraveled, on schedule. Cage's career began with 12-tone music, embraced percussion, noise, rhythmic structure, electronic tape, prepared piano, extended vocal techniques, graph music, multimedia, conceptual art, minimalism, chance music, continuum, collage, concrete poetry, found objects, amplified plants, and flying sopranos, ending at last with grand opera. More than that, he brought music together with visual art, dance, and theater. His career enveloped the century; no other composer came close.

"Cage is a music-philosopher, important for his *ideas,* not as a composer." That lame truism is what I *wish* had died August 12. It's repeated so
frequently, so blithely, by so many people who couldn't quote you a sentence of Cage, that it's clearly not true. So congealed is the cliché that when
Raphael Mostel wrote a 1990 article for the *Times* calling Cage "the most
important and influential composer of our time," the editors disallowed the
phrase, offering "music-philosopher" instead. (I love the *Times.* Xenakis is
a *romantic,* Feldman died a *minimalist-expressionist,* whatever that is, and
for one day Cage was officially a *minimalist;* a Saturday correction retracted
the term. Do they consult the *I Ching* over there, or just toss coins?)

On the contrary: Cage's music will live as long as civilization, but his
"philosophy," formed in the '30s, has already dated. He inherited his generation's materialism, as did Nancarrow and Babbitt. He mistrusted sym-
bolism and doubted music's potential for communication. Sound was
nature, existing for itself and not for people. His human-negating, non-
communicative, materialist approach to sound has never caught on, and
becomes less popular each year. If only his *philosophy* were important, his
reputational goose would be cooked.

Why did Cage use chance methods to compose, anyway? Forget randomness: it was a nonidea, a way of de-emphasizing what wasn't important. If I wanted to spell out a message for you using marbles, I'd line them
up carefully in rows and curves. But if it were the *marbles* I were proud of
and wanted you to notice, I'd toss them down randomly. Any *arrangement*
on my part would imply that I wanted you to notice my intentions, not the
marbles. Cage's chance music is that simple. As long as you don't expect it
to be something else, it's less arcane than the Beatles. He wanted you to
notice the sounds. But notes don't fall on paper randomly unless you find
a method to scatter them. Cage's chance procedures weren't the result of
sloppiness, but a fanatical attention to detail.

That's not to say there's no craft to Cage's music. He knew that to make
the sounds speak interestingly, he had to ask them interesting questions.
"What can be analyzed in my work," he said, "or criticized, are the questions that I ask." Different ways to conceptualize soundworlds can produce
remarkably different results, which is why "merely" random works like
Music of Changes, Atlas Eclipticalis, Williams Mix, and *Etudes Australes*
can have such diverse textures and tendencies. Structure in Cage's music isn't
moment-to-moment, but global, horizontal. To think of Cage's philosophy
as "anything goes" is the ultimate misunderstanding. In the marble analogy, acceptance of a random pattern doesn't mean you also have to accept a
sloppy or misspelled message. "If there are intentions," Cage said, "then

there should be every effort made to realize those intentions. Otherwise carelessness takes over."

Many young composers say that Cage "gave them permission" to be freer in their music, but I doubt he actually gave many go-aheads. What felt like permission, like his "philosophy," was that he knew the artist's appropriate attitude toward ideas: playful, nonattached. The short form of his principle was, "Get yourself out of whatever cage you find yourself in." He knew what psychologist James Hillman has said, that ideas taken literally harden and become neuroses, traps for the mind. (What better example than Cage's teacher Schoenberg, original victim of the 12-tone virus?) He didn't need chance; magic squares, star charts, and Thoreau's drawings did just as well. As a student, I asked him how he derived the chords in his String Quartet. "I found them," he smiled, "like sea shells on the beach." He knew what few 20th-century composers have known, that rationalization sucks music dry.

Literalize Cage's ideas, and either you think that using chance will justify your music, or you denounce Cage because you think he thinks so. (Cage has been called a charlatan by our most distinguished, Pulitzer Prize–winning charlatans.) Those who imitate Cage badly and those who don't take him seriously make the mistake of thinking his relation to chance is reified, theoretically indebted, like a serialist's relation to the 12-tone row. Far from being important for his ideas, Cage's legacy is that he knew that ideas don't matter.

Cage couldn't have articulated the creative attitude had he not learned it by writing great music. People are still amazed to learn how *pretty* the piano pieces are that he wrote in the '40s, such as *Dream, In a Landscape,* and *Experiences I.* How could you call a charlatan someone who had made so masterful a large-scale structure as *Sonatas and Interludes? The Seasons* of 1947 is an exotic, accessible orchestra work that could have served as a good composer's magnum opus. The *Three Dances* for two prepared pianos that this arid "philosopher" wrote in 1945 are a virtuosic, thrilling crowd pleaser. Few music-theater pieces of the '70s are as hilariously entertaining as *Songbooks.*

One difficulty in perceiving Cage's music was that he was never in step. Minimalism may have been a '60s movement, but Cage wrote some of its classics in the '40s *(Four Walls)* and '80s *(Hymnkus).* I had his 1950 String Quartet played at my wedding, and no guest raised an eyebrow; it's lovely, but it was written out of context, with no relation to the 12-tone music or neoclassicism prevalent at the time. There's no other piece like *Cheap Imitation,* a cheery rip-off of Erik Satie's *Socrate.* At my last public piano performance (years ago), I played two of the *Etudes Australes.* The score horrified me, for each hand was notated separately and used the entire key-board. Once I'd practiced, playing was like dancing, exhilarating, each arm gracefully choreographed. (Music that's fun to play will live forever, for performers call the shots.)

Europeras I–IV, one of the great art experiences of my life, floated singers above the stage and sent a blimp into the audience. *Four* is a string quartet that Thoreau would have enjoyed at Walden Pond. Little-known *Hymnkus* is Cage's late-life response to minimalism, a quietly rustling continuum of repetitions. Cage's last works, like *Two*^{2} for two pianos, seemed to take up where Morton Feldman left off, pianissimo and with a newly liberated, clock-scorning sense of time.

"Not important as a composer"—damn such ignorance. How many gor-geous works does a guy have to write to be more than a philosopher? Cage easily has more masterpieces than Schoenberg, possibly more than Stravinsky.

But if Cage's music transcended his philosophy, his significance as a composer was overshadowed by his value as a person. While extremely approachable, he was not easy to make small talk with. His conversation veered into unexpected channels. I once sat near him at a book signing where several people tried to hold his attention talking about music. My wife, Nancy, no musician, asked him to explain a comment he had made about the sex life of mushrooms, whereupon he chatted about their mating habits for 15 minutes. He enjoyed people in awe of the same things he was in awe of, while being awkward around those who were in awe of him.

He was cheerfully calm about his celebrity, as though public appearances were part of the job. Though so weak that he could no longer carry his bag, he had visited Austria, Italy, and Czechoslovakia in June, and was planning to be in Frankfurt August 28 for a mammoth 80th-birthday festival.

Cage changed my life in 1975 at the June in Buffalo symposium. More young composers were there than we had time to listen to, so Cage used chance procedure to allow them to talk about their work. An obnoxious young woman harangued him at regular intervals, saying it was stupid to use randomness this way. We rolled our eyes and wanted to wring her neck. Then, about the third day, Cage entered and said, "I've been thinking about it, and I've decided Mary's right. We'll drop the chance procedures." That moment I realized that artistic greatness and humility are adjacent in the web of human attributes.

Cage affected me in even more profound ways. His writings led me to take Chinese thought and the *I Ching* seriously. The pinhole he poked in my rationalist worldview became a canyon, opening me up to Zen, the unconscious, meditation, Jung, astrology, the Tarot, numerology. (If you doubt the relevance of these connections, there's a brilliant little book by Jung's assistant, Marie-Louise von Franz, *On Divination and Synchronicity: The Psychology of Meaningful Chance,* detailing the relation of randomness to the unconscious. Without mentioning Cage, she provides the psychological underpinning of his music.) If Cage did that for me, he did it for many other artists, too. He made the hidden side of the mind audible through music, and quietly started a spiritual revolution. My present view of reality dates to 1970, the year I discovered *Silence* and the Everest recording of *Variations IV.*

Everyone who met Cage (thousands did) has a story. He knew his position in music, comparable to that of Beethoven or Wagner in the last century, was a gift, and he shared it generously. His long, shaking, silent laughter was unpredictable and infectious. No other composer over 45 did I see at so many concerts. He made time for the work of dozens of young composers, and acted as though *they* were doing *him* a favor. I'm going to miss running into Cage, but the example he gave my generation is something we'll have forever. He was a great artist, and something rarer: a great man.

index

AACM. *See* Association for the Advancement of Creative Musicians

Abrams, Muhal Richard, 60, 61, 124

Adams, John, 2, 5, 123, 148, 213; *The Chairman Dances*, 211; *The Death of Klinghoffer*, 21, 107, 259; *Harmonielehre*, 80, 219; *Nixon in China*, 218–20

Adams, John Luther: *Coyote Builds North America*, 274; *In the White Silence*, 9

Ades, Thomas, 145

Adorno, Theodor, 1–8, 15*nn*1,3, 84, 118, 286

Aerosmith, 44

African Burial Ground (New York), 61–63

African drumming, xvi, 13

Afro Asian Music Ensemble, 69

Agnew, Spiro, 244

Ailey, Alvin. *See* Alvin Ailey Dance Company

Albany Symphony, 132

Albéniz, Isaac: *Iberia*, 256

Albert, Stephen, 2

Albert, Thomas, 248

Albrechtsberger, Johann Georg, 36

Allen, Gerri, 241

Alternative Museum (New York), 117

Alvin Ailey Dance Company, 53

Amadeus (film), 87

Amazeen, Lauren, 99

American Composers Forum, 189

American experimental tradition, 82

American Symphony Orchestra League, 107

"America the Beautiful," 253

"A Mighty Fortress Is Our God," 291

Amirkhanian, Charles, xiii, 10, 121, 240–41

AMM (improv group), 194

Anderson, Beth, 9, 119

Anderson, Laurie, xiii, 24, 116, 119, 134, 151, 191, 225, 233, 234, 235, 240–42; *Empty Places*, 228–32; *O Superman*, 12, 208

Andriessen, Louis, 208

The Andy Griffith Show, 77

Aristotle: *Poetics*, 149–51

artrock, xiii, 48, 247

Artusi, Giovanni Maria, 172

Ashley, Robert, 17–23, 31, 65, 107, 117, 122, 137, 145, 166, 191, 208, 259, 271–73, 283, 284; *Atalanta*, 17, 21, 23, 272; *eL/Aficionado*, 17, 19, 21–22; *Foreign Experiences*, 272; *The Immortality Songs*, 18, 21–22; *Improvement: Don Leaves Linda*, 17, 21–22, 259, 272; *Now Eleanor's Idea*, 17–19, 21–23, 271–73; *Perfect Lives*, 18, 19, 20, 21, 23, 166, 272, 284; *Purposeful Lady Slow Afternoon*, 272–73; *Van Cao's Meditation*, 134; *The Wolfman*, 18

Ashley, Sam, 273

Aspen music festival, 33

Association for the Advancement of Creative Musicians (AACM), 60, 62, 70, 112, 235

Aurobindo, Sri, 197

Austen, Jane, 271

Ayler, Albert, 13

Aznavour, Charles, 221

Babbitt, Milton, xiii, xiv, 3, 77, 85, 93, 105, 121, 124, 132, 137, 138, 139–40, 141, 149, 169–70, 171–72,

Babbitt, Milton *(continued)*
177, 179, 183, 208, 213, 263, 265,
276, 294; Piano Concerto, 158;
Reflections, 171
Bach, C. P. E., 36
Bach, Johann Sebastian, 60, 79, 82, 88,
102, 133, 171, 173, 186, 217; *The Art
of Fugue*, 257; *Goldberg Variations*,
77, 79, 150–51, 223; *The Well-
Tempered Clavier*, 186–87
Bach, P. D. Q., 112, 216
Bach, W. F., 36
Bad Medicine, 267
Bakunin, Mikhail, 126
Baldwin, Cliff, 50
Bang on a Can All-Stars, 273–74
Bang on a Can Festival, xvi, 9–10, 13,
129, 130, 138, 171–72, 293
Barber, Samuel, 32, 187
Barker, Bob, 65
Barker, Thurman, 59
Barriere, Jean-Baptiste, 214
Bartók, Bela, 33, 61, 123, 137, 144,
156, 217; *Music for Strings,
Percussion, and Celesta*, 250
Bassett, Leslie, 122
Baudelaire, Charles, 95, 226
Beatles, 25, 26, 27, 294; *Sgt. Pepper's
Lonely Hearts Club Band*, 74;
White Album, 25, 26
Beckett, Samuel, 193, 194; *Molloy*,
238; *Waiting for Godot*, 155
Beethoven, Ludwig van, 36, 48, 68, 79,
90, 100, 111, 145, 151, 165–66, 188,
199, 217, 220, 263, 264, 265, 284,
297; *Missa Solemnis*, 178; Piano
Sonata in B-flat, Op. 106,
"Hammerklavier," 165, 188; Piano
Sonata in F, Op. 57, "Appassionata,"
188, 256; String Quartet in F, Op.
135, 159; Symphony No. 5, 100,
263; Symphony No. 7, 74; Symphony
No. 9, 265; *Wellington's Victory*, 36
Beglarian, Eve, 6, 181, 191, 276–78;
Buncacan Song, 278; *Machaut a
Go-go*, 6, 278; *My Feelings Now*,
277; *No Man's Land*, 278;

Spontaneous Combustion 1, 277;
Wonder Counselor, 278
Behrman, David, 178
Beiser, Maya, 274
Bellini, Vincenzo, 259
Benary, Barbara, 206
Benny Hill (TV show), 223
Berg, Alban, 220; *Wozzeck*, 19, 259
Berger, Arthur, 177
Bergson, Henri, 286
Berio, Luciano, 39, 104, 197; *Sinfonia*,
101, 164, 275
Berlin Philharmonic Orchestra, 66
Berlioz, Hector, 100, 265; *Memoires*,
264; *Symphonie Fantastique*, 164
Bernstein, Leonard, 243; Mass, 40
Berry, Chuck, 45, 102, 221
Berwald, Franz, 89
B-52s, 25
Biber, Heinrich Ignaz Franz von, 204;
Mystery Sonatas, 204
the Bible, 226
Bidlo, Mike, 164
Bierstadt, Albert, 266
Billings, William, 185
Birdland, 233
Blacher, Boris, 197
Blackburn, Philip, 191
Black Panthers, 71
Blastula, 43
Blavatsky, Madame Helena, 197
bluegrass, 13
Blue Oyster Cult, 110
Bolcom, William, 2
Boosey & Hawkes (publisher), 179
Borbetomagus, 9
Boston Herald, 200
Boston Symphony Orchestra, 200
Boulanger, Nadia, 32
Boulanger, Richard, 215
Boulez, Pierre, 2, 4, 33, 39, 41, 46, 67,
102, 135, 137, 140–41, 142, 143,
160, 161, 171–72, 182, 208, 213,
259, 262, 263; *Le Marteau sans
maître*, 81, 141, 144, 152, 155; *On
Music Today*, 153; *Pli selon pli*, 159,
171; *Structures*, 147

Bowie, David, 256
Bowie, Lester, 235
Brahms, Johannes, 2, 7, 49, 78, 148,
    151, 168, 217, 248
Branca, Glenn, 42–50, 56, 58, 82, 108,
    137, 139, 170, 172; *Instrumental for
    Six Guitars*, 46–47; Symphony No.
    3, 178; Symphony No. 5, 48;
    Symphony No. 7, 49; Symphony
    No. 8, 43, 47, 48; Symphony No. 9,
    47, 48, 49; Symphony No. 10, 43,
    47, 48; *The World Turned Upside
    Down*, 48
Brant, Henry, 241, 264–66; *500:
    Hidden Hemisphere*, 253–55;
    Western Springs, 255
Braxton, Anthony, 13, 37, 60, 124
Brazelton, Kitty, 276; *Fishy-Wishy*, 6
Brecht, Bertolt, 26
Brennan, Patrick, 159
Brooklyn Academy of Music, 5, 28,
    69, 82, 115, 117, 119, 122, 134, 136,
    228, 232, 234, 235, 256, 258, 271,
    291, 292
Brooklyn Philharmonic, 49, 100, 291
Brooks, Richard, 51; *In Cold Blood*
    (film), 51
Brooks, William, 127
Brown, Earle, 53, 112, 149, 178, 185,
    195, 286, 287
Brown, James, 76
Brown, John Mason, 156
Brubeck, Dave, 112
Bruce, Neely, 182, 254
Bruckner, Anton, 48, 49, 166
Bruno, Giordano, 17–18, 19, 20
Bryars, Gavin, 175
Büchner, Georg, 48; *Woyzeck*, 48
Buckley, Lewis J., 254
Buckley, William F., 92
Buckner, Thomas, 20, 55, 273
Budd, Harold, 90, 148
Bumpurs, Eleanor, 62
Burton, Mary, 62
Bush, Philip, 186
Busoni, Ferruccio, 197
Butterfly Dance (Hopi), 245, 246

Buxtehude, Dietrich, 88
Byrne, David, 44, 52

Caccini, Giulio, 171, 219
Cage, John, xiii, xiv, xvi, xvii, 13, 23,
    24, 27, 32, 45, 49, 60, 68, 82, 83, 87,
    90, 108, 110–11, 116, 120, 121, 122,
    123, 125–27, 130–32, 135, 137, 139,
    149, 154, 160–61, 172, 175–76, 179,
    182–86, 188, 193, 194, 196, 207,
    211, 214, 216, 217, 231, 248, 249,
    252, 257, 262–64, 279, 280, 281,
    284, 286, 288, 290, 293–97;
    Apartment House, 1776, 185; *Atlas
    Eclipticalis*, 294; *Cheap Imitation*,
    295; *Concert for Piano and
    Orchestra*, 262–64; *Dream*, 295;
    Etudes Australes, 295–96;
    Europeras I–IV, 296; *Experiences I*,
    295; *Four*, 296; *4′33″*, 109, 126, 293;
    Four Walls, 295; *Hymnkus*, 131,
    295, 296; *In a Landscape*, 295;
    Music of Changes, 294; *Rozart Mix*,
    183; *The Seasons*, 295; *Second
    Construction in Metal*, 266; *Silence*,
    126, 196, 248, 297; *Sonatas and
    Interludes*, 295; *Songbooks*, 116,
    183, 290, 295; *String Quartet*, 295;
    Three Dances for Two Prepared
    Pianos, 295; *Two²*, 296; *Variations
    IV*, 111, 263, 297; *Williams Mix*,
    185, 294; *A Year from Monday*, 183
Cahill, Sarah, 280
Calder, Alexander, 195
Cale, John, 204, 205
Canadian Recording Industry
    Association, 74
Capote, Truman, 50–52, 55, 64; *In
    Cold Blood*, 50–52, 55, 64
Carnap, Rudolph, 162
Carpenter, John Alden, 160–61
Carter, Elliott, xiv, 3, 81, 85, 97, 102,
    108, 121, 128, 132, 138, 141, 144,
    159, 177, 180, 208, 263
Carter, Jimmy, 259
Castaneda, Carlos, 18, 67
Catler, Brad, 261

Catler, Jon, 261
Cavalli, Francesco, 89
Cedar Bar, 194
C. F. Peters (publisher), 122
Chamber Music Society of Lincoln
    Center, 193
Chanler, Theodore, 200, 201
Chatham, Rhys, xiii, xiv, xv, 4, 24, 46,
    110–14, 116, 117, 118; *An Angel
    Moves Too Fast to See*, 81; *Die
    Donnergötter*, 110; *Drastic
    Classicism* (also *Drastic Classical
    Music*), xiv, 110–11; *Guitar Trio*, 46,
    110; *Minerva*, 110, 113
Chelsea Hotel, 288
Childs, Lucinda, 258
Childs, Mary Ellen: *A Chording To*,
    250; *Carte Blanche*, 249–50; *Click*,
    250; *Parterre*, 249
Chinese medicinal music, 104
Chomsky, Noam, 3
Chopin, Frederick, 74, 90, 191; *Piano
    Sonata No. 2*, 187
Clapton, Eric, 25
climaxes, 249–50
Coleman, Anthony, 159, 176
Coleman, Ornette, 60, 123, 207; *Free
    Jazz*, 159
Collins, Nicolas, 75–76; *Dark and
    Stormy Night*, 81, 166–67, 236–38;
    Devil's Music, 75; *Tababo Fonio*,
    166–67, 236
Collins, Phil, 74
Coltrane, John, 60, 74, 268; *Ascension*,
    113
Columbus, Christopher, 29–30, 32
Composers Quartet, 280
Composer-to-Composer symposium
    (Telluride, CO), 240
conceptualism, xiii, xvi, 8, 11–12, 24,
    136, 139, 239
Conrad, Tony, xiii, 116, 284–85; *Early
    Minimalism*, 204–6, 285; *Flicker*,
    203, 285; *Four Violins*, 205, 285;
    Slapping Pythagoras, 206
Coomaraswamy, Ananda K., 105
Cook, Nancy, 288, 296

Cope, David, 119, 216–17; *New
    Directions in Music*, 217
Copland, Aaron, 32, 208; *Appalachian
    Spring*, 207; *Fanfare for the
    Common Man*, 207; *What to Listen
    for in Music*, 200
Cordero, Marghreta, 273
Corigliano, John, 2
Count Basie Orchestra, 291
counterpoetry, 51, 54
Cowell, Henry, xvi, 57, 82, 83, 123,
    129, 139, 174, 264–66, 278–81; *High
    Color*, 280–81; *New Musical
    Resources*, 36, 279, 281; *Persian Set*,
    279; *Quartet Romantic*, 280;
    Trickster Coyote, 279; *United
    Quartet*, 280
"crackerjack soup" singing style, 267
Crawford (Seeger), Ruth, 174
Creative Associates (SUNY Buffalo),
    290, 291–92
Crumb, George, 74; *Makrokosmos I*, 74
Crutchfield, Will, 118
Cunningham, Merce, 293
Curtis, Charles, 212

Dallapiccola, Luigi, 137, 154, 177, 197
Dante Alighieri, 18
Darmstadt, 141, 183, 212–13, 279
Davidovsky, Mario, 3, 96, 180, 265
Davidson, Tina, 249; *Blue Dawn (The
    Promise Fruit)*, 249
Davies, Hugh, 241
Davies, Peter Maxwell, 290; *Eight
    Songs for a Mad King*, 290
Davis, Anthony, 115
Davis, Miles, 284
Davis, Peter G., 102
Deak, John, 266
de Alvear, Maria, 191; *En Amor Duro*,
    68; *Sexo*, 66, 68; *Vagina*, 66–67;
    World, 66–69
Debussy, Claude, 33, 43, 89, 129, 187,
    220
Deep Listening, 179
Deep Purple, 110
De La Soul, 75

Del Tredici, David, 107
Dempster, Stuart, 91
Descartes, René, 262
Dewan, Brian, 283
Diamond, David, 235
Dickens, Charles, 271
Didkovsky, Nick, 181; *Amalia's Secret*, 133, 274
Die Reihe (journal), 279
Dine, Jim, 39
Dinkins, David, 62
Dissanayake, Ellen, 105
DJ music, 14, 204
Dodge, Charles, 217; *Rondeley*, 217
Dolden, Paul, 144
Dolphy, Eric, 260
the Dolls, 44
Donizetti, Gaetano, 259
Dove, Ulysses, 53
Downtown Ensemble, 234
Downtown music, xiii*ff.*, 1–15, 24, 39, 47–48, 49, 54, 93–94, 100, 131, 132–34, 149, 162, 163, 172–74, 178, 264–66, 275–76, 281
Dream Syndicate, 205
Dresher, Paul (and Ensemble), 273–75; *Double Ikat*, 274
Dreyblatt, Arnold, 285
Druckman, Jacob, xiii, 29
Drummond, Dean, 191
Dubuy, Frank G., 254
Duchamp, Marcel, 24, 127, 252
Duckworth, William, 9, 133, 172, 176, 179, 184, 185, 233; *Southern Harmony*, 178; *Time Curve Preludes*, 13, 247; *20/20: 20 New Sounds of the 20th Century*, 208–9
Dufay, Guillaume, 154
Dutilleux, Henri, 213
Dvořák, Antonin, 7, 48
Dwight, John Sullivan, 199
Dylan, Bob, 190

EAR magazine, 115, 120, 247
Eastman, Gerry, 291
Eastman, Julius, xvi, 103, 183, 206, 226, 289–93; *Crazy Nigger*, 289–92;

Evil Nigger, 289–92; *Gay Guerrilla*, 289–92; *Holy Presence, Jeanne d'Arc*, 292; *If You're So Smart, Why Aren't You Rich?*, 292; *Macle*, 292; Piano Sonata, 292; *Stay on It*, 290, 292; *Throughway*, 292
Echoes of God, 56
Eco, Umberto, 237
Edwards, Betty, 86–87; *Drawing on the Right Side of the Brain*, 86
Egyptian Book of the Dead, 58
Einstein, Albert, 257
Ellington, Duke, 62, 123, 133
Elliott, Gordon, 63
Emerging Voices festival (University of California, San Diego), 273–75
Emerson, Ralph Waldo, 156, 231
Eno, Brian, 256
Epstein, Paul, 172, 248
equal temperament, 186–88
Ernst, Max, 21
Evans, Brian, 216; *Marie Sets*, 216
Evelev, Yale, xiv, 232, 233
Experimental Intermedia (venue; Phill Niblock's loft), 5, 92, 117, 234, 250

Feldman, Morton, xvi, 68, 79, 80, 82, 101, 120–23, 129, 131, 137, 145, 148, 149, 168–69, 178, 183, 192–96, 197, 199, 207, 208, 212, 217, 265, 274, 281, 284, 286–88, 290, 294, 296; *For Samuel Beckett*, 193, 194, 195, 196; Oboe Concerto, 286, 287; *Rothko Chapel*, 286; *String Quartet II*, 193, 195; *The Swallows of Salangan*, 286; *Three Voices*, 193; *Triadic Memories*, 193; *The Turfan Fragments*, 263–64; *The Viola in My Life*, 193, 195; *Why Patterns?*, 193, 195, 286
Fell, Barry, 22
Fenley, Molissa, 291
Ferneyhough, Brian, 3, 93, 138, 273
Fibonacci series, 156, 172
Ficino, Marcilio, 18
Field, John, 192
Fine, Howard, 243

Finley, Karen, 93
First, David, 47, 276; *Jade Screen Test Dreams of Renting Wings,* 58, 128; *The Manhattan Book of the Dead,* 55–59; *Resolver,* 57
Fischer-Dieskau, Dietrich, 74
Fisher, Linda, 164; *Big Mouth,* 76
Flo and Eddie, 75
Fludd, Robert, 36
Fluxus, xiii, 24, 25, 26, 27, 28, 47
Forever Bad Blues Band, 260–62
Fortner, Wolfgang, 197
Foss, Lukas, 291, 292
fractal geometry, 153, 172
Franklin, Joseph, 91
Franz, Marie Louise von, 297; *On Divination and Synchronicity: The Psychology of Meaningful Chance,* 297
free improvisation, xiii, xvi, 8, 12, 85–86, 100, 116–18, 157
free jazz, 56, 247
Freeman, Betty, 200
Freud, Sigmund, 22, 166
Fried, Joshua, 165; *Travelogue,* 165
Frog Peak Music, 179
Frohnmeyer, John, 243
Fromm, Paul, 125
Frost, Robert, 117
Fulkerson, Gregory, 258
futurists (Italian), 160–61

gagaku, xvi, 13, 169
Galas, Diamanda, 108–9, 224–28; *Masque of the Red Death,* 225–28; *Wild Women with Steak Knives,* 226
gamelan, xvi, 6, 13, 98, 168, 169, 212, 248
Gandhi, Mahatma, 40, 220
Gann, Bernard, 288
Gann, Kyle, 81, 175–76, 275, 288–89; *Mountain Spirit,* 13
Gan-ru, Ge, 241–43
Garland, David, 53, 220–22, 281–83; *Control Songs,* 221; *Togetherness,* 281
Garland, Peter, 82, 172, 247, 281
Gaynor, Gloria, 277

Gena, Peter, xiii, xiv, xv, 172, 181, 287, 291, 292; *Beethoven in Soho,* 13; *McKinley,* 247; *Mother Jones,* 247
Geraldo (TV show), 63
Gershwin, George, 53; *Rhapsody in Blue,* 208
gesture music, 215
Gibson, Jon, 90
Gilmore, John, 60
"Girl from Ipanema," 158
Giteck, Janice, 91, 172; *Breathing Songs from a Turning Sky,* 13, 250; *Om Shanti,* 178, 248, 250
Glass, Philip, xiii, xv, 4, 5, 10, 28–33, 46, 49, 61, 89, 102, 107, 116, 119, 123, 129, 134, 139, 151, 194, 203–4, 205, 206, 208, 213, 220, 235, 247, 256–59, 265, 267; *Akhnaten,* 31, 32, 219, 259; *Einstein on the Beach,* xiv, 12, 31, 65, 118, 169, 175, 219, 257–59; *The Fall of the House of Usher,* 259; *Hydrogen Jukebox,* 29; *In the Upper Room,* 211; *Itaipu,* 256; *Low Symphony,* 256; *Music in Fifths,* 12, 32, 171; *Music in Similar Motion,* 30, 31; *Music in Twelve Parts,* 29; *Music with Changing Parts,* 30; *Satyagraha,* 31, 219, 259; *Songs from Liquid Days,* 29; *1,000 Airplanes on the Roof,* 29; *The Voyage,* 29–33, 259
Globokar, Vinko, 227
Gödel, Kurt, 231
Goebbels, Heiner, 235; *The Man in the Elevator,* 235
Golden Ratio, 156
Goldman Memorial Band, 254
Goode, Daniel, 118, 151, 178
Goodman, Alice, 219–20
Goodman, Nelson, 167; *Languages of Art,* 150
Gordon, Michael, 47, 48, 56, 172, 274, 275; *Four Kings Fight Five,* 128, 138, 144; *Thou Shalt!/Thou Shalt Not!,* 13, 129, 177–78, 247
Górecki, Henryk, 102, 199; *Symphony of Sorrowful Songs,* 9, 48

Gould, Glenn, 77
Graham, Dan, 45
Graham, John, 212
Grawemeyer Award, 139
Great Stalacpipe Organ (Luray
    Caverns, VA), 253
Greene, Ann T., 59, 61–63
Gregorian chant, 32, 101
Griffin, Johnny, 60
Griffith, Andy, 88
Griffiths, Paul, 141–43
Grove Dictionary of Music, 186
Gubaidulina, Sophia, 66
Guggenheim Award, 102, 121, 124, 139
Guinness Book of World Records, 101
Gulf War (first), 39
Guston, Philip, 194, 195
Gwiazda, Henry, 234

Hammer, M.C., 104
Handel, George Frederic, 118, 219; The
    Messiah, 41, 230; Orlando, 112
Hanrahan, Kip, 236
Harbison, John, 2, 108, 138
Harkness, Joan, 59
Harris, Roy, 254
Harrison, Lou, 123, 208, 248, 281
Harrison, Michael, 212
Harry, Deborah, 233–34
Hart, Mary Ann, 280
Hartmann, Karl Amadeus, 197
Hawking, Stephen, 30
Hawkins, Coleman, 284
Hawkins, Erick, 279
Haydn, Franz Joseph, 36, 49, 77–78,
    101, 111, 129, 154, 171, 182, 226;
    String Quartet Op. 50, No. 1, 159;
    Symphony No. 88, 100; Symphony
    No. 94, "Surprise," 100; Symphony
    No. 100, 159
Hayman, R.I.P., 222–24; Dreamsound,
    222–24
Heidegger, Martin, 161, 162
Helms, Jesse, 116, 243, 244
Henahan, Donald, 147, 202
Hendrix, Jimi, 56; "Purple Haze," 274
Henry Cow, 44

Henze, Hans Werner, 60
Hesse, Mary, 162
Hickock, Dick, 50–52
Hildegard von Bingen, 277
Hiller, Lejaren, 216; Algorithms III,
    216
Hillman, James, 81, 131, 262–64, 295;
    The Myth of Analysis, 87, 172–74;
    Puer Papers, 262
Hindemith, Paul, 82, 169, 173–74
Hines, Thomas, 130
Hitchcock, H. Wiley, 281
Hitler, Adolf, 22, 40, 229
Ho, Fred, 69–72; Journey Beyond the
    West, 69–70, 72; Yes Means Yes, No
    Means No, Whatever She Wears,
    Wherever She Goes, 71
Hoffman, Abbie, 193
Holiday, Billie, 61
Holland, Bernard, 126
Holland Festival (Amsterdam), 37
Holloway, Michael, 216
Holshouser, Will, 283
Holst, Gustave, 256
Hopi music, 94, 244–46, 267
Horton, Willie, 61
Houston, Cissy, 39
Houston, Thelma, 277
Hovda, Eleanor, 249; Ariadnemusic, 249
Hovhaness, Alan, 91, 115
Hudson, Ben, 212
Hughson, John, 62
Humbert, Jacqueline, 272–73
Hume, David, 155
Hussein, Saddam, 39
Hutchinson, Brenda, 191; Eee-yah!,
    166–67
Hwang, David Henry, 29–30
Hwang, Jason, 70
Hwong, Lucia, 115
hypnotism, 53

I Ching, 183, 185, 216, 294, 296
Ichiyanagi, Toshi, 23, 27
identity politics, 41–42
Ignace, Paul, 164
Impossible Music, 100

Impressionism, 168
International Computer Music
    Conference (Urbana, IL), 214–18
International Society for
    Contemporary Music (ISCM), 276
"In the Garden" (hymn), 54
Inuit throat songs, 114, 168
IRCAM, 152, 155
isorhythmic motet, 161
Ives, Charles, xvi, 32, 82, 88, 90, 118,
    123, 124, 160–61, 173, 196, 197,
    214, 228, 239, 253, 257, 264, 273,
    288; *Concord Sonata*, 144, 177, 188;
    Symphony No. 2, 238; Symphony
    No. 3, "Camp Meeting," 121, 123
I Wor Kuen, 71

Jackendoff, R., 154
Jackson, Michael, 74; "Bad," 74, 77
Jagger, Mick, 224, 272
James, William, 112
Jarvinen, Arthur, 247; *Egyptian Two
    Step*, 247
Jay, John, 243
Jenkins, Leroy, 59–63; *Editorial*, 61;
    The Mother of Three Sons, 59, 83;
    The Negros Burial Ground, 59–63
Jennings, Terry, 203, 206
Johnson, Dennis, 204; *November*, 206
Johnson, Stephen, 280
Johnson, Tom, xv, 116, 175, 178, 201–2
Johnston, Ben, 123, 148, 261; *Letter
    from Calamity Jane*, 191; *Visions
    and Spels*, 191
Jolas, Betsy, 66
Jones, A. M., 53; *Studies in African
    Music*, 53
Jones, Bill T., 59, 60, 61
Jones, Joe, 25
Joplin, Scott, 291
Jordanova, Victoria, 66
Jorgensen, Owen H.: *Tuning: The
    Perfection of Eighteenth-Century
    Temperament, the Lost Art of
    Nineteenth-Century Temperament,
    and the Science of Equal
    Temperament, Complete with*

*Instructions for Aural and
    Electronic Tuning*, 186–88
Josquin Desprez (attributed), 177;
    Absalon, fili mii, 177
Joy Buzzers, 56
Judson Church, 39
Juilliard School of Music, 39, 77
June in Buffalo (symposium), 183,
    290, 296
Jung, Carl Gustav, 40, 86, 161, 165,
    167, 172, 184, 213, 225, 297
just intonation, 116

Kagel, Mauricio, xiv, 13, 68, 279;
    Acustica, 111, 112
Kane, Jonathan, 261
Kant, Immanuel, 85, 104
Kantian fallacy, 84–85
Kayser, Hans, 42, 44, 47
Keane, David, 217; *La Aurora
    Estrellada*, 217
Kennedy, John, 193
Kermani, Elise, 191
Kerner, Leighton, xv, 218
Kernis, Aaron Jay, 144, 145
Kerouac, Jack, 188, 231
Keyserling, Count, 79
Kierkegaard, Søren, 194
Kiggel, Lancelot, 93
the Kinks, 44, 45
Kirchner, Leon, 3, 177
the Kitchen, 33–34, 37, 43, 45, 46, 62,
    66, 92, 99, 110, 116, 117, 196, 234,
    235, 255, 260, 261, 291
Kleeb, Hildegard, 68
Klein, Walter, 198
Kline, Franz, 194
Klucevsek, Guy, 221, 237, 250, 283
Knitting Factory, 5, 25, 108, 117, 221,
    222
Knowles, Alison, 24
Koch, Ed, 62
Komodo Whirligig Orchestra, 283
"kook composers," 265
Kooning, Willem de, 194
Kostelanetz, Richard, 127; *Conversing
    with Cage*, 183–84

Kosugi, Takehisa, 11; *Music for a Revolution*, 11
Kotik, Peter, 55, 185, 262–64
Koussevitsky, Serge, 200
Kramer, Hilton, 127
Kramer, Jonathan, 159; *The Time of Music*, 159
Krishnamurti, 107
Kronos Quartet, 119, 174, 193, 207, 209, 274
Kubera, Joseph, 58, 66, 262
Kuivila, Ron, 95; *Dulci Mura*, 251–53

LaBarbara, Joan, 193, 272–73
La Côte Basque (restaurant), 50, 54–55
Lam, Bun Ching, 70
La Montaine, John, 122, 123
Lancaster, Burt, 65
Lang, David, 13; *Press Release*, 274
Lauten, Elodie, 9, 148
League of Revolutionary Struggle, 71
Lehrer, Tom, 222
Leinsdorf, Erich, 287
Lennon, John, 24–25, 26, 27
Lentz, Daniel, 13; *The Dream King*, 13
León, Tania, 266
Lerdahl, Fred, 151–55
Levin, Robert D., 78
Levin, Todd, 178; *Prayer*, 178
Levine, Renee, 291–92
Leviticus (Old Testament book), 225, 226
Lewis, George, xiv
Lewis, Sinclair: *Elmer Gantry*, 65
liberalism, 160–63
Life magazine, 183
Lifton, John, 241
Ligeti, Gyorgy, 83, 138, 197, 208, 216; *Atmospheres*, 74; *Etudes*, 133
Lilly, John C., 231
Lincoln Center Festival, 193, 207, 208
Linn drum machine, 53
List, Garrett, 116
Liszt, Franz, 199
Locke, John, 231
Lockwood, Annea, xiii, 108, 118

Lohn, Jeffrey, 45–46
Long, Jhou, 70
Longo, Robert, 46
Lowell, Robert, 40
Lowitsky, Bella, 243
Lucier, Alvin, xiii, 49, 57, 58, 107, 131, 178, 182, 185, 264–66; *I Am Sitting in a Room*, 208
Lull, Raymond, 18
Luray Caverns (VA), 253

MacArthur, Mary, 116
MacArthur Award, 122, 142, 265
Machaut, Guillaume de, 276
Maciunas, George, 24, 27
MacLise, Angus, 203, 205
MacLow, Jackson, 24
Maderna, Bruno, 197
Madonna, 23, 174
Mahler, Alma, 27
Mahler, David, 91
Mahler, Gustav, 48, 172, 194, 198; Symphony No. 2, "Resurrection," 164; Symphony No. 6, 105
Malcolm, Janet, 278
Mamet, David, 122
Mannheim school, 171
Mao Tse-Tung, 25, 26
Mapplethorpe, Robert, 84
Marclay, Christian, 221
Marsalis, Wynton, 60
martial arts, 69
Martin, Billy, 283; *Stridulation for the Good Luck Feast*, 283
Martino, Donald, 3, 140
Martirano, Dorothy, 215
Martirano, Salvatore, 216; *L's G.A.*, 216
Martland, Steve, 274; *Horses of Instruction*, 274
Marx, Karl, 22
Mason, Daniel Gregory, 121, 122
Massenet, Jules, 229
Mathews, Max, 215
Matthew Effect, 142–43
Maxfield, Richard, xiii, 203
McClary, Susan, 28–29, 109
Meckler, David C., 274

Meckley, Diana, 167; *Strange Attractors*, 167
Mendelssohn, Felix, 2, 194
Messiaen, Olivier, 44, 126, 168–69, 178, 207, 239; *Oiseaux Exotiques*, 178
Metallica, 74
Metropolitan Opera, 20, 28–30, 32, 64, 141, 288
Metzger, Klaus-Heinz, 130
Meyer, Leonard, 170; *Music, the Arts, and Ideas*, 170
microtonality, 56*ff.*
Microtones (band), 261
Midtown, xvii, 2*ff.*, 32
Milhaud, Darius, 32, 33, 112
Miller, Alice, 96
Miniature, 234
minimalism, xiii, xv, xvi, 12, 44, 47–48, 54, 101, 118, 124, 128–29, 130–31, 132, 135, 136, 139, 147–49, 150, 166, 169, 170–72, 178, 194, 203–7, 216, 218–20, 248, 266, 275, 286, 293, 294, 295
Mitchell, Roscoe, 60; *L-R-G*, 112; "Nonaah," 158
Mizelle, Dary John, 118
Mobberley, James, 215; *Beams!*, 215
Mobil Oil, 92
Modern Music (journal), 182
Monet, Claude: *Water Lilies*, 196
Monk, Meredith, xiii, 95, 103, 137, 151, 191, 208, 225, 265, 291; *Atlas*, 138
Monk, Thelonious, 158, 160, 276
Monkey Chant (Balinese), 190, 225
Monkey Orchestra, 69
Monteverdi, Claudio, 21, 133, 170–72, 284; *Orfeo*, 284
Moondog, 234
Moore, Carman, xv, 38–42, 95, 118; *Mass for the 21st Century*, 39–42
Moore, Marianne, 40
Moore, Thurston, 43
Moorefield, Virgil, 48
Moorman, Wilson, 59
Morricone, Ennio, 13

Morris, Robert, 241
Moss, David, 237
Mostel, Raphael, 130, 294
Mozart, Wolfgang Amadeus, 6, 20, 36, 68, 77–79, 82, 85, 86, 87, 96, 109, 129, 134, 145, 157, 171, 180, 220, 226, 287; *Don Giovanni*, 177; Symphony No. 40, 78; Symphony No. 41, "Jupiter," 217
multiculturalism, 97–99, 103, 104–6
Mumma, Gordon, 130, 178, 185
Munch, Charles, 287
Murray, Charles: *The Bell Curve*, 95–97
musical literacy rates, 80
Music Critics Association, 77
Musicians Accord, 280
Music Mouse, 95
musique concrète, 216
Mussolini, Benito, 229
Mussorgsky, Modest, 192; *Pictures at an Exhibition*, 75
My Dinner with André (film), 228

Naked City, 113
Nancarrow, Conlon, xvi, 36–37, 54, 80, 82, 83, 108, 122, 123, 128, 144, 169, 197, 207, 208, 234, 252, 254–55, 264–66, 294; *Two Canons for Ursula*, 266
National Endowment for the Arts, 91, 92, 105–6, 241–44
National Public Radio (NPR), 90
Neill, Ben, 56, 129, 237; *Downwind*, 128
Nenets people, 67
Neoplatonism, 18–19
neoromanticism, 82, 128, 286
Nerval, Gerard, 226
Neuberg, Amy X, 273
New Age music, 151
New Complexity, 3
New Music America, xiv, 33, 60, 122, 232–36, 291
New Music Edition, 281
New Music New York, xiii, 12, 233, 236

New Romanticism, 152, 172. *See also*
  neoromanticism
New Yorker magazine, 82, 126, 155,
  200
New York Foundation for the Arts, 102
New York Herald Tribune, 200, 288
New York magazine, 102
"New York noise," 151
New York Observer, 126
New York Philharmonic, xv, 39, 132,
  182, 266, 288
New York Times, 81, 82, 95, 116, 118,
  124, 126–27, 130, 141, 143, 147,
  155, 170, 201, 202, 220, 294
Nguyen, Thi Hong Ngat, 277
Niblock, Phill, xiii
Nicholls, David, 279
Niemann, Edmund, 292
Niente, Al, 284
Nietzsche, Friedrich, 161; *Beyond
  Good and Evil*, 115
Nirvana, 274
Nixon, Richard Milhaus, dancing
  naked, 25, 26
Nono, Luigi, 2
Noska, Barbara, 248
Note Killers, 56
Nurock, Kirk, 175–76

Ockeghem, Johannes, 154; *Missa ma
  Maitresse*, 238
Offutt, Treva, 277
Oldenberg, Claus, 39
Oliveros, Pauline, xvi, 4, 13, 49, 68, 82,
  95, 108, 122, 123, 208, 212, 230, 241,
  243, 264–66
Ono, Yoko, xiii, 4, 11, 23–28; *Wall
  Piece for Orchestra*, 11, 24
open form, 111
Oppens, Ursula, 266
Orchestra Luna, 44
O'Rourke, Jim, 285
Ortiz, William, 119, 288
Ostrow, Elizabeth, 266
Oswald, John, 164; *Plunderphonics*,
  74–77
Overton, Hall, 39

Paik, Nam June, 11; *Danger Music No.
  5*, 11
Palestine, Charlemagne, xiii, 203,
  206–7; *Four Manifestations of Six
  Elements*, 206; *Godbear*, 206;
  Strumming Music, 206
Palestrina, Giovanni Pierluigi da,
  170–71
Palmer, Robert, 24
Pandemonium (Wesleyan University
  Steel Band), 254
Panharmonicon, 36
P'ansori epic (Korean), 190
Papp, Joseph, 243
Parades, Hilda, 275
Parker, Charlie, 291
Parsons, Geoffrey, 200
Pärt, Arvo, 199; *Miserere*, 208; *Passio*, 48
Partch, Harry, xvi, 17, 82, 90, 122, 123,
  137, 188–92, 258, 265, 281; *Barstow*,
  189, 192; *The Bewitched*, 189; *Bitter
  Music*, 189; *Castor and Pollux*, 138,
  189; *Delusion of the Fury*, 189; *The
  Dreamer That Remains*, 192;
  Finnegans Wake, 192; *Genesis of a
  Music*, 189–90; *The Jabberwocky*,
  192; *Li Po Songs*, 190; *On the
  Seventh Day Petals Fell in
  Petaluma*, 189; *Psalm 137*, 190; *U.S.
  Highball*, 189, 192; *Windsong*, 192;
  Y.D. Fantasy, 191
Parton, Dolly, 74, 77
Passchendaele battle, 93
Pataki, George, 52
Patelson's Music (store), 179
Patten, Tom, 187–88
Pattison, Robert, 221
Parenti, Susan, 191
Parkinson, Stephen, 274; *Paradise
  Canyon*, 274
Paul Revere and the Raiders, 44
Penderecki, Krzysztof, 44, 46
performance art, 68, 99, 103, 105
Peri, Jacopo, 171, 219
Perle, George, 124, 148, 154, 177
Perloff, Marjorie, 130
Perot, Ross, 28

Perry, Edmund, 62
Persichetti, Vincent, 33, 39
Peterson, Wayne, 123, 138
Pickett, Wilson, 75
Pierce, Joshua, 175–76
Plains Indian music, 267–68
Plato, 149–51
pluralism, 117–18, 152
"Poetry in Motion" (MTA campaign), 95
Polansky, Larry, 241–42; *51 Melodies*, 81; *Lonesome Road Variations*, 144
Pollitt, Barbara, 223
Pollock, Jackson, 194, 195, 287
Porter, Andrew, 200
Poss, Robert, 237
postminimalism, xvi, 13, 14, 101, 113, 124, 132, 150–51, 172, 178–79, 247–50
postmodernism, 136, 145
postserialism, 68
Pound, Ezra, 152
Pousseur, Henri, 164; *Votre Faust*, 164
Powell, Bud, 21
Powell, Jarrad, 91
Pran Nath, Pandit, 211
Previte, Bobby, 283
The Price Is Right (TV show), 65
Prince, Richard, 46
Prokofiev, Sergei, 187
Prometheus, 173
Public Broadcasting System (PBS), 20, 53
Public Theater, 28
Puccini, Giacomo, 197
"Puff, the Magic Dragon," 244
Pulitzer Prize, 61, 96, 120–25, 139, 142, 265, 273, 295
Pythagoras, 205

Rachmaninoff, Sergei, 74, 89; *Rhapsody on a Theme of Paganini*, 74
radio, classical, 88–90
the Ramones, 44
Ran, Shulamit, 121, 138
Ranaldo, Lee, 43
Rands, Bernard, 123

rap, 40, 75–76, 100–1
Reagan, Ronald, 7, 60, 119, 229, 259
Redmond, Layne, 95
Reich, Steve, xiii, 4, 5, 10, 46, 56, 122, 123, 134, 147, 151, 179, 194, 203–4, 206, 207–9, 213, 247, 265; *The Cave*, 107, 207; *Come Out*, 12, 101; *The Desert Music*, 207; *Drumming*, xiv, 12, 171, 207, 274; *Music for 18 Musicians*, 12, 207; *Piano Phase*, 12, 81, 172, 249; *Tehillim*, 207; *Triple Quartet*, 207, 209
Reed, Ralph, 193
Relache Ensemble, 91, 248–50
Reynolds, Roger, 124, 181, 241, 273
Reynolds, Willard, 21
Ricki Lake (TV show), 63
Riley, Terry, xv, 39, 107, 123, 204, 205, 208, 213, 264–66; *In C*, 90, 132, 133, 266; *Persian Surgery Dervishes*, 12
Roach, Max, 71
Robbe-Grillet, Alain, 147
Robertson, Brian, 74–75, 76
Robinson, Marilynne, 220
Rochberg, George, 137
Rockwell, John, 81, 116, 126–27
Rolnick, Neil, 178; *Sanctus*, 178
roots-rock reggae, 114
Rorty, Richard, 155; *Contingency, Irony, and Solidarity*, 160–63
Rosenboom, David: *Is Art Is*, 240; *Layagnanam*, 240; *Systems of Judgment*, 238–40
Rothko, Mark, 194, 287
Rothstein, Edward, 83, 124, 126, 202
Roulette (venue), 5, 92, 234, 276
Rouse, Christopher, 2
Rouse, Mikel, 8, 10, 47, 56, 57, 144, 172, 191; *Copperhead*, 133; *Dennis Cleveland*, 63–66; *Failing Kansas*, 50–55, 64, 178; *High Frontier*, 128; *Hope Chest*, 129; *Living Inside Design*, 51; *Quick Thrust*, 13; *Quorum*, 53
Rubinstein, Anton, 80
Rudhyar, Dane, 44, 174, 210–12, 214, 267; *Culture, Crisis, and Creativity,*

210; *The Magic of Tone and the Art of Music*, 47, 210
Rudy's bar (New York), 127
Ruggles, Carl, 82, 131, 154
Rzewski, Frederic, 82, 107, 123, 148, 234, 255–57; *Andante con moto*, 256; *Bumps*, 255; *De Profundis*, 255–56; *The Turtle and the Crane*, 255

Sadra, I Wayan, 241–42
Salieri, Antonio, 36
Sam Ash (musical equipment store), 167
Sammartini, Giovanni Battista, 171
sampling, 73–77, 164–67
Sandoval, Carlos, 37
Sandow, Greg, xiv, xv, 116, 221
San Juan Pueblo music, 246
Sankaran, Trichy, 240; *Layagnanam*, 240
Sartre, Jean-Paul, 155
Satie, Erik, 130, 217, 255; *Socrate*, 250, 295; *Vexations*, 174–76
Saul, John Ralston, 66, 93–96; *The Doubter's Companion*, 95–96; *Voltaire's Bastards*, 64–65, 93–95
Scelsi, Giacinto, 145, 196–99; *Anahit*, 197; *Konx-Om-Pax*, 198; *Quattro pezzi su una nota sola*, 198; *Uaxuctum*, 198
Schenkerian theory, 160
Schick, Steve, 274
Schickele, Peter, 100
Schiff, David, 81, 141
Schillinger, Joseph, 53
Schillinger technique, 53
Schoenberg, Arnold, xiii, 31, 32, 33, 60, 68, 82, 84, 103, 125, 126, 148, 151–52, 155, 168–69, 173, 176, 184, 194, 195, 197, 257, 294, 296; *Moses und Aron*, 141; Piano Concerto, 168; *Pierrot Lunaire*, 81, 139; String Quartet No. 1, 156; String Quartet No. 3, 168; Violin Concerto, 112
Schubert, Franz, 6, 82, 96, 98, 164, 165, 221; *Der Winterreise*, 73

Schuller, Gunther, 265
Schumann, Robert, 150
Schumpeter, Joseph, 163
Schwantner, Joseph, 2, 108, 138
Scott, Stephen, 247
Scriabin, Alexander, 154, 211, 214, 239
Seeger, Charles, 174
S.E.M. Ensemble, 24, 262–64
serialism, 118, 128, 135, 136, 139, 140, 141, 147–49, 153–55, 156, 160, 165, 168, 194, 213, 286. *See also* twelve-tone music
Sessions, Roger, 3, 103, 177, 201, 265
Seuss, Dr. (Theodor Seuss Geisel), 34, 189
Shapey, Ralph, 122, 123–24, 183; *Fromm Variations*, 178; *Three for Six*, 178
Sharp, Elliott, 134
Shaw, George Bernard, 200, 288
Shea, David, 176
Shepp, Archie, 71
Shono, Susumu, 130
Shostakovich, Dmitri, 80
Sibelius, Jan, 199, 200
Simmons, Doug, xiv, xv, xix
Simpson, O. J., 102
Sinatra, Frank, 221
Singleton, Alvin, 61
Skymusic Ensemble. *See* Moore, Carman
Sloboda, John A., 151
Smith, Leo, 60, 241
Smith, Patty, 233
Smith, Perry, 50–52
Smith, Stuart, 80
Smith, William O., 91
Snake Dance (Hopi), 246
Snake River (WY), 218
Soldier String Quartet, 237
Sollberger, Harvey, 124
Sonami, Laetitia de Compiegne, 191
sonata form, 165–66
Sondheim, Stephen, 44; *Anyone Can Whistle*, 44
Sonic Youth, 43, 49
Sony, 78

Soundings (journal), 281
Source magazine, 119, 189
Sowerby, Leo, 122, 123
Speach, Bernadette, 287
Speculum Musicae, 157
Spiegel, Laurie, 90, 95; *Music for Signals*, 216; *Sound Zones*, 81
Spies, Claudio, 139–40
Spinoza, Benedict de, 286
Spoleto Festival, 196
Sprinkle, Leland W., 253
"squeakfart music," 215
Squire, J.C., 257
Staebler, Gerhard, 241–42
Stanley, Lawrence, 75–77
Starr, Ringo, 25
"Star-Spangled Banner," 229
the Static, 46
Steiger, Rand, 275
Stein, Gertrude, 40, 200–1, 289
Stewart, Mark, 285
Stewart, Michael, 62
stochastic music, 153
Stockhausen, Karlheinz, 2, 13, 20, 25, 46, 100, 111–12, 114, 129, 137, 138, 143, 175, 208, 212, 213, 287; *Gesang der Jünglinge*, 192; *Gruppen*, 255, 279; *Klavierstück XI*, 164, 238; *Kurzwellen*, 111, 112; *Opus 1970*, 111; *Zyklus*, 108
Stone, Carl, 73, 75, 172; *Shing Kee*, 73, 81, 164–65, 167
Strauss, Richard, 213
Stravinsky, Igor, 36, 82, 100, 103, 129, 139, 144, 148, 161, 168–69, 176, 194, 256, 257, 278, 296; *Concerto for Piano and Winds*, 168; *Pulcinella*, 275; *Requiem Canticles*, 168, 195; *Le Sacre du Printemps*, 7, 74, 164, 208; *Symphony of Psalms*, 168
structural listening, 84–86
Studio PASS, 239
Subotnik, Rose Rosengard, 84–86; *Developing Variations*, 84–86
Sugiura-Nancarrow, Yoko, 264–65

Sultan, Grete, 175
Supové, Kathleen, 276–78
"Surfin' U.S.A.," 165
Sutton, Sheryl, 258
Suzuki, Daisetz, 184
Svard, Lois, 133–34, 175–76
Swartz, Steven, 288
Swed, Mark, 131, 208
"Swing Low, Sweet Chariot," 227–28

Takahashi, Aki, 193
Talking Heads, 44, 52
Tan Dun, 70, 145
Tanglewood festival, 139
Taos pueblo, 266–68
Taruskin, Richard, 139–40
Taylor, Cecil, 56, 60
Tchaikovsky, Pyotr Ilich, 80; *Romeo and Juliet*, 80
Teitelbaum, Richard, xiii, 279
Temier people (Malaysia), 223
Tenney, James, 82, 131, 241
Thatcher, Margaret, 272
[THE] (duo), 239
Theater of Eternal Music, 205–6, 285
Theoretical Girls, 45, 46
Third Stream music, 162
Thomas, Augusta Read, 144
Thomson, Virgil, 199–202, 254, 288–89; *Four Saints in Three Acts*, 200–1; *The Mother of Us All*, 200, 218, 289
Thoreau, Henry David, 127, 231, 295
Threadgill, Henry, 61
Thunderbird American Indian Dancers, 279
Tibetan Book of the Dead, 18, 58
Tin Pan Alley, 53
Tirez Tirez, 52–53
Toch, Ernst, 122
Tolstoy, Leo, 105; *Anna Karenina*, 105
Tommasini, Anthony, 199–202; *Virgil Thomson: Composer on the Aisle*, 199–202
tonal flux, 190
Tone Deaf, 46

Torke, Michael, 144
Tosati, Vieri, 198–99
totalism, xvi, 13–14, 54, 56, 101, 104,
    127–29, 132, 178–79, 275
Tourtelot, Madeline, 189, 192
Tower, Joan, 2
Trimpin, 33–38, 90–93, 95, 236,
    264–66; Contraption IPP 71512,
    33–34; *PHFFFT-ARRRRGH*, 90–91
Truax, Barry, 216; *Riverrun*, 216
Trump, Donald, 233
Tsumagari, Bobbi, 99
Tudor, David, 185, 262
Turetzky, Bertram, 275
Turner, Rita, 153
Twain, Mark, xvii, 153, 271
twelve-tone music, xiii, 2–3, 4, 82, 83,
    85, 96, 112, 122, 124, 137–38, 143,
    145, 153–55, 159, 160, 164, 168,
    173, 176, 177, 180, 184, 187, 194,
    199, 208, 212, 235, 247, 248, 293,
    295. *See also* serialism
The Twilight Zone, 157
Twining, Toby, 95
Twisted Tutu, 275–78
2 Live Crew, 240–44; *As Nasty as
    They Wanna Be*, 241
Tyranny, "Blue" Gene, 19, 226; *The
    Intermediary*, 81, 167; *Nocturne With
    and Without Memory*, 134, 178;
    Somewhere in Arizona 1970, 167

Uitti, Frances-Marie, 196, 198–99
ultramodernism, 247
United States Coast Guard Band, 254
UPIC system, 215
Uptown music, xiii, xvii, 2*ff.*, 32, 39,
    83, 93, 131, 136–40, 149, 172–74,
    177–78
Urlinie, 160
U.S. Military Academy Band, 254

Valkanas, Alene, xiv
Van Gogh, Vincent, 194
Varèse, Edgard, 23, 113, 121, 131, 196;
    Déserts, 263; *Ionisation*, 108

Velvet Underground, 24, 204
Verdi, Giuseppe, 20, 190, 197; *La
    Traviata*, 34, 259
Victoria, Queen, 40
Vierk, Lois V., 119, 172; *The Attack
    Cat Polka*, 248–50; *Go Guitars*, 13;
    Timberline, 248–49
Village Voice, xivff., xvii, 8, 13, 39, 56,
    88, 116, 117, 127, 160

Wada, Yoshi, 24
Wagner, Richard, xvii, 100, 125, 148,
    150, 151, 168, 177, 212, 264, 265,
    297; *Lohengrin*, 284; *Das
    Rheingold*, 48; *Der Ring des
    Nibelungen*, 21, 175; *Tristan und
    Isolde*, 164, 284
Wahman, Jerome, 53
Waldrep, Mark, 235; *Piano Maps*, 235
Walker, George, 61; *Lilacs*, 61
"wall of sound" pieces, 215, 216
Walsh, Michael, 126
Warhol, Andy, 231
Warner Bros. cartoons, 76
Watts, Robert, 11; *Trace*, 11
Webern, Anton, 2, 137, 167, 195, 212;
    Variations Op. 27, 188
Weill, Kurt, 26; *Three-Penny Opera*,
    221
Weinstein, David, 100
well temperament, 187–88
WFMT (radio station, Chicago), 89
White, William Braid, 187; *Modern
    Piano Tuning*, 187
Whitehead, Alfred, 149
Wilde, Oscar, 167, 255–56
Wildmon, Donald, 92
Wilkerson, Edward, 235
Wilson, Robert, 258
Winfrey, Oprah, 63
Winsor, Phil, 216; *Dulcimer Dream*,
    216
Wittgenstein, Ludwig, 151, 158, 160,
    231; *Tractatus Logico-
    Philosophicus*, 46
The Wizard of Oz, 70

WNCN (radio station, New York), 89
WNYC (radio station, New York),
    248, 282
Wodnicki, Adam, 216
Wolfe, Julia, 13
Wolff, Christian, 111, 178, 185, 286;
    For 1, 2, or 3 People, 183; Snowdrop,
    133
Wolpe, Stefan, 11, 23, 154
women composers, 119, 234–35
Woolf, Randall, 276–77; One Tough
    Lama, 277
Wordsworth, William, 286
Workman, Reggie, 71
World Casio Quartet, 56, 57
world music, 115, 124, 163
World War I, 93
WRR (radio station, Dallas), 90
Wuorinen, Charles, 3, 61, 96, 107,
    139–40, 142, 172, 265, 276
Wyatt, Scott, 216; Circulation, 216
Wyckoff, Laurel, 249

X, Malcolm, 71
Xenakis, Iannis, xv, 60, 109, 208, 211,
    215–16, 227, 239, 294; Mycenes
    Alpha, 215; Pithoprakta, 270

Yamada, Norman, 176
Yanni, 10
Yano, Akiko, 73, 75
Yarrow, Peter, 244
Yates, Frances, 17, 19
Yi, Chen, 49, 70

Young, La Monte, xv, 4, 24, 43, 49, 57,
    58, 78, 82, 103, 107, 122, 123, 129,
    139, 160–61, 181, 199, 204–5, 208,
    239, 260–62, 265, 285; The Base
    9:7:4 Symmetry in Prime Time . . . ,
    269–71; Composition 1960 #7, xiii,
    11–12; Composition 1960 #15, 11;
    For Brass, 212; For Guitar, 212;
    Romantic Symmetry (over a 60
    cycle base), 270; The Second Dream
    of the High-Tension Line Stepdown
    Transformer, 212; Trio for Strings,
    12, 212; The Well-Tuned Piano, 204,
    210–14, 260; Young's Dorian Blues
    in G, 260

Z, Pamela, 191
Zappa, Frank, 15, 144
Zarlino, Gioseffo, 172
Zaslaw, Neal, 78
Zazeela, Marian, 205; Ruine Windoe
    1992, 270
Ziporyn, Evan, 47, 128; LUVTime,
    128, 129
Zorn, John, xvi, 10, 12–13, 48, 49, 93,
    108, 110–14, 116, 119, 122, 134,
    145, 149–51, 159, 161, 221, 232–33,
    235, 283; Archery, xiv, 12, 111; The
    Big Gundown, 13; Cobra, 12,
    111–12; For Your Eyes Only, 100;
    Hu Die, 113; Pool, 12; Spillane,
    149–50
Zuni music, 246, 267
Zwilich, Ellen Taaffe, 2, 93, 107–8, 138

text

10/13 aldus

display

aldus

compositor

international typesetting and composition

printer and binder

thomson-shore, inc.